CW00432824

lots of love

Andrew
xxx

An MRM Publication

Copyright © 2020 MRM Promotions

The COUCH POTATOES GALAXY OF BRITISH TV QUIZZES

Cover Morph. Dawn French & David Jason
(as the Vicar of Dibley & Del Boy).

  =

Someone in our village told me this week that the surname we shared
is probably the most important one in the country. I asked her why.

LEWIS

She spelt it out to me!
London - England-Wales-Scotland-Ireland-Scotland

We learn something every day.

MIKE LEWIS

Illustrations by Andrew Western

THE COUCH POTATOES GALAXY OF BRITISH TV QUIZZES

Most of us have spent a great amount of our lives in front of 'The Box'. Many excellent programmes have occupied our leisure time and, most certainly, several others have not reached our own expectations.

This quiz book covers British-made TV programmes of all types. If your favourite is not included, let me know and I will make a note to include it in volume 2! The 400/500 programmes included in this book are certainly not a selection of all my own personal top shows. Hopefully when you look through the pages it may trigger action to try to dig up episodes of some long-forgotten, vintage shows to watch. In some instances I have 'given a clue to answers by inserting pictures.

For over 30 years I have written and presented quizzes as part of The Inquizitors team, alongside my wife Mo and son Rob. We have produced quizzes for groups ranging from about 10 people right up to round 450. Much of the information in this book has been dug out of our archives. But as Inquizitors quizzes are multi-media, we can only cover 'words and pictures' elements here, but hopefully, you'll find enough varied teasers to enjoy, whilst perhaps learning some interesting facts too! The information was correct as at August 2020.

I will happily accept any comments or ideas for further quiz books. Meanwhile, I am very indebted to Rob, Katie and Mo for their strenuous proof checking labours. However, even with all of their efforts there may still be a few errors remaining. Please advise me if you find anything and I will amend it for the next print run. Thank you for buying the book.

My email address is inquizitors3@gmail.com

Mike Lewis

Many thanks to Andrew Western for his fabulous cover illustrations and many other super paintings throughout the book.

Would you like a portrait or a pet portrait painted?
E-mail contact : andrew.western1961@gmail.com
Web: https://www.facebook.com/andrew.western.14
or www.artistsandillustrators.co.uk/andrew-western

Thank you to Wikipedia and IMDB for providing some very useful programme information.

My gratitude to Mr Chris Streets, Mr Andrew Hollowood, Dr Indra da Costa and all of the Bristol NHS team who cared and fought for me, against the odds, 12 years ago!

Lots of love to my wife Mo who has been left alone for many hours as I have been writing this book. Mo is, without doubt, my great tower of strength.

This book is dedicated with much love to:
Puss, Tilly, Jess, Poppy, Pebbles and Wilma.
The happiness and pleasure they have given to us will never be forgotten.

CONTENTS

CONTENTS

A much loved British TV sitcom created and written by John Sullivan. 64 episodes over 7 series were broadcast on BBC One in the UK from 1981-1991. Also 16 sporadic Christmas specials were aired up until 2003. Episodes are still regularly repeated on UK Gold.

1. The 1996 episode *Time on Our Hands* was originally billed as the last ever episode. It holds the record for the highest UK audience for a sitcom episode. How many watched? A) 18 million B) 21.4m   C) 22m   D) 24.3m

2. What was the name of the spin-off series, located in Shropshire, that ran from 2005 to 2009, starring Boycie and Marlene?

3. Del Boy, Rodney and Grandad lived in a council flat in a high-rise tower block in Peckham, South London. What was its name?

4. When Grandad died which character was introduced and what was his family link to Del Boy and Rodney?

5. The first series began on 8 September 1981. It attracted an average of how many million viewers? A) 4m   B) 5m   C) 7m   D) 10m

6. What is the first sentence uttered by Del in the first episode? A) Grandad stop arguing with the plonker will ya? B) Are you two at it again are ya? C) Will you two stop causing a commotion will ya?

7. What 1982 episode featured the famous chandelier incident?

8. Who sang the iconic theme tune?

9. Who was the only actor to return for the prequel series *Rock & Chips*?

10. How did Trigger get his nickname and what name does he call Rodney?

TRIVIA: Over a dozen Reliant Regals (the 3-wheeled vans) were used during the series.

WHO AM I?
I APPEARED IN JUST TWO EPISODES OF OFAH

First shown on 29 June, and with a regular audience of three to five million, The Chase is one of ITV's most successful daytime shows ever. It has been nominated six times at the National Television Awards, winning in 2016, 2017, and 2019. Contestants play against a professional quizzer, known as the "chaser", who attempts to prevent them from winning a cash prize. 14th series in 2020.

1. From Series 14 in 2020 there will 6 Chasers. Can you name them all?

2. In the first round the contestants answer as many questions as they can within one minute. What is the round called?

3. Which Chaser is known as The Dark Destroyer?

4. After celebrity programmes, a new spin-off was introduced in 2017. What was the show called?

5. A further big-money version of the show was introduced in November 2019. What is that show called?

6. What game-show is broadcast by the BBC in direct opposition to *The Chase* most days?

7. In 1997 Bradley Walsh presented 50 episodes of which other well known TV game-show?

8. As of June 2020 which Chaser had the highest win percentage, clocking up an impressive 82.4%?

9. In February 2019 contestant Judith carved a unique record for the show. Did she; A) Get 0 points in the cash builder; B) Win £70,000 playing on her own against Jenny Ryan or C) Scored 30 steps in the Final Chase?

10. True or False? Bradley Walsh released an album entitled *Chasing Dreams* in 2016 and it became the biggest selling debut album by a British artist, selling 111,650 copies.

THE CHASE TRIVIA

The most steps set for The Chaser was 28. This has happened twice, and on both occasions the Chaser was only able to get 27 steps and the contestants won. The least steps set for The Chaser was 7.

ONLY FOOLS AND HORSES ANSWERS: 1. D) 24.3m; 2. The Green, Green Grass; 3. Nelson Mandela House; 4. Uncle Albert, Grandad's long-lost brother; 5. C) 7 million; 6. B), Are you two at it again are ya?; 7. A Touch of Glass; 8. John Sullivan the writer; 9. Nicholas Lyndhurst (as Freddie Robdal); 10. He looks like a horse, he calls Rodney 'Dave' for some unknown reason. WHO AM I? Nervous Nerys (Andree Bernard).

British medical drama series that airs weekly on BBC One. It is the longest-running emergency medical drama television series in the world. Casualty follows the professional and personal lives of the medical and ancillary staff of Holby City Hospital's emergency department. There had been 34 series and 1,178 episodes pre Covid-19 .

1. In which fictional hospital is *Casualty* set?

2. From 1986 - 2010 the exterior filming was done in an English city. From 2011 it moved to a city in Wales. What are the 2 *Casualty* cities?

3. What was MacKenzie 'Big Mac' Chalker's job in the show before he became an emergency care assistant?

4. Who helped assist Megan's death?

5. In what number series did Tess arrive?
A) 16   B) 17   C) 18   D) 19.

6.Why did Dixie get suspended in 2014?

7.Why did Nick Jordan leave in 2013?

8. To which country did long-running character Lisa 'Duffy' Duffin move?

9.Which pictured *Cagney and Lacey* star has appeared in 3 episodes of *Casualty*?

10. In 2014 Matt Bardock's character is killed when a vehicle explodes. Which character did Matt play?
A)   Iain Dean
B)   Martin 'Ash' Ashford
C)   Jeff Collier
D)   Josh Griffiths

THE CHASE; 1. Mark Labbett, Shaun Wallace, Anne Hegerty, Paul Sinha, Jenny Ryan, and Darragh Ennis; 2. The Cash Builder; 3. Shaun Wallace; 4. The Family Chase; 5. Beat the Chasers; 6. Pointless; 7. Wheel of Fortune; 8. Anne Hegerty; 9. B) Win £70,000 playing on her own against Jenny Ryan; 10. True (It reached No .10 in the album charts).

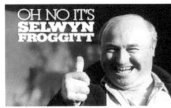

OH NO IT'S **SELWYN FROGGITT**

A situation comedy based around the members of a working men's club in the fictional Yorkshire town of Scarsdale which ran on the ITV network. Mostly written by Alan Plater, a pilot was launched in 1974 and the show of 30 minute episodes ran for 3 series and 22 episodes. Renamed 4th series was a flop.

1. Which long-established comedian and actor played Selwyn Froggitt?

2. If he approved of something, what was the memorable one-word catchphrase that Selwyn uttered?

3. When ordering at the bar a second catchphrase from the series became very well known. What was it?

4. What daily newspaper was he often seen carrying, but hardly ever seen reading?

5. What was Selwyn's role on the committee of his local working men's club?

6. A sequel was made, simply called Selwyn. What role did he play in that less successful series?

7. Rosemary Martin played Vera Parkinson, Selwyn's brother's girlfriend in the 1st series. Which *Open All Hours* actress took over?

8. This is Selwyn's brother Maurice played by Robert Keegan. In which 2 television Police series was Keegan most familiarly known?

9. What outer garment of clothing was Selwyn often seen wearing?

10. The show was a big success in the ratings. What was the reputed peak level of viewers?   A) 12million   B) 16m   C) 23m   D) 29m

Walter Williams, when told that Williams was too common a surname to use professionally, adopted the name Maynard after seeing a sign advertising Maynard's Wine Gums.

CASUALTY: 1. Holby City Hospital; 2. Bristol and Cardiff; 3. Porter; 4. Tess and Charlie; 5. C) 18; 6; Taking a patient out of hospital without permission; 7. His girlfriend Yvonne Rippon died; 8. New Zealand; 9. Sharon Gless; 10. C) Paramedic Jeff Collier.

A detective series produced by Yorkshire Television (later ITV Studios) for ITV from 6 December 1992 until 5 April 2010, initially based on the Frost novels by R. D. Wingfield. The show starred David Jason in a very different role and ran for a remarkable 15 series and 42 episodes.

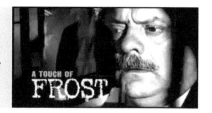

1. The final episode of the drama was watched by how many viewers?
    A) 4.8 million   B) 5.6 million   C) 8.3 million   D) 15.3 million.

2. The leading character is Detective Inspector 'Jack' Frost . What are his actual forenames? A) William Edward B) Robert John C) David John

3. What award had been made to Jack Frost for an act of heroism, making him the Chief Constable's 'blue-eyed boy'?

4. Frost's boss had a love-hate relationship with him. Who was the social climbing Superintendent superbly played by Bruce Alexander?

5. Who wrote the novels upon which the show was initially based?

6. The series was set in which fictional South Midlands town?

7. Whose death played a role in Frost's decision to retire?

8. Matt Bardock, who was also killed off in _Casualty_, played the Chief Constable's nephew, shot in the line of duty. What was his name?

9. Frost made his debut in _Care and Protection_. What type of incident was he investigating, which led to a grisly discovery in Denton woods?

10. On Frost's wedding day to Christine Moorhead in 2010 her ex-husband, in a drunken fit of jealousy, tried to kill Jack by speeding into the side of his car in a 4x4. However he missed, and instead killed DS George Toolan. Which actress played the role of Jack's intended, Christine?

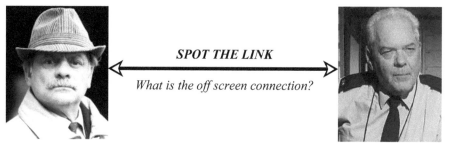

SPOT THE LINK

What is the off screen connection?

OH NO, IT'S SELWYN FROGGITT: 1. Bill Maynard; 2. 'Magic'; 3. 'A pint of cooking and a bag of nuts'; 4. The Times; 5. Concert Secretary - booking turns!; 6. Holiday camp director; 7. Lynda Baron; 8. Z Cars and Softly, Softly; 9. A donkey jacket; 10. D) 29 million.

Also known as Ab Fab this BBC TV show is a sitcom based on the French and Saunders sketch "Modern Mother and Daughter". First series on BBC2, the following 4 on BBC1. Ran from 1992-2004 plus 20th anniversary specials. 39 episodes including 7 specials.

1. Name the theme song, written by Bob Dylan and Rick Danko, and also identify the two credited performers of the song.

2. The main character was a heavy-drinking, drug-abusing PR agent. What was the character's name?

3. In the first episode called Fashion, Eddie called Shikani to channel her a colour for the day. What colour was channeled?

4. In 2000, the show was ranked at what number on the 100 Greatest British Television Programmes by the British Film Institute?
A) 3rd   B) 10th   C) 17th   D) 47th

5. In 2012 Jennifer Saunders stated that Dawn French and her had been inspired by which female pop band?

6. What was Patsy doing when she broke her ankle?

7. Daughter Saffron is a cynical student and aspiring writer. Who played her?

8. What year was *Absolutely Fabulous : The Movie* released?

9. Which 'Dame' starred in the show? Sadly she died in 2018 at the age of 93?

10. Name the 4 'special guests' (pictured below) who featured in the show?

A TOUCH OF FROST: 1. C) 8.3 million; 2. A) William Edward; 3. The George Cross; 4. Superintendent Stanley Mullett; 5. R.D. Wingfield; 6. Denton; 7. DS George Toolan; 8. DS Clive Barnard; 9. Looking for a missing child who turned up safely but a severed arm was found attached to a strongbox; 10. Phyllis Logan. SPOT THE LINK: David Jason (DI Frost) & Arthur White (PC Ernie Trigg) are brothers.

British science fiction television programme produced by the BBC since 1963. It originally ran until 1989. The programme was re-launched in 2005, and since then has been produced in-house by BBC Wales in Cardiff. 38 series & seasons and 861 episodes as of August 2020.

1. How many actors have played the Doctor on BBC-TV, and can you name them all?

2. The Doctor has which Type No of Tardis?

3. How many operators is the Tardis designed to have?

4. Is there a swimming pool in the Tardis?

5. What fruit does the Doctor say you should never eat because they are squishy?
A) Pears   B) Bananas   C) Oranges   D) Apples

6. In Season 5 in *The Unicorn and the Wasp*, which author do the Doctor and Dr Noble meet? A) Jane Austen B) Charles Dickens C) Agatha Christie

7. What was the Doctor's nickname whilst attending the Prydonian Academy on Gallifrey?

8. Which Doctor said 'I've never been slapped by someone's mother?'

9. The Ice Warriors come from which planet?

10. How did Sec describe the Daleks' confrontation with the Cybermen?
A) Sport
B) Extermination
C) Pest control
D) Simple

Hugh Grant was once approached to play the Doctor. He turned down the role, thinking the show would not take off. He expressed deep regret in 2007, after seeing how successful the show had become. He had played the Doctor in Comic Relief: Doctor Who - The Curse of Fatal Death (1999).

ABSOLUTELY FABULOUS: 1. This Wheel's on Fire by Julie Driscoll and Adrian Edmondson; 2. Edina Monsoon; 3. Green; 4. C) 17th; 5. Bananarama; 6. Putting it into a Jimmy Choo; 7. Julia Sawalha; 8. 2016; 9. Dame June Whitfield; 10. Debbie Harry, David Haye, Stella McCartney, Dale Winton.

British detective drama television series set during (and shortly after) the Second World War. It ran from 2002 - 2015. 8 series, 28 episodes. Each episode ran for 90 to 100 minutes, filling a two-hour time slot on ITV when commercials are included. The series is also notable for its attention to historical detail.

1. Who played the leading character, Detective Chief Superintendent Foyle?

2. The first 6 series were set in which historical Sussex coastal town?

3. What was the name of Foyle's driver and why doesn't he drive himself?

4. True or False? Christopher Foyle was a widower. His wife had been Margaret.

5. Fill in the blank. Sam Stewart married Adam Wainwright who had worked as a …. ……. during the war and went on to become an MP.

6. What was the occupation of Sam's father?

7. Sam Stewart' appeared in every episode. Which actress played her?

8. What was the name of Foyle's usual sergeant?

9. Outside his work, Foyle had what particular hobby?

10. At the end of series six, Foyle retired and decided to go where?
A) Australia   B) Canada   C) USA   D) Wales

WHAT MAKE OF CAR ……
was used to chauffeur
DCS Foyle around (left)?

DR WHO: 1. 1st - William Hartnell, 2nd - Patrick Troughton, 3rd - Jon Pertwee, 4th - Tom Baker, 5th - Peter Davison, 6th - Colin Baker, 7th - Sylvester McCoy, 8th - Paul McGann, 9th - Christopher Eccleston, 10th - David Tennant, 11th - Matt Smith, 12th - Peter Capaldi, 13th - Jodie Whittaker; 2. A Type 40; 3. 6; 4. Yes; 5. A) Pears; 6. C) Agatha Christie; 7. Theta Sigma; 8. 9th played by Christopher Eccleston; 9. Mars; 10. C) Pest control.

A British sitcom produced by Granada Television for the BBC, which ran for three series from 1998–2000, and specials from 2006–2012. A total of 25 episodes. Most episodes appear to take place in real time and all action takes place within the Royles' council house home. Unlike most UK sitcoms of the time, the show was filmed in 16 mm film using a single camera production style, instead of the multi-camera production style, and was not filmed in front of an audience.

1. What was the title of the theme song and who performed it?

2. What was Jim Royle's mocking catchphrase?

Question 3

3. Jim and Twiggy decorated the dining area for Baby David's christening by scraping off the wallpaper. What song did they scrape along to?

4. Where did Barbara work part time?

5. The Queen of Sheba featured Nana's declining health and death. Which actress played Nana?

6. What were Denise and David's kids called?

7. Which of Anthony's girlfriends gave birth on Christmas day?

8. In the 2009 Christmas special, *The Golden Egg Cup,* Dave was driving Twiggy's car. What song do the family sing-along with during the journey?

9. Which 2 members of the cast co-wrote every episode and what show did they both narrate?

10. Who lives next-door to the Royles and constantly battles with her weight,

HINT: *CORRY CARL HELL*

'My arse!'

FOYLE'S WAR: 1. Michael Kitchen; 2. Hastings; 3. Samantha Stewart, apparently it seems he does not like to drive; 4. False, it was Rosalind; 5. Code breaker; 6. Vicar; 7. Honeysuckle Weeks; 8. Sergeant Paul Milner; 9. Fly-fishing; 10. C) USA. WHAT CAR? A 1936 Wolseley 14/56 Series II.

ALL CREATURES GREAT & SMALL

A British television series made by the BBC and based on the books of a veterinary surgeon based in the Yorkshire Dales. It ran for 7 series from 1978, with 90 episodes being broadcast. Additionally 3 Christmas specials were also produced. Revived very successfully in 2020 on Channel 5 with a new cast.

THE LAST LETTER OF ANSWER 1 IS THE FIRST LETTER OF ANSWER 2 AND SO ON

1. What was the pseudonym used by the writer of the books?

2. What was Siegfried Farnon's younger brother's first name?

3. In 2020 a new series of All Creatures Great and Small appeared. Who played the main role, originally acted by Christopher Timothy?

Darrowby

4. Which market town is England's highest, set 850 feet above sea water, and is used as the location for Darrowby Cattle Market?

5. What was the name of the building that housed the vets in the series?

6. What was housekeeper Mrs Hall's first name? A) Elsie   B) Edna   C) Emily

7. Which village, containing both the vets' practice and the Drovers Arms was renamed Darrowby for the show?

8. The housekeepers for the vets 1985 special and series 4, episodes 1–5 was Mrs .... ? (Fill in the surname).

9. The real name of the vet played by Christopher Timothy was Alf ..... ? (Fill in the surname).

10. Mrs Pomphrey was brilliantly portrayed by Marguerita Scott. A) What was the name of her pampered Pekingese dog B) Which Dame played Mrs Pomphrey in 2020, but sadly died shortly afterwards?

STRANGE! *The character of Siegfried was based on a real-life vet called Donald Sinclair. By a remarkable coincidence, the character of Basil Fawlty in Fawlty Towers was also based on a real-life hotelier called Donald Sinclair.*

THE ROYLE FAMILY: *1. Half the World away by Oasis; 2. My arse! (well I gave you a clue); 3. Mambo No 5 by Lou Bega; 4. A bakery; 5. Liz Smith; 6. David and Norma; 7. Saskia; 8. LDN by Lily Allen; 9. Caroline Aherne and Dave Cash. Gogglebox; 10. Cheryl Carroll.*

The BBC's UK charity. Since 1980 it has raised over £1 billion for disadvantaged children and young people in the UK. When adjusting for the year 2020's inflation this totals £1,493,556,399 from 1980-2019.

1. Who is the mascot for BBC Children in Need?

2. Who was the long-standing host for 35 years until he sadly died in 2014?

KEEP DONATING AND HELP **CHILDREN IN NEED**

3. The BBC's first broadcast charity appeal took place in 1927, in the form of a 5-minute radio broadcast on Christmas Day. How much did it raise? A) £10,678 B) £6,123 C) £3,419 D) £1,342

4. In 1980 the first appeal using the new format was used. Who were the two female presenters alongside the long-established male lead?

5. Which presenter and radio DJ was the main presenter for just one year in 2015?

6. The first official single record for the charity *(Almost Seems) Too Late To Turn* was released in 1985. It got to No 80 in the charts. Who sung the song?

7. 2009, the familiar mascot was joined by another bear, a brown female bear, what was her name?

8. What particular challenge has Matt Baker spearheaded since 2011, raising an incredible £8.5 million in 2019?

9. In 2019 *Children in Need* issued an album for the first time. It was called *Got It Covered* and featured many stars. Who covered Coldplay's *Yellow*?

10. In 1997, 2000, 2001, 2004, 2009, 2010 and 2014 the *Children In Need* single reached number one in the UK charts. Name the performers.

Pudsey Bear appeared in 1985, and instantly transformed the Children in Need brand. He was created by BBC designer Joanna Ball, and took his name from her home town in Yorkshire.

ALL CREATURES GREAT AND SMALL: 1. James Herriott; 2. Tristan; 3. Nicholas Ralph; 4. Hawes; 5. Skeldale House; 6. B) Edna; 7. Askrigg; 8. Greenlaw; 9. Wight; 10. A) Trickii-Woo; B) Dame Diana Rigg.

CALL THE MIDWIFE

A BBC period drama series about a group of nurse midwives working in London's E End in the late 1950s and 1960s. The first series, set in 1957, premiered in the UK on 15 January 2012. There have been 9 series and 78 episodes. It has won numerous awards and nominations .

1. To what order and denomination do the sisters belong?

2. In which district of London is the programme set?

3. Who is the creator and co-producer of Call the Midwife?

4. Which actress and activist narrates the programme?

5. In 2017 the Christmas Special was set during which weather phenomenon?

6. Which character took leave of absence to overcome their alcoholism?

7. Fred discovers Sister Evangelica had passed away in her sleep, where had she died?

8. Who plays the doctor - Patrick Turner - in the series?

9. After the opening episode the BBC commissioned a second series due to excellent viewing figures. What were the viewer numbers of the first ever episode? A) 4 million B) 6 million C) 8 million D) 10 million.

10. Can you name the 5 actors from the show pictured below? Also, name the characters that they play.

BBC CHILDREN IN NEED: 1. Pudsey Bear; 2. Sir Terry Wogan; 3. D) £1,342 (equates to about £69,000 today; 4. Sue Lawley and Esther Rantzen; 5. Dermot O'Leary; 6. Clannad; 7. Blush; 8. The Rickshaw Challenge; 9. Jodie Whittaker; 10. Lou Reed & Various Artists, S Club 7 (twice), Girls Aloud, Peter Kay's Animated All-Star Band, JLS and Gareth Malone's All Star Choir.

A British sitcom, written by Dick Clement and Ian La Frenais, broadcast on BBC1 from 1974 to 1977. There were three series, and two Christmas specials and a feature film. Ranked No 35 on the 100 Greatest British Television Programmes compiled by the British Film Institute in 2000. 21 Episodes. A sequel was shown 2016/2017.

PORRIDGE

1. What is the name of the judge who sentenced Fletch and ended up sharing a cell with him?

2. Harry Grout ('Grouty') was an antagonistic, influential villain in HMP Slade, He actually appeared in only 3 episodes, but who played the role?

3. What was the name of Godber's girlfriend who dumped him in Series 2?

4. What did Mr Mackay do immediately before he joined the prison service? A) Ran a boarding house in Peebles with his wife Marie   B) Was a police officer   C) Was a security guard   D) Was a whisky taster.

5. In *Just Desserts* what was stolen from Fletcher?

6. Warren, who is illiterate, was chosen to steal the exam questions for Godber's History exam. Which paper did he mistakenly steal? A) Geography   B) English   C) Biology   D) Chemistry.

7. In *The Final Stretch*, what is the name of the prisoner with whom Godber is planning to fight?

8. In *A Storm in a Teacup*, what dropped into Fletcher's cup of tea?

9. What is the name of the rotund young man from the Midlands who had a calm and personable manner and shared a cell with Blanco?

10. With whom was the Governor's secretary, Mrs Jamieson, having an affair?

WHO IS THIS?
What relation is he to Norman Stanley Fletcher, and in which prison could you have found him on TV from 2016/17?

CALL THE MIDWIFE : 1. Order of St Raymond. Anglican; 2. Poplar; 3. Heidi Thomas; 4. Vanessa Redgrave; 5. The big freeze of 1963; 6. Trixie Franklin; 7. In an armchair by the fire; 8. Stephen McGann; 9. D) 10 million; 10. Camilla 'Chummy' Noakes (Miranda Hart); Fred Buckle (Cliff Parisi); Sister Julienne (Jenny Agutter); Rev Tom Hereward (Jack Ashton); Sister Evangelina (Judy Parfitt).

A British television series broadcast on BBC1 between 9 January 2006 and 10 April 2007. The series combines elements of speculative fiction and police procedural, featuring a police officer from the Greater Manchester Police from the year 2006 who wakes up in 1973 after being involved in a road accident. 2 series, 16 episodes.

LIFE ON MARS

1. The star of the show is Detective Chief Inspector Sam Tyler. Which former Master played the role?

2. In episode 1, what make and model of car ran Sam down after he stopped on a motorway slip road in the present day?
A) Vauxhall Cavalier   B) Saab 90   C) Fiat Mirafiori   D) Rover 2000

3. In the very first episode, Gene Hunt introduced himself to Sam by saying: 'I'm Gene Hunt. I'm your DCI. It's 1973. Almost dinnertime. I'm having _____!' A) Doughnut B) Shandy   C) Kippers   D) A pie and a pint

4. In the first series, Sam met Marc Bolan (the lead singer from T-Rex). What apt piece of advice did he give him?

5. In the penultimate episode, what was Gene Hunt forced to dress up as, allowing him to sneak into the police station?

6. A classic quote from Gene Hunt in the 2nd series, fill in the missing word: 'This is why birds and CID don't mix. You give a bloke a _____ , it's a dream come true. You give a girl one, she moans it doesn't go with her dress'.

7. In both series, Sam regularly talked to the barman at their local pub as he seemed to have a deeper insight into Sam's situation than could possibly be expected. What was this barman's name?

8. Throughout the two series, Sam received phone calls from a mystery caller. What number did he trace the calls to?
A)   London 2015   B) Hyde 2612   C) Manchester 1973   D) Bristol 1973

9. Who played DCI Gene Hunt?

10. How long was each episode? A) 30 minutes   B) 40m   C) 45m   D) 60m

PORRIDGE: 1. Rawley; 2. Peter Vaughan; 3. Denise; 4. A) Ran a boarding house with his wife Marie; 5. A tin of pineapple chunks; 6. C) Biology; 7. Jarvis; 8. A bottle of pills; 9. Lukewarm (played by Christopher Biggins); 10. Mr Barrowclough. WHO IS THIS? Nigel Norman Fletcher is the grandson of Norman Stanley Fletcher, who is sent to Wakeley Prison.

An English comedy drama series, produced by Yorkshire Television for the ITV network, first broadcast between 7 April 1991 and 4 April 1993. It is an adaptation of the 1958 novel of the same name, and its sequels, by H. E. Bates. 3 series were made containing a total of 20 episodes of approximately 50 minutes.

The Darling
Buds *of* May

1. What was 'Pop' Larkin's first name?

2. The Larkins' farm was set in rural England. In which county?

3. What was 'Ma' Larkin's first name, and how many children did her and 'Pop' have?

4. What sort of local business did Mariette and Charley purchase?

5. The frustrated romantic Rose moved to which country with a boyfriend?

6. Which actress portrayed 'Ma' Larkin and in which series did she then play a nun for 4 years?

7. Moray Watson played a retired army officer. What rank was he?

8. Who was the local spinster with whom 'Pop' often dallied?
A) Edith Pilchester B) Angela Snow
C) Mrs Daws D) Mrs Kinthley.

9. What car was Pop's pride and joy?

10. One of the most iconic scenes sees Pop and Ma enjoying a meal together in an unusual place. Where?

The Inquizitors present

QUIZ QUESTIONS IN READY ROUNDS

INQUIZITION
151+

Mike Lewis
Rob Lewis
Mo Lewis

ALSO AVAILABLE FROM AMAZON

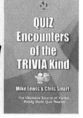

QUIZ
Encounters
of the
TRIVIA Kind

Mike Lewis & Chris Smart

The Ultimate Source of Varied, Ready Made Quiz Rounds

LIFE ON MARS 1. John Simm; 2. A) Vauxhall Cavalier; 3. Hoops; 4. Drive carefully; 5. A squirrel; 6. A gun; 7. Nelson; 8. B) Hyde 2612; 9. Philip Glenister; 10. D) 60 mins.

A British game show involving word and number tasks, Countdown is one of the longest-running game shows in the world, along with the original French version. Over 7,000 episodes and 81 series (plus specials) have been broadcast since its debut on 2 November 1982. The programme is shown in a teatime slot.

1. *Countdown* has had five presenters. Can you name all of them?

2. *Countdown* is based upon the French game, *Des Chiffres et des Lettres*. What does that title mean in English?

3. How many years did Richard Whiteley present the show before his death?
A) 15   B) 18   C) 22   D) 27

4. In 2008, Carol Vorderman left the show rather acrimoniously. Which mathematics graduate took her place?

5. What word starts with **E** and ends with **E** but only has one letter in it?

6. A word I know, six letters it contains, remove one letter, and twelve remains. What am I?

7. Solve this religious conundrum - **OH MY KNOB** (4,4).

8. Find the longest word you can make from these letters? **GYHDNOEUR.**

9. Insert addition, subtraction, multiplication and division to get the the answer **177** from these numbers - **100, 50, 9, 4,7, 8.**

10. On each episode, what is the prize for defeating the reigning champion?

The Countdown set

THE DARLING BUDS OF MAY: *1. Sidney; 2. Kent; 3. 6; 4. A brewery; 5. France; 6. Pam Ferris, Call the Midwife; 7. Brigadier; 8. A) Edith Pilchester; 9. A 1926 yellow Rolls Royce; 10. In the bath.*

A British espionage television programme created in 1961. The series ran from 1961 until 1969, screening as one-hour episodes for its entire run. The Avengers was produced by ABC Television for ITV, Rediffusion and Thames Television, who produced under the ABC name. ITV produced a sequel series, The New Avengers (1976–1977). 6 seasons 161 episodes.

1. The first series focused on Dr David Keel aided by John Steed . Who was the actor who played Dr Keel and had also starred in *The Lotus Eaters*?

2. Steed's most famous female assistants were Cathy Gale, Emma Peel and Tara King. Who were the 3 actresses who played these women?

3. Steed developed into a stereotypical English gentleman. What 3 items of clothing depicted this image?

4. Cathy Gale's innovative leather outfits were ideal for many of the athletic fight scenes that she was involved with. What was the novelty song that her and Steed took into the top 5 when it was re-released in 1990?

5. Two of Steed's assistants starred in James Bond films. Name the stars and the films.

6. In Series 6 a government official in a wheelchair who gave Steed his orders was introduced in *The Forget-Me-Knot*. Name the character.

7. From the 4th season onwards, Steed's signature cars were six vintage green racing or town cars. What make were they?

8. Patrick McNee reprised the role of Steed in *The New Avengers*. He had two new partners, Mike Gambit and Purdey. Who played those two roles?

9. A stage version of *The Avengers* was produced in 1971, directed by Leslie Phillips. Who played Steed?
A) Martin Shaw   B) Simon Oates   C) Robert Hardy

10. Finally, a 1998 film starring Uma Thurman as Emma Peel and Ralph Fiennes as John Steed was a monumental flop. Who played the villain?
A) Sean Connery B) Roger Moore C) Pierce Brosnan

Sir Sean Connery
1930-2020

COUNTDOWN: 1. Richard Whiteley, Des Lynam, Des O'Connor, Jeff Stelling, Nick Hewer; 2. Numbers and Letters; 3. C) 22; 4. Rachel Riley; 5. An envelope; 6. Dozens; 7. Hymn Book; 8. Greyhound or Hydrogen; 9. 100+50-9 = 141; 4x7=28, 141+28+8 = 177; 10. A teapot styled to resemble the 30-second time clock used in each round.

A British sitcom television series created by David Croft and Jeremy Lloyd and originally broadcast on BBC One. A parody of BBC wartime drama Secret Army, 'Allo 'Allo was launched with a pilot on 30 December 1982. followed by nine series between 7 September 1984 until its conclusion on 14 December 1992.

1. 'Allo 'Allo focuses on René Artois, a café owner in Nouvion and a reluctant member of the town's local French Resistance cell. What was Renee's codename?

2. One storyline follows the efforts of a Gestapo agent to find a stolen painting and unmask Resistance members. What is the agent's name and what is the title of the painting?

3. What are the names of the two stranded British airmen, shot down over Nouvion, waiting to be smuggled out of France?

4. Michelle 'of the Résistance' Dubois had a very well-known catchphrase. What was it?

5. Who was the 'policeman', played by Arthur Bostrom, who could speak perfectly in English, but who mangled his words when speaking in French?

6. Which star of the *Carry On* film series was frequently seen in the series?

7. Who is the head waitress in Café René, passionately in love with Rene and who is found kissing and hugging him nearly every episode?

8. Which character treats his 'little tank' as if it's a living thing, naming it Hubert after himself and showing excessive affection towards it?

9. Who was the German officer who accidentally escaped from the PoW camp, and was smuggled to England?

10. Madame Edith is tone deaf but insists on treating cafe customers to displays of her talents. What indispensable item must the customers have taken with them whilst patronising 'Café René'?

FINE ART
This is a section of which famous painting?

THE AVENGERS: 1. Ian Hendry; 2. Honor Blackman, Diana Rigg and Linda Thorson; 3. Savile Row suit, bowler hat and umbrella; 4. Kinky Boots; 5. Honor Blackman (Goldfinger) and Diana Rigg (On Her Majesty's Secret Service); 6. Mother; 7. Bentley; 8. Gareth Hunt and Joanna Lumley; 9. B) Simon Oates; 10. A) Sean Connery.

THE WONDERFUL WORLD OF SIR DAVID ATTENBOROUGH

1. What was Sir David Attenborough's relationship to the late Lord Richard Attenborough?

2. After leaving Cambridge University, which branch of the British military did he go into?

3. What animals does Sir David Attenborough admit to NOT liking?

4. Which of the following is NOT the name of a TV series made by Sir David Attenborough? A) The Life of Mammals B) State of the Planet C) Life in the Undergrowth D) Life

5. In what year did Sir David receive his knighthood?
A) 1965 B) 1975 C) 1985 D) 1995

6. This is a species named after Sir David, is it A) Sitana Attenboroughii B) Euptchia Attenboroughi C) Trigonopterus Attenboroughi D) Pristimantis Attenboroughi

7. In 2012, Sir David was among British cultural icons picked by artist Sir Peter Blake for a new version of The Beatles' Sgt. Pepper's Lonely Hearts Club Band album cover. True or False?

8. What 13 part series was the first produced in 1979 and has become a benchmark of quality in wildlife film-making and has influenced a generation of documentary film-makers?

9. In 1975 Attenborough presented a BBC children's series about crypto zoology which featured mythical creatures such as the griffin and kraken. What was that called?

10. In 1969 to what position was Attenborough promoted, making him responsible for the output of both BBC channels?

'ALLO 'ALLO: 1. Nighthawk; 2. Herr Otto Flick, The Fallen Madonna (with the Big Boobies); 3. Fairfax and Carstairs; 4. 'Listen very carefully, I will say zis only once'; 5. Officer Crabtree; 6. Kenneth Connor as Monsieur Alfonse; 7. Yvette Carte-Blanche; 8. Lieutenant Hubert Gruber; 9. Captain Hans Geering; 10. Earplugs (or cheese).
FINE ART: Fallen Madonna With the Big Boobies.

 A British police procedural TV series on ITV from 16 August 1983 - 31 August 2010. Originated from a one-off drama, Woodentop. Won several awards, incl BAFTAs, a Writers' Guild of Great Britain award, Best Drama at Inside Soap Awards in 2009, the series' 4th consecutive win. 26 series, 2425 episodes.

1. What was the name of the police station?
A) Sun Spot   B) Sun Hill   C) Sun Road   D) Bent Street

2. What rank was Jack Meadows? A) DC B) DS C) DI D) DCI

3. Where was Cathy Bradford an inspector for 6 years before Sun Hill?
A) Scotland   B) Spain   C) Hong Kong   D) France

4. Can you name the five characters from the show pictured left?

5. The finale was watched by how many viewers? A) 2m   B) 3m   C) 4m   D) 6m

6. Billy Murray played which character from 1995 to 2004? He was a cold police officer, notably having murdered DS John Boulton.

7. In 2000 one spin-off series of six episodes starred which character?
A) Burnside   B) Carver   C) Stamp   D) Meadows

8. Which character was initially perceived to be the comical oddball of the relief? *He spent his time carrying out light duties like serving as the station's collator and was Federation representative? In the show for 24 years.*

9. Trudie Goodwin played which PC, later promoted to Sergeant from 1983 to 2007. She left after her relationship with DC Jim Carver came to an end.

10. Which female DI with a know-it-all air that could be irritating, was subjected to a private prosecution for manslaughter following a raid on a crack dealer's house. She was in the show for almost a decade.

SIR DAVID ATTENBOROUGH: 1. Younger brother; 2. Navy; 3. Rats; 4. B) State of the Planet; 5. C) 1985; 6 Sitana Attenboroughii ; 7. True; 8. Life on earth; 9. Fabulous animals; 1 0. Director of Programmes.

THE BRITISH COMEDY QUIZ

1.   1966 - 1971. 33 episodes + 1 short

2. 1977 - 1981. 22 episodes

3. 1984 - 1986. 22 episodes

4. 1956 - 1961. 63 episodes

5. 1976 - 1979. 9 episodes

6. 1986 - 1987. 14 episodes

7. 1983 - 1986 22 episodes

8. 1956 - 1960 60 episodes
1971-1972

9. 1986 - 1991 40 episodes

10. 1977 - 1980 30 episodes

THE BILL: 1. B) Sun Hill; 2. D) DCI; 3. C) Hong Kong; 4. Sgt Bob Cryer, PC Reg Hollis, PC (later Sgt) June Ackland, Chief Super Brownlow, DC Jim Carver 5. C) 4m; 6. DS Don Beech; 7. A) Burnside; 8. PC Reg Hollis; 9. June Ackland; 10. DI Sally Johnson.

The Gentle Touch was A British police drama series by LWT for ITV from 1980 to1984 - 5 series, 56 episodes.. C.A.T.S Eyes was a spin-off made by TVS for ITV that ran from 1985-1987. 3 series, 30 episodes.

1. Both shows had a central, leading character. In *The Gentle Touch*, she became the first female lead in a Police drama series on TV. Who was she and who played her?

2. What happened to Maggie's husband, a police constable, in the first episode of *The Gentle Touch*?

3. Detective Sergeant Jimmy Fenton was played from 1980-1982 by an actor more remembered for a long-running medical series. Who was he?

4. In which fictitious police station was the show set?
A) Dock Green   B) Seven Dials   C) Sun Hill   D) Newtown

5. The title of the last episode in 1984 was:
A) Exit Laughing   B) The Last Laugh   C) Rough Rendevous   D) Fair Cop

6. Maggie joined an all-female private detective agency called 'Eyes' in Kent. That was a front for a Home Office team - C.A.T.S. What does the acronym represent?

7. Nigel Beaumont was the ministry officer overseeing their activities. He was played by Don Warrington, who is best remembered for which comedy series?

8. In which county is most of the filming done for the series?
A) East Sussex B) Hampshire   C) Kent   D) Essex

9. Leslie Ash starred as a streetwise computer expert. What was her name?
A)   Frederica 'Fred' Smith B) Tessa Robinson C) Pru Standfast D) Sandra Williams

10. Actress Jill Gascoine died in Los Angeles, aged 83 in 2020. A charity was set up at a Beverly Hills Gala, she attended with her husband Alfred Molina, to raise funds to fight which disease?

The Gentle Touch was the first British series to feature a female police detective as its leading character.

THE BRITISH COMEDY QUIZ: 1. All Gas and Gaiters; 2. A Sharp Intake of Breath; 3. Duty Free; 4. Hancock's Half Hour; 5. Ripping Yarns; 6. Dear John; 7. Just Good Friends; 8. Whack-O; 9. Brush Strokes; 10. Citizen Smith.

An English comedy-drama about seven English construction workers who, in series 1, leave England to search for employment overseas. Subsequent series filmed in locations in and outside the UK. 5 Series, 40 episodes. ITV from 1983-1986 and BBC1 from 2002-2004.

1. In series 1 seven out-of-work construction workers from various parts of England were forced to work in West Germany. In which city?

2. The unofficial 'leader' of the men was a Geordie played by Tim Healy. What is his character's name?

3. Can you name the other 6 characters who made up the 'Magnificent 7' in the first and second series?   An electrician from the Black Country, an insecure young newly-wed, an aggressive Geordie bricklayer, a womanising joiner from London, a Bristolian brickie and a Scouse ex-con plasterer.

4. Sadly, the actor who played the London joiner died aged 32 in 1985. What was his name?

5. Which related character took his place from Series 3 and who played the part?

6. What was Neville's wife's name?

7. In the second series the boys reunited to help Barry with his house. In which English town (now a city) was the house located?

8. The boys then helped Dennis, now working for a crooked businessman Ally Fraser, to renovate Thornely Manor. Falling foul of the locals Fraser then invited the boys to his Spanish villa to refurbish his swimming pool. Who played Fraser?

9. The show was revived on BBC1. Which real-life landmark were the boys persuaded to dismantle to be reconstructed in the Far East? A) St James Park, Newcastle   B) Middlesbrough Transporter Bridge   C) The Angel of the North

10. In series 4, to which capital city were the team posted to completely refurbish the British ambassador's new residence?

THE GENTLE TOUCH / C.A.T.S.EYES: 1. DI Maggie Forbes played by Jill Gascoine; 2. He was murdered; 3. Derek Thompson (Charlie Fairhead in Casualty); 4. B) Seven Dials; 5. A) Exit Laughing; 6. Covert Activities Thames Section ; 7. Rising Damp; 8. C) Kent; 9. A) Frederica 'Fred' Smith; 10. Alzheimer's disease.

A British TV game show based on the American Family Feud. The programme ran on ITV from 1980 to 1984. Then from 1987-2002. In July 2020, it was announced that the show will return after 18 years later in the year. To date there have been 22 series and 545 episodes. Also All Star Family Fortunes ran from 2006-2010 and 2010-2015.

1. There were 4 hosts for the show between 1980 and 2002. Can you name them and also name the new Italian presenter for 2020?

2. What was the name of the large computer screen used during 1980-1984?

3. Who hosted *All Star Family Fortunes*, a celebrity version of the show?

4. Contestants are asked to guess the results of surveys in which people would be asked open-ended questions. How many surveyed? A) 50 B) 100 C) 200 D) 500

5. How much was the top cash prize in 'Big Money' in the first series in 1980?

NOW FOR SOME TYPICAL FAMILY FORTUNES QUESTIONS.

We asked 100 people to name various things. 5 points if you match their top selection, 4 points for the second, 3 points for the third, two points for the fourth and one point for the fifth. No other answers score points.

6. Name a country whose name starts with the letter 'I'.

7. Name something that you fill with water.

8. Name a word used in a TV weather report.

9. Name something that is worn by both men and women.

10. Name something that you might catch.

CHALLENGE			41
	152		

TOWEL	18	TURKEY	0
BREAD	28	TURKEY	0
CHICKEN	58	TURKEY	21
HIGGINS	14		
TENNIS	13		
TOTAL	131	TOTAL	152

SOME ACTUAL ANSWERS! A type of bean: 'Lesbian..'; A number you might have to memorise: 'Seven..'; A medieval weapon: 'Hand-grenade..'; A reason for kneeling: 'To be beheaded..'; Someone who works early hours: 'A burglar..'

AUF WIEDERSEHEN PET: 1. Düsseldorf; 2. Dennis Patterson; 3. Barry Taylor, Neville Hope, Oz Osborne, Wayne Norris, Brian 'Bomber' Busbridge and Albert Moxey; 4. Gary Holton who played Wayne Norris; 5. His illegitimate son Wyman Norris played by Noel Clarke; 6. Brenda; 7. Wolverhampton; 8. Bill Patterson; 9. B) Middlesbrough Transporter Bridge; 10. Havana.

A 1987 series adapted by Malcolm Bradbury from the 1974 Tom Sharpe novel of the same name for Channel 4 in four episodes. Total running time 200 minutes. The series won an International Emmy and two BAFTA Awards including Best Actor. The show was repeated on the UK channel GOLD .

PORTERHOUSE B·L·U·E

1. Who memorably played the Head Porter of Porterhouse, a fictional college of Cambridge University, in *Porterhouse Blue*?

2. The title song *Dives in Omnia* (cod-Latin for 'Excess in everything') was sung by:
A) Enya   B) The Flying Pickets   C) Il Divo   D) Blake

3. What is a 'Porterhouse Blue'?
A) A Rowing award B) A soulful hymn C) A stroke brought on by over-indulgence

4. Appointed as Master, Sir Godber Evans, egged on by his zealous wife, Lady Mary, announced sweeping changes to centuries of college tradition. Who played the roles of Sir Godber and Lady Mary?

5. What got stuck in the chimney and caused an explosion that demolished the Bull Tower and killed Mrs Biggs and Zipser in their moment of passion?

6. How did Sir Godber Evans die?

7. Who paid a visit to their bank and discovered they had been left a nest egg of shares inherited from a previous master which is worth a fortune?

8. What mode of transport was used by Skullion?

9. Skullion gave a shocking revelatory interview on former student Cornelius Carrington's live television show. Who played Carrington?

10. In the finale Skullion drools joyfully as the old traditions are restored to college. What had happened to him?

TRIVIA FACT: Some of the more irreverent scenes, such as the one where Skullion races around the college quad bursting the gas-filled condoms that Zipser has released, were filmed at a mansion near Peterborough because none of the Cambridge colleges would allow them to be filmed there due to allegations of tarnishing the reputation of the university.

FAMILY FORTUNES: 1. Bob Monkhouse, Max Bygraves, Les Dennis and Andy Collins; Gino D'Acampo; 2. Mr Babbage; 3. Vernon Kay; 4. B) 100; 5. £1,000; 6. 5pts - Italy, 4pts - Iceland, 3pts - India, 2pts - Iraq 1pt - Iran; 7. 5pts - Bath, 4pts - Kettle, 3pts - Glass, 2pts - Hot water bottle, 1pt - Balloon; 8. 5pts - Rain, 4pts - Sunny, 3pts - Cloudy, 2pts - Temperature, 1pt - Cold; 9. 5pts- Trousers, 4pts - T Shirt, 3pts - Jeans, 2pts - Glasses, 1pt - Track suit; 10. 5pts - Fish, 4pts - A Cold, 3pts - Bus, 2pts - Ball, 1pt - Train.

 A British comedy panel show aired on BBC 1, made by Zeppotron. Informally abbreviated as WILTY. First broadcast on 16 June 2007, 13 series have followed, 113 x 30 minute episodes. In all rounds teams gain a point for correctly guessing whether a statement is true or not, if they guess incorrectly the opposing team gets a point. Won several Best British TV Panel Show awards.

1. Since 2009 Rob Brydon has presented the show. But which neighbour of Victor Meldrew's was in the chair for the first two series?

2. The two team captains have been in place since the beginning, who are they and which famous comedian had turned down the offer to be a team captain?

3. Which TV Quiz hostess is married to one of the team captains?

4. In Series 1 one round comprised of the showing of clips from a TV show , a statement being read out about the show by a member of one team, and the other team then having to guess whether it is true or false. Name the round.

5. What round comprises a guest comes onto the set, being introduced by first name, remaining standing in silence as the round continues, while panellists on one team tell the opposing team about their relationship to the guest? *Only one account out of three told is genuine, the opposing team has to work out which it is.*

6. Which of the following guests has appeared most times on the show as at October 2019? A) Clare Balding B) Henning When C) Rhod Gilbert D) Jo Brand

NOW PLAY THE GAME WITH FOUR QUESTIONS. JUST ANSWER TRUE OR LIE

7. When David Mitchell was a child of around 5 he was scared of the sun as somebody had said he would go blind if he looked at it. True or Lie?

8. Lee Mack had to stop listening to Vienna by Ultravox as it made his baby daughter cry. True or Lie?

9. Rob Brydon invented a theatrical agent, Richard Knight, to represent himself by using a different voice whilst negotiating on the phone. True or Lie?

10. The first horse that Lee Mack rode was 3 times Grand National winner Red Rum. True or Lie?

TRIVIA: Rob Brydon once stole Catherine Zeta-Jones's dinner money when they were both pupils of Dumbarton House School,Swansea. At the school gates Catherine's mum told him she had forgotten to give her daughter her lunch money,could Rob pass it on to her? Brydon completely forgot and bought sweets instead.

PORTERHOUSE BLUE: 1. David Jason; 2. B) The Flying Pickets; 3. C) A stroke brought on by over-indulgence; 4. Ian Richardson and Barbara Jefford; 5. Gas filled condoms; 6. Skullion hits him resulting in a fall; 7. Skullion; 8. A bicycle; 9. Griff Rhys Jones; 10. He had a Porterhouse Blue having become Master.

A soap opera is a serial that deals with domestic situations and is often characterized by melodrama, ensemble casts and sentimentality. 'Soap opera' originated from radio dramas originally being sponsored by soap manufacturers.

CORONATION STREET. MATCH THE CHARACTERS (left) WITH THE ACTORS (right)

1. GAIL PLATT	**A. PAT PHOENIX**
2. LEANNE BATTERSBY	**B. BARBARA KNOX**
3. YASMEEN NAZIR	**C. VIOLET CARSON**
4. VERA DUCKWORTH	**D. JANE DANSON**
5. SUZIE BIRCHALL	**E. JEAN ALEXANDER**
6. HILDA OGDEN	**F. SHELLEY KING**
7. ELSIE TANNER	**G. CHERYL MURRAY**
8. RITA FAIRCLOUGH	**H. SHERRIE HEWSON**
9. ENA SHARPLES	**J. LIZ DAWN**
10. MAUREEN HOLDSWORTH	**K. HELEN WORTH**
11. DANNY BALDWIN	**L. WILLIAM ROACHE**
12. ALAN HOWARD	**M. CHRIS BISSOM**
13. NICK TILSLEY	**N. STEPHEN HANCOCK**
14. EDDIE YEATS	**P. FRED FEAST**
15. CHRISTIAN GATLEY	**Q. BEN CARTWRIGHT**
16. KEN BARLOW	**R. BRADLEY WALSH**
17. ERNEST BISHOP	**S. ALAN BROWNING**
18. VIKRAM DESAI	**T. ANDREW TURNER**
19. NEIL CLIFTON	**U. WARREN JACKSON**
20. FRED GEE	**V. GEOFFREY HUGHES**

WOULD I LIE TO YOU?: 1. Angus Deayton; 2. Lee Mack & David Mitchell, Alan Carr turned down the offer; 3. Victoria Coren Mitchell (married to David Mitchell); 4. Telly Tales; 5. This is My…. ; 6. C) Rhod Gilbert; 7. True; 8. True; 9. True; 10. True.

ANTIQUES ROADSHOW

A British television programme broadcast by the BBC in which antiques experts travel to various regions of the United Kingdom (and occasionally in other countries) to appraise antiques brought in by local people. It has been running since 1979. Clocked up 42 series and 827 episodes

1. There have been 6 presenters since the show began (3 of them in the first year). Can you name them?

2. A spin-off programme, *20th Century Roadshow*, focusing on modern collectibles, aired between April and June 2005. Who hosted that show?
A) Huw Edwards B) Joanna Lumley C) Naga Munchetty D) Alan Titchmarsh

3. What was the most valuable item to ever appear on the show featured on 16 November 2008 and worth around £1m?
A) Model of Angel of the North statue   B) A Rolls-Royce car
C) A painting by Lowry   D) A Faberge egg

4. Identify the expert (left) who was also a senior director at Sotheby's.

5. Which of the following was not a location used in 2019?
B) Battle Abbey   B) Aerospace Bristol   C) Buckfast Abbey   D) Cromer Pier

6. At Lichfield Cathedral 2005 Lord Nelson's sword pistol was valued at
A) £2,000   B) £5,000   C) £20,000   D) £75,000

7. In a 2003 episode Michael Aspel arrived in the Citroen 2CV with the grandfather clock sticking up through its roof. What location?
A) Sudeley Castle   B) Berkeley Castle   C) Windsor Castle   D) Cardiff Castle

8. Can you name this expert (right) who specialises in the art, architecture, design and decorative arts of the 19th and 20th centuries?

9. What is the vintage item pictured to the left?

10. Who first earned fame as a ceramics expert on the BBC's Antiques Roadshow and then appeared on shows like *Put Your Money Where Your Mouth Is?*

CORONATION STREET: 1. K; 2. D; 3. F; 4. J; 5. G; 6. E; 7. A; 8. B; 9. C; 10. H; 11. R; 12. S; 13; U; 14; V; 15. T; 16. L; 17. N; 18. M; 19. Q; 20. P.

A British television detective drama series. A prequel to the long-running Inspector Morse. After a pilot episode in 2012, the first series was broadcast in 2013, and six more series have followed, with the exception of the year 2015 to make a total of 7 series and 30 episodes. Set in the 1960s & 1970s in Oxford, England, the series centres on the early career of Endeavour Morse (Shaun Evans) after he has left Lonsdale College of Oxford University late in his third year without taking a degree.

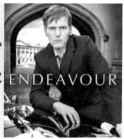

1. Who played Morse in this series?

2. Morse spent a short time in which army unit as a cipher clerk, before joining the Carshall-Newtown Police?

3. During the pilot episode, he tendered his resignation but which superior took him under his wing to be his new 'bag-man', replacing a corrupt DS?

4. In Series 1 the young Morse began to solve a string of complex multiple-murders, much to the envy and annoyance of Chief Superintendent Reginald Bright. Who brilliantly portrayed Bright in the series?

5. At the end of Series 2 Morse was wrongly arrested by officers from another force. On what charge?

6. What happened to Morse's original Sergeant's Exam paper, and how does it affect his result?

7. Who did Morse ask to marry him in series 4?

8. At the end of Series 4, Morse and Thursday averted a nuclear power plant disaster. Thursday was promoted to DCI, Morse to DS. What were they both also awarded?

9. In Series 5, now a DS, Morse was assigned a new DC, and initially was annoyed with his lack of focus. The DC was then killed in the line of duty. His name?

10. What was significantly different about Morse's physical appearance in Series 6?

TRIVIA: *Abigail Thaw, daughter of John Thaw who played Inspector Morse, appears in several episodes of Endeavour as Dorothea Frazil. Frazil is a type of ice; when combined with the character's first initial the name could be read as De-ice, which in turn could be interpreted as to 'thaw'.*

ANTIQUES ROADSHOW: 1. Bruce Parker, Angela Rippon, Arthur Negus, Huw Scully, Michael Aspel, Fiona Bruce; 2. D) Alan Titchmarsh; 3. A) A model of the Angel of the North statue; 4. Hilary Kay; 5. A) Battle Abbey; 6 C) £20,000; 7. A) Sudeley castle; 8. Paul Atterbury; 9. A washboard; 10. Eric Knowles.

BREAD — *A British television sitcom, written by Carla Lane, about a close-knit, working-class family in Liverpool, England. It was produced by the BBC and screened on BBC1 from 1 May 1986 to 3 November 1991. In 1988, the ratings for the series peaked at 21 million viewers. Bread is frequently repeated on digital television.*

1. Who wrote this hugely successful sit-com?

2. Money was collected before meals at the dinner table. In what receptacle?
A) Wooden Box   B) China Cockerel Egg Basket   C) Piggy Bank   D) Cash Box

3. Prayers were also said before meals. Which denomination were the Boswells? A) Protestant   B) Baptist   C) Roman Catholic   D) Presbyterian

4. Who was Joey's great love interest? A) Sandra B) Roxy C) Alexa D) Coleen

5. Who did the family frequently visit next door?

6. Billy got the girl over the road pregnant. What was her name?
A) Jennifer   B) Jenny C) Jill   D) Julie

7. When Nellie shouted 'She is a tart!' To whom is she referring?

8. The only Boswell daughter was Aveline, a colourful model. Who did she marry and incur the wrath of her staunchly Catholic mother?

9. What was the name of the family dog?
A) Mungo B) Mickey B) Midge D) Mongy

10. What was the name of the clerk (left) who spent all seven series enduring the various tales the Boswells spun to get more dole money. She perfected her catchphrase "Next!"?
A) Elsie B) Martina C) Celia D) Leonora

SPOT THE FACE FROM THE CAST:

Pictured in 2020, who is this former cast member who Mrs Boswell likened to a an open pastry case containing a sweet or savoury filling?

ENDEAVOUR: *1. Shaun Evans; 2. Royal Corps of Signals; 3. DI Fred Thursday; 4. Anton Lesser; 5. The Murder of Chief Constable Rupert Standish; 6. It goes "missing", automatic failure; 7. Joan Thursday (daughter of Fred); 8. The George Medal; 9. George Fancy; 10. He has grown a moustache.*

A British soap opera set in Emmerdale (known as Beckindale until 1994), a fictional village in the Yorkshire Dales. The series originally aired during the afternoon until 1978. Then moved to an early-evening prime time slot. At the time of writing it has notched up nearly 9,000 episodes.

SOAP WATCH

EMMERDALE

1. In what year did the show change its name from *Emmerdale Farm*?

2. Who is the show's longest serving character, notching up 34 years in 2020?

3. In which county is the show set?

4. Where was Belle Dingle born on Christmas Day 1998?

5. Which major storyline killed off 4 characters in 1993 and gave the show its highest ever ratings?

6. Who played Mandy Dingle between 1995 and 2001 before presenting *You've Been Framed*?

7. What was the occupation of Marlon Dingle, a character in Emmerdale since 1996?

8. The episode on 16th December 2019 was dedicated to which actress who played Annie Sugden and who had died aged 100?

9. Which half of a well-known comedy duo made his debut as pensioner Derek in September 2019?

10. How did *Emmerdale* celebrate its 40th anniversary on 17 October 2012?

TRIVIA: *Locales close to Emmerdale (situated in West Yorkshire) are market town Hotten (7½ miles away), Connelton (2¾m) and Robblesfield (3m). Emmerdale itself was called Beckindale until 1994, when it was renamed after the Sugdens' farm of the same name. It bears the (fictional) Ordnance Survey grid reference 981674.*

BREAD: 1. Carla Lane; 2. B) China Cockerel Egg Basket; 3. C) Roman Catholic; 4. B) Roxy; 5. Grandad; 6. D) Julie; 7. Lilo Lil; 8. Oswald Carter (a Protestant vicar); 9. D) Mongy; 10. B) Martina. **SPOT THE FACE FROM THE CAST:** Eileen Pollock who played Lilo Lil always described as 'A tart' by Nellie Boswell.

A British comedy game show which initially ran from 18 January 1979 to 12 March 1990 on BBC One. Then from 1979 until 1983, and from 1984 until 1990. A revival was produced by the BBC from 26 December 1997 to 28 December 1999. Finally it appeared on ITV from 7 January 2001 to 10 August 2002. A total of 17 series, 266 episodes.

1. Name the 3 hosts of *Blankety Blank* during its main runs.

2. What was the famous consolation prize awarded on the show?

3. Who hosted the last version of the show on TV, a Christmas Special for ITV on 24 December 2016?

4. Which famous centenarian fundraiser (left) appeared as a contestant in 1983?

5. Which of these celebrities did **NOT** appear on the final show, a 1999 Christmas Special?

A) Donald Sinden   B) Honor Blackman   C) Barbara Windsor   D) George Baker

FILL IN THE BLANKS FOR ANSWERS 6-10

6. The local market trader caused a stir yesterday after slipping his *(BLANK)* into a local ladies shopping bag.

7. Delilah cut off Samson's hair to sap his strength, but I just heard that first she cut off his *(BLANKS)* to slow him down.

8. Annie Oakley won the hearts of the Wild West with the biggest pair of *(BLANKS)* you ever saw.

9. My old man's a *(BLANK)*.

10. Talking about a hot dog on BBC Look North, the presenter said 'There's nothing like a big, hot *(BLANK)* inside you on a night like this'.

TRIVIA: Only seven celebrities appeared as panellists alongside all three hosts of the series: Wendy Richard, June Whitfield, Barbara Windsor, Ruth Madoc, Thora Hird, Sarah Greene and Kathy Staff.

EMMERDALE: 1. 1989; 2. Eric Pollard; 3. Yorkshire; 4. In a pigsty; 5. A plane crash; 6. Lisa Riley; 7. Chef; 8. Sheila Mercer; 9. Tommy Cannon (Cannon & Ball); 10. With its first-ever live episode.

Budgie was a popular British television series starring Adam Faith which was produced by ITV company London Weekend Television. It was broadcast between 1971 and 1972. The series was originally shot in black and white and set out as one hour stories. There were 2 series, 26 episodes recorded.

1. Name the actor who starred as *Budgie,* and also recall the title of his first number one single record from November 1959.

2. A main character was a Glaswegian gangster played by a renowned character actor who went on to play a Procurator Fiscal in a small Scottish town in 46 episodes. Name the actor and the series?

3. Budgie failed to unload thousands of stolen ballpoint pens he has unwisely bought from a fence for a silly price. What was the problem?

4. Budgie accidentally stole the wrong Ford Transit which was full of pornography. Who owned the van and where was its heading?

5. In yet another hare-brained disaster Budgie arranged a pornographic film show in a hotel. He scarpered when the film turns out to be:
A) Coronation Street B) Laurel & Hardy C) Fanny Craddock cooking show

6. Budgie's girlfriend Hazel went on to appear in Emmerdale Farm as Ruth Merrick Sugden and in Crossroads as Rita Hughes. What was the actresses name? A) Lynn Dalby   B) Adrienna Posta;   C) June Lewis

7. What was Budgie's real name? A) Tom Wren B) Jack Daw C) Ronald Bird

8. John Rhys-Davies had 270 acting credits including *Raiders of the Lost Ark*. He appeared in 6 episodes of *Budgie*. And his gangster character's name in the show was: A) Laughing Spam Fritter B) Cold Turkey C) Cheddar Cheese

9. All but two episodes of Budgie were written by the same writing partnership: A) Ray Galton & Alan Simpson B) Keith Waterhouse & Willis Hall C) Dick Clement & Ian Le Frenais

10. What sort of club did Charlie Endell run? A) Country   B) Strip   C) Chess

ADAM FAITH TRIVIA: 1. Towards the end of his musical career Adam had a backing group in an attempt to bring his music closer to the Mersey sound that was so popular at the time. What was this band called? 2. On his 1960 hit Made You, which other hit maker of the time played lead guitar?

BLANKETY BLANK: 1. Terry Wogan, Les Dawson, Paul O'Grady; 2. A Blankety Blank chequebook and pen; 3. David Walliams; 4. Captain Sir Tom Moore; 5. D) George Baker (he appeared on the first episode on 18/1/79; 6. Phone number; 7. Legs; 8. Pistols (or Guns); 9. Dustman; 10. Sausage.

A sit-com shown on BBC1. The first episode was broadcast on 27 August 2012, in a late time slot of 10:20pm. It follows the trials and tribulations of Mr Khan, a loud-mouthed, patriarchal, cricket-loving, self-appointed community leader, and his long suffering wife and 2 daughters. The title is a play on words of the Orson Welles film Citizen Kane. The show ran for 5 series and 34 episodes.

1. Who wrote and starred in *Citizen Khan*?

2. Where was the inner-city suburb of Birmingham in the show?

3. In 2013 and 2014 the show won 2 Royal Television Society Awards for Best performance in a comedy – Adil Ray, and Best Comedy Programme. True or False?

Transformation!

4. What was Mr Khan's first name?

5. What colour was Mr Khan's Mercedes car, and what is displayed on the bonnet?

6. In October 2015 Adil Ray, as Mr Khan, took over the train announcements at Birmingham New Street station for an hour. True or False?

7. Kris Marshall played Dave in the first series. Who took over the part?
A) Matthew Cottle   B) Phil Nice   C) Felix Dexter

8. Mr Khan had two daughters. What were their names?
A) Razia & Shobu   B) Alia & Shazia   C) Haniya & Yameena

9. Amjad was training to be to a Police Community Support Officer. Mr Khan called him: A) Toy Policeman   B) Hobby Bobby   C) PC Plodder

10. When his younger daughter had a boyfriend, Scab, from a wealthy home, Mr Khan tried to impress his parents. Who plays A) Scab and B) Scab's father?

BUDGIE: 1. Adam Faith, What Do You Want; 2. Iain Cuthbertson, Sutherland's Law; 3. Stamped with the logo of Her Majesty's Government; 4. The Police, heading to the incinerator; 5. B) Laurel & Hardy; 6. A) Lynn Dalby; 7. C) Ronald Bird; 8. A) Laughing Spam Fritter; 9. B) Keith Waterhouse & Willis Hall; 10. B) Strip Club.
ADAM FAITH TRIVIA: 1. The Roulettes; 2. Joe Brown.

Mixed set of questions covering categories including Drama, Children's TV, Comedy, Soaps, Cookery programmes, Sci-Fi, News Years, Catchphrases, Crime shows and some more! There are 3 sets of mixed questions in the book.

All Kinds of Everything

1

A Miscellaneous Round

1. The expression 'well jel' meaning very jealous was made famous after regular use in what part soap opera, part reality show?

2. What colour is Mr Strong's hat in the *Mr Men*? A) Blue   B) Red   C) Green

3. Who played barmaid Michelle Connor in *Coronation Street*?

4. Who played the title role in *Dr Quinn, Medicine Woman*?

5. On Deal or No Deal what was the highest 'blue' amount of money?
A) £500   B) £750   C) £1000

6. In what year did *Ready Steady Cook* make its debut on BBC2 and who was the presenter until 2000?

7. In *The Kumars at No 42* what is the real life relationship between the actors who played Sanjeev Khumar and his grandmother Sushila (Ummi)?

8. In which sit-com were Eddie Booth and Bill Reynolds neighbours?

9. What is the name of *Bob the Builder*'s female business partner?

10. What car did Roger Moore drive in *The Saint*?
A) Aston Martin   B) Jaguar   C) Volvo

11. What long-standing star of Coronation Street had an uncredited role as an urchin in the 1968 musical film Oliver?
A) Helen Worth   B) Bill Roache   C) Barbara Knox

12. Who does the voiceover on *Love Island*?

13. Where is *Strictly Come Dancing* filmed?

14. Which girl band performed during the opening minutes of the *Channel 5* launch in 1997?

15. What *Cold Feet* character was killed going to an auction to buy a house?

CITIZEN KHAN: 1. Adil Ray; 2. Sparkhill, East Birmingham; 3. True; 4. It is never revealed; 5. Yellow, the Pakistan flag; 6. True; 7. A) Matthew Cottle; 8. B) Alia & Shazia; 9.B) Hobby Bobby; 10. A) Tyger Drew-Honey B) Harry Enfield.

ITV 12 episodes 1992-1993.   BBC 52 episodes 1960-1963.   ITV 4 episodes 2016-17

1. Name the three actors who have appeared as Maigret in the three TV series?

2. Maigret's first name is rarely used, even by his wife. What is it?
A) Georges   B) Jules   C) Victor   D) Marius

3. The writer of the Maigret novels commented 'At last, I have found the perfect Maigret!' when the BBC version was launched in 1960. Who wrote the novels and who was playing the part?

4. In 1988 there was another one-off on ITV starring a major star as Maigret. Who played the role somewhat idiosyncratically?
A) Richard Harris   B) Alan Bates   C) Maurice Denham   D) Robert Powell

5. Variety called the 1992 Maigret series 'clever and soaked with procedure and atmosphere' and noted that the production values were 'first class'. Where was the series filmed as post-WWII France?
A) Birmingham   B) Munich   C) Budapest   D) Dublin

6. In 2016 the first episode saw Maigret under heavy pressure from his superiors and the press because he has failed to catch a serial killer of women. The story was titled Maigret .... A) At the Crossroads   B) Sets a Trap   C) Afraid   D) Hesitates

7. Maigret does have some vices. Which is the odd one out - Drinking, Gambling, Gourmandizing, Smoking.

8. Maigret cannot drive or swim. True or False?

9. Do you know the first name of Madam Maigret?
A) Marie   B) Charlotte   C) Louise   D) Hazel

10. Which Maigret actor was the first person to be Pipe Smoker of the Year in 1964? Also awarded Best Actor in 1962.

TRIVIA ABOUT THE WRITER: Georges Simenon weighed himself before and after writing each of his novels. This was partly to measure how much each novel made him sweat. He reckoned that writing a book cost him one-and-a-half litres of sweat.

ALL KINDS OF EVERYTHING 1: *1. The Only Way Is Essex; 2. C) Green; 3. Kym Marsh; 4. Jane Seymour; 5. B) £750; 6. 1994, Fern Britton; 7. Sanjeev Bhaskar and Meera Syal are husband and wife; 8. Love Thy Neighbour; 9. Wendy; 10. Volvo P1800 (STI); 11. Helen Worth; 12. Iain Stirling; 13. Elstree Studios; 14. The Spice Girls; 15. Rachel Bradley.*

A British game show, hosted by Noel Edmonds, which aired from 31 October 2005 to 23 December 2016 on Channel 4. The programme was regularly aired daily – for its first eight series. The show was then aired six days a week for a year, with breaks in production between July and August . A total of 13 series. 3003 episodes.

1. Since 2014, contestants can win prize money ranging from between 1p and £500,000. How many boxes were used prior to 2014?
A) 20   B) 21   C) 22   D) 23

2. How many contestants won £250,000, and how many were women?

3. On 12 February 2014 Roop Singh was the first winner offered what?

4. The original studio set for the show was converted from an old paintworks factory and its associated warehouses. In which city?

5. What name is given to the show's quasi-fictional antagonist who talks to Noel via the old Bakelite telephone on the player's desk, and also regularly talks to the player?

6. Noel Edmonds played the game for the first time to raise money for charity, winning £26,000 for Children's Hospice on the 10-year anniversary show in 2015. Who was the guest host on the show?
    A) Alan Carr B) Stephen Mulhern C) Sarah Millican D) Alexander Armstrong

7. Box 23 contains 5 cards, Double, +£10,000, Half, Nothing and ....what?

8. 2009 *X Factor* runner-up Olly Murs was a contestant on *Deal or No Deal* in the same year. How much did he win?
                A) £10   B) £2,000   C) £15,000   D) 50,000

9. The highest amount of money won by a celebrity on DOND won £70,000. Who was the celebrity?
        A) Katie Price   B) McFly   C) Louis Walsh   D) Joan Collins

10. The winner of many daytime TV awards, how much prize money was given away as at February 2015? A) £10 million B) £20m C) 30m D) £40m

In one show in 2008, one contestant who only had two boxes remaining (50p and £750), was given a banker offer of £0 (and twelve eggs). He rejected the offer but did swap boxes and won £750.

MAIGRET: 1. Rupert Davies, Michael Gambon, Rowan Atkinson; 2. B) Jules; 3. Georges Simenon, Rupert Davies; 4. A) Richard Harris; 5. C) Budapest; 6. Sets a Trap; 7. Gambling; 8. True; 9. C) Louise; 10. Rupert Davies.

Formerly known as Crossroads Motel and Crossroads King's Oak, a British TV soap opera that ran on ITV over two periods – originally 1964 -1988, followed by a short revival from 2001 -2003. The series regularly attracted huge audiences during this time, with ratings as high as 15 million viewers. Episodes: original series 4,510 , revived series 320.

CROSSROADS

1. The Crossroads Motel was located on the outskirts of the small village of A)
A) King's Oak B) Queen's Elm C) Princes Poplar

2. Who said the first words, 'Crossroads Motel, may I help you?' in Episode 1 in November 1964? A) Meg Richardson B) Benny Hawkins C) Jill Richardson

3. Meg may not have realised it at the time, but she was leaving a sinking ship when she sailed into the sunset. Where and when did she go?
A) Wolverhampton 1982 B) Kidderminster 1983 C) New York 1981

4. In which unlikely spot did Meg briefly turn up almost two years later at Jill and Adam's honeymoon ? A) Sorrento   B) Vienna   C) Marbella

5. What caused Miss Diane's death?
A) Brain haemorrhage   B) Car crash C) Cancer

6. How did Benny's plan to marry Maureen Flynn end? A) She ran off with a car salesman B) Knocked off her bicycle and died   C) Allergic to woolly hats

7. Who wrote the theme? A) Paul McCartney B) Tony Hatch C) Ron Grainer

8. Doris Luke was played by an actress who gained fame for her wrinkled stockings in a long-running sit-com. Who was she and what was the sit-com?

9. Name this character (left), played by Ronald Allen, who appeared in the show from 1969-1985 .

10. The show launched several singles into the UK charts. Marilyn Gates' nightclub song hit number 17 in 1968 by which actress member of the cast? (Clue: Went on to be a Corrie star).

DEAL OR NO DEAL: 1. 22; 2. 9, 7 of them women; 3. Box 23 (he would have won £500,000 if he had accepted the swap!); 4. Bristol; 5. The Banker; 6. C) Sarah Millican; 7. Money Back; 8. A) £10; 9. C) Louis Walsh (all the others have appeared on the show); 10. £40 million.

Crime drama shows have always been very popular on our TV screens. Going right back to New Scotland Yard, Dixon of Dock Green and many more, right up to Gangs of London. Here is a round covering 10 such shows.

WATCHING
—THE—
DETECTIVES

1. Both Endeavour Morse and 'Jack' Frost won awards for bravery. What were they?

2. Stratford Johns will be forever associated with his famous police role on TV. It began on Z Cars and moved through Softly, Softly : Task Force into an eponymous series from 1971-1975. What was the role?

3. Which actor moved from being a DS in the Channel Islands to a DCI in a fictional English county with some deadly villages?

4. Peter Davison played Albert Campion in a British television mystery drama broadcast for two series from 1989 -1990. Who wrote the books?
A) Agatha Christie   B) Ngaio Marsh   C) Margery Allingham   D) Dorothy L Sayers

5. Two famous TV detectives have had their faces morphed. (left). Name both of them.

6. A British detective television series, broadcast on BBC1, adapted from novels by Dame Ngaio Marsh, featured which actor as Chief Inspector Roderick Alleyn?

7. DCI Roseanne "Roz" Huntley was an intelligent and ambitious officer leading a major murder hunt and determined to get her career back on track; the scale and speed of her fall is almost Shakespearean. In what series?

8. In which series was WPC Shirley Trewlove at the heart of the police team?

9.The Tunnel was a British–French crime drama television series adapted from the 2011 Danish-Swedish crime series The Bridge. Who played Detective Chief Inspector Karl Roebuck of Northbourne Police?

10. John Woodvine had a regular role in the seminal British drama series Z-Cars as Det Insp. Witty (1968–69) and also in Softly, Softly. In which series, named after a famous building, did he play a Chief Superintendent in 1972-3?

CROSSROADS: 1. A) Kings Oak; 2. C) Jill Richardson; 3. C) New York in 1981; 4. B) Vienna; 5. A) Brain haemorrhage; 6. B) She was knocked off her bicycle and died; 7. B) Tony Hatch; 8. Kathy Staff, Last of the Summer Wine (Nora Batty); 9. David Hunter; 10. Sue Nicholls.

A British sitcom following holidaymakers who spent a week (usually) in Benidorm, Spain. It is the same people who go at the same time of year, by coincidence of course. Produced by Tiger Aspect for ITV the show aired for ten series from 1 February 2007 until 2 May 2018. 74 episodes were shown.

1. What was the name of the all-inclusive hotel the series centres around?

2. Which holidaymaker agreed to meet a girl he met on the Internet, but his date turned out to be a man dressed as a woman?

3. What was the name of the hairdressing salon in Benidorm, and which duo operate the business?

4. Geoff had a sister with an alcohol problem, what was her name?

5. Joyce Temple Savage was an air-hostess with BOAC and then a cruise ship manager before she ran the Solana Resort . What actress portrayed Joyce?

6. Madge was Janice's mother. She was a sharp-tongued, sun-worshipping grandmother! Rarely seen without a fag, she was normally either sun-bathing or driving around insulting people. What mode of transport did she use?

7. Which barman got himself dates with all the ladies?

8. High on pills, who did Maggie mistake a famous singer for?

9. In Series 8 Tiger and Joey took on a mountain challenge with little provisions. They asked a passing stranger, Grenville Titcombe, for water. Who played the guest role of Titcombe?

10. Donald* died from a heart attack in his sleep in 2015. Where did his widow Jacqueline and friends Troy and Kenneth try to scatter his ashes?

*TRIVIA: Geoffrey Hutchings (Mel) and * Kenny Ireland (Donald) had to be written out of the series after their deaths. In both cases, their characters died off-screen.*

WATCHING THE DETECTIVES: 1. Morse won the George Medal and Frost the George Cross; 2. Charlie Barlow (initially DCI then DCS; 3. John Nettles (Bergerac to Midsomer Murders); 4. C) Margery Allingham; 5. George Baker (Wexford) & Nathaniel Parker (Lynley); 6. Patrick Malahide; 7. Line of Duty (series 4); 8. Endeavour; 9. Stephen Dillane; 10. New Scotland Yard.

A British crime drama television series filmed and set in the Calder Valley, West Yorkshire, in Northern England. The first series debuted on BBC One on 29 April 2014, and the second series debuted on 9 February 2016. In May 2015, Happy Valley won the BAFTA Award for Best Drama Series. Two series 12 episodes. More planned.

HAPPY VALLEY

1. Catherine Cawood was a strong-willed police sergeant in West Yorkshire, still coming to terms with the suicide of her teenage daughter, Becky, eight years earlier. Who won the best actress award in 2014 for playing her?

2. In which part of England was the series set?

3. For what crime was Tommy Lee Royce originally serving 8 years in prison?

4. Where did Catherine find Ann Gallagher?

5. When in Disguise, what book was Tommy Lee Royce seen carrying?

6. What was the Name Of DS John Wadsworth's mistress?

7. In Series 2 Catherine was back at work. How was she awarded for rescuing Ann Gallagher ? A) George Medal B) George Cross C) Queen's Police Medal

8. Ryan, developed a friendship with a new Teaching Assistant who was secretly a prison groupie infatuated with Royce. What was her assumed name? A) Miss Wealand B) Miss Brodie C) Miss Shackleton

9. Catherine successfully ensures how many female victims of human trafficking were taken to safe houses? A) 4 B) 13 C) 21

10. When Catherine approaches the suspected killer he flees to the edge of a bridge. What follows? A) He confesses and is arrested B) He confesses and jumps to his death C) He names the real killer and is arrested.

BENIDORM: 1. Solana; 2. Geoff; 3. Blow 'n' Go, Kenneth and Liam; 4. Pauline; 5. Sherrie Hewson; 6. Mobility scooter; 7. Mateo; 8. Tom Jones; 9. Angus Deayton; 10. From the cliff overlooking Benidorm.

A British sit-com about a committee man. He has numerous schemes and committees organized around the neighbourhood. He is so obsessive about every detail of everything he does, he is driving his long-suffering wife slowly crazy. Then the new neighbour arrives! The show ran on BBC1 from 1984 and 1989. 4 Series. 27 episodes.

1. *Ever Decreasing Circles* was written by John Esmonde and Bob Larbey. They had written another smash hit comedy series for Richard Briers. Which series? A) Brush Strokes   B) The Good Life   C) Please Sir!

2. An undercurrent running throughout the series is the unresolved sexual tension and flirting between Paul and Ann. Who played the roles?

3. Richard Briers plays an obsessive, middle-aged man at the centre of his local suburban community in East Surrey. What was his name?

4. Who are the long-standing friends and neighbours of Martin's, who always wear 'his and hers' matching outfits?

5. What kind of business did Paul run?

6. What did Martin always do when he walked into the house through the front door?

7. Who won the annual pub snooker tournament?

8. What is the name of the house that Martin and Ann lived in?
A) Meadow View   B) Brooksmead   C) Home Sweet Home

9. For five years Martin, Ann, Howard and Hilda always went on holiday together. What was the name of the hotel in 'The Black Forest' where they went? A) Hotel Glockenspiel   B) Black Forest Hotel   C) Hotel Bavaria

10. Martin liked to send notices out to everyone in his clubs and associations. What were they produced on: A) Photocopier B) Handwritten C) Manual printing press.

WHO'S BEEN MORPHED?
Two faces merged together. Who are they?

HAPPY VALLEY: 1. Sarah Lancashire; 2. Calder Valley, West Yorkshire; 3. Drug related offences; 4. In Lynn Dewhurst's cellar; 5. Tolstoy's War and Peace; 6. Vicky Fleming; 7. C) Queen's Police Medal; 8. A) Miss Wealand; 9. 21; 10. B) He confesses and jumps to his death .

A British TV quiz show based on an American show of the same name. A solo player and a team of two answer trivia questions, clued up with an initial letter of the answer, to complete a path across or down a game board of hexagons. Ran from 1983-1995. 16 series, 1541 episodes. Occasional Specials made since Series ended.

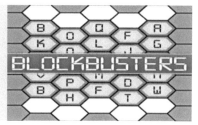

1. The show has had 5 presenters from 1983-2019, can you name them?.
A) 1983-95, B) 1997, C) 2000-01, D) 2012 and E) 2019.

2. With what memorable hit from 1978 is Bob Holness still frequently wrongly attributed with playing the saxophone solo?

3. Bob Holness presented the show on ITV for 10 years. He then presented it on another TV channel for 2 years (1994-5). Which channel?

4. The winner of the match went on to play which bonus round?

NOW FOR SOME BLOCKBUSTERS STYLE QUESTIONS

5. What 'H' was the place where England's Harold II lost his life?

6. What 'O' is an audience reaction of enthusiastic applause often executed standing up?

7. What 'TDF' is an annual European sporting event, basically a bike race?

8. What 'OOB' is where you should not go, or is it an exhausted kangaroo?

9. What 'BTP' involved the destruction of 342 chests of tea?

10. What 'SA' is a religious movement founded by William Booth?

11. What 'ST' is a popular breed of toy dog?

12. What 'GOITMS' according to Noel Coward is what mad dogs and English men do?

13. What 'FPAAP' Is the name of the house band on the TV show Friday Night with Jonathan Ross?

14. What 'TCOTLB' was an Historical Event occurred on October 25, 1854?

15. What 'TFWOM' is what Nancy Wilkinson became on TV In 1972?

EVER DECREASING CIRCLES: 1. B) The Good Life; 2. Penelope Wilton and Peter Egan; 3. C) Martin Bryce; 4. Howard and Hilda Hughes; 5. Hairdressing Salon; 6. Turns the telephone around; 7. Howard Hughes; 8. Brooksmead; 9. A) Hotel Glockenspiel; 10. C) Manual printing press. MORPHED: Richard Briers & Peter Egan.

The UK channels and independent production companies output a significant amount of TV drama which is shot all over the UK. TV dramas span all genres; they can be a one-off or a series whose air time is usually capped at an hour. Many have been immensely successful in the UK and around the world.

DRAMA

1. What was the title of the series from 1976-77, that starred Gemma Jones working her way up from servant to proprietress at the Bentinck Hotel?

2. Which star of *Pink Panther* films starred on ITV from 1963/5 as Dr Roger Corder who consults at 162 Harley Street, London and St Damian's Hospital?

3. What comedy-mystery-drama series was filmed on location in Plockton, near Kyle of Lochalsh and in the surrounding areas from 1995-1997?

4. What 1986 award-winning BBC mini-series, adapted from Fay Weldon's novel, concerned Ruth and Bobbo, on the verge of separation. Bobbo was having an affair with novelist Mary Fisher and Ruth plans to get her revenge?

5. What 60s series starring Patrick Wymark focused on power struggles between trade union and management at an aircraft factory, Scott Furlong Ltd, as well as including political in-fighting within the management. What series succeeded it?

6. *Reilly: Ace of Spies*, was a 1983 ITV mini-series about Sidney Reilly, a Russian-born adventurer and a great spy. Who played the title role?

7. *Rome* was a British-American-Italian production,scheduled for 5 seasons. However, after just 2 seasons, 2005-7, it was halted due to high production costs. What was the cost of the 2 seasons? A) £25m   B) £63m   C) 89m

8. *Lipstick on your Collar* was a 1993 serial centred around British Military Intelligence in Whitehall including contemporary songs. Who wrote the serial and who had a number 3 hit record with the same title in 1959?

9. In the 2014 2-part drama *The Lost Honour of Christopher Jefferies*, about the tragic murder of Joanna Yeates, who played the award winning title role?

10. *The Durrells* is based upon Gerald Durrell's three autobiographical books about his family's four years (1935–1939) on which Greek Island?

BLOCKBUSTERS: 1. A) Bob Holness, B) Michael Aspel, C) Lisa Tarbuck, D) Simon Mayo, E) Dara O'Briain; 2. Saxophone solo in Baker Street by Gerry Rafferty (actually played by Raphael Ravenscroft); 3. Sky One; 4. Gold Run; 5. Hastings; 6. Ovation; 7. Tour De France; 8. Out of bounds; 9. Boston Tea Party; 10. Salvation Army; 11. Shih Tzu; 12. Go out in the midday sun; 13. Four Poofs and a Piano; 14. The Charge of the Light Brigade; 15. The first winner of Mastermind.

British serial crime drama series broadcast on ITV for 3 series from 2013 - 2017. A total of 24 episodes. All 3 series had positive reviews for writing, cinematography and character development. Series 1 nominated for 7 BAFTA awards. Series 3 won award for best Crime Drama at the National Television Awards in early 2018

1. In Series 1 what was the name of the 11-year old boy murdered and found on the beach beneath the cliffs?

2. In which 2 seaside towns was the majority of the series filmed?

3. Which mysterious member of the community had the murdered boy's missing skateboard hidden in their cupboard? Who played the character?

4. Throughout the murder enquiry DI Hardy attempts to cover up which serious health problem?
A) Cancer   B) Multiple sclerosis   C) Heart condition

5. What is the name of the Latimer's new baby?
A) Daniel   B) Elizabeth   C) Mark

6. What were the names of the 2 girls who went missing in Sandbrook?
A) Lisa & Laura   B) Pippa & Laura   C) Pippa and Lisa

7. Why is Joe Miller's confession excluded from his trial?

8. What relation was Nigel Carter to Susan Wright?

9. Who was the vicar, Rev Paul Coates, dating?

10. There are 6 women characters from Broadchurch pictured below. Can you name the actresses and then link them to one of these 6 TV shows: i) Coronation Street ii) Line of Duty iii) Birds of a Feather iv) Howard's Way v) London Spy vi) Frankie

A	B	C	D	E	F
JOCELYN KNIGHT	CLAIRE RIPLEY	TRISH WINTERMAN	SUSAN WRIGHT	KAREN WHITE	CS ELAINE JENKINSON

DRAMA: 1. Duchess of Duke Street; 2. Herbert Lom; 3. Hamish McBeth; 4. The Life and Loves of a She-Devil; 5. The Plane Makers, The Power Game; 6. Sam Neill; 7. B) £63m; 8. Dennis Potter, Connie Francis; 9. Jason Watkins; 10. Corfu.

A British television magazine and chat show programme. Broadcast live on BBC One weeknights at 7:00 pm, it features topical stories and studio guests. Launched with a pilot series in 2006, then a full series from 2007. Now notched up over 3,000 episodes.

1. The first long-running male/female duo hosted the show from 2007-2010. Who were they, and before them which 2 women who had hosted?

2. In 2010, it was announced the show was being revamped with an hour-long Friday episode, to be hosted by whom?

3. After some further changes another duo was established in 2011 and lasted until 2019. Who were the new long-running pair?

4. On 26 January 2015, the draw for a major UK sporting event was held live on the show for the first time. This has been repeated since. What tournament is involved?

5. On 1 February 2016, to whom did the show broadcast a one-hour tribute?

6. Who left the show in Spring 2020 to spend more time with his family, but reassured viewers that he will continue to work with the BBC?

7. *The One Show* moved location again to Broadcasting House in January 2014. Where had it been broadcast from for the previous 7 years?

8. Which former UK Prime Minister's daughter did not have her contract renewed when the BBC refused to accept an apology for an alleged off camera racist comment after filming?

9. Which annual charity challenge, linked to the *One Show*, involving 6 young people, has raised tens of millions for *Children in Need*?

10. Which two long-term presenters have entered *Strictly Come Dancing* and come 2nd in 2010 and 5th in 2011 respectively?

BROADCHURCH: 1. Danny Latimer; 2. West Bay , Dorset and Clevedon, Somerset 3. Susan Wright played by Pauline Quirke; 4. C) Heart condition; 5. B) Elizabeth; 6. C) Pippa & Lisa; 7. Because Ellie beat him up whilst in custody; 8. He is her son; 9. Becca Fisher; 10. A) Charlotte Rampling (v); B) Eve Myles (vi); C) Julie Hesmondhalgh (i) D) Pauline Quirke (iii); E) Vicky McClure (ii); F) Tracey Childs (iv).

A British mystery drama programme that aired on ITV from 8 January 1989 to 13 November 2013. The programme ran for 13 series and 70 episodes in total; each episode was adapted from a novel or short story by Dame Agatha Christie that featured Hercule Poirot.

1. Who was recommended to play Poirot by Agatha Christie's family, who had seen him as Blott in Tom Sharpe's *Blott on the Landscape*?

2. Which Hercule Poirot novel is titled *Le Crime du Golf* in France?

3. Hercule Poirot, Ariadne Oliver, Colonel Race and Superintendent Battle all appeared together in which Agatha Christie story?
A) *Death on the Nile* B) *Why Didn't They Ask Evans?* C) *Cards on the Table*

4. Match the correct year each of the listed 5 titles was first published:

A. *The ABC Murders*	**i) 1941**
B. *Death on the Nile*	**ii) 1975**
C. *Evil Under the Sun*	**iii) 1952**
D. *Curtain*	**iv) 1933**
E. *Mrs McGinty's Dead*	**v) 1936**

5. There were 70 BBC adaptions of Poirot stories in this series. What was the first one shown in January 1989?
A) *Adventures of the Clapham Cook* B) *The Veiled Lady* C) *Wasp's Nest*

6. Which future star of Inspector Lynley Mysteries was Chris Davidson in *The Affair at the Victory Ball* in March 1991?

7. Three acting sisters have each appeared in an episode: *The King of Clubs*, *Jewel Robbery at The Grand Metropolitan*, and *Dead Man's Folly*. Name them.

8. Christopher Gunning won a BAFTA award for the series in 1990. What for?

9. Which brother of Poirot's star is a former newsreader turned radio presenter?

10. In the last story *Curtain* what does Poirot do to James Norton before he dies?

THE ONE SHOW: *1. Adrian Chiles and Christine Bleakley, Nadia Sawalha and Myleene Klass; 2. Chris Evans; 3. Alex Jones and Matt Baker; 4. The FA Cup; 5. Sir Terry Wogan; 6. Matt Baker; 7. BBC Media Village, White City; 8. Carol Thatcher; 9. The Rickshaw Challenge with Matt Baker; 10. Matt Baker and Alex Jones.*

CRITICAL:

An historical drama series about the reign of Queen Elizabeth II, produced by Left Bank Pictures and Sony Pictures Television for Netflix. It grew out of Morgan's film The Queen (2006) and his stage play The Audience (2013), and is credited as based on the latter. 3 seasons, 30 episodes from 2016. More scheduled.

HERE ARE 10 ACTORS WHO HAVE APPEARED IN THE CROWN. CAN YOU NAME THE REAL LIFE PEOPLE THEY ARE PORTRAYING IN THE SERIES?

1. Olivia Colman; 2. Josh O'Connor; 3. Gillian Anderson; 4. Erin Doherty; 5. Jason Watkins; 6. Helena Bonham-Carter; 7. Matt Smith; 8. Emma Corrin; 9. Anton Lesser; 10. Marion Bailey.

AGATHA CHRISTIE'S POIROT: 1. David Suchet; 2. Murder on the Links; 3. C) Cards on the Table; 4. A(v), B(iv), C(i) D(ii), E(iii); 5. A) Adventures of the Clapham Cook; 6. Nathaniel Parker; 7. Cusack; Niamh, Sorcha, Sinéad; 8. Best Original Television Music; 9. John Suchet; 10. Shoots him dead.

A British game show, presented by Warwick Davis and airing daytime on ITV from 14 November 2016. On each episode, five contestants attempt to win up to £125,000 by filling in the lists of 10 items each. To date there have been 4 series and 200 episodes.

FOOTBALL

Name the last 10 different teams to win the English FA Cup.

GEOGRAPHY

Name the 10 US States that have two words in their name.

SCIENCE

Name the 10 elements in the Periodic Table that have fewer than 6 letters in their name.

MOVIES

Name the next 10 Animated Classics Disney feature films released from 1950.

ONLY FOOLS AND HORSES
Name the 10 characters who have appeared in most episodes.

THE CROWN: 1. Queen Elizabeth II; 2. Prince Charles; 3. Margaret Thatcher; 4. Anne, Princess Royal; 5. Harold Wilson; 6. Princess Margaret; 7. Prince Philip, Duke of Edinburgh; 8. Princess Diana; 9. Harold MacMillan; 10. Queen Elizabeth, The Queen Mother.

BAND of GOLD

A British television crime drama series that first broadcast on ITV on 12 March 1995. Produced by Granada Television, the series revolves around the lives of a group of sex workers. Three series of Band of Gold were produced (the third entitled Gold with not too many returning characters). Last episode was on 1 December 1997. 3 Series. 18 Episodes.

1. In which city's Red Light District was the series based?

2. Which renowned writer created and wrote the series?

3. Debts forced mother of 3 Gina, onto the street where she was murdered. Who played Gina? A) Ruth Gemmell B) Cathy Tyson C) Sam Morton

4. Carol had a tryst with which police detective in charge of the murder investigation? A) DI Barlow B) DCI Newall C) DCS Dalgleish

5. Rose and Carol gave up the street and ran a cleaning company with financial support from Anita. What was it called?
A) Magic Maids B) Clean Game C) Scrubbit

6. Who murdered Curly and George Ferguson? A) Tracy B) Collette C) Anita

7. What happened to Tracy at the end of Series 2?

8. And what happened to Carol?

9. Which award winning actress played Rose?

10. In Series 3, entitled *Gold* and regarded as a spin-off, who perished in a fire, as the series ends on a final dramatic and tragic note?
A) Carol B) Rose C) Charlie

TENABLE: *FOOTBALL - Arsenal, Manchester United, Wigan Athletic, Manchester City, Chelsea, Portsmouth, Liverpool, Everton, Tottenham Hotspur, Wimbledon.* **GEOGRAPHY** *-New Hampshire, New Jersey, New Mexico, New York, North Dakota, North Carolina, Rhode Island, South Dakota, South Carolina, West Virginia.* **SCIENCE** *- Tin, Gold, Iron, Lead, Neon, Zinc, Argon, Boron, Radon, Xenon.* **MOVIES** *- Cinderella, Alice in Wonderland, Peter Pan, Lady and the Tramp, Sleeping Beauty, One Hundred and One Dalmatians, Sword in the Stone, The Jungle Book, The Aristocats, Robin Hood.* **ONLY FOOLS & HORSES** *- Derek Del Boy Trotter, Rodney Trotter, Trigger, Uncle Albert, Boycie, Mike Fisher, Grandad, Cassandra Trotter, Marlene, Mickey Pearce.*

A British detective drama produced for ITV, first airing in 2006 (pilot) then 2007 (series 1). It was a spin-off from Inspector Morse and, like that series, it is set in Oxford. On 2 November 2015, ITV announced the show would end after its 9th series, following the decision made by the 2 main stars to retire. 33 episodes.

1. Lewis was assisted by a DS, portrayed by Laurence Fox, who was promoted to Inspector before the seventh series. What was his name?

2. The series also starred a forensic pathologist Dr Laura Hobson, likewise reprising her role from Inspector Morse. Who played Dr Hobson?

3. Who made a very brief cameo appearance in several episodes, including one as a porter at Wadham College?

4. DI Lewis returned to Oxford after two years' absence and is reluctantly assigned by his new boss, DCS Innocent, to the murder of an Oxford mathematics student, shot while participating in what sort of study? A) Maths B) Sleep C) Cancer

5. In 2014-15 Detective Sergeant Elizabeth 'Lizzie' Maddox was introduced as Hathaway's DS. Which established TV star played the role?

6. Lewis is called out to deal with a noise complaint and is shocked to meet a rock star, Esme Ford, whom he had once admired. Joanna Lumley played Esme but what was the name of the band? A) Ford Classics B) Yep C) Midnight Addiction

7. A bishop visiting St Gerard's College was found dead after drinking poisoned wine. What was the title of the episode?
A) Wild Justice B) Poor Vintage C) Early Communion.

8. Paul Yalland, a controversial visiting lecturer at the college of criminology is found hanged. Which American actor played the role and had a UK number one hit 36 years previously.

9. After seven years of ducking the question, Lewis finally embarks on a relationship with whom?

10. Who is the character *(pictured left)* that appeared in the first 8 series of Lewis?

BAND OF GOLD: 1. Bradford; 2. Kay Mellor; 3. A) Ruth Gemmell; 4. B) DCI Newall; 5. C) Scrubbit; 6. A) Tracy; 7. She commits suicide in her parents house; 8. Carol inherits Curly's factory and all his wealth; 9. Geraldine James; 10. C) Charlie

 *A British reality series that premiered on Channel 4 on 7 March 2013. The programme features a number of families and groups of friends from different places around the UK watching TV shows in their homes and commenting. 15 series, 234 episodes.*

1. There have been two narrators for the show. Can you name them?

2. In 2014 the show won a BAFTA TV Award for "Reality & Constructed Factual Programme". True or false?

3. Who are the odd ones out?
A) Jenny & Lee B) Mary & Marina C) Donald & Jacqueline D) John & Beryl

4. Which member of the Moffatt family went on to take part in *I'm A Celebrity...Get Me Out Of Here?* The family were then axed from the show before series 9.

5. A version of the show featuring only children was launched as a Christmas special on Christmas Day 2015, and was followed by a full-length series, which began airing on 17 June 2016. What is the show's title?

6. *Celebrity Gogglebox* was launched in 2014. Who is the odd one out?
A) Noel Gallagher B) Naomi Campbell C) Ellie Goulding D) Liam Gallagher

 7. The first couple cast for *Gogglebox* in 2013 are pictured left. Both sadly passed away, one in 2017 the other in 2020. Name the much loved couple?

8. What is the surname of the family from Manchester who have been regulars since 2014 and have four rottweilers and, seemingly, always a plate of cakes or snacks on the table that remain uneaten?

9. Who are the pair of 'older' ladies from Bristol who have appeared since 2016 and keep viewers amused with their wine drinking and cheeky comments?

10. One favourite but eccentric pair on the show live in Wiltshire. They met at the age of 21, she was a model and he was studying at Wimbledon Art School. That was over 30 years ago. What are their names?

LEWIS: 1. James Hathaway; 2. Clare Holman; 3. Colin Dexter (who wrote the Morse novels) 4. B) Sleep; 5. Angela Griffin; 6. C) Midnight Addiction; 7. Wild Justice; 8. David Soul; 9. Dr Laura Hobson; 10. DCS Jean Innocent (played by Rebecca Front).

A sitcom produced by British production company Hat Trick Productions for Channel 4. The show originally aired over three series from 21 April 1995 until 1 May 1998, including a Christmas special, for a total of 25 episodes. Received several BAFTA awards. ranked second to Fawlty Towers in a list of 'the greatest British sitcoms' compiled by a panel of comedy experts for the Radio Times.

1. Who was the eponymous star of the show who died a few days before his 46th birthday?

2. The show was set on a fictional, remote island off Ireland's west coast. What was the island's name?

3. Ardal O'Hanlon brilliantly portrayed the dim curate sent to Craggy Island after an incident referred to as the Blackrock Incident. What was his name?

4. The third priest sent to the island as a punishment for his alcoholism and womanising, particularly for an incident at a wedding in Athlone, is Father Jack Hackett. Name a few of the random words he frequently shouted out.

5. Ted had to pay a forfeit to Father Dick Byrne after cheating at a football match. What did Byrne choose as the forfeit?

6. By what name did Dougal call the Bishop, incurring his wrath?

7. The housekeeper was characterized as being hyperactive, repressed and very persistent, occasionally to the point of being manic and angry, especially when someone refuses the offer of a cup of tea. Can you name her?

8. In the *A Christmassy Ted* episode, Ted and Dougal, together with 6 other priests found themselves stuck in what section of a large department store?

9. Father Noel Furlong appeared in three episodes of the show, in *Hell* and *Flight Into Terror* in series 2; and in *The Mainland* in series 3. Who played the part?

10. *Speed 3* was the 3rd episode of the 3rd series and the 20th episode overall. It parodied the action-thriller film *Speed* and its sequel *Speed 2: Cruise Control*. What type of vehicle, normally driven by Pat Mustard, is involved in the plot?

GOGGLEBOX: 1. Caroline Aherne and Craig Cash; 2. True; 3. C) Donald & Jacqueline (not cast members); 4. Scarlett; 5. Gogglesprogs; 6. C) Ellie Goulding only one NOT to appear on Celebrity Gogglebox); 7. Leon and June Bernicoff : 8. Malone; 9. Mary and Marina; 10. Giles

Takes place on the 2nd Saturday in September on BBC Two (1st half) and BBC One (2nd half). The concert is traditionally lighter, with popular classics followed by a second half of British patriotic pieces. First broadcast on TV in 1947

1. What is the more formal name of the Proms?

2. In what year were the Proms founded? A) 1895 B) 1905 C) 1915 D) 1925

3. What is the venue for *The Last Night of the Proms*?

4. To which part of Edward Elgar's *Pomp & Circumstance March No 1* do the audience joyously participate in the singing?

5. How many ticket stubs from previous concerts must Prommers present to qualify for a standing Last Night ticket, either in the Arena or Gallery?
A) 1 B) 3 C) 5 D) 6

6. With what is Sir Henry Wood's bust adorned with by representatives of the Promenaders, who often wipe an imaginary bead of sweat from his forehead or make some similar gentle visual joke?

7. Which 12-times conductor, between 1988 and 2018, was noted for his humorous Last Night speeches, but who also addressed the deaths of Diana, Princess of Wales, Mother Teresa, and Sir Georg Solti in his 1997 speech?

8. True or False? The Proms never missed a year, even during two World Wars.

9. Just months before his death in 1918, Sir Charles Hubert Hastings Parry signed over copyright for one of his compositions to British suffragettes so they could use it as an official anthem. Name the tune used at *The Last Night of the Proms*.

10. Which famous American composer, born in 1918, was also well-known as a conductor, concert pianist and teacher? His works are often heard at The Proms.

TRIVIA: The world of the Proms is littered with arcane rituals that can puzzle outsiders. When the lid of the piano is raised prior to a piano concerto. There is a cry of 'Heave-Ho'. The arena promenaders always do the "heave", while the gallery do the "ho".

FATHER TED: 1. Dermot Morgan; 2. Craggy Island; 3. Father Dougal McGuire; 4. Drink! Feck! Arse! Girls! Knickers!; 5. Kick Bishop Brennan Up the arse!; 6. Len (his Christian name); 7. Mrs (Joan) Doyle; 8. The largest lingerie section in Ireland; 9. Graham Norton; 10. A milk float.

A British survival reality show produced by ITV. The format sees a group of celebrities living together in a jungle camp. Each member undertakes challenges to get food and treats for the group, and to avoid being voted out by viewers. The winner is crowned 'King or Queen of the Jungle'. 19 series, 359 episodes.

1. In which country was the show filmed before 2020 when it had to move due to Covid-19?

2. Ant and Dec have hosted the show every year except in 2018 when Ant took a year off. Who replaced him?

3. To gain food or treats for the camp, what Trials take two formats: eating trials, or physical/mental tasks?

4. What challenge involves two or more celebrities going into the jungle to perform a task that requires then to open a container and release something nasty?

5. Name the odd one out. A) Carol Thatcher B) Harry Redknapp C) Amir Khan D) Jacqueline Jossa

6. In 2019, why did some viewers criticise Adele Roberts' elimination?

7. In 2012, the decision by Nadine Dorries to enter the show was a source of criticism that led to her suspension from which body?

8. Where was the 2020 show's base?

9. Who won the very first *I'm A Celebrity...Get Me Out Of Here* back in 2002?

10. Hilarious contestant, Paul Burrell, finished where in the 2004 series?
A) First   B) Last   C) Quit the show   D) Runner-up

TRIVIA: *In recent years as the celebrities fly in in the helicopter, The Batman Begins theme is played. Also when the last challenge, the 'Superhero', is happening, the theme from The Avengers (2012) is played.*

LAST NIGHT OF THE PROMS: 1. Henry Wood Promenade Concerts; 2. A) 1895; 3. Royal Albert Hall; 4. Land of Hope and Glory; 5. C) 5; 6 A laurel chaplet; 7. Sir Andrew Davis; 8. True; 9. Jerusalem; 10. Leonard Bernstein.

A British romantic sitcom which follows the relationship between two former lovers who meet unexpectedly, after not having been in contact for 38 years. It was aired on BBC One from 12 January 1992 to 14 December 2005, running for nine series and three specials. 67 episodes.

1. A Second Lieutenant and a Middlesex Hospital nurse met in the summer of 1953 and fell head over heels in love, but then Lionel was posted to Korea. Who played the roles when they meet again 38 years later?

2. Why did the relationship fail in 1953 after Lionel went to Korea?

3. After Korea, Lionel married Margaret, they later divorced, and earned a living doing what? A) Civil servant   B) Accountant   C) Coffee planter

4. Jean also married and had one child. After her husband's death, Jean opened a secretarial agency called what? A) Type for You   B) Secs Galore   C) Take It Down

5. Lionel's irrepressible father Rocky played by Frank Middlemass had a favourite saying. What is it? A) Rock on! B) Rocky times ahead C) On the rocks

6. Rocky married Madge, as much a character as he is, when he was 85 and she was 78. They travelled the world, were country and western music fans, tooled about in her classic Cadillac convertible, and hung out at the local pub, where Madge sang. Which *Carry On* star played Madge until she died before Series 9 was filmed?

7. In Series 2, Lionel signed copies of My Life in Kenya and Alistair had 'stacked' the queue with people paid to ask him to sign the book. Where did the signing take place in London? A) Blackwells   B) Waterstones   C) The Bookworm

8. In the midst of wedding preparations during Series 4, while shopping for the perfect dress Jean managed to be accused of what?

9. Lionel found the letter that he had sent to Jean from Korea, the one that was lost in the post. Where did he find it?

10. What part of London did the Hardcastle's reside?
A) Knightsbridge B) Peckham C) Holland Park

Geoffrey Palmer (who sadly died in November 2020) and Dame Judi Dench

I'M A CELEBRITY...GET ME OUT OF HERE!:1. Australia; 2. Holly Willoughby; 3. Bushtucker Trials; 4. Dingo Dollar; 5. C) Amir Khan has not been King or Queen of the Jungle; 6. A typing error meant that app votes were not counted; 7. The Conservative party; 8. Gwrych Castle in Abergele, North Wales; 9. Tony Blackburn; 10. D) Runner-up.

A British soap opera created by Julia Smith and Tony Holland which has been broadcast on BBC One since 1985. Set in Albert Square in the East End of London in the fictional borough of Walford, the programme follows the stories of local residents and their families as they go about their daily lives. 6124 Episodes as at

MATCH THE EASTENDERS EVENT TO THE CORRECT YEAR

1. Den Watts shot and falls into the canal	A. 1985
2. Arthur Fowler wrongly imprisoned	B. 1986
3. Queen Victoria public house burnt down	C. 1987
4. Reg Cox is murdered in his flat	D. 1989
5. Bianca Butcher gives birth in the Queen Vic	E. 1995
6. The funeral of Shakil Kazem after stabbing	F. 1998
7. Den Watts hands Angie divorce papers	G. 2006
8. Episode featuring only Dot and Ethel	H. 2009
9. Pauline died from a brain haemorrhage.	I. 2010
10. Danielle killed by speeding car on Turpin Rd	J. 2018

AS TIME GOES BY: 1. Judi Dench and Geoffrey Palmer; 2. He wrote to give her his mailing address, the letter went astray. She assumed he had lost interest in her, he decided she must have lost interest in him; 3. C) Coffee planter; 4. A) Type for you; 5. A) Rock on; 6. Joan Sims; 7. B) Waterstones; 8. Shoplifting; 9. On display in the Imperial War Museum; 10. C) Holland Pk.

A BBC television sitcom that first aired on BBC1 from 1979 to 1981. A special edition appeared in 2007. All episodes and the 2007 special written by Peter Spence, the creator, while the final episode in 1981 was written by Christopher Bond, the script associate. The title is a play on the phrase "to the manner born," from Shakespeare's Hamlet . 3 series 22 episodes.

1. Who played Audrey fforbes-Hamilton, an upper-class woman who, upon the death of her husband, had to move out of her beloved manor house to the old lodge?

2. The manor was then bought by Richard DeVere, a nouveau riche millionaire supermarket owner who had originally came from which country?

3. Which estate was used for the exterior shots for the series?

4. How much did Richard DeVere pay for Grantleigh Manor?
A) £676,000   B) £776,000   C) £876,000   D) £976,000

5. When Audrey learned that Richard was taking Marjory to the Summer Hunt Ball, she refused to attend and instead stayed at home playing which game with Brabinger? A) Cluedo   B) Cribbage   C) Draughts   D) Scrabble

6. What was the cause of Richard breaking his leg?

7. The actress who played Marjory Frobisher also starred as Margaret Thatcher in *Anyone For Denis?* Who is she?

8. What is the name of the butler who moved to the Lodge with Audrey, where he helped her keep up the standards of behaviour suited to an aristocrat?

9. Where were Richard and Audrey when she asked him to marry her?
A) By Marton fforbes-Hamilton's grave
B) The estate church   C) In the lodge

10. In the 2007 special Richard gave Audrey a dog for a silver wedding anniversary present. It was the same type as her long since departed Bertie. Which breed was it?
A) Corgi   B) Bassett hound   C) Beagle

TRIVIA: The final episode held the record until 1996 for the biggest-ever audience for a single programme on British TV, with an audience of over 27 million viewers. The record was broken 15 years later by the series Only Fools and Horses (1981) with 27.6 million viewers.

EASTENDERS: 1D, 2E, 3I, 4A, 5F, 6J, 7B, 8C, 9G, 10H.

A British talent show competition, part of the global Got Talent franchise created by Simon Cowell. Shown on ITV every year in late Spring to early Summer. Premiered on 9 June 2007. Contestants of any age can audition for the televised contest with whatever talent they wish to demonstrate. 14 series, 185 episodes.

NAME THE WINNERS AND FIND THE ODD ONE OUT!

2007   2012   2017   2018

2013   2019   2009

2008   2014   2015

2011   2007

TO THE MANOR BORN: 1. Penelope Keith; 2. Czechoslovakia; 3. Cricket St Thomas; 4. C) £876,000; 5. D) Scrabble; 6. Richard fell during skiing practice; 7. Angela Thorne; 8. Brabinger; 9. By Marton fforbes-Hamilton's grave; 10. C) Beagle (named Bertie the second).

A TV adaptation of Douglas Adams' novel was broadcast in January/February 1981 on BBC Two. Initially thought by the BBC to be unfilmable, the series won a Royal Television Society Award as Most Original Programme of 1981, and several British Academy Television Awards. 6 Episodes.

1. Who played Arthur Dent?

2. Which day of the week could Arthur Dent never get the hang of?
A) Mondays   B) Tuesdays   C) Thursdays   D) Sundays

3. What is the official name of the restaurant at the end of the universe?
A) McDonalds   B) Milliways   C) The Duck & Goose   D) Cafe Lou

4. Who played Trillian and what did she dress up as at the fancy dress party where she met Arthur; was it Charles Darwin or Albert Einstein?

5. Who created the Pan Galactic Gargie Blaster?
A) Zaphod Beeblebrox   B) Arthur Dent   C) Ford Prefect   D) A Mouse

6. What job was being done by Marvin the depressed robot, whom was left on Magrathea 40 million years ago?

7. According to The Guide, Planet earth is:
A) Damp   B) Uninhabitable   C) Blue   D) Harmless

8. What is a Strag?
A) A Non-Hitch-Hiker   B) A Non-Human   C) A Non-Vogan   D) A Really Cool Dude.

9. How did Ford prefect get his name? A) He thought it was inconspicuous B) Arthur named him after his favourite car   C) He thought a Ford prefect was a funny looking car D) His parents named him

10. What is the answer to the ultimate question of Life, The Universe, and Everything?
A) 22   B) 32   C) 42   D) 52

TRIVIA: Douglas Adams' head appears as a planet during Slartibartfast's (Bill Nighy's) tour of the galaxy.

BRITAIN'S GOT TALENT: 2007 - Paul Potts; 2012 - Ashleigh and Pudsey; 2017 - Tokio Myers; 2018 - Lost Voice Guy; 2013 - Attraction; 2019 - Colin Thackery; 2009 - Dliversity; 2008 - George Sampson; 2014 - Collabro; 2015 - Jules O'Dwyer and Matisse; 2011 - Jai McDowall; 2007 - Susan Boyle is the odd one out. A runner-up.

A joint UK and French crime drama series created by Robert Thorogood. Shown on BBC1. First shown on 25 October 2011. Has enjoyed high ratings, leading to repeated renewals. To date there has been 9 Series, 72 episodes.

1. Name the four actors who have played the leading role of the DI in the series?

2. What is the fictional Caribbean Island upon which the show is set?

3. How did Detective Sergeant Camille Bordey join the team?

4. Richard Poole was murdered at the start of series three and Humphrey Goodman came to replace him, but by whom was Richard murdered?

5. In the third episode of series two, a woman is found drowned at a luxury clinic and Richard thinks it's murder, but how long does the Commissioner give him to solve it?
A) 24 hours   B) 48 hours   C) A week   D) A month

6. What is the name of the ghost when Eolith gets killed?

7. French actress Elizabeth Bourgine (left) has been in the show playing a restaurateur since it began in 2011. What is the name of the character she plays?

A) Camille Bordey B) Catherine Bordey
C) Florence Cassell D) Madeleine Dumas

8. Selwyn Patterson, the Commissioner, has also appeared in the show since it began. Who played the role and in which seventies sit-com did he star alongside Leonard Rossiter?

9. *Death in Paradise* consistently features in the most watched shows on TV. On average, how many viewers did Series 9 attract?
A) Over 5 million B) Over 6m C) Over 7m D) Over 8m

10. In the Series 1 episode *Music For Murder* a comeback concert for a popular band ends abruptly with the death of the lead singer as he is revealed onstage, shot to death. Which former Boyzone member played the bass player Eddie?

HITCH HIKERS GUIDE TO THE GALAXY: 1. Simon Jones; 2. C) Thursdays; 3. B) Milliways; 4. Sandra Dickinson, Charles Darwin; 5. A) Zaphod Beeblebrox; 6. Car park Attendant (and still depressed); 7. D) Harmless; 8. A) A Non-Hitch-Hiker; 9. A) He thought it was inconspicuous; 10. C) 42.

A British sit-com, Baby Cow Productions produced it for BBC Wales. 3 series totalling 20 episodes broadcast from 13 May 2007-1 January 2010 on BBC Three, later on BBC One. A Christmas Day 2019 special for BBC One had 18.49m viewers, the most watched comedy in 17 years.

1. The romance between Gavin and Stacey formed the basis for this hugely successful series. Where were Gavin and Stacey living when the first series began?
A) Harlow and Cardiff B) Billericay and Barry C) Braintree and Swansea

2. Who wrote the show and what roles did they play in the programme?

3. What was the name of the electronics company that Stacey works for?
A) Bedmore's Electrics B) Shocking Blue C) Barry Island Bargains

4. Where did Gavin and Stacey go on their honeymoon?

5. What was Nessa's codename 'on the airwaves'?
A) Desmond Tutu B) Robert Mugabe C) Nelson Mandela

6. When singing *Islands in the Stream* with Bryn; besides Gwen, to whom does Nessa dedicate her performance?

7. Which footballer did Smithy repeatedly ask about during the pub quiz?
A) Alan Shearer B) Paul Gascoigne C) Gary Lineker

8. Who did Bryn insist on singing along with in the car?
A) James Blunt B) George Ezra C) Andy Williams

9. How much was the toll when Smithy used the Severn Bridge?
A) £3.25 B) 4.50 C) £5.10

10. Who gets stuck with the Bounty when Nessa and Dave give out Celebrations chocolates? A) Smithy B) Pam C) Gwen

TRIVIA: Gavin and Stacey's surnames (Shipman and West) are named after the famous British serial killers Dr. Harold Shipman (one of the most prolific serial killers ever, believed to have had least 200 victims) and Fred West. Also Pete Sutcliffe has the same first and last name as the man known as 'The Yorkshire

DEATH IN PARADISE: 1. Ben Miller, Kris Marshall, Ardal O'Hanlon, Ralf Little; 2. Saint Marie; 3. She was undercover involving the first case; 4. Sasha Moore; 5. A) 24 hours; 6. Mama Beth; 7. B) Catherine Bordey; 8. Don Warrington, Rising Damp; 9. D) Over 8 million; 10. Keith Duffy.

A British quiz show, first broadcast on BBC Two then BBC One from 2000-2017. The game begins with a team of 9 contestants, who take turns answering general knowledge questions within a time limit to create chains of 9 correct answers in a row. At the end of each round, the players then vote one contestant, "the weakest link", out of the game. 13 series 1694 episodes. Presented by Anne Robinson.

GENERAL KNOWLEDGE QUESTIONS,
ANSWERS BEGIN WITH THE INITIAL LETTERS OF T-H-E-W-E-A-K-E-S-T-L-I-N-K

1. In what US State is the city Nashville? **(T)**

2. Who is the main character in *Catcher in the Rye*? **(H)**

3. The name of the fictional borough of Melbourne where *Neighbours* is set. **(E)**

4. What war time song contains the lyrics, 'Keep smiling through Just like you always do, 'Til the blue skies drive the dark clouds far away'? **(W)**

5. New Orleans is nicknamed 'The Big.......' Complete the description. **(E)**

6. What hymn is traditionally sung before the FA Cup Final at Wembley **(A)**

7. The book .... *Remembered* is about US actress Katherine Hepburn who died in 2003. **(K)**

8. Cotton buds packaging contains a warning not to insert them into what part of the body? **(E)**

9. On which river does the city of Worcester stand? **(S)**

10. Road signs in the UK that warn the road user are what shape **(T)**

11. What 'L' is the name given to the poet who wins the Nobel Prize? **(L)**

12. The island of Sri Lanka lies off the coast of which Asian country? **(I)**

13. In the human body what is the name of the main olfactory organ? **(N)**

14. At the seaside, novelty shops sell hats with the slogan '....... Me Quick' **(K)**

GAVIN AND STACEY: 1. B) Billericay and Barry; 2. James Corden and Ruth Jones, Smithy and Nessa; 3. A) Bedmore's Electrics; 4. Greece; 5. B) Robert Mugabe; 6. Dave'; 7. C) Gary Lineker; 8. A) James Blunt; 9. C) £5.10; 10. C) Gwen.

Award-winning British sitcom by Victoria Wood. Two series were broadcast on BBC One from 1998 - 2000, 16 episodes. Set in the canteen of a fictional factory in Manchester, featuring caterers and regular customers as the main characters. Depicts lives and social and romantic interactions of the

1. What is the name of the firm which employed the canteen staff?

2. Bren played by Victoria Wood was the central figure in an all-star cast. What was her surname and what was the TV quiz show she entered?

3. What was the name of Anita's blow-up friend?

4. When Prince James, Duke of Danby visits what special food did Bren prepare for him to take away and, as he leaves, what did he tell Stan to keep doing?

5. What was Jane's normal order each day just as the shutters go up?

6. Canteen regular Bob regularly asked for bacon or liver, but had a memorable punch line when he was kept waiting for a cup of tea. Can you remember it?

7. Where had Jean and Dolly previously worked together?

8. Who organised the Millennium Dinner?

9. Towards the end of her time working at the canteen, who showed interest in becoming a lap dancer?

10. Norman, the bread delivery man was agoraphobic. How did he say he got into that state?

11. Bren's mother was played brilliantly by Julie Walters.
A) What her character was known as   B) Her character's actual name
C) In the final episode who did she say was Bren's father?

12. At the end of the very last episode when all the main cast are gathered in the canteen, after finding money that Petula has left, what familiar request did Tony make to Bren?

TRIVIA:

- *To research for this show, Victoria Wood got first-hand experience by working on the early morning canteen shift at the James Halstead factory in Whitefield, Manchester.*
- *Victoria Wood insisted that the title 'dinnerladies' should be spelled with a lower-case D.*

THE WEAKEST LINK: 1. Tennessee; 2. Holden Caulfield; 3. Erinsborough; 4. We'll Meet Again; 5. East; 6. Abide With Me; 7. Kate; 8. Ears; 9. Severn; 10. Triangular; 11. Laureate; 12. India; 13. Nose; 14. Kiss.

A British medical comedy drama series. The programme is set in the fictional seaside village of Portwenn, Cornwall with most interior scenes shot in a converted local barn. Nine series aired between 2004 and 2019, with a television film airing on Christmas Day in 2006. One final series to film. 70 episodes.

1. What is the fictional name of the hill on which Doc Martin's surgery is located?
A)   Roscarock Hill B) Primrose Hill C) Harbour Hill

2. Martin has a very particular phobia. What is it?

3. What kind of car does Martin drive?

4. Pauline takes over as receptionist at the surgery at the start of Series 2 after Elaine goes on an extended trip with her boyfriend. How are the girls related?

5. When Martin worked in London, what was his job?

6. What's the name of the doctor who was Martin's predecessor in town? A) Dr Finlay   B) Dr Kildare   C) Dr Sim

7. In 2 pilot episodes for Sky, Martin's surname is Bamford. How was the doctor's new surname Ellingham selected?

8. What names are given to Martin and Louisa's son?
A) Martin Paul   B) James Henry   C) James Martin

9. Mrs Tishell wears a neck brace due to suffering from: A) Torticollis B) Back ache C) Whiplash

10. PC Penhale has two disorders, one causes him to become nervous in crowds, and the other means he falls asleep at random times. What are the medical terms for these problems?

TRIVIA: Although the fictional Dr Martin Ellingham hates dogs with a fiery passion and is often seen chasing strays from his surgery, the actor who portrays him, Martin Clunes, is a great lover of dogs and brings them with him to filming every day.

dinnerladies: *1. HWD Components; 2. Furlong, Totally Trivia; 3. Malcolm; 4. Bacon sandwiches, Whitewashing the baskets; 5. 12 rounds of white, low fat spread; 6. Just give us a tea bag and I'll suck it on the way; 7. Cafe Bonbon; 8. Phillipa; 9. Twinkle; 10. He fell off a diving board in Guernsey; 11. A) Petula Gordino B) Bren Furlong C) Either called Kevin or Keith; 12. 'Make us a brew then, eh?'.*

Brookside was a British soap opera set in Liverpool, England. The series began on the launch night of Channel 4 on 2 November 1982 and ran for 21 years until 4 November 2003. A total of 2915 It was filmed in real, brand-new houses in a real cul-de-sac.

1. Bobby and Sheila Grant were played by 2 actors who had huge success as man and wife in a sit-com. Who are they and what was the sit-com?

2. With a little help from the media, a campaign to Free George Jackson in 1984 was organised. Why was he in prison?

3. The first and last episodes of Brookside started in exactly the same way - what was happening in the scenes?
A) Paper boy delivering B) Milkman delivering
C) Dog bounding across the grass

4. In 1999 father and son Greg and Jason Shadwick were killed when an explosion rocked the Close. What was the apt name of the night club that was bombed?

5. What did a frustrated Billy Corkhill do when his marriage to Doreen reached breaking point?
A) Got drunk regularly B) Held Doreen hostage
C) Drove aggressively around the Close churning up neighbours' gardens

6. Michael Starke played the loveable rogue Sinbad, but what was his character's real name?

7. What was controversial about the relationship between couple Nat and Georgia Simpson, who moved to the close in 1996?
A) She used to be a man   B) He was a bigamist   C) They were brother and sister

8. In 1993 Mandy Jordache killed abusive husband Trevor and buried him under the patio with help of daughter Beth. How was his body discovered?

9. In the 1,000th episode, Sue and Danny Sullivan plunged to their deaths from scaffolding at the new Parade. Who pushed them?

10. What was Brookside originally intended to be called? As a clue it was handyman Stan's surname in *dinnerladies*!

The last resident to leave Brookside Close, Jimmy Corkhill, added the letter 'd' to the word 'Close', symbolically signalling the end of the soap.

DOC MARTIN: 1. B) Primrose Hill (Roscarrock Hill in real life); 2. Haemophobia; 3. Lexus; 4. Cousins; 5. Chief of Vascular Surgery; 6. C) Dr Sim; 7. Anagram of the writer's name, Minghella; 8. B) James Henry; 9. A) Torticollis; 10. Agoraphobia and Narcolepsy.

A British sitcom produced by Thames Television and first aired between 1976 and 1979. A spin-off from Man About the House, George and Mildred left their flat and move to a new upmarket estate in Hampton Wick. Their arrival horrifies a snobbish neighbour who fears their presence will devalue his home. 5 series. 38 episodes.

1. What was George and Mildred's surname?

2. What was the surname of the family next door?

3. What was the name of the neighbours' sons?

4. What was the name of George and Mildred's dog?
A) Ruffles B) Truffles C) Snuffles

5. What was the name of the neighbour who just wanted them to move away?

6. Who played the Ropers?

7. What game did George and Tristram play when George was babysitting him?

8. George's brother had a document suggesting that George was a ...... What?

9. What did Mildred accidentally donate to the church jumble-sale?

10. What foolish thing did George say to Mildred in the final episode?

TRIVIA

Which character is pictured in 2020 (left)

ANAGRAM TO SOLVE
GENDERED MARIGOLD

BROOKSIDE: 1. Ricky Tomlinson and Sue Johnston, The Royle Family; 2. He was wrongly convicted of a warehouse robbery; 3. B) Milkman delivering; 4. The Millennium Club; 5. C) drove aggressively around the Close churning up neighbours' gardens; 6. Thomas Sweeney; 7. C) They were brother and sister; 8. Jimmy Corkhill and Eddie Banks discovered Trevor's body after an underground leak forced the area to be dug up.; 9. Barry Grant; 10. Meadowcroft.

A British historical drama series set in the early 20th century the series first aired on ITV in the UK on 26 September 2010. Set in a fictional Yorkshire country between 1912 and 1926, it depicts the lives of the aristocratic Crawley family and their domestic servants in the post-Edwardian era. 6 Series, 52 Episodes.

1. The first series began the day after the heir to Downton Abbey was lost in what iconic event?

2. In series 2 the Dowager Duchess told Lady Edith, 'Don't be .... Dear, it's very middle class!'. What is the missing word?

3. The Earl of Grantham had owned 3 Golden Labrador retriever dogs over the 6 series. After what did he name them?
A) English historical figures   B) Ancient Egyptian figures   C) Family ancestors

4. In series 3 Alfred Nugent arrived at Downton in 1920. What career did he pursue when he left?

5. Where did her aunt bundle Lady Edith off to give birth in the 4th series?
A) Harley Street   B) America   C) Switzerland

6. In series 5 Mrs Beryl Patmore learnt that her nephew was shot in the war. Why was he shot?

7. In series 3 Robert learnt from his lawyer, George Murray, that the investment he made in what company has become worthless, and that he had lost his own and most of Cora's money?

8. In series 4 whose valet, Alex Green, brutally attacked Anna and afterwards went off to a concert as if nothing had happened?

9. In series 5 who memorably stated, 'I am going upstairs to take off my hat'?

10. In series 4 kitchen maid Daisy and the cook Mrs Patmore fell out over which 'new-fangled' invention?

Anagram to solve
RECTORY WARBLE

GEORGE AND MILDRED: 1. Roper; 2. Fourmile; 3. Tristram and Tarquin; 4. B) Truffles; 5. Jeffrey Fourmile; 6. Brian Murphy and Yootha Joyce; 7. Poker; 8. An Army deserter; 9. George's porn collection; 10. 'I love you too, Beryl' (a lady frien'ds name. Sadly Yootha Joyce's death meant no more episodes - so we will never know!). CHARACTER: Tristram (Nicholas Bond Owen). ANAGRAM - GEORGE AND MILDRED.

A British sitcom originally broadcast on BBC 1 from 16 October 1989 to 24 December 1998, then revived on ITV from 2 January 2014 to 18 December 2017. A total of 12 series and 128 episodes. The title comes from the idiom "birds of a feather flock together", meaning that people having similar characters, backgrounds, interests, or beliefs will congregate.

Birds of a Feather

1. How are the two leading characters, Sharon Theodopolopodous and Tracey Stubbs, related to each other?

2. Why did Sharon, a common, fun-loving, large and loud-mouthed character from a council flat in Edmonton, move into her sister's luxury home in Chigwell?

3. Tracey loved her husband Darryl, who made most of his money by robbing banks. However, what was his legitimate business?

4. When Darryl was finally released in series 7, Tracey trusted him when he asked for a cheque on the company account. What was the result of this?

5. What unscrupulous or criminal activities was Sharon willing to indulge in:
A) Illegally subletting her council flat whilst living with Tracey   B) Taking drugs
C) Selling stolen merchandise   D) Fiddling her VAT   E) All of them!

6. Who was the sisters' neighbour; a wealthy, snobbish, man-eating , middle-aged woman striving to create the impression that she is a glamorous beauty?

7. When she was 17, Dorien had a daughter, Naomi, who was raised by Lionel. They reunited fifty years later. What was Naomi's job?

8. In series 7 Darryl and Chris were released from prison. Chris felt remorseful for his crimes and not treating Sharon better, so he got a honest job as:
A) A petrol station cashier   B) A road sweeper   C) A pizza delivery man

9. In series 10 in 2014 Garth found a job in a sandwich shop. What was it called?
A) Knuckle Sandwiches B) Scrummy Yummy C) Seedy McCrusty's

10. What was the title of the 2017 Christmas Special?
A) Feeling Glad All Over B) Big Donkey C) The House For The Rising Sons

DOWNTON ABBEY: 1. The sinking of the Titanic; 2. Defeatist; 3. B) Ancient Egyptian figures; 4. Chef; 5. C) Switzerland; 6. Cowardice and desertion; 7. the Canadian Railway; 8. Lord Gillingham's; 9. Lady Mary; 10. Electric mixer. ANAGRAM - ROBERT CRAWLEY

A BBC religious programme presenting religious songs and hymns of Christian denominations around the UK. From November 2014, the programme adopted a magazine format. The intention was to reflect the wider Christian audience across the country. Over 2300 episodes.

ON 29 SEPTEMBER 2019 SONGS OF PRAISE VIEWERS WERE ASKED TO VOTE FOR THEIR FAVOURITE HYMN.
A Top 10 was selected from the tens of thousands of votes.
Your task is to select the <u>top 10</u> as chosen the viewers
There are 30 well-known hymns listed below, including the selected top 10. If you match the hymn that was Number 1 you get 10 points for that. For number 2 selection you get 9 points. Number 3 - 8pts, No. 4 - 7pts, No. 5 - 6pts, No. 6 - 5 pts, No. 7 - 4pts, No. 8 - 3pts, No. 9 - 2pts, No.10 - 1pt. A maximum of 55 points can be notched up.
Good luck with your selection - there are some surprises!

1. Abide With Me	16. In Christ Alone
2. All People That On Earth Do Dwell	17. Jerusalem
3. All Things Bright and Beautiful	18. Lead Us Heavenly Father
4. Amazing Grace	19. Lord of All Hopefulness
5. And Can It Be	20. Love Divine, All Love Excelling
6. Be Still, For the Presence of the Lord	21. Make Me A Channel For Your Peace
7. Be Thou My Vision	22. Morning Has Broken
8. Dear Lord and Father of Mankind	23. Nearer My God To Thee
9. For All the Saints	24. O Happy Day
10. Great Is Thy Faithfulness	25. O Jesus I Have Promised
11. Guide Me O Thou Great Redeemer	26. Shine Jesus Shine
12. Here I Am Lord	27. Tell Out My Soul
13. How Great Thou Art	28. The Day Thou Gavest, Lord, Is Ended
14. I the Lord of Sea and Sky	29. The King of Love My Shepherd Is
15. I Vow To Thee My Country	30. The Lord's My Shepherd

BIRDS OF A FEATHER: 1. They are sisters; 2. To support her when their husbands are imprisoned for armed robbery; 3. Building conservatories; 4. Darryl defrauds her out of her business assets; 5. E) All of them; 6. Dorien Green; 7. She is a Vicar; 8. B) A pizza delivery man; 9. C) Seedy McCrusty's; 10. C) The House For The Rising Sons.

A British situation comedy that aired as twenty episodes over three series from 1993 to 1996 produced for the BBC by Lenny Henry's production company, Crucial Films. The first two series were shot on film and directed in the style of a drama series. Due to budgetary and time constraints, the third series was shot on videotape and was directed more like a traditional sitcom.

QUESTIONS ABOUT CHEF AND OTHER FAMOUS TV CHEFS

1. Lenny Henry starred as the talented, arrogant, tyrannical and obsessed chef who has endlessly inventive insults for his staff. What was his name?

2. The kitchen was in a gourmet restaurant in English countryside, one of the few in the United Kingdom to have received a two-star rating from Michelin. It's name?
A) Le Château Anglais   B) Lox, Stock & Bagels   C) Mustard's Last Stand

3. Lucinda was promoted to sous chef at the start of Series I, being the most talented and capable of the kitchen staff. Which outnumbered actress played Lucinda?

4. Which celebrity chef was born Phyllis Nan Sortain Pechey?

5. Before becoming famous which chef went to prison for breaking into and burgling musician Paul Young's house?

6. The principal writer of *Chef* is pictured. He also acted in the series and other TV shows. What is his name?
A) Bruce Montague   B) Peter Tilbury   C) Gary Parker

7. In *Chef* what was the name of the kitchen labourer who often dealt with the presentation of food and also has a liking for marijuana?   A) Wayne   B) Gaston   C) Piers

8. Delia Smith is famous for her role as joint majority shareholder at which football club?

9. In 1994, at just 32 who became both the youngest chef and the first British chef to be awarded three Michelin stars?

10. Famous Austrian-American chef Wolfgang shares is last name with a character in a William Shakespeare's play, what's the name?

SONGS OF PRAISE: Number 1. 10 POINTS for - 17. Jerusalem; Number 2. 9 POINTS for - 13. How Great Thou Art; Number 3. 8 POINTS for - 16. In Christ Alone; Number 4. 7 POINTS for - 8. Dear Lord and Father of Mankind; Number 5. 6 POINTS for - 1. Abide With Me; Number 6. 5 POINTS for - 15. I Vow to Thee My Country; Number 7. 4 POINTS for - 11. Guide Me O Thou Great Redeemer / Jehovah; Number 8. 3 PTS for 4. Amazing Grace; Number 9. 2 PTS for 6. Be Still For the Presence of the Lord; Number 10. 1 PT for 14. I the Lord of Sea and Sky

THE FORSYTE SAGA

26 Episodes. Originally on BBC2. A Sunday night repeat run on BBC1, starting 8 September 1968, secured the programme's success; Pubs closed early, streets were deserted. The Church rescheduled evening worship so that the huge audience could be ready for the start of the show at 7:25pm. 18 million tuned in for the final episode in 1969. Then adapted by Granada Television for the ITV network in 2002 and 2003. 10 Episodes.

1. Young Jolyon left his wife for the governess of his daughter June, and they ran off together to live in sin and later have two children. What was her name?
A) Irene   B) Helene   C) Helene

2. With whom did Soames fall in love?

3. Who played Soames Forsyte   A) In the 1967 version and   B) In the 2002 version?

4. Who did June plan on marrying as she was so in love with him, but was then jilted and left heart-broken?

5. In the BBC version Young Jolyon was played by a famous film star. He had appeared in films like *Genevieve, Reach For The Sky* and *Some People.* Who was he?

6. During the Boer War, how many Forsytes joined to help the cause?

7. How did Phillip Bosinney die?

8. Which of these women was married multiple times? A) Irene   B) Helene   C) Holly

9. Which actor played Jolyon 'Jon' Forsyte and went on to play the title role in *Nicholas Nickleby*, appear in 161 episodes of *Countdown*, be featured on *This Is Your Life* and honoured with an OBE? *(Extra clue - he is a face in question 10)*

10. Can you identify the Forsyte actors below? 3 appeared in 1967 and 3 in 2002.

A   B   C   D   E   F

FORSYTE 1967 ANAGRAM - CASE EROTIC
Wrote the music used for the series, Halcyon Days, from
The Three Elizabeths and also The Dam Busters March

CHEF: 1. Gareth Blackstock; 2. Le Château Anglais; 3. Claire Skinner; 4. Fanny Cradock; 5. Gino D'Acampo; 6. B) Peter Tilbury; 7. C) Piers; 8. Norwich City; 9. Marco Pierre White; 10. Wolfgang Puck.

A BBC comedy sketch show that ran from 1994 to 1997, with specials in 2000 & 2014. Loosely structured, it relied on character sketches, running gags, and many catchphrases. The number and relative brevity of its sketches set it apart from other comedy sketch shows. 5 Series 40 Episodes.

1. Name these five characters from the show?

2. What catchphrase was most associated with Ken and Kenneth?

3. One of the cast went on to star in Harry Potter films and in the eponymous TV role as Father Brown. Who is he?

4. In satirical adverts presented by a northern boy, he claimed, 'They're great for your teas!'. To which product was he referring?

5. Paul Whitehouse created 'The Fast Show' with which other comedian?

6. Jesse was another character in the show. Which of these was one of his tips?
A) 'Today, I have been mostly doing nudist archery' B) 'This week, I have been mostly eating raspberry poptarts' C) 'This week, I have been mostly wearing toilet roll earrings'

7. On to 'Channel 9 News'. Weathergirl Poula Fisch had only one word for the weather. What was it?

8. Which of these movie stars made the mistake of going into 'suit you sir' Ken and Kenneth's tailors' shop?   A) Johnny Depp   B) Bradley Cooper   C) Hugh Grant

9. No matter what occasion, Insecure Woman was only concerned with one thing; what was it? Arabella Weir used the phrase as the title for her best selling novel.

10. Rowley Birkin QC, gives hilarious, if completely nonsensical, monologues from his fireside. How did Rowley usually finish his ramblings?

THE FORSYTE SAGA: 1. B) Helene; 2. Irene; 3. A) Eric Porter B) Damian Lewis; 4. Phillip Bosinney; 5. Kenneth More; 6. 4 (Holly, June joined as nurses. Jolly and Val Dartie as a dare; 7. He was hit by a carriage; 8. A) Irene; 9. Martin Jarvis; 10. A) Martin Jarvis B) Gina McKee C) Rupert Graves D) Nyree Dawn Porter E) Ioan Gruffudd F) Susan Hampshire.
FORSYTE 1967 ANAGRAM - Eric Coates.

A British sports entertainment game show, an adaptation of the American programme and its format, American Gladiators, and was produced by LWT for ITV from 10 October 1992 to 1 January 2000, with a revival made for Sky 1 between 2008 and 2009. 4 contestants, 2 male and 2 female, compete against the show's 'Gladiators'. 13 Series 135 Episodes (inc specials).

MATCH THE GLADIATOR WITH THE CORRECT PORTRAYER

1	ACE	A	JANE OMOROGBE
2	AMAZON	B	MICHAEL VAN WIJT
3	BLAZE	C	JENNIFER STOUTE
4	COBRA	D	JOHN SERU
5	HUNTER	E	JUDY SIMPSON
6	JET	F	MARK GRIFFIN
7	LIGHTNING	G	KIM BETTS
8	NIGHTSHADE	H	JEFFERSON KING
9	REBEL	J	DIANE YOUDALE
10	RHINO	K	MIKE LEWIS
11	RIO	L	EUNICE HUTHART
12	SARACEN	M	MARK SMITH
13	SHADOW	N	SHARRON DAVIES
14	TROJAN	P	JAMES CROSSLEY
15	VULCAN	Q	MICHAEL WILSON
16	WOLF	R	WARREN FURMAN

THE FAST SHOW: 1. Ron Manager, Insecure Woman, Ken & Kenneth, Poula Fisch; 2. Ooh! Suit you Sir; 3. Mark Williams; 4. Cheesy Peas; 5. Charlie Higson; 6. B) 'This week, I have been mostly eating raspberry pop-tarts'; 7. Scorchio; 8. A) Johnny Depp; 9. Does my bum look big in this?; 10. "I'm afraid I was very, very drunk."

A British television talent show created by John de Mol and based on the concept The Voice of Holland. It began airing on BBC One on 24 March 2012. There are five different stages to the show: producers' auditions, blind auditions, battle phase, knockouts, and live shows. The winner receives a record deal with Polydor Records. From 2017 the show switched to ITV.

1. There have been 4 presenters. Name them.

2. In the 9 seasons there have been 13 judges. Can you also name them?

The first 8 winners of the voice and their coaches. Can you marry them up?

2012	2013	2014	2015
2016	2017	2018	2019

A	B	C	D	E	F

GLADIATORS: 1R, 2N, 3L, 4Q, 5P, 6J, 7G, 8E, 9C, 10M, 11A, 12K, 13H, 14F, 15D, 16B.

A British sitcom centered on a small grocer's shop in Balby, Doncaster, created and written by Roy Clarke for the BBC. It ran for 26 episodes in four series, which premiered in 1976, 1981, 1982 and 1985. The programme developed from a television pilot broadcast in Ronnie Barker's comedy anthology series, Seven of One (1973). Open All Hours ranked eighth in the 2004 Britain's Best Sitcom poll. A sequel, entitled Still Open All Hours, began airing in 2013

Open All Hours
(See page 284). 26 Episodes were made.

1. What was the full name of the shop owner?

2 For whom did he have uncontrollable lust?

3. Which character, played by Barbara Flynn, whose name is never mentioned, was occasionally receptive to Granville's interests?

4. Delphine Featherstone was a regular customer in the shop. Due to her long black coat and black hat, by what name was she known behind her back. Who played the role?

5. Which character, known for her indecisiveness and an implied unhappy marriage, tends to 'mother' Granville?

6. In what type of musical genre was the theme for the television comedy 'Open All Hours' played? A) Orchestral B) Cockney duo C) Brass band

7. What was the family relationship between shopkeeper and his dogs body?

8. Arkwright bought an ice cream van to transform it into a mobile grocer's van for Granville. A sign on the van showed what part of Yorkshire the van had originated? Was it:
A) Pontefract   B) Leeds   C) Normanton

9. In one episode, Granville took delivery of a bread order from 'Formula One', the bread man. Which future 'Only Fools and Horses' co-star played this delivery man?
A) Paul Barber (Denzil) B) John Challis (Boycie) C) Roger Lloyd-Pack (Trigger)

10. Arkwright claimed to sell marital aids in his shop, but this was actually a con to sell which product? A) Oysters B) Baked beans C) Jamaican Ginger cake

***HAFT FAT SKY** is an anagram of an actress who excelled in playing 'battleaxes' and appeared in 7 episodes of Open All Hours as Mrs Blewett*

THE VOICE: 2012 - Leanne Mitchell and A (Tom Jones); 2013 - Andrea Begley and B (Danny O'Donoghue); 2014 - Jermain Jackman and C (will.I.am); 2015 - Stevie McCrorie and D (Ricky Wilson); 2016 - Kevin Simm and D (Ricky Wilson); 2017 - Mo Adeniran and E (Jennifer Hudson); 2018 - Ruti Olajugagbe and A (Tom Jones); 2019 - Molly Hocking and F (Olly Murs).

A British baking competition, in which a group of amateur bakers compete against each other, attempting to impress a group of judges with baking skills. Initially on BBC Two, until its growing popularity led to BBC One. After its 7th series, Love Productions signed a 3-year deal with Channel 4 to produce the series. Totals 10 series. 94 Episodes and 28 specials.

Hope you find this round a piece of cake!

1. Mary Berry has published more than 75 cookery books. True or False?

2. Before filming commences a cake is baked in every oven to test it's working! But what type of cake? A) Chocolate Brownie B) Red Velvet Cake C) Victoria Sponge

3. How many bakers are there at the start of the Bake Off?

4. A 19th century Quaker,Henry Chalkley, is credited with inventing a simple sponge cake with pink icing that could be easily mass produced and sold cheaply. After which area of London is this cake named? A) Whitechapel B) Poplar C) Tottenham

5. Kendal mint cake is not really a cake! What are the four main ingredients used in its production?

6. Scotch pancakes are generally smaller and thicker than English pancakes. By what other name are they generally known - particularly in parts of Scotland?

7. A rich fruit cake, usually topped with a distinctive circular pattern of almonds, is named after which Scottish city?

8. A flat, round cake made with flaky pastry and packed with currants is often called the unappetising name 'squashed fly cake'. What name is more familiar?

9. Which popular spiced bun, named after the area of London where it was first produced in the 18th century, is made by rolling up dough, spread with a mixture of butter, sugar and currants?

10. Named after a Derbyshire market town, what is the famous British tart that consists of a short-crust pastry case lined with jam and filled with frangipane and, in some variations, topped with fondant icing and half a glacé cherry.

SOLVE THE CLUE TO FIND A FAVOURITE BREAKFAST PASTRY
ARSONIST is calorie-free

OPEN ALL HOURS: 1. Albert Arkwright; 2. Nurse Gladys Emmanuel ; 3. The milk woman; 4. The Black Widow, Stephanie Cole; 5. Mavis; 6. C) Brass band; 7. Uncle and nephew; 8. C) Normanton; 9. B) John Challis (Boycie); 10. C) Jamaican ginger cake. ANAGRAM is Kathy Staff (famous as Nora Batty).

A British comedy-drama television series based on a one-woman show. Premiered on 21 July 2016 for digital channel BBC Three. Final series on 8 April 2019. It received widespread acclaim and won numerous awards. Shows then broadcast on BBC1 and 2. Just 2 series and 12 episodes.

1. In what city was *Fleabag* set?

2. Who created and starred as the main character of *Fleabag*?

3. Where does Fleabag meet the Priest?

4. What creature stalks the Priest?

5. Which Academy award winning actress played Fleabag and Claire's godmother?

6. What is the name of the Godmother's Art Collection?

7. The programme is particularly noted for breaking the ..... Wall? What is the missing word?

8. What did Fleabag and the priest drink when she visited his house for the first time?

9. Who won the Woman in Business award?

10. Hugh Dennis was a recurring character. What was his job?

TRIVIA
British actresses Jodie Comer and Phoebe Waller-Bridge both won lead actress Emmys on the same night for, respectively, Killing Eve (2018) and Fleabag (2016), both series being original creations of Phoebe Waller-Bridge.

CONNECTION
Look at these 5 pictures of TV shows and find the link

THE GREAT BRITISH BAKE OFF: 1. True; 2. C) Victoria Sponge; 3. 12; 4. C) Tottenham; 5.Sugar, glucose, water and peppermint oil; 6. Drop or dropped scones; 7. Dundee; 8. Eccles cake; 9. Chelsea bun; 10. Bakewell tart. ARSONIST CLUE: Croissant - Anagram minus the C (calorie).

A BBC sitcom about the British militia called the Home Guard during the Second World War. Broadcast from 1968 to 1977. Ran for nine series and 80 episodes in total. The series regularly gained audiences of 18 million viewers, and is still repeated worldwide. 3 'lost' episodes were filmed with a new cast in 2019.

1. What was the name of Captain Mainwaring's unseen but formidable wife?

2. The theme song 'Who Do You Think You Are Kidding Mr Hitler?' was the last song sung by which popular British music hall entertainer and comedian?

3. Location filming for Dad's Army was almost all completed in which county?
A) Sussex   B) Kent   C) Norfolk   D) Suffolk

4. In the 1971 film of Dad's Army, Mainwaring, Wilson and Pike worked at Martin's bank. What was the bank named in the TV series?

5. Much to Mainwaring's chagrin, Sergeant Arthur Wilson eventually inherited which title upon an uncle's death?

6. Corporal Jack Jones fought two campaigns in the Sudan, climaxing at the Battle of Omdurman in 1898. He also served in India and saw action in both the Boer War and the Great War. Why was he invalided out in 1915?

7. Private James Frazer began making coffins back in Scotland and became an undertaker. What was his job in Walmington before be became funeral director?

8. In the Great War, Private Charles Godfrey was a conscientious objector - a fact that horrified Mainwaring. However, it emerges that he volunteered for the medical corps and earned which bravery award at the Battle of the Somme?

9. Private Frank Pike was set to enter the RAF. However, after his going-away party he revealed he was excluded from active service. For what reason?

10. The platoon met in the church's parish hall. What was the name of the church?
A) St Joseph's B) St Stephen's C) St Aldhelm's D) St George's

PUT THAT LIGHT OUT!

FLEABAG: *1. London; 2. Phoebe Waller-Bridge; 3. At an engagement party; 4. A fox; 5. Olivia Colman; 6. The Sexhibition; 7. Fourth (character speaking directly to camera); 8. M&S canned gin and tonic; 9. Belinda Friers; 10. Bank manager.* *CONNECTION* *- Tom Hiddleston featured in all of them; Suburban Shootout (2006), Galapagos (as voice of Charles Darwin) (2006), Casualty (2007), Wallander (2008), Night Manager (2016).*

GRANDSTAND

BBC SPORT

A British sport programme. Broadcast from 1958 to 2007. The show dominated Saturday afternoons on BBC1 and covered nearly every major sporting event in Britain; FA Cup Final, Wimbledon, Grand National and the Boat Race, major global events; Olympic Games, Paralympic Games, Commonwealth Games and FIFA World Cup. Over 3500 Episodes.

1. Whilst there were several occasional hosts on the show, there were only five main presenters of the programme during its long history. Can you name them?

2. The 1967 Grand National was won by a horse with odds of 100/1, following a 23rd fence pile up in which every other horse fell or was remounted – the fence was subsequently named in his honour. Name of the winner please.

3. Golfer Tony Jacklin hit a notable televised first in Britain during the Dunlop Masters on 16 September 1967. What did he achieve?

4. Which Welshman scored what is regarded as 'the greatest try in history', playing for the Barbarians v All Blacks in a rugby union international match at Cardiff Arms Park on 27 January 1973?

5. The first known streaker at a major sporting event during an England v France Rugby Union match at Twickenham on 20 April 1974. Who was it? Erica Roe   B) Michael O'Brien   C) Samantha Fox

6. What did Cambridge achieve in both the 1978 and 1984 University Boat Races?

7. A fight broke out on air between staff in the newsroom behind presenter Des Lynam on 1 April 1989. What was the reason for the incident?

8. Which jockey won all seven races on British Champions' Day at Ascot on 28 September 1996?

9. With 96 fatalities and 766 injuries, the worst disaster in British sporting history occurred on 15 April 1989. Where did this awful event take place?

10. From 1981 Grandstand also appeared on Sundays. Which two Formula 1 drivers suffered fatal accidents during the San Marino Grand Prix on 30 April & 1 May 1994 ?

DAD'S ARMY: 1. Elizabeth; 2. Bud Flanagan; 3. C) Norfolk (in Thetford) ; 4. Swallow Bank; 5. Honourable; 6. Due to failing eyesight; 7. He ran a philately shop (stamps); 8. Military Medal for venturing into No-Man's Land and saving several lives; 9. He has an extremely rare blood group; 10. C) St Aldhelms.

A sitcom produced in the UK by BBC Scotland in partnership with BocPix and RTÉ. The show adopts an informal production style, production mistakes and tomfoolery are edited into each episode. Hammered by critics, the show has been a huge ratings success. 3 Series. 36 Episodes, including 18 Specials.

1. At the beginning of each episode Agnes Brown broke the fourth wall, with an introductory monologue. Who played Mammy in addition to writing the scripts?

2. What is Grandad's name? A) George Brown B) Albert Brown C) Harold Brown

3. Which of the Brown Boys was born on his parents' wedding day?

4. Who married fellow hairdresser Dino Doyle, in a private ceremony at the end of Series 3?

5. What was the name of Cathy's psychology teacher?

6. What names were given to Dermot and Maria's triplets?

7. Who said to Mammy he wanted 'no cake, no decorations, no brass band, and please Mammy, no tears'?

8. Maria came from a wealthy family. Her mother Hilary was a snob and disliked Agnes intensely; but what was her father's occupation?

9. When Agnes saw Dino wearing suspenders, she used a malapropism and tells Rory that she thinks he is a A) Transtesticle B) Tandem-rider C) Shoving leopard

10. Winnie McGoogan once asked Mr. Foley for a quickie as she had misread the menu. What did she mean to ask for?

'BROWN BOYS' TRIVIA
What are the first names of these Browns?
A) Lead singer of Hot Chocolate
B) Famous English Landscape Gardner and Architect (1716 - 1783)
C) The Scots-born British Prime Minister from 2007 to 2010?
D) American Abolitionist and Activist executed in 1859?
E) Central hero of the Peanuts cartoon by Charles Schulz

GRANDSTAND: 1. Peter Dimmock, David Coleman (who took over from Dimmock after just three programmes), Frank Bough, Des Lynam and Steve Rider; 2. Foinavon; 3. A hole in one; 4. Gareth Edwards; 5. B) Michael O'Brien (modesty covered by a policeman's helmet!); 6. Their boat sunk; 7. April Fool's Day joke; 8. Frankie Dettori; 9. Hillsborough Stadium, Sheffield; 10. Roland Ratzenberger and Ayrton Senna.

A British quiz show where contestants can win £1m. Originally created and formerly produced by David Briggs, and made for the ITV network. The original series aired from 4 September 1998 to 11 February 2014. Four years after the original series ended, ITV announced that the show would be revived to commemorate the 20th anniversary of the programme. 35 Series. 630 Episodes.

£100 - In children's stories, how many wishes are granted by a genie or fairy?
A) 1   B) 2   C) 3   D) 4

£200 - Trigonometry is a branch of which subject?
A) Biology   B) Economics   C) Psychology   D) Mathematics

£300 - Lily Savage was a persona of which TV personality? A) Paul O'Grady   B) Barry Humphries   C) Les Dawson   D) Brendan O'Carroll

£500 - Which of these is a hat? A) Pork Pie   B) Crisp   C) Sausage Roll   D) Scotch Egg

£1,000 - Which iconic horror film involves a couple whose newborn child is replaced at birth with the Antichrist? A) The Shining   B) Jaws   C) The Exorcist   D) The Omen

£2,000 - Which of these is a religious event celebrated in Hinduism? A) Diwali
B) Ramadan   C) Hanukkah   D) Whitsun

£4,000 - British athlete Katarina Johnson-Thompson became a world champion in which athletics event in 2019? A) Heptathlon   B) Marathon   C) 100 metres
D) 400 metres hurdles

£8,000 - Which of these have to pass a test on 'The Knowledge' to get a licence?
A) Taxi drivers   B) Bus drivers   C) Police officers   D) Ambulance drivers

£16,000 - Which toxic substance is obtained from the pressed seeds of the castor oil plant? A) Sarin   B) Strychnine   C) Ricin   D) Cyanide

£32,000 - In the opera by Rossini, what is the first name of 'The Barber of Seville'?
A) Tamino   B) Alfredo   C) Figaro   D) Don Carlos

£64,000 - The Twelve Apostles is a series of peaks connected to which mountain?
A) Aoraki Mount Cook   B) K2   C) Table Mountain   D) Mont Blanc

£125,000 - Which king wrote a famous denunciation of smoking? A) Richard I
B) William I   C) George I   D) James I

£250,000 - What was the occupation of the composer Borodin?   A) Naval captain
B) Chemist   C) Lawyer   D) Chef

£500,000 - Who was the first man to travel into space twice? A) Vladimir Titov
B) Michael Collins   C) Gus Grissom   D) Yuri Gagarin

£1,000,000 - Tirich Mir is the highest point in which mountain range? A) Sierra Madre
B) Hindu Kush   C) Ural Mountains   D) Western Ghats

MRS BROWN'S BOYS: 1. Brendan O'Carroll; 2. C) Harold Brown; 3. Mark; 4. Rory Brown;
5. Professor Thomas Clowne; 6. John, George and Ringo; 7. Trevor; 8. He is a solicitor;
9. A) Transtesticle (instead of transvestite); 10. A quiche.
BROWN BOYS TRIVIA: A) Errol; B) Lancelot (Capability); C) Gordon; D) John; E) Charlie.

A British sitcom written by John Cleese and Connie Booth, broadcast on BBC2 in 1975 and 1979. Two series of six episodes each were made. Ranked 1st on 100 Greatest British TV Programmes by the British Film Institute in 2000 and, in 2019, named it 'greatest ever British TV sitcom' by Radio Times.

1. In *The Builders*, who did Sybil want to do the work?

2. In *The Psychiatrist*, who did Miss Tibbs and Miss Gatsby think the psychiatrist had come to see?

3. *In The Anniversary,* who pretended to be Sybil?

4. In *The Hotel Inspectors*, Basil sucks up to Mr Hutchinson, thinking he is reviewing the hotel. What does he actually do?

5. Which music did Sybil describe as a racket when Basil had it playing loudly in Reception?

6. What was the name of the horse on which Basil placed a bet in *Communication Problems*?

7. In the episode *The Wedding Party*, what book was Basil Fawlty reading in bed?
A) Kama Sutra   B) Lady Chatterley's Lover   C) Jaws

8. In *Basil the Rat*, the health inspector Mr Carnegie, after an exhaustive listing of problems in the kitchen, informed Basil and Sybil that the hotel had many flaws to be corrected urgently. What had to be removed from the water tank?

9. In *The Kipper and the Corpse* episode where did Basil hide away at the end?

10. In *The Psychiatrist* episode the Abbotts asked Basil how often he and Sybil 'managed it'. Basil, indignant, replied 'Average'. What were the Abbots really asking?

GUEST APPEARANCES
Name these 5 characters and the episode they appeared in!

WHO WANTS TO BE A MILLIONAIRE?: £100 - C) 3; £200 - D) Mathematics); £500 - A) Pork Pie; £1,000 - D) The Omen; £2,000 - A) Diwali; £4,000; - A) Heptathlon; £8,000 - A) Taxi Drivers; £16,000 - C) Ricin; £32,000 - C) Figaro; £64,000 - C) Table Mountain; £125,000 - D) James I; £250,000 - B) Chemist; £500,000 - C) Gus Grissom; £1,000,000 - C) Hindu Kush. If you got all these right, enter the real thing!

A British reality singing competition series based on the Masked Singer franchise from South Korea. Premiered on ITV on 4 January 2020. On 19 August 2020 it was announced that series two, would be filmed without an audience due to Covid-19 restrictions. Jonathan Ross, Davina McCall, Rita Ora and Mo Gilligan (Ken Jeong not able to travel) would be the panel. Joel Dommett hosting.

ALL OF THE CONTESTANTS OF SERIES ONE. REMEMBER WHO WAS IN EACH COSTUME?
Pictures in the order in which each act finished.

1. QUEEN BEE   2. HEDGEHOG   3. OCTOPUS   4. MONSTER

5. FOX   6. UNICORN   7. DUCK   8. DAISY

9. TREE   10. CHAMELEON   11. PHARAOH   12. BUTTERFLY

FAWLTY TOWERS: 1. Mr Stubbs; 2. The Major (Gowen); 3. Polly; 4. He is a spoon salesman; 5. Brahma (Third Racket!); 6. Dragonfly; 7. C) Jaws; 8. Two dead pigeons; 9. In a laundry basket; 10. Going on holidays. **GUEST APPEARANCES** - A) Mrs Richards (Communication Problems); B) Harry Hamilton (Waldorf Salad); C) Mrs Peignon (The Wedding Party); D) Lord Melbury (Touch of Class); E) Dr Price (Kipper and the Corpse).

A British darts-themed game show which featured 3 pairs of contestants comprising an amateur darts player and a quizzer, competing to win cash and prizes. The original ITV series aired on ATV in 1981, then Central from 1982 - 1995. A revival produced by Granada Yorkshire aired in 2006. 16 Series. 354 Episodes (incl 11

1. Who hosted the original shows from 1981 - 1995 and who presented the revival in 2006?

2. The show sported an animated mascot, an anthropomorphic large brown bull who wore a red and white striped shirt and blue trousers. What was his name?

3. *Bullseye* was created and owned by Andrew Wood and a man who had also compéred *Sunday Night at the London Palladium.* Who was the former host of the Sunday variety show?

HERE ARE A FEW QUESTIONS FROM BULLY'S CATEGORY BOARD

4. Art - In which Spanish city did the Joan Miro museum open in 1975?

5. Bible - After Jesus was arrested, which apostle disowned him three times?

6. Books - Who wrote the true-crime book *In Cold Blood*, often called the first non-fiction novel?

7. Britain - Which is the only town in England with a name ending with an exclamation mark?

8. Showbiz - Who, in 1978, became the first woman to have a wholly self-penned number one single in Britain, with a song based on a novel of 1847?

9. Pot Luck - In computing what is RAM short for?

10. Sport - How many players are on each side of the net in beach volleyball?

> *JIM BOWEN (1937-2018) TRIVIA*
> He worked as a binman. Then eventually earned a degree in maths and education and began a career as a teacher. After ten years of teaching, Bowen had become a deputy headmaster by the time he decided to turn his stand-up hobby a career. The rest is history.

THE MASKED SINGER: *1. Nicola Roberts; 2. Jason Manford; 3. Katherine Jenkins; 4. CeeLo Green; 5. Denise Van Outen; 6. Jake Shears; 7. Skin; 8. Kelis; 9. Teddy Sheringham; 10. Justin Hawkins; 11. Alan Johnson; 12. Patsy Palmer.*

A British satirical puppet show. First broadcast in February 1984, the series was produced for Central Independent Television on ITV network. Won numerous awards, including 10 BAFTA Television Awards, and 2 Emmy Awards in 1985 and 1986 in the Popular Arts Category. 18 Series. 131 Episodes.

CAN YOU RECOGNISE THESE SPITTING IMAGE PUPPETS?

ANAGRAMS OF PEOPLE LAMPOONED BY SPITTING IMAGE

A) Nikon nickel

B) Clancy tempura

C) Eugenio milky

D) Anne acrotic

E) Carolynn Lilith

F) Antidote scowl

BULLSEYE: 1. Jim Bowen, Dave Spikey; 2. Bully; 3. Norman Vaughan; 4. Barcelona; 5. Peter; 6. Truman Capote; 7. Westward Ho!; 8. Kate Bush (Wuthering Heights); 9. Random Access Memory; 10. 2

A British sitcom based on a series of novels written by David Nobbs. It was produced from 1976 to 1979. Some of its subplots were considered too dark or risqué for television and were toned down or omitted. The Legacy of Reginald Perrin followed in 1996. 3 Series. 21 Episodes. A series, Reggie Perrin ran for two series from April 2009 to November 2010.

1. Reginald Perrin, aged 46, was driven to bizarre behaviour by the pointlessness of his job. Where did he work?

2. Who played the title role in the series *The Fall and Rise of Reginald Perrin*, and who portrayed him in the *Reggie Perrin* series which followed in 2009?

3. Who wrote the novels upon which the series was based?
A) David Nobbs   B) John Barron   C) David Croft

4. Perrin lived on the 'Poets Estate' in a south London suburb called Climthorpe, at what address?
A) 12 Yeats Close   B) 12 Coleridge Close   C) 12 Tennyson Close

5. Reggie fantasised about his secretary, Joan Greengross. The actress who played her has had a long-running role in Coronation Street and had a number 17 hit in the UK charts in 1968 with *Where Will You Be.* Who was she ?

6. After Reggie commited a few reckless acts, including getting out of his car in the lion enclosure at a safari park, he faked suicide by leaving clothes and personal effects on a beach with *Broadchurch* connections. Where was the beach?

7. Who was Reggie's oppressive boss, played brilliantly by John Barron, who 'Didn't get where I am today' for many varied reasons?

8. Reggie only found fulfilment as a buck-toothed farm labourer. What animals did he look after?

9. In Series 2 Reggie opened a shop called Grot, where he sold useless products like square hoops, confident that it would be a great success. It was, What was the shop called? A) Bilge   B) Hogwash   C) Grot

10. In Series 3 Reggie was hired by CJ's brother FJ, working directly under CJ. What was the company called?
A) Amalgamated Aerosols   B) Come and Go   C) A Salt and Battery

SPITTING IMAGE: 1. Ant & Dec; 2. Margaret Thatcher; 3. Boris Johnson; 4. Kanye West; 5. Mark Zuckenberg; 6. Vladimir Putin; 7. Greta Thunberg; 8. Donald Trump; 9. Meghan Markle; 10. Noel Gallager. ANAGRAMS: A) Neil Kinnock; B) Paul McCartney; C) Kylie Minogue; D) Hillary Clinton; E) Clint Eastwood.

A British music chart programme, made by the BBC and originally broadcast weekly between 1 January 1964 and 30 July 2006. It was the world's longest running weekly music show. The programme would always end with the No 1 record, the only record that could appear in consecutive weeks. It would include the highest new entry and highest climber and omit any song going down 2267 Episodes

1. 5 dance troupes appeared on the show. Can you remember who they were?

2. What was the first song performed on the first TOTP on 1 January 1964?
A) I Wanna Be Your Man - Rolling Stones   B) I Only Want To Be With You - Dusty Springfield   C) Glad All Over - Dave Clark 5

3. A Mancunian model became the regular disc girl until 1967. Who was she and which famous band member did she later marry?

4. In 2003 the show played more up-and-coming tracks ahead of any chart success, and also featured interviews with artists and a music news feature called *24/7*. Which former children's TV presenter was the new producer of TOTP?

5. The last edition of TOTP was on 30 July 2006. Which woman co-presented its hour-long swan-song with Jimmy Savile (the main presenter on the first show)?

CONSECUTIVE WEEKS AT NUMBER 1 IN THE UK

Match the 10 songs below with the correct number of consecutive weeks at No 1

1. I WILL ALWAYS LOVE YOU - WHITNEY HOUSTON (1992)	A-16 WEEKS
2. CATHY'S CLOWN - THE EVERLY BROTHERS (1960)	B-15
3. 19 - PAUL HARDCASTLE (1985)	C-13
4. BAND OF GOLD - FREDA PAYNE (1970)	D-10
5. BOHEMIAN RHAPSODY - QUEEN (1975)	E-9
6. SHAPE OF YOU - ED SHEERAN (2017)	F-8
7. (EVERYTHING I DO) I DO IT FOR YOU - BRYAN ADAMS (1991)	G-7
8. DO THEY KNOW IT'S CHRISTMAS - BAND AID 20 (2004)	H-6
9. LOVE IS ALL AROUND - WET WET WET (1994)	J-5
10. WONDERFUL LAND - THE SHADOWS (1962)	K-4

THE FALL AND RISE OF REGINALD PERRIN: 1. Sunshine Desserts; 2. Leonard Rossiter, Martin Clunes; 3. A) David Nobbs; 4. B) 12 Coleridge Close; 5. Sue Nicholls; 6. West Bay, Dorset; 7. John Barron; 8. Pigs; 9. Grot; 10. A) Amalgamated Aerosols.

There have been many superb British drama programmes. Drama is a category of narrative fiction (or semi-fiction) intended to be more serious than humorous in tone. Drama is usually qualified with additional terms that specify its particular genre; police crime drama, political drama, legal drama, historical drama, domestic drama or comedy-drama. Here, we are able to cover just a few of these programmes.

DRAMA
2

1. In 1986, who played Percy Toplis, the Monocled Mutineer, in a 4 part serial by Alan Bleasdale that caused a lot of accusations of BBC bias to the left wing?

2. *The House of Elliott* was a costume drama that ran from 1991-1994 on BBC. In what decade was the drama, written by Jean Marsh and Eileen Atkins, set?

3. In which production was the actor portraying the Virgin Mary 9 years younger that the actor playing Jesus, her son?

4. Britain's first sci-fi serial about the return to earth of a new rocket-ship and its crew, who have become the first humans to travel into space, brought fear to living rooms across Britain in 1953. What was its name?

5. Can you recall the title of a 1987 British television serial set in the 1930s, and starring Nigel Havers as Ralph Ernest Gorse, a seducing conman?

6. Can you name the crime drama on ITV from 1994 to 2000 which portrayed the activities of customs officers from the London City & South Collection Investigation Unit of HM Customs and Excise?

7. Which star of *Shirley Valentine* played the title role in *Ambassador*, which ran for 2 series in 1998/9 about the new British ambassador to the Republic of Ireland?

8. Who was the Barman at the Winchester Club frequented by Arthur Daley in *Minder* on ITV between 1979 and 1994?

9. What were Pauline Quirke, Michelle Collins, Gwyneth Strong, Frances Barber and Lesley Manville in 1998/9?

10. *Peak Practice* ran from 1993-2002. It was about a GP surgery in Cardale, a fictional town in the Derbyshire Peak District. In which country had Dr Jack Kerruish (Kevin Whately) set up a clinic before returning to the UK to join The Beeches team?

TOP OF THE POPS: 1. The Go-Jo's, Pan's People, Ruby Flipper, Legs and Co, Zoo; 2. B) I Only Want To Be With You - Dusty Springfield; 3. Samantha Juste, Mickey Dolenz (The Monkees); 4. Andi Peters; 5. Edith Bowman.
CONSECUTIVE WEEKS AT NUMBER ONE: 1D, 2G, 3J, 4H, 5E, 6C, 7A, 8K, 9B, 10F.

A British crime drama series, starring Patricia Routledge as the title character, Henrietta "Hetty" Wainthropp, that aired for four series between 3 January 1996 and 4 September 1998 on BBC One. The series, by writers David Cook and John Bowen, spawned from a pilot episode entitled *Missing Persons* aired by ITV in 1989. A total of 28 episodes.

1. Who played Hetty Wainthropp and her young sidekick Geoffrey Shawcross in this gentle crime series?

2. We all remember Patricia Routledge as Hyacinth Bucket, but in which American series did her young co-star appear in 65 episodes a few years later?

3. In which county did most of the filming take place?
A) Yorkshire   B) Lancashire   C) Derbyshire

4. When the first series began Hetty had a part-time job working where? A) In the Newsagents   B) In the Post Office C) In the Supermarket

5. On what milestone birthday did Hetty decide to embark on new pursuits?

6. In the first episode Geoffrey stole what from the Post office counter?

7. What was the name of the investigation bureau that Hetty launched?

8. Geoffrey moved into the spare room vacated by Hetty and Robert's son. What happened to the son?

9. In *Lost Chords* what did the Blainthorp Music Festival finalists mysteriously lose?

10. The final episode of the fourth series was the final episode of *Hetty Wainthropp Investigates* and did leave several issues in the air. In *For Love Nor Money* what kind of establishment did Marianne work at before she disappeared?
A) Cinema   B) Victorian Living Museum   C) Wildlife Conservation Park

---

DAME PATRICIA ROUTLEDGE
Can you name the show or films featuring Dame Patricia below?

| 1990-1995 | 1967 | 1971 | 1974 | 1985 |

DRAMA: 1. Paul McGann; 2. 1920s; 3. Jesus of Nazareth (Olivia Hussey and Robert Powell); 4. The Quatermass Experiment; 5. The Charmer; 6. The Knock; 7. Pauline Collins; 8. Dave (Harris); 9. Real Women; 10. Africa.

A British fantasy series, starring Geoffrey Bayldon in the title role, and created by Richard Carpenter for London Weekend Television. The first series, produced and directed by Quentin Lawrence, was screened in the UK on ITV in 1970. The second series, directed by David Reid and David Lane, was shown in 1971. Each series had thirteen episodes.

1. Catweazle, pursued by Norman soldiers, jumped into a castle moat and through total immersion in water travelled in time to arrive in which year?
A) 1949   B) 1959   C) 1969

2. Catweazle hid out in a Water Tower on which farm?
A) Hexwood Farm B) Scatterbrook Farm C) Woodlands Farm

3. What did Catweazle call the abandoned Water Tower he made his home? A) Castle Howard B) Castle Saburac C) Castle Hogwarts

4. The 14 years old farmer's son (played by Robin Davies) befriended Catweazle. What was his nickname?

5. What was Catweazle's familiar toad called?

6. Catweazle had an athame (a so-called witch's ceremonial knife with a double-edged blade) around his neck. What was it called?

7. What did Catweazle call a 'telling-bone'?

8. In Series 2 the central location was a Manor House. Lord and Lady Collingford's son is Catweazle's new friend. What is his name? A) Rodney   B) Gary   C) Cedric

9. What was the name of the abandoned railway station?

10. How did Catweazle depart at the end of, what was to be, the final episode?

TOADS

In traditions and legends toads have long been associated with witches and magicians. Witches were allegedly able to transform themselves into toads, kept them as pets or even used parts of them as ingredients for magic potions. Symbolically toads are related to the moon and the earth and in general to the female/maternal principle. In popular belief the toad is a spirit and a guardian of treasure that protects the house against misfortune. In China it stands for fertility and wealth.

HETTY WAINTHROPP INVESTIGATES: 1. Patricia Routledge and Dominic Monaghan; 2. Lost; 3. B) Lancashire; 4. B) In the Post Office; 5. 60th; 6. A Children's Charity Box; 7. Wainthropp Detective Agency; 8. He emigrated to Australia; 9. Their voices; 10. B) Victorian Living Museum. DAME PATRICIA ROUTLEDGE: 1990 - Keeping Up Appearances; 1967 - To Sir With Love; 1971 - Sense and Sensibility; 1974 - Steptoe and Son; 1985 - Marjorie and Men.

A British game show version of charades which was broadcast on ITV from 1979 to 1992. The show featured two teams of celebrities. A revived version was broadcast by BBC One in 1997 over 30 episodes. Returned for a special Comic Relief episode in March 2011. The programme has been repeated on satellite TV. 18 Series, 333 Episodes.

1. The show had 3 main presenters,
A) from 1979-1983   B) 1984-1992   C) 1997. Who were they?

2. There were 3 Boys' Captains and 3 Girls' captains. Can you name them?

3. The programme shared a theme tune with which other TV show?

4. How long was given to act out the charade?

5. The infamous impossible long song titles reserved for some comedian to mime were traditionally how many words?

CAN YOU NAME SOME GUEST STARS WHO APPEARED ON GIVE US A CLUE

A	B	C	D
E	F	G	H

CATWEAZLE: 1. C) 1969; 2. A) Hexwood Farm; 3. B) Castle Saburac; 4. Carrot; 5. Touchwood; 6. Adamcos; 7. The telephone; 8. C) Cedric; 9. Duck Halt; 10. In a hot air balloon.

A British detective fiction drama series, set in an unnamed city in the West of England, featuring the down-at-heel private detective Eddie Shoestring, who presents his own show on Radio West, a local radio station. Broadcast on BBC1, Shoestring had two series, between 30 September 1979 and 21 December 1980, a total of 21 episodes.

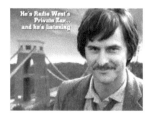

1. Who played the title role?

2. In which West Country city was Shoestring filmed?

3. Down-at-heel private detective Eddie Shoestring formerly worked as what before he had a nervous breakdown? A) Accountant B) Computer expert C) Clerk

4. On which radio station did Eddie Shoestring present his own show?

5. What was the name of the receptionist, played by Liz Crowther?

6. Shoestring drove a Hillman Hunter before changing to a bright orange car. What make was that? A) Vauxhall Viva B) Morris Marina C) Ford Cortina Estate

7. In *Find the Lady* rock singer Toola asked Eddie to dissuade Mole, her sacked bass player, that his beauty queen girlfriend Chrissie had been killed by the band's manager Malcolm Kenrick. Who played Toola?

8. Shoestring's landlady, as a barrister, sometimes provided legal advice for Eddie's cases. What was her name? A) Erica Bayliss B) Molly Tasker C) Maddy Hopkins

9. In the last ever episode of *Shoestring*, Dangerous Game, Pete Johnson, a market trader who dealt in stolen goods, gave his little son Mike a present, an electric racing game called Lunar Race 2000. What happened when Mike played the game?

10. In the real world, Bristol's first independent radio station was started on 27 October 1981. What name was it given?

AMATEUR SLEUTHS

Can you work out who the TV crime solvers are?

A) HECKLERS SHOLOM   B) ISIAH TANAGRA
C) AMPLER JASMINES   D)BEVY MERCHANDISERS

GIVE US A CLUE: 1. Michael Aspel, B) Michael Parkinson, C) Tim Clark; 2. Lionel Blair, Norman Vaughan, (1980 stand in for Lionel), Christopher Blake; Una Stubbs, Liza Goddard, Julie Peasgood; 3. Grange Hill; 4. 2 minutes; 5. 24; A) Faith Brown; B) Bernard Cribbins; C) Marti Caine; D) Bob Holness; F) Leslie Crowther; G) Mary Parkinson; G) Bernie Winters; H) Eve Ferret.

ADRIAN MOLE

The Secret Diary of Adrian Mole aged 13¾ was a British series based on the book of the same name written by Sue Townsend. It began on 16 September - 21 October 1985. The Growing Pains of Adrian Mole followed, it aired from 5 January to 9 February 1987. Series 6 episodes in each series.

1. Which of these was not one of Adrian's New Year's resolutions at the start of the story? A) Stop squeezing spots B) Hang up trousers C) Get a paper round

2. Adrian's family had a pet dog. But what was it called?

3. Adrian had an American pen-pal. Can you name him?

4. On New Years Eve, at the start of the book, what did the dog get drunk on? A) Cherry Brandy B) Cooking Sherry C) Advocaat

5. What is the name of the old person whom Adrian looks after?

6. What is the name of Adrian's humanities teacher?
A) Mr Gnome B) Miss Elf C) Ms Dwarve

7. The old man who Adrian looks after has false teeth. In which year did he get his teeth? A) 1946 B) 1956 C) 1966

8. Barry Kent has been taking 25p a day from Adrian in exchange for not being beaten up. Who finds out, gets Adrian's money back, and tells him that Barry will not bother him again. Who did this deed?

9. Two actresses played Adrian's mother, one in series one, and the other in the second series. Name the two actresses.

10. What football item did Adrian steal from Mr. Cherry's shop?

TRIVIA

Which actress, who starred in The Killing of Sister George and Bold as Brass, appeared as Grandma Mole?

SHOESTRING: 1. Trevor Eve; 2. Bristol; 3. B) Computer expert; 4. Radio West; 5. Sonia; 6. C) Ford Cortina Estate; 7. Toyah Willcox; 8. A) Erica Bayliss; 9. It is faulty and blows up, leading to the hospitalising of the boy; 10. Radio West. AMATEUR SLEUTHS: A) SHERLOCK HOLMES;

A round of mixed questions about British TV. This covers categories including Drama, Children's TV, Comedy, Soaps, Cookery programmes, Sci-Fi, News Years, Catchphrases, Crime shows and more! There are 3 sets of these questions throughout the book

All Kinds of Everything
2
A Miscellaneous Round

1. Which octogenarian singing Knight was on the Piers Morgan Show in October 2020?

2. In which fictional retirement home did Diana Trent and Tom Ballard live?

3. In *The Sister*, Nathan is a lost soul who harbours a terrible secret that he's desperate to keep buried. Which *Being Human* star played the role of Nathan in this October 2020 psychological thriller?

4. Who presents *Dragon's Den*?

5. Which Scottish singer played herself in *Absolutely Fabulous*?

6. Which comedy cricket drama starred 'Rodney's father in law and Vera' ?

7. Which two mischievous puppets appeared with Chris Evans in *The Big Breakfast*?

8. Which Scot played a popular transgender barmaid in *Rab C Nesbitt* ?

9. What happened to the Rovers Return pub in Coronation Street in 1979 and which regular was knocked unconscious?

10. Bernard Bresslaw as Popeye Popplewell uttered the famous catchphrase 'Well I only asked' in which military sit-com?

11. What was the highest rated British TV series on the IMDB Top 250 TV series List in 2012, being ranked 5th?
A) The Office   B) Black Mirror   C) Sherlock

12. In 2013 where in Indiana did Sir Trevor McDonald visit to present a two part documentary?

13. Which Big Brother winner went on to host two series of the show?

14. Which sci-fi series released the interactive Netflix film Bandersnatch in 2018?

15. In *Emmerdale* on New Years Day in 2004, who died when The Woolpack pub's chimney came crashing down in a storm?

ADRIAN MOLE: 1. C) Get a paper round; 2. The Dog ; 3. Hamish Mancini; 4. A) Cherry Brandy; 5. Bert Baxter; 6. B) Miss Elf; 7. A) 1946; 8. His Grandma; 9. Julie Walters, Lulu; 10. A Kevin Keegan key ring. TRIVIA: Beryl Reid.

A BBC1 British science fiction, time travel, sitcom. An accidental time traveller, leads a double life through the use of a time portal, allowing him to travel between London in the 1990s and 1940s during WW2. Ran from 1993-1999. 6 series, 59 episodes. A special was made in 2016.

1. What is the name of the time traveller played by Nicholas Lyndhurst?
A) Darren Thrush B) Charlie Dunnock C) Gary Sparrow

2. What is the name of the 1940's pub that Gary walks into?

3. The pub landlord was suspicious of Gary as he should be in the forces, but isn't. The landlord's daughter, however, took a fancy to Gary. A) What is her name and B) Name the 2 actresses who played her in 3 series each?

4. At the end of series two, Gary decided to stop travelling back in time. Why does he resume his trips?

5. Gary frequently pretended, while in wartime London, to have written many modern pop songs. Which song did George Formby want to record?
A) When I'm 64 by The Beatles B) Wouldn't It Be Nice by The Beach Boys
C) My Old Man's A Dustman by Lonnie Donegan

6. True or False? Gary meets his own son, now older than him.

7. Learning that the small passageway where his time-slip portal exists, is being redeveloped, how does Gary resolve the problem?

8. What's the name of the shop where Gary flogs the memorabilia he brings back from the 1940s?
A) Ration Passion B) War & Peace C) Blitz and Pieces

9. Who does Gary encounter when he accidentally travels back to Victorian times?
A) Jack the Ripper B) Queen Victoria C) Charles Dickens

10. Goodnight Sweetheart returned for a one-off special in 2016, but how did Gary Sparrow re-open the portal and get back to his time-travelling ways?
A) He sang Goodnight Sweetheart on karaoke B) He held himself as a newborn baby
C) He heard Love Me Do by The Beatles

All the episode titles of Goodnight Sweetheart are names of songs from the 1940's.

ALL KINDS OF EVERYTHING 2: 1. Sir Cliff Richard; 2. Bayview Retirement Home near Bournemouth; 3. Russell Tovey; 4. Ewan Davis; 5. Lulu; 6. Outside Edge; 7. Zig and Zag; 8. David Tennant; 9. A lorry crashed into it;, Alf Roberts was KO'd 10. The Army Game; 11. C) Sherlock; 12. Indiana State Prison Death Row; 13. Brian Dowling; 14. Black Mirror; 15. Trisha Dingle.

A British variety and stand-up comedy series. The show was originally a one-off Christmas special in 2015, before the BBC announced that they had ordered a full series in 2016. The show features celebrity guests, musical performances, comedy sketches from McIntyre, guest comics and some regular fun and games involving people in the audience. Now 5 series and 33 episodes broadcast.

1. What segment of the show involves McIntyre taking a celebrity's phone and sending an awkward text message to all of their contacts. Then, at the end of the show, checking the phone to see what replies have come through?

2. What is the popular part of the show when a member of the public is told to come to the theatre (suitably disguised) and asked to do various jobs that turn out to be fake. This eventually leads them backstage, then either the walls of the fake room fall down or the person opens a door to see the audience?

3. From the third series a new segment was introduced. Michael goes into a home of a celebrity or audience member at midnight, without them knowing, and sneaks into their bedroom to play a game-show at midnight. What is it called?

4. The fifth series was broadcast live from The London Palladium. In which theatre had the previous four series been filmed?

5. In series 5, episode 4, which 2 superstars surprise some karaoke-singing audience members with Kylie-aoke and Robbie-aoke?

6. In series 2, episode 4, which TV presenters both hand over their phones in the first ever double phone text game?

7. In the *Sport Relief Special* in 2018, which famous sportsman was caught out at midnight for some fun and games?

8. Which former Labour party Shadow Home Secretary 'invited' his contacts via text message to a Hot Tub Party?

9. The show won the BAFTA award for Best Entertainment Performance in which year? A) 2016 B) 2017 C) 2018

10. On which ITV talent show did Michael McIntyre appear as a judge in 2011?

GOODNIGHT SWEETHEART: 1. C) Gary Sparrow; 2. Royal Oak; 3. A) Phoebe; B) Dervla Kirwan and Elizabeth Carling; 4. To invest money in the 1940s, to become rich in the 1990s; 5. A) When I'm 64 by The Beatles; 6. True (Phoebe bore him a son, Michael. He was a pauper, 20 years older than Gary, who returned to change history); 7. He buys the shop now built over the old passageway; 8. C) Blitz and Pieces; 9. A) Jack the Ripper; 10. B) He held himself as a newborn baby.

A British game show based on the short-lived American game show of the same name. It originally aired on ITV in the United Kingdom between 12 January 1986 and 23 April 2004 (Daytime TV in 2002). A revival premiered on ITV on 7 April 2013 and still continues. A total of 24 Series, 413 Episodes.

'Say what you see!' And solve the catchphrases

1. AID <
   AID
   AID

2. **SKTTY**

3. M O
   E K

4. **TUMMY**

5. MUST GET HERE
   MUST GET HERE
   MUST GET HERE

6. U͟BC͟U

7. 1,2,3,4,5
   US

8. *REVILO*

9. *ACRIML*

10. **HOROBOD**

NAME THE CATCHPHRASE HOSTS

A

B

C

D

MICHAEL McINTYRE'S BIG SHOW: 1. Send To All; 2. Unexpected Star of the Show; 3. Midnight Gameshow; 4. Theatre Royal, Drury Lane; 5. Kylie Minogue, Robbie Williams; 6. Marvin and Rochelle Humes; 7. Andy Murray; 8. Ed Balls; 9. B) 2017; 10. Britain's Got Talent.

A British sketch show first broadcast on BBC Two in 1990 in the 9 pm slot on Thursday nights which became the traditional time for alternative comedy on television. Enfield was already an established name but the series gave greater presence to his frequent collaborators Paul Whitehouse and Kathy Burke – so much so that, in 1994, the show was retitled Harry Enfield & Chums. 4 Series, 28 Episodes.

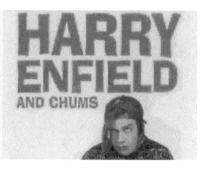

NAME THE CHARACTERS

CATCHPHRASES TO MATCH TO SOME OF THE CHARACTERS ABOVE

A) I'm having a fag; B) I HATE you; C) You dirty bugger;
D) Lulu lolly; E) Young man; F) Hello peeps

CATCHPHRASE: 1. First Aid; 2. Pie in the sky; 3. OK by me; 4. Upset tummy; 5. Three Musketeers; 6. Be seeing you; 7. Count on us; 8. Oliver Twist; 9. Criminal; 10. Robin Hood. **CATCHPHRASE HOSTS:** A) Roy Walker; B) Nick Weir; C) Mark Curry; D) Stephen Mulhern.

A British panel show produced by Hat Trick Productions for the BBC. Regularly broadcast since 1990, it is loosely based on the BBC Radio 4 show The News Quiz and has a topical and satirical remit. The programme was shown on BBC Two for its first ten years, before moving to BBC One. 59 Series. 524 Episodes.

1. Which one of the captains has not missed a single show?

2. Which team captain has notched up most wins?

3. When Angus Deayton was sacked, after a kiss and tell story appeared in the tabloid press, Paul Merton wore a T shirt with what message: A) TV Host Sordid Sex Shame B) Have I Got Boobs For You C) TV's Deayton Drug Romp With Vice Girl.

4. Which politician was a Guest Host in 2003 and earned a BAFTA nomination?

5. To date which guest has appeared the most times?

6. In 2003 Bruce Forsyth hosted a spoof game show based on HIGNFY. What was it called?
A) Play Your Iraqi Cards Right B) Have I Got Unbroadcastable News for You
C) The Generation Election.

7. In 1993 Roy Hattersley pulled out late in the day and was replaced with what?

8. As part of a very long running joke, which 'celebrity' has Ian been likened too and has mimicked as part of a one-off round?

9. What is Paul Merton's greatest educational achievement?

10. The 26 April 2013 edition prompted over 100 complaints to the BBC and Ofcom for its perceived anti-Scottish stance. During a section discussing Scottish independence. Ian Hislop had suggested what would be the new Scottish currency

ODD ONE OUT
From these 4 celebrities

HARRY ENFIELD AND CHUMS: 1. Mr You-Don't-Want-To-Do-It-Like-That; 2. Stavros; 3. Wayne & Waynetta Slob; 4. Il Postino Pat; 5.Smashie & Nicey; 6. Harry & Lulu; 7. Julio Geordio; 8. Loadsamoney; 9. Tim Nice But Dim; 10. Randy Old Ladies; 11. Kevin the Teenager; 12. Old Gits. CATCHPHRASES: A3, B11, C12, D6, E10, F2.

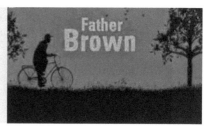

A British detective period drama which began airing on BBC One on 14 January 2013. It features a crime-solving Roman Catholic priest. Loosely based on short stories by G K Chesterton. Apart from soap operas, it is the third-longest-running daytime drama series on BBC TV. 8 Series 90 Episodes.

1. The Series is set in: A) The mid 40s B) The mid 50s C) The mid 60s.

2. The series is set in a fictional Cotswold village where Father Brown is priest at St Mary's Catholic Church. A) Wood Green B) St Mary Mead C) Kembleford.

3. In the period the show is set, the country still applied the death penalty as a sentence for capital crimes such as murder. Is Father Brown for or against Capital punishment?

4. Who is Lady Felicia's chauffeur? It is not a secret that he uses marijuana and has cracksman skills, which Father Brown frequently utilises.

5. Who is the Irish parish secretary, who often does a number of things around the presbytery for Father Brown? She is the stereotypical church gossip and always knows everybody's business despite claiming else-wise.

6. Which actress played the character, who is the topic of the previous question? She also had another starring role alongside another Brown!

7. Other than Father Brown, name the only character created by GK Chesterton that regularly appeared in the TV series. He was a French jewel and art thief whose brilliant mind poses a tricky puzzle for Father Brown.

8. Name the third Inspector of the series. Unlike his predecessors, he is openly rude to Father Brown (and most everyone else) whereas the others were just frustrated with the priest.

9. Mark Williams brilliantly portrays Father Brown. He is a versatile actor but which daytime quiz did he host in 2014 and 2015?

10. In the original Father Brown TV series in 1974, which acclaimed film star played the title role?

BERETS SLOUCH	*This is an anagram of the first Father Brown book title and also a TV episode in January 2013.*

HAVE I GOT NEWS FOR YOU: 1. Ian Hislop; 2. Paul Merton; 3. C) TV's Deayton Drug Romp With Vice Girl; 4. Boris Johnson; 5. Alexander Armstrong; 6. A) Play Your Iraqi Cards Right; 7. A tub of lard (named Rt Hon Tub of Lard); 8. Jimmy Somerville; 9. Metalwork CSE, ungraded; 10. Mars Bars. ODD ONE OUT: Bradley Walsh (has not been guest presenter).

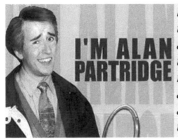

BBC sitcom features the eponymous Alan Partridge, a tactless and inept radio DJ and television presenter, after he has been left by his wife and dropped from the BBC after the events of his chat show. The show follows Partridge as he lives alone in a roadside hotel and presents a graveyard slot on local Norwich radio, all the while desperately pitching ideas for new television shows. 2 Series. 12 Episodes.

1. Apart from his low-standard show having falling ratings, why was Alan Partridge dismissed from the BBC?

2. In series one he was divorced from his wife Carol. Where was he living?

3. Whilst desperately trying to get back on television AP was reduced to working the graveyard shift on: A) Radio Bristol B) Radio Norwich C) Radio Luton

4. When Alan was nearly bankrupt he chose to fire the entire staff of his company. The name of the company was :
A) L C Partridge B) Peartree Productions C) Pheasant Pluckers

5. Throughout the episode *Basic Alan*, Partridge was desperately bored and does various things to pass the time. This included a walk along a busy dual carriageway to a petrol station to buy several bottles of what?
A) Windscreen Washer Fluid B) Tizer C) Mouthwash

6. In the episode *Watership* Alan made various unsympathetic and ill-advised comments about which group of workers, leading to him being crushed by a dead cow thrown from a bridge?

7. In the Series 2 episode *Brave Alan,* AP made friends with Dan at the BP garage. Who played Dan?

8. Dan owned a furniture store, and arranged for Alan to present which awards?
A) Cromer Crab Awards B) Best Broads Boat Awards C) Colman's Mustard Bravery Awards.

9. True or False? In 1998 *I'm Alan Partridge* won the Best TV Sit-Com award at the British Comedy Awards.

10. In the final episode 14,000 copies of Alan's book were being pulped whilst which song is playing in the background?
A) Money, Money, Money B) Windmills Of Your Mind C) Paperback Writer

---

FATHER BROWN: 1. B) The mid 50s; 2. C) Kembleford; 3. Against capital punishment; 4. Sid (Sydney); 5. Mrs Bridgette McCarthy; 6. Sorcha Cusack (Hilary Nicholson in Mrs Brown's Boys); 7. Hercule Flambeau; 8. Inspector Mallory ; 9. The Link; 10. Kenneth More.
ANAGRAM: The Blue Cross.

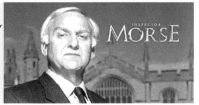

A British detective drama series based on a series of novels by Colin Dexter. The series was made by Zenith Productions for Central Independent Television, and first shown in the UK on the ITV network of regional broadcasters between 1987 and 2000. 7 Series, 5 Specials. 33 Episodes.

1. Why was Morse named Endeavour?

2. What is the name of A) The first Inspector Morse novel and B) What is the name of the first TV episode of Inspector Morse?

3. Which actor connects Max the pathologist in the early episodes of Inspector Morse and the Trotters in *Only Fools and Horses*?

4. Who appeared in a cameo role in all but 3 of the episodes of Inspector Morse?

5. Morse drove a red Jaguar Mark II. What was the registration number? A) EM 123   B) 248 RPA   C) IM 999

6. Who was Morse's boss, played by James Grout?

7. Many guest stars appeared throughout the 7 series. Which actor, more renowned for comedy, played the reptilian Master of Lonsdale College in *Death Is Now My Neighbour*?

8. To which Oxford University College did young Morse receive a scholarship and whilst there as a student what was his nickname?

9. In Deceived By Flight a member of The Clarets cricket team dies. Lewis goes undercover as what?

10. What was the name of the final Inspector Morse episode? At the end of the episode Lewis visits him at the morgue, how does he say a final farewell?

Can you solve this Morse Code message?
.--- --- .... -. / - .... .- --

I'M ALAN PARTRIDGE: 1. For punching Chief Commissioning Editor Tony Hayers in the face with a stuffed partridge; 2. Linton Travel Tavern; 3. B) Radio Norwich; 4. B) Peartree Productions; 5. A) Windscreen Washer Fluid; 6. Farmers; 7. Steven Mangan; 8. C) Colman's Mustard Bravery Awards 9. True (It won 4 awards at the British Academy and British Comedy Awards); 10. B) Windmills On Your Mind.

C●MIC RELIEF

An operating British charity, founded in 1985 in response to famine in Ethiopia. The concept is to get British comedians to make the public laugh, whilst raising money to help people in need in Africa, and in the UK. The highlight of Comic Relief's appeal is Red Nose Day, a biennial telethon. First held 5th February 1988. Sport Relief also held biennially.

1. At the end of the 2015 Red Nose Telethon it was announced that in the 30 year history of *Comic Relief* the Red Nose Day and Sport Relief had raised more than.... what amount of money?

2. Who were the two principal founders of *Comic Relief*?

3. Which TV character played *Deal or No Deal* on Noel Edmonds' TV show for a Comic Relief sketch in 2007?

4. In 1986 Cliff Richard revived one of his number one hits for *Comic Relief*. It reached the top of the charts for a second time. Who also performed on the hit single with Cliff?

5. In the year 2000 which author wrote two special books, raising £18 million for Comic Relief?

6. 3,307,000 special Red Noses were purchased in 1993, but what edible item did they resemble?

7. In 1999 which top movie star appeared in a special episode of The Vicar of Dibley?

8. In 2009 Gary Barlow, Fearne Cotton, Cheryl, Chris Moyes, Denise van Outen and other stars climbed a mountain and raised £3.5 million. Which mountain?

9. In 2002 Comic Relief launched a Fairtrade chocolate bar made by workers in Ghana. It was called?
A) Rubble B) Bubble C) Dubble D) Hubble

10. In 2014 a special episode of Only Fools and Horses was made for Sport Relief. Which former footballer turned celebrity guest starred in the 10 minute sketch?

INSPECTOR MORSE: 1. His father was obsessed with Captain James Cook, so he was named after HMS Endeavour; 2. A) Last Bus to Woodstock; B) The Dead of Jericho; 3. Peter Woodthorpe played Max and also Reg Trotter, Del Boy's father; 4. Colin Dexter; 5. B) 248 RPA; 6. Chief Superintendent Strange; 7. Richard Briers; 8. St John's College, Pagan; 9. College porter; 10. A Remorseful Day, Kisses him on the forehead and says 'Goodbye Sir'. MORSE CODE - John Thaw.

A BBC sitcom about a Royal Artillery concert party based in India, during the last months of the Second World War. It was written by Jimmy Perry and David Croft, who had both served in similar roles during that war. It was first broadcast on BBC 1 in eight series between 1974 and 1981, totalling 56 episodes

1. In 1975 two characters from the series, Gunner Lofty Sugden and Battery Sergeant Major Williams, duetted on a UK number one hit. Name the song and the two actors who performed on the record?

2. 'Nobby' Clark did a whistling act in the show, including bird sounds. The actor who played Nobby became a regular in *Only Fools & Horses*, until his death at just 50. In his will he asked that his character not to be killed off but serving 5 years in prison for embezzling money from brewery. Can you name him?

3. Initially, the British soldiers were stationed at the Royal Artillery Depot in Deolali, where soldiers were kept before being sent to fight at the front lines. In which country is Deolali?

4. The only exception to the Sergeant Major's callous treatment of the troops was Gunner Parkin. Why did he treat him differently?

5. Lieutenant-Colonel Reynolds was the most senior officer in charge of the concert party. He thought army life in Asia was very hard, but he sat around most of the time sipping what drink? A) Lemonade   B) Pink Gin   C) Lager

6. George Layton starred in the first two series before his Jewish character was demobbed back to England. What was his nickname?
A) Manny B) Immanuel C) Solly

7. What was the name of the bald, bespectacled concert party pianist who spoke with a very upper-class accent, and what does the Sergeant Major call him?

8. Rangi Ram was the concert party's Indian bearer and very proud to be of service to the army. He got shouted at more often than anyone else. Who played the role in the first 5 series before he also sadly died? *(Extra clue: also starred in Last of the Summer Wine from 1973-75).*

9. The series is no longer repeated on British television, on the assumption it would offend viewers, but how many viewers did it attract in its prime?
A) Up to 10 million   B) Up to 12 million   C) Up to 14 million   D) Up to 17 million

10. 'Pretty Boy' Me Thant was a Burmese smuggler, bribed by GHQ at 20 pieces of gold a week to keep away from, and avoid assaulting, the local British troops. Which actor, well known for the Pink Panther films, played the role?

COMIC RELIEF: 1. Over £1 billion; 2. Richard Curtis and Lenny Henry; 3. Catherine Tate's Nan; 4. The Young Ones and Hank Marvin; 5. JK Rowling; 6. A tomato; 7. Johnny Depp; 8. Mount Kilimanjaro; 9. C) Dubble; 10. David Beckham.

A British programme launched in February 1957 when both TV and Rock 'n' Roll were in their infancy. The BBC's first attempt at a Rock 'n' Roll programme and much imitated since. It aired live at five past six on Saturday evening, beginning immediately after the abolition of the Toddlers' Truce, when TV had closed 6pm -7pm, so children could be put to bed. 96 Episodes, last 27 December 1958.

Lonnie Donegan was a mainstay on the programme. Below there is a list of 10 of his biggest hits. Their highest chart position was from 1-10. Match up the songs with their highest UK chart position.

SONG / YEAR IN CHARTS	CHART POSITION
A. THE PARTY'S OVER - April 1962	1
B. I WANNA GO HOME - May 1960	2
C. BATTLE OF NEW ORLEANS - June 1959	3
D. ROCK ISLAND LINE/JOHN HENRY - Jan 1956	4
E. BRING A LITTLE WATER SYLVIE/DEAD OR ALIVE - Sep 1956	5
F. DON'T YOU ROCK ME DADDY-O - Jan 1957	6
G. MY OLD MAN'S A DUSTMAN - March 1960	7
H. LORELEI - August 1960	8
J. DOES YOUR CHEWING GUM LOSE ITS FLAVOUR - Feb 1959	9
K. THE GRAND COOLIE DAM - April 1958	10

CAN YOU NAME THESE STARS OF THE 6.5 SPECIAL?

| A | B | C | D | E |

TRIVIA: The budget for each show was £1,000. Even in 1957 £1,000 was not very much money with which to create a television show. This lack of money meant that Jack Good was restricted to mainly British Artists singing cover versions of American songs. The Mudlarks, The King Brothers, Jim Dale, who later became one of the presenters, Tommy Steele, Vince Eager and Marty Wilde all made career helping appearances.

IT AIN'T HALF HOT MUM: 1. Whispering Grass, Don Estelle and Windsor Davies; 2. Kenneth MacDonald; 3. India; 4. He believes Parkin is his illegitimate son, having had an affair with Parkin's mother some years before; 5. B) Pink Gin; 6. C) Solly; 7. Gunner 'Paderewski' Jonathan Graham, Mr La-De-Dah Gunner Graham; 8. Michael Bates; 9. D) Up to 17 million; 10. Burt Kwouk.

A British sitcom created and written by Roy Clarke and originally broadcast by the BBC from 1973 to 2010. It premiered as an episode of Comedy Playhouse on 4 January 1973, and the first series of episodes followed on 12 November 1973. Repeats of the show are broadcast in the UK on Gold, Yesterday, and Drama. 31 Series. 285 Episodes.

1. The show centred on a trio of old men and their youthful misadventures. Around which small Yorkshire town was the series filmed?

2. The original trio consisted of the mischievous and impulsive Compo Simmonite, easy-going everyman Norman Clegg, and uptight and arrogant Cyril Blamire. Who played the roles?

3. *Last of the Summer Wine* won the National Television Award for Most Popular Comedy Programme in which year? A) 1979   B) 1989   C) 1999   D) 2009

4. Which vehicle did Wesley call his 'Ferrari in overalls'?

5. In later episodes the 'third man' was one Herbert 'Truly' Truelove. What was his former job?

6. The actresses who portrayed hen-pecked husband Howard Sibshaw's shrewish wife Pearl and his busty love interest Marina, died within 5 weeks of each other in 2019. Can you name the actresses who played the roles?

7. What was the name of the café frequented by the trio of aged delinquents?

8. We quite often see the women, Ivy, Nora, Pearl, Edie and Glenda having coffee and cake discussing their husbands' faults. What type of cake was favourite?

9. For three series Foggy Dewhurst was not present. What was the reason given in the show for his absence?

10. Compo had two passions in life, his ferrets and who?

CAN YOU NAME THE ACTORS WHO PLAYED THE CHARACTERS BELOW?

A - Edie Pegden   B - Foggy Dewhurst   C - Nora Batty   D - Seymour Utterthwaite   E - Ivy

THE SIX-FIVE SPECIAL: A9, B5, C2, D8, E7, F4, G1, H10, J3, K6. STARS OF 6.5 SPECIAL: A) Jim Dale; B) Joan Regan; C) Wee Willie Harris; D) Petula Clark; E) Trevor Peacock (comedy & scriptwriter for the show - later starred in The Vicar of Dibley).

A British soap opera which began airing on Channel 4 on 23 October 1995. It was created by Phil Redmond, who had previously conceived the soap opera Brookside. The programme is set in the fictional village of Hollyoaks, a suburb of Chester. A total of 5,443 Episodes (as at Sept 2020).

1. Who were the two main characters that appeared in the original *Hollyoaks*?

2. What was the surname of a group of 5 brothers that moved to the village with their mother?

3. In 2011, India and Bex were both murdered, and Lynsey narrowly escaped the same fate. But who was the twisted murderer?

4. What is the name of the local pub in the show. How is it usually known?

5. The Boxing Day episode in 2011 was based upon Doug attempting to commit suicide. Who came back as an angel and showed Doug what the village would be like if he was not around?

6. Who murdered Texas on her wedding day?

7. In 2018, the show featured a self-harming storyline which won Best Storyline and Best Single Episode at The British Soap Awards in 2018. Which character continued to self-harm, leading to her death of sepsis in 2019?

8. In 2016, 'Point of View' week, focused on the Police suspects for the killer of Motor Neurone Disease victim Patrick Blake, who had been found buried in the woods. Who did kill him?

9. In 2014 Sienna Blake's car got stuck on the tracks after a car chase with her father, causing the train to smash into it and derail, killing 2 characters. Name them?

10. On 21 December 2009, the show's time-line moved forward six months into May 2010. The episode featured the second wedding of which couple?

> *TRIVIA: Unusually for a British soap, the majority of characters tend not to be in the programme for longer than two years, and even fewer have been on for longer than five years.*

LAST OF THE SUMMER WINE: 1. Holmfirth; 2. Bill Owen, Peter Sallis, Michael Bates; 3. C) 1999; 4. Land Rover; 5. Policeman; 6. Juliette Kaplan (Pearl) and Jean Fergusson (Marina); 7. Sid's Café; 8. Chocolate Éclair; 9. He took over an egg-painting business; 10. Nora Batty.
CHARACTERS: A) Dame Thora Hird; B) Brian Wilde; C) Kathy Staff; D) Michael Aldridge; E) Jane Freeman.

A British sitcom created and written by Roy Clarke. It originally aired on BBC1 from 1990 to 1995. The central character is an eccentric and snobbish lower middle class social climber, Hyacinth Bucket (Patricia Routledge), who insists that her surname is pronounced "Bouquet". The show comprised five series and 44 episodes, four of which are Christmas specials.

1. What was the specialist social function to which Hyacinth would invite a large number of guests, many of whom don't know her all that well - but are extremely well-to-do, so she can fulfil the most important task in her life - to impress?

2. Richard and Hyacinth had a son away at 'university' (polytechnic actually!) What was his name and when he calls what is he usually requesting?

3. Who were the four Walton sisters and what connects their names?

4. How did Onslow turn on his television set?

5. *The Three Piece Suite* was a 1991 episode. Why was Hyacinth so anxious that the neighbours, especially Mrs Barker-Finch, saw the new suite being delivered?

6. Elizabeth's brother was frightened about being invited to Hyacinth's for coffee. What did he fear she would do when she saw him?

7. What did Violet's husband Bruce like to do?

8. In the 1993 Chrismas Special, who danced with Hyacinth on the QE2 cruise?

9. Who got scolded by his wife for his efforts to avoid 'The Bucket Woman'?

10. What was the feature on Hyacinth's Royal Doulton china tea set?

MEMBERS OF THE CAST IN 2020
Who did they portray?

A- Marion Barron   B- David Griffin   C- Judy Cornwell   D- Jeremy Gittins   E - Josephine Tewson

HOLLYOAKS: 1. Ben & Lisa; 2. Roscoe; 3. Silas; 4. The Dog (The Dog in the Pond); 5. Steph; 6. Will; 7. Lily Drinkwell; 8. His grand-daughter Nico; 9. Carmel McQueen & Sonny Valentine; 10. Calvin Valentine & Carmel McQueen.

 A 1976 BBC adaptation of Robert Graves's 1934 novel I, Claudius and its 1935 sequel Claudius the God. Written by Jack Pulman. I, Claudius follows the history of the early Roman Empire, narrated by the elderly Roman Emperor Claudius, from the year 24 BC to his death in AD 54. 12 Episodes.

1. The knighted actor who portrayed Claudius has continued as a phenomenal stylish actor on stage, film and TV. Can you name him?

2. A raptor dropped a bloodied animal into the young Claudius's arms. Name the animal that was seen to represent Rome.

3. The opening title sequence featured a creature moving across a mosaic picture of Claudius. What kind of creature was it?

4. Livia, the manipulative wife of the Emperor Augustus, would stop at nothing to see that her son became Emperor. Who was her son?

5. Which close friend of Claudius frequently told him to 'Trust no one'?

6. Another acclaimed knighted actor, Sir John Hurt, played whom in the series?

7. At his first wedding ceremony, Claudius's family were all very amused. What was so funny?

8. How did Livia finally poison Augustus?

9. Claudius married Agrippinilla and adopted her son. He was, later in his life, linked with popular legend - he fiddled whilst Rome burnt! What was his name?

10. Which of the following was NOT one of Claudius's so-called defects?
A) A limp   B) A tendency to drool   C) Stupidity   D) A stammer

ROMAN NUMERALS
The numbers below are equivalent to:

1.	2.	3.	4.	5.
XCIX	XLI	CCCLVIII	MMDCCXCII	DCCCXLV

KEEPING UP APPEARANCES: 1. Candlelight Suppers; 2. Sheridan, Money; 3. Hyacinth, Violet, Daisy and Rose, named after flowers; 4. Slaps it on the top; 5. The delivery van had a royal crest on the side; 6. She will sing at him; 7. Dress in women's clothes; 8. Onslow; 9. Michael, the Vicar; 10. Hand painted periwinkles. MEMBERS OF THE CAST IN 2020: A) Mrs Partridge the Vicar's wife; B) Emmet; C) Daisy; D) Michael Partridge the Vicar; E) Elizabeth.

Can you match the correct year that each of the listed programmes below was first shown on British TV?

What Year Was It?

1. TOMORROW'S WORLD	A. 1952
2. THE FLOWERPOT MEN	B. 1955
3. NEW FACES	C. 1956
4. THE SOOTY SHOW	D. 1961
5. ROBIN'S NEST	E. 1965
6. POSTMAN PAT	F. 1966
7. BALLYKISSANGEL	G. 1971
8. BODYGUARD	H. 1973
9. POINTS OF VIEW	J. 1976
10. ONE MAN AND HIS DOG	K. 1977
11. ALL GAS AND GAITERS	L. 1981
12. AN ISLAND PARISH	M. 1984
13. THE LENNY HENRY SHOW	N. 1985
14. OWEN MD	P. 1993
15. ROCK AND CHIPS	R. 1996
16. WAKING THE DEAD	S. 2000
17. SHARPE	T. 2003
18. WHACK-O	U. 2007
19. ALBION MARKET	V. 2010
20. BLUE MURDER	W. 2018

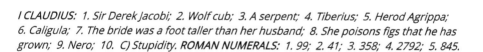

I CLAUDIUS: 1. Sir Derek Jacobi; 2. Wolf cub; 3. A serpent; 4. Tiberius; 5. Herod Agrippa; 6. Caligula; 7. The bride was a foot taller than her husband; 8. She poisons figs that he has grown; 9. Nero; 10. C) Stupidity. ROMAN NUMERALS: 1. 99; 2. 41; 3. 358; 4. 2792; 5. 845.

A British action/drama series first aired 8 July 1967, it ran to 24 May 1972. The plots concerned an agent of a state secret service dealing with internal security threats to the UK. Portrayed as being similar to MI5, Callan's fictional 'Section' has carte blanche to use ruthless methods in interrogation. 4 Series. 44 Episodes.

1. The series pilot episode entitled *A Magnum for Schneider* aired as one part of a drama anthology in February 1967. What was the name of the anthology?
A) ITV Playhouse   B) Armchair Theatre   C) BBC Sunday Night Theatre

2. The downbeat cover for the Section's headquarters was the scrap metal business named what: A) Charlie Hunter   B) Fred Flintstone   C) George Cole

3. Who was cast in the title role?

4. The series began with Callan having an ordinary job before returning to his occupation as Government agent. What was his ordinary job?

5. A rather odious individual, played by Russell Hunter, was usually on hand to assist Callan with various assignments. His nickname was what?

6. There was a colleague, played by Anthony Valentine, who was ruthless and sadistic in the way he performed his duties. What was the name of the character?

7. In the episode *The Carriers* Callan was compromised after Lonely caused a burglary job to go wrong. What did he do?

8. The Section used a series of colour-coded files. What did a Red File indicate?

9. Which British Prime Minister cited it as his favourite programme in contemporary interviews?

10. The Section head always went under a codename. A) What was the codename? B) What was Callan's regular alias?

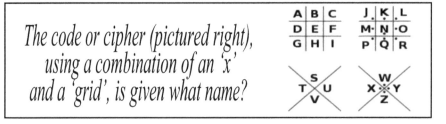

The code or cipher (pictured right), using a combination of an 'x' and a 'grid', is given what name?

A	B	C		J	K	L
D	E	F		M	N	O
G	H	I		P	Q	R

WHAT YEAR WAS IT?: 1E, 2A, 3H, 4B, 5K, 6L, 7R, 8W, 9D, 10J, 11F, 12U, 13M, 14G, 15V, 16S, 17P, 18C, 19N, 20T.

A British sitcom created by Brian Cooke and Johnnie Mortimer. On ITV from 15 August 1973 to 7 April 1976. Considered daring at the time featuring a man sharing a London flat with two single women. Made by Thames Television and recorded at its Teddington studio in Greater London. It is regularly repeated on ITV3. 6 Series. 39 +1 short Episodes.

1. Chrissy and Jo lived in a London flat together and worked for the same firm. The women found a stranger, student chef Robin Tripp, asleep in their bath the morning after a farewell party for their departed flatmate Eleanor. Who were the 3 stars?

2. What skills did Robin have that impressed the two girls so much they wanted him to be their new flatmate?

3. The landlord was a miserly, spiteful and unkempt man under the thumb of his domineering and sexually frustrated wife. What were their names?

4. What did Chrissy tell the landlord about Robin to eliminate his objections to the mixed-sex living arrangement?

5. Robin's friend played by Doug Fisher, was a lovable rogue. He moved into the loft apartment above the trio's apartment and was a frequent source of trouble. What was the character's name?

6. The landlord's friend was a dodgy builder named Jerry. The actor portraying him died in 1988, aged just 54, after falling from a horse and suffering serious injuries, leading to a heart attack, whilst filming in 1988. Who was the much loved actor?

7. Robin's brother Norman Tripp, played by Norman Eshley, appeared in the final three episodes of the sixth and final series, and started a romance with Chrissy. In which comedy sequel did he play estate agent Jeffrey Fourmile?

8. In the episode, *Match of the Day*, Robin caught a cold from the landlord and is annoyed as he is due to play in a football match. The girls gave him various remedies to get him fit but as he walks out on to the pitch, what did he discover?

9. In Series 2 Chrissy invited the Ropers up for a meal, not realising Robin had invited his German friend Franz Wasserman. But George had a grudge against the Germans and will not stop taking about the war. Who played Franz?

10. In Series 6 why didn't George want to go to Norman and Chrissy's wedding?

TRIVIA: Richard O'Sullivan quit showbiz in the mid-nineties, he occasionally does commercials and voiceovers.

CALLAN: 1. B) Armchair Theatre; 2. A) Charlie Hunter; 3. Edward Woodward; 4. Office worker; 5. Lonely; 6. Toby Meres ; 7. Stole a few items; 8. An especially dang. 9. Harold Wilson; 10. A) Hunter (Charlie when contacted from the outside world); B) David Tucker. CODE: Pigpen Code.

A British game show adapted from the French show *Intervilles*, and was part of the international *Jeux sans frontières* franchise. The series was broadcast on BBC1 from 7 August 1966 to 30 July 1982, thereafter a number of specials were broadcast until 25 December 1988. An episode was made by TVS for ITV which aired on 28 May 1990 as part of its ITV Telethon. 23 Series.

1. A Welsh version, *Gemau Heb Ffiniau* was broadcast from 3 August 1991 to 24 December 1994 on S4C. *Gemau Heb Ffiniau* was the inspiration for a Peter Gabriel song; what does it mean?

2. In April 1999, Channel 5 bought the rights to the show and started filming on 15 August in Reading, Berkshire with new presenters Keith Chegwin and Lucy Alexander. Which WBC heavyweight title-winning boxer was the referee?

3. *It's A Knockout* featured teams representing a town or city competing tasks in absurd games, generally dressed in what clothing?

4. How could teams double their points score in one round?

5. The first two presenters in the first two series in 1967 and 1968 each stayed for just one series. Both were well-established TV presenters. Can you name them?

6. A rugby league commentator with an eccentric northern mode of speech that was either loved or hated then took over as presenter for 12 years. Who was he?

7. Who was the man who presented the show from 1972-1988 but was jailed when found guilty of committing multiple sexual offences?

8. The Grand Knockout Tournament of 1987 raised over £1 million for charities. It featured four teams of celebrities. Can you name the four non-participating team captains who came from a very prominent family?

9. Whose team, including Dame Kiri Te Kanawa, Nicholas Lyndhurst, Tessa Sanderson and John Cleese, won the *Grand Knockout Tournament*?

10. The theme tune for the show was by Herb Alpert and the Tijuana Brass. What was it called? A) Rubber Band   B) Bean Bag   C) Greasy Pole   D) The Interceptor

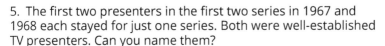

MAN ABOUT THE HOUSE: 1. Richard O'Sullivan, Sally Thomsett and Paula Wilcox; 2. His culinary skills (as a trainee chef); 3. George and Mildred Roper; 4. She tells him Robin is gay; 5. Larry Simmonds; 6. Roy Kinnear; 7. George & Mildred; 8. It was actually a rugby match; 9. Dennis Waterman; 10. He had a darts match.

A British police procedural and legal programme that was broadcast from 2009 to 2014 on ITV. Law & Order: UK is based in London the first American drama television series to be adapted for British television. Whilst the episodes are adapted from scripts and episodes of the parent series. The show ran for 8 Series, a total of 53 Episodes.

1. Which character did Bradley Walsh play in the series?

2. Why did Detective Inspector Natalie Chandler leave?

3. Which Kaiser Chiefs song has also been the name of an episode?

4. What happened to Detective Inspector Wes Layton as he was on his way to a dinner with his wife to celebrate his birthday?
A) He was assassinated   B) He was diverted to a murder
C) He had a collision with a motor bike

5. The opening narration for the show: In the criminal justice system, the people are represented by two separate yet equally important groups: The police who investigate crime, and the Crown Prosecutors who prosecute the offenders. These are their stories. Who was the narrator?
A) Robert Glenister B) Philip Glenister C) Bradley Walsh D) Peter Davison

6. What was Detective Sergeant Joe Hawkins' specialist area?

7. What comedy duo are Matt and Ronnie known as?

8. Ben Daniels played a senior crown prosecutor employed by the London CPS. His sidekick was Alesha Phillips. Who played the roles?

9. In what department of the Metropolitan Police Force do the Police detectives carry out their duties?

10. Detective Inspector Wes Layton was replaced in the final episode. DI Elizabeth Flynn was played by an actress who had previously worked in another crime series with an aristocratic, Oxford-educated Detective Inspector. Name the Scottish actress?

ANAGRAM TIME
BAWLED RASHLY

IT'S A KNOCKOUT: 1. Games Without Frontiers; 2. Frank Bruno; 3. Large foam rubber suits; 4. By playing their Joker; 5. McDonald Hobley and Katie Boyle; 6. Eddie Waring; 7. Stuart Hall; 8. Anne, The Princess Royal; Andrew, Duke of York; Prince Edward, Sarah, The Duchess of York; 9. Anne, The Princess Royal's team; 10. B) Bean Bag.

A British panel game show based on the short-lived US version of the same name. Call my Bluff ran for 23 years, from October 1965 to December 1988, with brief revivals in 1996, 2003 and 2011. The game comprised two teams of three (a captain and two guests) who would compete to earn points by determining the correct definitions to obscure words. 37 Series. 1,097 Episodes.

Find the right description for each word - A, B or C

WORD	A	B	C
1. ROUSTABOUT	Roundabout on a canal for boats to turn round	A device to turn kebab meat	An unskilled worker or labourer
2. PINTLE	Small boat used by Incas	A pin that holds a hinge together	Small shrew-like creature
3. DASHIKI	Japanese plant like horseradish	A loose, brightly coloured shirt from Africa	A pair of small drums used in Indian music
4. CATCHPOLE	Medieval officer who arrested debtors	A Scottish election agent	A large stick use to vault canals
5. POLLEX	Bitchy name for goldsmith apprentices	Astronomers refer to it as the double star system	Another name for the thumb
6. GLABELLA	Small metal covering for the toes of footwear	The space between the eyebrows	A plinth for a book to be read by reader
7. CERUMEN	Another name for earwax	Colloquial term in Sudan for camel's milk	Babylonian deity believed to habit oak trees
8. CONTUBERNIUM	Small unit of 8 soldiers	Herbaceous plant or small shrub	Thin silk or crepe dress
9. FRIABLE	Can be cooked in oil or dripping	Crumbly	Capable of being pronounced
10. TRAGUS	A trailer used to transport Roman slaves	Small cartilage projection at front of ear	Used in India as a symbol of resistance

LAW AND ORDER : UK: 1. DS Ronnie Brooks; 2. To care for her mother, who was in the late stages of a terminal disease; 3. I Predict A Riot ; 4. A) He was assassinated; 5. A) Robert Glenister; 6. Child protection; 7. Morecambe and Wise; 8. Ben Daniels and Freema Agyeman; 9. Murder Investigation Unit (referred to as MIU); 10. Sharon Small (was Sergeant Barbara Havers in Inspector Lynley Mysteries). *ANAGRAM: Bradley Walsh*

A British crime drama series, produced by TVS and Meridian Broadcasting, in association with Blue Heaven productions, for broadcast on ITV. 12 series were broadcast between 2 August 1987, and 11 October 2000. Created by renowned author Ruth Rendell, the first 6 series focused entirely on Rendell's main literary character Chief Inspector Wexford. 84 episodes in all.

1. What was DCI Wexford's first name?

2. Actually filmed in Romsey, Hampshire, the series was located in which fictional Sussex town?

3. Wexford (George Baker) was married to Dora (Louie Ramsay). What are their 2 daughters names?

4. One of the most memorable episodes was called *Kissing the Gunner's Daughter*. Where did the saying originate?

5. Christopher Ravenscroft played Wexford's right hand man. What was his character's name?

6. What was the name of the local pub?

7. In the Episode *Put On and Cunning* a world famous musician drowns in the grounds of his country estate. What instrument was he renowned for playing? A) Violin   B) Trumpet   C) Flute   D) Percussion

8. What was the profession of Wexford's youngest daughter?

9. The writer of the theme music for the series was the drummer in a top British instrumental band. Who is he?

10. Wexford had a guilty secret. Was it that: A) He'd had an affair in the first year of marriage   B) He preferred one of his daughters over the other   C) He'd cheated during his Police entry exams   D) He had once given a criminal a false alibi.

Anagrams of Ruth Rendell Novels. Can you work out the titles?

A) AIMS SOIL   B) AGED ROAR   C) EVENTIDE HOLE

CALL MY BLUFF: 1. C) An unskilled worker or labourer; 2. B) A pin that holds a hinge together; 3. B) A loose, brightly coloured shirt from Africa; 4. A) Medieval officer who arrested debtors; 5. C) Another name for the thumb; 6. B) The space between the eyebrows; 7. A) Another name for earwax; 8. A) Small unit of 8 soldiers; 9. B) crumbly; 10. A) A trailer used to transport Roman slaves.

A football highlights and analysis programme, typically broadcast on BBC One on Saturday evenings, during the Premier League season. It is one of the BBC's longest-running shows, having been on air since 22 August 1964. Now completed 51 Series. Over 5,000 Episodes.

1. The title *Match of the Day* was first used in June 1964 as the highlights of which sporting event?

2. What was the estimated audience for the first *Match of the Day* that showed highlights of Liverpool v Arsenal?
A) 1.3 million   B) 700,000   C) 310,000   D) 20,000

3. In what year were slow-motion replays first introduced?
A) 1965   B) 1967   C) 1969   D) 1971

4. *Match of the Day 2* launched in the 2004/5 season. Who was the first host?

5. There have been 5 main presenters of *MOTD* so far. Can you name them?

6. Alan Shearer and Ian wright have frequently appeared together as pundits. How many goals did they score between them in the Premier League?

7. Who was the first female commentator?

8. Who netted the Goal of the Season in these three seasons?
A) 1970/71 for Coventry City   B) 2009/10 for Wigan Ath   C) 2019/20 for Spurs

9. In August 2014, as part of the 50th anniversary celebrations for the programme which commentator returned for one last commentary?

10. Which pundit on the show from 1992 - 2014 was known for his outspoken views, particularly on teams' defensive performances, frequently criticising what he believed was 'diabolical' or 'shocking" defending'?

PREMIER LEAGUE APPEARANCES
Can you name the ten players who have notched up the most appearances in the Premier League before the start of the 2020/2021 season.

RUTH RENDELL MYSTERIES: 1. Reg; 2. Kingsmarkham; 3. Sylvia and Sheila; 4. A method of corporal punishment in the Royal Navy - to be flogged or beaten while restrained over a cannon.; 5. Inspector Mike Burden; 6. The Olive and Dove; 7. C) Flute; 8. Sheila is an actress; 9. Brian Bennett; 10. B) He preferred one of his daughters over the other. **NOVEL TITLES:** A) Simisola B) Road Rage C) The Veiled One

WHO SAID THAT!

There have been many catchphrases used on TV. Many have proved to be memorable. Below we list 20 catchphrases and 20 British TV characters. All you have to do is to match them up.

CATCHPHRASE	CHARACTER
1. My Arse!	A. Wilberforce C Humphries (Are You Being Served?)
2. Listen very carefully I will say this only once!	B. Zebedee (Magic Roundabout)
3. You dirty old man!	C. Nessa Jenkins (Gavin & Stacey)
4. Hello campers!	D. Brian Potter (Phoenix Nights)
5. Boom! Boom!	E. Selwyn Froggitt (Oh No It's Selwyn Froggitt)
6. Everybody out!	F. Gladys Pugh (Hi-De-Hi)
7. You silly moo!	G. Carol Beer (Little Britain)
8. What's occurring?	H. Captain George Mainwaring (Dad's Army)
9. I have a cunning plan!	J. Harold Steptoe (Steptoe & Son)
10. Garlic bread!	K. Michelle Dubois ('Allo 'Allo!)
11. Magic!	L. Alf Garnett (Till Death Us Do Part)
12. Am I bovvered!	M. Cupid Stunt (Kenny Everett TV Show)
13. Computer says no!	N. Basil Brush (Basil Brush Show)
14. I'm free!	P. Baldrick (Blackadder)
15. Time for bed!	Q. Mrs Joan Doyle (Father Ted)
16. You stupid boy!	R. Jim Royle (The Royle Family)
17. It's all done in the best possible taste!	S. Lauren Cooper (Catherine Tate Show)
18. Who rattled your scrotum?	T. Arthur Daley (Minder)
19. Nice little earner!	U. Paddy Fleming (The Rag Trade)
20. You will, you will, you will, you will!	V. Twinkle (dinnerladies)

MATCH OF THE DAY: 1. Wimbledon tennis; 2. D) 20,000 (about half of the attendance at Anfield for the match); 3. C) 1969; 4. Adrian Chiles; 5. Kenneth Wolstenholme (1964-7), David Coleman (67-73), Jimmy Hill (73-88), Des Lynam (88-99), Gary Lineker (1999-; 6. 373 (Shearer 260, Wright 113); 7. Jacqui Oatley; 8. A) Ernie Hunt B) Maynor Figuroa C) Son Heung-min; 9. Barry Davies; 10. Alan Hansen. **PREMIER LEAGUE APPEARANCES:** Gareth Barry (653), Ryan Giggs (632), Frank Lampard (609),David James (572), James Milner (5380, Gary Speed (535), Emile Heskey (516), Mark Schwarzer (514), Jamie Carragher (508), Phil Neville (505).

A 1970s British police drama about two members of the Flying Squad, part of the Metropolitan Police specialising in tackling armed robbery and violent crime in London. The title comes from "Sweeney Todd", Cockney rhyming slang for "Flying Squad". Produced by Thames Television subsidiary Euston Films for broadcast on the ITV network, it began as a television film Regan . 4 Series. 53 Episodes.

1. Who were the two main characters and which actors played the roles?

2. Stephanie Turner, who played Carter's late wife, went on to star as which female TV cop heroine and what fate befell her in the second series?

3. What was Regan's favourite drink?

4. In the second series episode *Trojan Bus*, Regan briefly whistled the theme-tune to which police series after a particularly elementary piece of detective work?

5. Regan had an ex-wife, Kate, and daughter, Susie, who lived in Ruislip. In the last episode of the first series what happened to Susie?

6. Detective Chief Inspector Frank Haskins was Regan's immediate superior. In series 2, *Golden Fleece* episode, an informant was paid to frame Haskins by planting money in his greenhouse. Haskins was suspended, then exonerated. Who played the Chief Inspector?

7. What was the name of the main antagonist Regan and Carter are trying to catch and who played the role?

8. In the opening scene of series 1 entitled *Ringer* what was the name on the side of the ambulance converted into a florists van as part of a plot to spring a prisoner?
A) Darling Buds   B) Blooming Lovely   C) Florries   D) Loose Leaf

9. *Hearts and Minds* was the last episode to be filmed. It featured a famous comedy duo, a quid pro quo for Waterman and Thaw's appearance in a sketch in their Christmas show on the BBC. Who were they?

10. Scotland Yard's real Flying Squad apparently lost an important surveillance technique when The Sweeney copied the method in an episode. What was it?

WHAT DO THESE WORDS MEAN IN COCKNEY RHYMING SLANG?
A) TROUBLE   B) LOAF   C) CHINA   D) SYRUP   E) TURKISH

CATCHPHRASES: 1R, 2K, 3J, 4F, 5N, 6U, 7L, 8C, 9P, 10D, 11E, 12S, 13G, 14A, 15B, 16H, 17M, 18V, 19T, 20Q.

A British reality music competition to find new singing talent. Created by Simon Cowell, the show opened on 4 September 2004 with 445 episodes broadcast over fifteen series as of 2 December 2018. Produced by Fremantle's Thames and Cowell's production company Syco Entertainment. It was broadcast on ITV in the UK.

15 WINNING ACTS AND THEIR DEBUT SINGLES.
CAN YOU MATCH THEM UP CORRECTLY?

PERFORMER	SONG AND YEAR
1. JOE McELDERRY	A. AGAINST ALL ODDS (2004)
2. JAMES ARTHUR	B. THAT'S MY GOAL (2005)
3. LOUISA JOHNSON	C. A MOMENT LIKE THIS (2006)
4. SHAYNE WARD	D. WHEN YOU BELIEVE (2007)
5. RAK-SU	E. HALLELUJAH (2008)
6. SAM BAILEY	F. THE CLIMB (2009)
7. LITTLE MIX	G. WHEN WE COLLIDE (2010)
8. LEONA LEWIS	H. CANNONBALL (2011)
9. MATT CARDLE	J. IMPOSSIBLE (2012)
10. BEN HAENOW	K. SKYSCRAPER (2013)
11. STEVE BROOKSTEIN	L. SOMETHING I NEED (2014)
12. MATT TERRY	M. FOREVER YOUNG (2015)
13. ALEXANDRA BURKE	N. WHEN CHRISTMAS COMES AROUND (2016)
14. DALTON HARRIS	P. DIMELO (2017)
15. LEON JACKSON	R. POWER OF LOVE (2018)

THE SWEENEY: 1. Detective Inspector Jack Regan played by John Thaw, Detective Sergeant George Carter played by Dennis Waterman; 2. Insp. Jean Darblay in Juliet Bravo, she is murdered in error by a gang of diamond smugglers; 3. Scotch whisky; 4. Dixon of Dock Green; 5. She is abducted; 6. Garfield Morgan; 7. Frank Kemble played by Brian Blessed; 8. C) Florries; 9. Morecambe and Wise; 10. Roadside tent as erected by telephone engineers, who would place them over open manholes in the street to protect them from the weather.
COCKNEY RHYMING SLANG: A) Wife (trouble and strife); B) Head (Loaf of bread); C) Mate (China plate); D) Wig (Syrup of fig); E) Laugh (Turkish bath).

A genre that uses speculative, fictional science-based depictions of phenomena that are not fully accepted by mainstream science, such as extraterrestrial life forms, alien worlds, extrasensory perception and time travel, along with futuristic elements such as spacecraft, robots, cyborgs, interstellar travel or other technologies.

SCI FI

1. Which actor playing *Dr Who* teamed up with a young alien, Turlough?

2. In *Hitch-Hikers Guide to the Galaxy*. Who created the Pan Galactic Gargle Blaster?

3. What is Lady Penelope's surname in *Thunderbirds*?

4. Which number in *The Prisoner* was served by a mute dwarf butler?

5. Which *Doomwatch* hero was killed trying to defuse a bomb?

6. In 1973 which group of individuals were Homo Superior?

7. Which *Red Dwarf* character's first love was a Sinclair ZX81?

8. From which planet did Husky originate in 1962 *Space Patrol*?

9. Who was *Adam Adamant*'s arch enemy?

10. Name the sole survivor in the spaceship in *The Quatermass Experiment*?

11. When Dr Who returned in 2005, it filmed under which secret codename?

12. What was Hermione Granger's original surname in JK Rowling's early notes for the Harry Potter books?

13. Daleks first appeared in *Dr Who*? A) 1960   B) 1962   C) 1963   D) 1966

14. What does TARDIS stand for?

15. In the British-Italian show *Space 1999*, who played John Koenig?

16. What organization did *Captain Scarlet* work for?

17. Name the 'Paranoid Android' with a 'Brain the size of a planet'?

18. For whom did Joe 90 work when he was undercover?

19. In Thunderbirds who mainly operated Thunderbird 5?

20. What did W.A.S.P. Stand for in *Stingray*?

THE X FACTOR: 1F, 2J, 3M, 4B, 5P, 6K, 7H, 8C, 9G, 10L, 11A, 12N, 13E, 14R, 15D.
Years 2004-2014 all number ones in the UK charts. The rest reached the top 10.

A British television quiz show presented by Victoria Coren Mitchell. Teams compete in a tournament of finding connections between seemingly unrelated clues. Aired on BBC Four from 15 September 2008 to 7 July 2014, before moving to BBC Two from 1 September 2014. 15 Series, 309 Episodes. 31 Specials.

1. CONNECTIONS. Find a link between the 4 pictures.

2. SEQUENCES. What goes in the missing box?

5	17	53	?

3. CONNECTIONS. Find a link between the 4 pictures.

4/5. MISSING VOWELS. Double Song Titles

WDN H RTFG LSS   MLL WYLL WSB MRN

6/7. SEQUENCES. What goes in the missing boxes?

Z	V	R	?

N12	E3	S6	?

8. CONNECTIONS. Find a link between the 4 pictures.

9/10. MISSING VOWELS. Places of Entertainment

MS MN TRCD   BN GH LL

SCI-FI: 1. Peter Davison; 2. Zaphod Beeblebox; 3. Creighton- Ward; 4. Number Two; 5. Toby Wren; 6. Tomorrow's People; 7. Holly; 8. Mars; 9. The Face; 10. Victor Carroon; 11. Torchwood; 12. Puckle; 13. C) 1963; 14. Time and Relative Dimensions in Space; 15. Martin Landau; 16. Mysterons; 17. Marvin; 18. World Intelligence network; 19. John; 20. World Aquanaut Security Patrol.

A BBC television sitcom shown on BBC1 from 1 January 1980 to 30 January 1988. Set in 1959 and 1960 in Maplins, a fictional holiday camp. The title was the greeting the campers heard and in early episodes was written Hi de Hi. The series gained large audiences and won a BAFTA as Best Comedy Series in 1984. There were 9 Series; 58 Episodes.

1. In which fictional Essex seaside town was Maplins located?

2. Complete the lyrics from the sit-coms signature tune, Holiday park; 'Well, if you're feeling lonely, and getting in a ....'

3. Which subject did Jeffrey Fairbrother formerly teach at Cambridge University?
A) Archaeology   B) History   C) Economics   D) English Literature

4. To Joe Maplin's horror he hears that the local authority are planning to build what next door to the camp?
A) Abbatoir   B) Crematorium   C) Hospital   D) Zoo

5. A Goof from the show featured Ted Bovis singing a Tom Jones song in 1959 that was not written until 1968. What was the song? A) It's Not Unusual   B) Green Green Grass of Home   C) Delilah   D) Sexbomb

6. Jeffrey Fairbrother was succeeded by Clive Dempster, an ex-serviceman. In what branch of the forces did Clive serve?   A) Army   B) Royal Navy   C) RAF

7. Just before the unveiling of Joe Maplin's statue a drunken member of staff defaces the statue and paints it like a clown. Who was the perpetrator?
A) Spike Dixon   B) Ted Bovis   C) William Partridge

8. Who had been voted most popular girl Yellowcoat in 1959?
A) Gladys Pugh   B) Sylvia Garnsey   C) Tracey Bentwood

9. Which disqualified jockey was the camp's riding instructor?

10. In the last ever Episode Peggy finally becomes a Yellowcoat but she is hospitalised and diagnosed with: A) Nervous exhaustion   B) Flu   C) Appendicitis   D) Pregnancy

MISSING CHARACTER ANAGRAM
Who is often mentioned but never seen?
CHRISTMAS CAT

ONLY CONNECT: 1. Football, Woolworths, Heinz, Dr Pepper - All poker games; 2. 5, 17, 53 - 161 (multiply by 3 and add 2); 3. Bob Hope, Irving Berlin, George Burns, Captain Sir Tom Moore - All Centenarians; 4. Wooden Heart and Heart of Glass; 5. Mellow Yellow and Yellow Submarine; 6. N - Alphabet backwards 3 letters between; 7. W9 - Compass points on the face of a clock; 8. Tom Moore, Banksy, Zoe Ball, James Hunt - England team in 1966 World Cup Final; 9. Amusement Arcade, 10. Bingo Hall.

A BBC television drama series, which ran from 1971 to 1980. The show covers the rise of a fictional shipping company, the Onedin Line. The series also illustrates some of the changes in business and shipping, such as from wooden to steel ships and from sailing ships to steamships. It shows the role ships played in international politics, uprisings and the slave trade. 8 Series. 91 Episodes.

1. In which northern city is *The Onedin Line* set?

2. The 8 series covered the period of rise for the Onedin Line which was:
A) 1840-1850 B) 1860-1886 C) 1886-1898 D) 1901-1921

3. Who is the owner of the line, also name his partner and brother?

4. The theme music Adagio of Spartacus and Phrygia was written by which Soviet Armenian composer?

5. Which historically contemporary event was part of the story in Series 1? It was about an epidemic that destroyed most of the vineyards of Europe.

6. In Series 2 James charters which ship for a voyage to the West Indies with a man named Jessop? A) Star of Bethlehem B) Charlotte Rhodes C) Pelican

7. In Series 3 Samuel Plimsoll supports Robert in his bid to become a councillor; for which political party?

8. What did Samuel Plimsoll invent, it was also used in the storyline for the series?

9. James Onedin's first ship was portrayed by a schooner of the same name. What was she called?

10. Which actress played Anne and in the series ignored the doctor's warning not to get pregnant, knowing how much James wanted a son and heir, and died giving birth to a daughter, Charlotte?

Several actors boosted their careers in The Onedin Line. Can you name the 4 pictured below?

HI-DE-HII: 1. Crimpton-on-Sea; 2. Stew; 3. A) Archaeology; 4. C) Hospital; 5. C) Delilah;
6. C) RAF; 7. A) Spike Dixon; 8. B) Sylvia Garnsey; 9. Fred Quilley; 10. A) Nervous exhaustion.
MISSING CHARACTER: Miss Cathcart (Peggy Ollerenshaw's supervisor and nemesis).

A British game show for the BBC. Its creator, Bill Wright, drew inspiration from his experiences of being interrogated by the Gestapo during World War II. The show featured an intimidating setting and challenging questions. Four and in later contests five or six contestants face two rounds, one on a specialised subject of the contestant's choice, the other a general knowledge round. 14 Regular series, 19 Specials, 978 Regular Episodes, 58 Specials.

1. *Mastermind* first aired on BBC1 between 1972-1997. Name the presenter?

2. What was his catchphrase?

3. After being dropped by BBC1 in 1997 *Mastermind* had brief spells on radio and the Discovery channel. A new BBC Two version premiered in 2003, with a new host. Who was the new question master?

4. The highest overall Mastermind score is 41 points, set in 1995, with a specialist subject of *Life of Martin Luther King Jr*. Who is the record holder?

5. The 2004 champion is now a Chaser on ITV's The Chase. Which one?

6. The lowest score in the specialist subject round is jointly held by Simon Curtis and Steve Ferry when answering questions on The Life & Films of Jim Carrey and The Thirty Years' War respectively. How many did they score?

7. Contestants sit in a chair, lit by a solitary spotlight in an otherwise dark studio. What upholstery covers the chair?

8. *The Two Ronnies* did a superb spoof of the show in 1980, featuring Ronnie Corbett as a contestant, Charlie Smithers. What was his specialist subject?

9. Can you name the first winner of mastermind in 1972?
A) Elizabeth Wilkinson B) Fred Housego C) Patricia Owen D) Roger Pritchard

10. What is the form of the tie-breaker if scores are level?

MORPH!
Two faces have been morphed.
Can you name the two celebrities?

THE ONEDIN LINE: 1. Liverpool; 2. B) 1860-1886; 3. James Onedin (and Robert); 4. Aram Khachaturian; 5. Phylloxera; 6. A) Star of Bethlehem; 7. Liberal; 8. Plimsoll line (a line on a ship's hull indicating the maximum safe depth when loaded); 9. Charlotte Rhodes; 10. Anne Stallybrass. ACTORS: A) Jane Seymour; B) Warren Clarke; C) Jill Gascoine; D) Kate Nelligan.

A British police drama series set in 1960s North Riding of Yorkshire. Broadcast on ITV in 18 series from 1992 and 2010. Made by ITV Studios (formerly Yorkshire Television) at Leeds Studios and on location. Heartbeat first aired on Friday 10 April 1992 (it was later moved to Sunday evenings). The 372nd and final episode aired on Sunday 12 September 2010.

1. The show's theme song, *Heartbeat* was a 1992 No 2 hit for Nick Berry. It was originally recorded by which singer and reached number 30 in 1959?

2. *Heartbeat* was set in which fictional Yorkshire village?

3. Which cast member actually lived in the village in which the show was set?

4. It was truly heartbreaking to see Nick lose his beloved wife after she gave birth to their daughter. From what disease did Kate die?

5. What was the name of the actor who played PC Phil Bellamy?

6. *Heartbeat* was a British television series based on the 'Constable' series of books by which author?

7. Oscar Blaketon played the crotchety Police Sergeant. He later owned the Aidensfield Arms. Where did he briefly work in between?

8. Joseph McFadden played a new PC Joe Mason. What country was he from?

9. Who was *Heartbeat*'s resident petty criminal? What was his dog's name?

10. Which doctor was killed in an explosion at the Aidensfield Police House?

GONE BUT NOT FORGOTTEN
These stars of Heartbeat have gone to the great theatre in the sky. What were their characters names?

| Derek Fowlds | William Symons | Geoffrey Hughes | Bill Maynard & Tramp | Peter Benson | Stuart Golland | Frank Middlemass |

MASTERMIND: 1. Magnus Magnusson; 2. 'I've started so I'll finish'; 3. John Humphrys; 4. Kevin Ashman; 5. Shaun Wallace; 6. Just 1 point; 7. Black leather; 8. Answering the question before last; 9. A) Elizabeth Wilkinson (the others all won too!); 10. The contestant with the fewest total passes wins. If contestants have the same score and number of passes, a five-question tiebreaker is played. **MORPHED IMAGE:** Magnus Magnusson and John Humphrys.

Butterflies

A British sitcom series written by Carla Lane that was broadcast on BBC2 from 1978 to 1983. The day-to-day life of middle-class Parkinson family treated in bittersweet style. Ria's unconsummated relationship with Leonard as she still loves her husband, Ben. Ria has raised two teenage sons, but is dissatisfied! 4 Series. 30 Episodes.

1. What was *Butterflies* called in the USA?

2. The theme song *Love is Like a Butterfly** was sung by Clare Torry, but which Country Music superstar wrote the song?

3. In which Gloucestershire town was *Butterfies* set and filmed?

4. Who were cast as the Parkinson family; Ben, Ria, Russell and Adam?

5. What was Ben Parkinson's profession and how did his hobby play a role in the title of the sit-com?

6. The cast, minus the sadly demised Michael Ripper, reunited for a 13 minute special in 2000. What charity benefitted from the reunion?

7. In Series 1 why did Russell chain himself to the statue of 'The Lovers'. What was Ria's reaction to the protest?

8. In Episode 2 Ria was involved with another protest, this time against fox hunting. How many turned up for her mass protest?

9. In Series 4. Ben and Ria went to Paris. When they returned what unwanted substance did they discover in the house?

10. Ria's charlady, Ruby, was going through a crisis. She told Ria that she has a compulsion to do what?

> ** Love is like a butterfly*
> *As soft and gentle as a sigh*
> *The multicolored moods of love are like its satin wings*
> *Love makes your heart feel strange inside*
> *It flutters like soft wings in flight*
> *Love is like a butterfly, a rare and gentle thing*

HEARTBEAT: 1. Buddy Holly; 2. Aidensfield; 3. William Symons (PC Alf Ventrass (Sadly died in 2019); 4. Leukaemia; 5. Mark Jordon; 6. Nicholas Rhea; 7. The Aidensfield Post Office; 8. Scotland; 9. Claude Jeremiah Greengrass (Played by Bill Maynard), Alfred; 10. Helen Walker. GONE BUT NOT FORGOTTEN: Oscar Blaketon, PC Alf Ventress, Vernon Scripps, Claude Greengrass & Tramp, Bernie Scripps, George Ward, Dr Alex Ferrenby.

Since television became a mass medium in the 1960s, children's TV has been a key part of the schedules, fulfilling a mission to inform, educate and entertain. Obviously it was the "entertain" bit that appealed to us as kids. But which show was best?

CHILDREN'S TELLY

1. Which whistling characters lived on a blue moon?

2. Cut Throat Jake was the mortal enemy of which pirate?

3. What was the nickname of *Grange Hill* pupil Samuel McGuire?

4. Which is the purple Teletubby?

5. What kind of creature was George in *Rainbow*?

6. Which *Watch With Mother* favourite duo made a comeback in 2001?

7. Who had an Eskimo bride named Nooka?

8. Which iconic character keeps Colley's Mill, rides a tricycle, and values tradition?

9. What is the registration number of *Postman Pat*'s van?

10. Who wore a hat. Pinky or Perky?

11. Who lived in a basket with Andy Pandy and Teddy?

12. Who lived in *Ivor the Engine*'s boiler?

13. What was the name of the wooden woodpecker bookend in *Bagpuss*?

14. Eamonn Andrews was the first presenter of which children's programme?

15. What was the name of the star locomotive on the *Chigley* steam railway?

16. Who were the 3 friendly little aliens who slept on the ceiling?

17. A female singer provided the opening and closing lines on *Teletubbies.* A) Who was she and B) Who replaced her in 2015?

18. What colour was Roobarb?

19. Which town's clock always told time 'never too quickly, never too slowly'?

20. Name the teen drama series aired between 1989-2006 set in Newcastle.

BUTTERFLIES: 1. Maggie; 2. Dolly Parton; 3. Cheltenham; 4. Wendy Craig, Geoffrey Palmer, Andrew Hall and Nicholas Lyndhurst; 5. Ben was a dentist, he was a lepidopterist (collecting and studying butterflies); 6. Children in Need; 7. In protest against its sale to an American buyer, Ria then also chained herself to the statue; 8. Just Leonard and an old tramp; 9. Pot (Marijuana); 10. Steal things, shoplifting.

A British drama series produced by Ecosse Films for BBC Scotland and broadcast on BBC One for 7 series between February 2000 and October 2005 with 64 episodes in total. Loosely based on Sir Compton Mackenzie's Highland Novels, set in the same location but in the 1930s and 1940s.

1. Who painted the famous Monarch of the Glen?

2. How were Golly and Duncan related?
A) Father and son B) Uncle and nephew C) Distant cousins

3. Who played Hector and Molly MacDonald?

4. How many children were born to Molly and Hector? A) 1   B) 2   C) 3

5. The fictional estate in Compton Mackenzie's novels was near Ben Nevis, the series was filmed in and around the Cairngorms, Badenoch and Strathspey, with Ben Nevis replaced by fictional Ben Bogle. What was the estate's name?

6. The first 5 series focused on Archie MacDonald as he tried to restore his childhood home. What was his occupation in London before returning to Scotland?

7. In 2003 a young actor joined the cast as Ewan Brodie and was featured in 20 episodes. He had formerly been a professional footballer, won the cheese rolling at Coopers Hill twice, and then in 2012 went on to star in *Line of Duty*. Who is he?

8. The manor's 'gilly' (steward) was nicknamed 'Golly', why? A) His last name is McGonagle B) After a dance, he was with a girl, and when she removed his pants she said, 'Golly!' C) Archie called him that when he was a boy

9. Who moved to New Zealand at the end of the last series?

10. What was Archie's last sound, at the end of the last series?
A) A scream   B) Bugger!   C) A huge sigh

TRIVIA SPOT
*BEN NEVIS is the highest mountain in the UK.
How many metres (or feet) above sea level is the summit*

*CHILDREN'S TV: 1. The Clangers; 2. Captain Pugwash; 3. Zammo; 4. Tinky Winky;
5. Hippopotamus; 6. Bill and Ben; 7. Noggin the Nog; 8. Windy Miller (in Camberwick Green);
9. PAT 1; 10. Perky; 11. Looby Loo; 12. Idris the Dragon; 13. Professor Yaffle; 14 . Crackerjack;
15. Bessie; 16. The Bumblies; 17. A) Toyah Willcox, B) Antonia Thomas; 18. Green; 19.*

A British sketch comedy which was broadcast on BBC2 from 1979 to 1982. Originally shown as a comedy alternative to the Nine O'Clock News on BBC1, it featured satirical sketches on current news stories and popular culture, as well as parody songs, comedy sketches, re-edited videos, and spoof television formats. 4 Series 27 Episodes

Not the Nine O'Clock News

1. The show was supposed to air on April 2, 1979. What event was called a couple of days before the air date, so the programme was put on hold for six months?

2. Which famous woman was the first choice to fill the female role in the programme, eventually handed to Pamela Stephenson?

3. *Prof Timothy Fielding:* I'm sorry, I'm sorry! Can I put this into some sort of perspective? When I caught Gerald in '68 he was completely wild. *Gerald:* Wild? I was absolutely livid! Who was Gerald?

4. In the football hooliganism sketch the experts reached an inevitable conclusion that the one drastic course of action that the authorities must take was what?

5. The Prime Minister at the time complained when, by adroit image editing, the programme implied that they had crashed a car. Who was the PM?

6. Which comedy pair met on the show in 1979, married in 1989, and still together?

7. The success of the programme led to Rowan Atkinson getting the lead role in which sit-com?

8. Whose career path includes: Oxford University, the Edinburgh Fringe, the Royal Court Theatre, London, Bristol Old Vic, associate director, Sheffield Crucible Theatre, TV star, number 3 hit record, Film director, West End director?

9. Which Welshman formed a successful comedy double act with another member of the cast and has had a very successful career on stage and screen?

10. The programme is credited with bringing what form of comedy to British television? A) Surreal   B) Slapstick C) Alternative

MONARCH OF THE GLEN: 1. Sir Edwin Landseer; 2. C) Distant cousins; 3. Richard Briers and Susan Hampshire; 4. C) Jamie, Lizzie, and Archie are the MacDonald children but Jamie died; 5. Glenbogle; 6. Restaurateur; 7. Martin Compston; 8. B) After a dance, he was 'canoodling' with a girl, and when she removed his pants she said, 'Golly!'; 9. Fergal; 10. A) A scream.

A British series that was produced at Wembley Studios by Associated-Rediffusion for the ITV network between 16 September 1959 and 22 June 1967. No Hiding Place carried on from where the TV series Murder Bag and Crime Sheet left off. Murder Bag featured 55 episodes. Crime Sheet 17 episodes. Originally 30 minute episodes No Hiding Place was extended to 60 minutes. 10 Series. 236 Episodes.

1. Raymond Francis was the star of the show. What character did he play?

2. The star's son went on to become a well-known face on both small and big screen, in addition to being a caricaturist who has had several exhibitions at the National Theatre. Who is he?

3. The actor who played Detective Sergeant Russell took advice and wore built up shoes for his audition. He got the part and went on to star in 2349 episodes of *Coronation Street* and many other films and TV shows. Can you name him?

4. Originally the writers wanted to further promote the main character, but were told it was not possible. Why was that?

5. A decision was made to cancel the series in 1965, but there were so many protests from the public, and the police, that it started again for another two years. The main character appeared in all episodes of *Murder Bag, Crime Sheet* and *No Hiding Place* except the very last episode. Why did he not appear in that episode?

6. Where were the detectives based in *No Hiding Place*?

7. The stirring theme music for the show was composed by a man who had written dozens of themes for TV and films. He had a Top 10 hit with *Sucu Sucu* in 1961. Who was he?

8. What recreational habit did DCS Lockhart have?

9. What was Lockhart's original sidekick's character's name who 'retired' at the height of the show's popularity? He was played by Eric Lander.

10. As the titles rolled and the theme music played what make of police car bearing the two detectives screeched out of Police HQ?
A) Wolseley 6/90   B) Ford Granada   C) Morris 1000

NOT THE 9 'O' CLOCK NEWS: 1. The General Election; 2. Victoria Wood; 3. A gorilla; 4. Cut their goolies off!; 5. Margaret Thatcher; 6. Billy Connolly and Pamela Stephenson; 7. Blackadder; 8. Mel Smith; 9. Griff Rhys Jones; 10. C) Alternative.

A British sitcom produced by Big Talk Productions. The show premiered on BBC Two on 28 June 2010 and ended on 28 April 2014. The series revolves around a Church of England priest, who becomes the vicar of a socially disunited inner-city London church after leaving a small rural Suffolk parish. There were 3 Series and 19 Episodes.

1. What was the name of the Anglican priest who moved from a rural parish to the inner city? A) Adam Smallbone B) Timothy Farthing C) Gabriel Stokes

2. What was the name of the inner city parish?

3. Who played the vicar's wife, solicitor Alex?
A) Dawn French B) Olivia Colman C) Marion Barron

4. Which real life priest, who also had a spell in pop band The Communards, was cited as an inspiration for the character of the leading man?

5. In the first episode the vicar was overwhelmed after his church sermons in London experience a large increase in attendance. What was the reason for the boost?

6. On which BBC TV programme did the vicar make a controversial comment about homosexuality in the Church?

7. The vicar and his curate attended an house blessing for an elderly resident of a care home to scare off a laughing ghost, the visit was mistaken for what?

8. What special Festive Service was a disaster when the congregation was boosted by revellers from the local pubs and clubs?

9. What happened in Archdeacon Robert's taxi as Adam is presiding over Ellie Pattman's wedding?

10. Following his resignation and the church's closure Adam became a house husband and worked part time at the local convenience store. He retired to bed, broken hearted until Alex organised what?

Lord
help me to remember
that nothing is going to happen
to me today that you and I
together can't handle.
Amen

NO HIDING PLACE: *1. Detective Chief Superintendent Tom Lockhart; 2. Clive Francis; 3. Johnny Briggs; 4. He would no longer be expected to visit the crime scene, thus hindering the potential of the storylines; 5. He had the mumps; 6. The original New Scotland Yard; 7. Laurie Johnson; 8. He took snuff; 9. DS (later DI) Harry Baxter ; 10. Wolseley 6/90.*

A competitive cooking show produced by the BBC (originally BBC2, since 2009 BBC1). Masterchef initially from 1990 -2001, revived in 2005 as MasterChef Goes Large. In 2008, the name reverted to MasterChef but with same format.The series currently appears in 4 versions: the main MasterChef series; Celebrity MasterChef; MasterChef: The Professionals & Junior MasterChef. Total of 424 Episodes + 211 Celebrity. 27 series + 15 Celebrity.

1. Who was the original American-British presenter of the show until 2000?

2. The new version of the show in 2001 did not revive ratings as hoped and was cancelled after one series. Which chef presented this version?

3. Finally the show settled on two presenters who continue to the present time. Who are they, from which country does one of them hail, and what did the other formerly sell in Covent Garden?

4. Who provides the voiceover for the 2020 series?

5. Thomasina Miers won the first of the new shows in 2005. What's the name of her chain of Mexican restaurants? A) Wahaca B) Chiquita C) Chimichanga

6. Since 2005 how many of the 16 winners have been female?

7. Which EastEnders actor won *Celebrity Masterchef* in 2018?

8. Which former Scottish international footballer turned TV pundit won the *Sport Relief Does Masterchef* in 2010?

9. Who is the odd chef out from *Celebrity Masterchef* 2020?
A) Lady Leshurr B) Judy Murray C) Crissy Rock D) Zandra Rhodes

10. True or False? Thomas Frake won the 2020 *Masterchef* title with a menu comprising: Monkfish scampi, Ox cheek and salted caramel custard tart dessert.

NAME THAT DINNER!
A Starter, a Main Course and a Dessert in Anagram form
CLOCK WARPAINT   DISUNION ROOSTERS   DRUMMING DUPES

REV: 1. A) Rev Adam Smallbone; 2. St Saviour in the Marshes in Hackney, East London; 3. B) Olivia Colman; 4. Rev Richard Coles; 5. A rumoured good Ofsted report on the local church school, with parents desperate to get their children enrolled; 6. The One Show; 7. An exorcism; 8. Midnight mass; 9. His wife Alex gives birth to a daughter; 10. A reunion of Adam's parishioners for an Easter Day service and the baptism of his daughter Katie in the closed church.

ALF GARNETT was ranked 49th on the list of the 100 Greatest Characters. He appeared in BBC1 sitcoms Till Death Us Do Part (1965-1975; 7 Series, 54 Episodes) and its follow-on and spin-off series Till Death... and In Sickness and in Health (1985-1992; 6 Series, 47 Episodes).

1. In which area of London did Alf Garnett live?

2. What was the name of Alf's wife played by Dandy Nichols, who died in 1986 whilst filming the comeback series *In Sickness And In Health*?

3. Alf Garnett often referred to his wife as a what?

4. Which actress played Alf's daughter Rita; and who played her layabout (Scouse git!) husband Mike?

5. What is the nickname of the London football team Alf supports and which team did he hate?

6. When Alf and Elsie Garnett retired, to which seaside town did they move?
A) Hastings   B) Eastbourne   C) Brighton   D) Weymouth

7. What was the name of the young, gay, black care worker assigned to look after Alf's wife in the first series of *In Sickness and in Health* and what was Alf's nickname for him?

8. Which character jilted Alf Garnett at the altar in the 4th series?
A) Mrs Winston   B) Mrs Stubbs   C) Mrs Hollingberry   D) Mrs Hall

9. Who wrote and performed the theme song for *In Sickness and in Health*?

10. Else dies of natural causes. Left alone after the mourners have gone home, Alf, the belligerent old curmudgeon who always treated his wife appallingly, gently touches the handle of her (now empty) wheelchair and sobs .... What?

IN SICKNESS & IN HEALTH - ODD ONE OUT
Name the 6 actors below and find the odd one out!

A   B   C   D   E   F

MASTERCHEF: 1. Loyd Grossman; 2. Gary Rhodes; 3. John Torode and Greg Wallace, Australia, Vegetables; 4. India Fisher; 5. A) Wahaca; 6. 7; 7. John Partridge; 8. Alan Hansen; 9. D) Zandra Rhodes (she appeared in 2019); 10. True. NAME THAT DISH: Prawn Cocktail, Tournedos Rossini, Summer Pudding.

WHAT HAPPENED WHERE ON TV?

ON LOCATION

1. In which South London district was *Citizen Smith* (Robert Lindsay) set?

2. Who stood in Ten Acre Field at Scatterbrook Farm?

3. Arden House, Tannochbrae was the home of which Doctor?

4. What 70s Police series was set in a fictitious Midlands town, Broadstone?

5. Which children's character lived at 52, Festive Road?

6. Name the hospital in the *Doctor in the House* series in 1969/70?

7. Which funereal sit-com was set in a fictional Lancashire town, Oldshaw?

8. Which magical sleuth lived in a windmill in West Sussex?

9. Which English city was the setting for *Spender*?

10. What medical serial was set in Oxbridge General Hospital?

11. What links Grassington and Askrigg?

12. What series starred a small town doctor/police surgeon in Warwickshire?

13. In which country did *The District Nurse* work?

14. On which islands does DI Jimmy Pérez carry out his duties?

15. HMS Hero was the setting for which seventies drama series?

16. Which sit-com flat-mates lived in Huskisson Street?

17. Which female detective works for Northumberland & City Police?

18. Which bulbous pink figure covered with yellow spots lived at Crinkley Bottom?

19. In which county was Fletcher a prisoner in the Cat C Prison Slade in *Porridge?*

20. Little Clogborough-in-the-Marsh was the setting for which 70s sit-com featuring Arthur Lowe?

ALF GARNETT: 1. Wapping; 2. Else; 3. A silly moo; 4. Una Stubbs, Anthony Booth; 5. The Hammers (West Ham United), Tottenham Hotspur; 6. B) Eastbourne; 7. Winston, Marigold; 8. C) Mrs Hollingberry; 9. Chas and Dave; 10. "Silly old moo!". *ODD ONE OUT:* A) Hugh Lloyd, B) Anthony Booth, C) Patricia Hayes, D) James Ellis; E) Harry Fowler, G) Irene Handl Odd one out is B) Anthony Booth who opted out of appearing in the series.

A British black comedy-drama spy thriller series, produced from 8 April 2018 in the UK by Sid Gentle Films for BBC America and BBC iPlayer. The series follows Eve Polastri a British intelligence investigator tasked with capturing psychopathic assassin Villanelle. 3 Series. 24 Episodes.

1. Who stars as an agent with MI5 who becomes obsessed with a notorious assassin the title role?

2. Oksana Astankova / Villanelle, is a psychopathic, skilled assassin who becomes obsessed with the MI6 officer who is tracking her. Who skilfully plays the part?

3. In what city did we first meet Villanelle?

4. What did Eve get in trouble for eating the first time we meet her?

5. How did Bill Pargrave (played by David Haig) die in Berlin?

6. What was the name of the season 2 finale episode?
A) At Last   B) In Ruins   C) I'm Yours   D) You're Mine

7. How many known kills does Villanelle have?

8. Who wrote Killing Eve?

9. The Buckinghamshire village where Villanelle tracks Frank down is also used as the setting for which highly successful British sit-com?

10. What did Eve accidentally leave in Berlin?

CAST OF KILLING EVE ACTORS
Actors names from the Series with vowels removed

1) SND RH	3) FNS HW	5) HR RTW LTR
2) JDC MR	4) DR R NB YD	6) DR NSC RBR GH

ON LOCATION: 1. Tooting; 2. Worzel Gummidge; 3. Doctor Final; 4. Hunters Walk; 5. Mr Benn;
6. St Swithins; 7. In Loving memory; 8. Jonathan Creek; 9. Newcastle-upon-Tyne;
10. Emergency Ward 10; 11. Both have been the fictional town of Darrowby - the former in 2020 series and the latter in 1978 series; 12. Dangerfield; 13. Wales; 14. Shetland; 15. Warship; 16. The Liver Birds; 17. DCI Vera Stanhope; 18. Mr Blobby; 19. Cumbria; 20. The Last of the Baskets.

A television advertisement (also called a television commercial, commercial, advert, TV advert or simply an ad) is a span of television programming produced and paid for by an organization. It conveys a message promoting, and aiming to market, a product or service. There have been many memorable ads. How many can you remember?

1. In the 1960s which product cleaned 'a big, big carpet for less than half a crown'?

2. Who used the slogan 'Exceedingly' good cakes' for half a century?

3. Which Danish drink is 'probably the best lager in the world'?

4. In 1979 who liked his Remington shaver so much that he bought the company?

5. From 1968 to 2003, and since 2016, which action man jumped on to moving trains, swung from helicopters and jumped off cliffs just to deliver a box of chocolates?

6. What was the Brooke Bond chimps reply to the question, 'Dad, do you know the piano's on my foot?'

7. The original campaign for which coffee brand ran for 12 x 45-second instalments between 1987 and 1993? It starred Anthony Head and Sharon Maughan as Tony and Sharon, a couple who begin a slow-burning romance over a cup of the advertised coffee.

8. For a decade who played Prunella Scales' long-suffering daughter in Tesco ads on TV?

9. Which actress, who includes The Bodyguard and Line of Duty in her TV credits, played a shop assistant in 1987 in the first British ad for condoms?

10. What was whispered in your ear if you didn't use Lifebuoy soap in the 1960s?

NAME THE PRODUCTS
Some classic TV ads to identify

A *B* *C* *D* *E* *F*

KILLING EVE: 1. Sandra Oh; 2. Jodie Comer; 3. Vienna; 4. Croissant; 5. He was repeatedly stabbed on the dance floor; 6. D) You're Mine; 7. 19; 8. Phoebe Waller Bridge; 9. The Vicar of Dibley (Turville in Buckinghamshire); 10. B) Her suitcase. *MISSING VOWELS ACTORS:* 1) Sandra Oh 2) Jodie Coer 3) Fiona Shaw 4) Darren Boyd 5) Harriet Walter 6) Adrian Scarborough

A British BBC police procedural series created by Jed Mercurio, produced by World Productions. The first series premiered on 26 June 2012 and was BBC Two's best-performing drama series in ten years with a consolidated audience of 4.1 million viewers. The fourth series moved to BBC 1 on 26 March 2017. It was included in a list of the Top 50 BBC Two shows of all time[12] and in a list of the 80 best BBC shows of all time. 5 Series to date. 29 Episodes.

LINE OF DUTY

1. In Series 1, Detective Chief Inspector Tony Gates is suspected of corruption and faced an internal affairs investigation that added further complications to his troubled home-life. Who played Gates?

2. In Series 2 DC Georgia Trotman died in hospital. How did she die?

3. In Series 3 Sergeant Danny Waldron left an envelope containing a list of names. He addressed the envelope to whom?

4. In Series 4 Detective Chief Inspector Roz Huntley is the Senior Investigating Officer of Operation Trapdoor, and at the centre of an AC-12 investigation for mishandling evidence. In error sample KRG-13 was changed to what?

5. In Series 5 Detective Sergeant John Corbett was an undercover police officer, uncontactable for several months. He first appeared as John Clayton, the gang leader of an organised crime group which had hijacked a police convoy transporting seized drugs. Who played the role?

6. What does Ted Hastings hate?

7. What was Detective Inspector Matthew 'Dot' Cottan's nickname in the criminal underworld?

8. Why did Detective Inspector Kate Fleming not want to investigate the death of DS Jayne Akers?

9. What incriminating evidence did AC-12 have on DCC Mike Dryden?

10. The Caddy finally realised the game was up during interrogation. Complete the text message he sent to activate planned action. "Urgent …. Required".

AS SEEN ON TV: 1. 1001; 2. Mr Kipling; 3. Carlsberg; 4. Victor Kiam; 5. Cadbury's 'Milk Tray Man'; 6. 'You hum it son and I'll play it'; 7. Nescafé Gold Blend; 8. Jane Horrocks; 9. Gina McKee; 10. B.O. NAME THE PRODUCTS: A) Cadbury's Dairy Milk; B) British Telecom; C) Go Compare; D) Hamlet; E) Cinzano; F) John Lewis.

A British sitcom that has aired on BBC One since 2006. The show was cancelled by the BBC in 2009, whilst the third series was still airing, but the decision was later reversed due to a combination of strong DVD sales and an online petition. Now notched up 10 series and 79 Episodes + the pilot.

1. Who played a fictional version of himself: an unambitious man in his late thirties living as a lodger in a flat in the London Docklands?

2. In an attempt to impress Lucy with his intellectual prowess which television quiz programme did he and Daisy appear on?

3. Which former member of a comedy duo has played Lee's dad Frank in a number of episodes?

4. Lee used to work in what kind of vehicle?

5. Which country did Lee pretend he's moved to when he finds out he might be a dad?

6. Daisy (Katy Wix), was an incredibly dimwitted young woman. What is her job?

7. Who played Barbara, Lucy's accident-prone cleaner?

8. In which country did Daisy think Santa Claus lives and what did Lee tell her counts as one of her 5-a-day?

9. Which US state did Kate come from?

10. Which football team did Lee support?

NAME THE MYSTERY YEAR

5 POINTS: The Statue of Liberty celebrated her 100th birthday.

4 POINTS: Halley's Comet made its 75th yearly visit.

3 POINTS: Cary Grant, Phil Lynott, James Cagney and Harold Mcmillan die.

2 POINTS: Mike Tyson becomes youngest ever heavyweight boxing champ.

1 POINT: The Chernobyl disaster. Maradona's 'Hand of God' goal.

LINE OF DUTY: 1. Lennie James; 2. She was thrown out of a window; 3. DS Steve Arnott; 4. KRG-30; 5. Stephen Graham; 6. Bent coppers; 7. The Caddy; 8. She was having an affair with her husband; 9. Photos of him enjoying sexual affairs with a minor; 10. Exit.

The BBC's news and current affairs programme, that provides 'in-depth investigation and analysis of the stories behind the day's headlines. Newsnight broadcasts on weekdays. It began on 28 January 1980 and was the first programme to be made by direct collaboration between BBC News and the current affairs department.

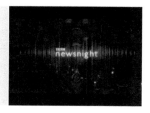

1. The first presenter in 1980 remained for 17 years. Who was he?

2. Which prolific composer wrote the theme music for the show? *He also provided brilliant music for Bergerac, Blue Planet, Gandhi, Groundhog Day and more*

3. Who was the first principal female presenter in the show?
A) Emily Maitlis B) Kirsty Wark C) Olivia O'Leary D) Emma Barrett

4. In May 1997 who asked Michael Howard, the then Home Secretary, the same question 12 times. 'Did you threaten to overrule him' ?

5. In 2019 *Newsnight* was awarded Interview of the Year and Scoop of the Year for Emily Maitlis' interview with which member of the Royal Family?

6. In 2001 the programme was accused of political bias handling whose resignation over the Hinduja affair, with only Labour supporters on a panel?

7. 1 May 2020 Emily Maitlis broke BBC rules of impartiality, stating as a fact the country was outraged by whom breaking Coronavirus lockdown rules?

8. In 2011 an investigation into a paedophile was allegedly dropped as it conflicted with BBC tribute programmes prepared after his death. Who?

9. In 2005 editor Peter Barron replaced which popular report with a weather report, arguing that information was available on the Internet?

10. After the Brexit vote in 2016 Andrew Rosindell MP argued for a return to broadcasting 'God Save the Queen' at the end of BBC programmes each day. That evening Kirsty Wark said she was delighted to oblige - and played what?

MATCH THE EVENT TO THE CORRECT YEAR

EVENT	YEAR
1. Air France Concorde crashes in Gonesse, France killing 113	A) 1980
2. Nude, Green Leaves and Bust by Picasso sells for $106.5m	B) 1990
3. Ian Gow is assassinated by the Provisional IRA	C) 2000
4. New South Wales declares state of emergency as bush fires rage	D) 2010
5. Indian politician Sanjay Gandhi killed in a plane crash	E) 2020

NOT GOING OUT: 1. Lee Mack; 2. Pointless; 3. Bobby Ball; 4. An ice cream van; 5. New Zealand; 6. Hairdresser; 7. Miranda Hart; 8. Wales; 9. California; 10. Wigan Athletic. NAME THE MYSTERY YEAR: 1986.

An English sitcom that was created and written by Simon Nye. It was first broadcast on ITV in 1992 for 2 series. Men Behaving Badly became highly successful after being moved to a post-watershed slot on BBC1 from 1994. It has won the Comedy Awards' best ITV comedy, and the first National Television Award for Situation Comedy. A total of six series were made, 42 Episodes, including a Christmas Special and the Last Orders trilogy.

1. Who played Gary Strang?

2. Lesley Ash played Deborah Burton. True or False?

3. Gary and Tony fantasized about their ideal women. Which of their favourites had a cameo role in the Comic Relief Special in 1999?

4. In series 2 Gary thought Tony may be gay because he had a collection of whose records?

5. Which kind of company employed Gary?

6. What was the name of the pub often frequented by Gary and Tony?

7. In the episode *Drunk* in Series 4 Gary and Tony spent the night in the pub getting drunk on a selection of foreign beers. What was the name of the Russian lager? A) Plip B) Plop C) Slop D) Slip

8. Which of the two main female characters was a nurse?

9. Before Tony, who was Gary's room-mate and who played the role?

10. What did Gary want to name his and Dorothy's baby in the last of the final trilogy episodes?

THE STARS OF MBB IN OTHER ROLES
Can you name the other TV shows they appeared in?

A   B   C   D

NEWSNIGHT: 1. Peter Snow; 2. George Fenton, 3. C) Olivia O'Leary; 4. Jeremy Paxman; 5. Prince Andrew, Duke of York; 6. Peter Mandelson; 7. Dominic Cummings; 8. Jimmy Savile; 9. Market Report; 10. The Sex Pistols version. MATCH THE EVENT: 1C, 2D, 3B, 4E, 5A.

A British, six episode series based on the 1862
French historical novel of the same name by
Victor Hugo. The series was produced by the BBC
and BBC Studios handled the distribution. It was
broadcast in the UK between 30 December 2018
and 3 February 2019

LES MISERABLES

1. Dominic West starred as Jean Valjean. Which serial killer did he portray in *Appropriate Adult* in 2011, earning a BAFTA award for Best Actor?

2. For what crime was Jean Valjean serving a 19-year prison sentence?

3. Valjean became M Madeleine and Mayor of Montreuil-sur-Mer. He had a tense relationship with the new chief of police. What is the chief's name?

4. Valjean was treated cruelly by the police chief when he was a prison guard What brave act by Madeleine makes the chief think he was Valjean?

5. Forced into prostitution, Fantine sold her hair and what else to pay board for her daughter Cosette?

6. Honouring his promise to Fantine, Valjean bought Cosette's freedom for 1,500 Francs from whom?

7. The Thénardiers and their accomplices lured Valjean into a trap, but he is able to fight them off. Who then alerted the police, who arrested the Thénardiers and their accomplices?

8. In which establishment was it written, 'Revel if you can, eat if you dare'?
A) The prison B) ABC group's cafe meeting place C) Thénardier's Inn

9. How did Javert commit suicide?

10. Who spent time with her adoptive father Valjean on his deathbed?

WHO AM I?

Which actor links the following roles?
5 POINTS: BISHOP MYRIEL
4 POINTS - STANLEY BALDWIN
3 POINTS - STUART BIXBY
2 POINTS - ALAN BUTTERSHAW
1 POINT - BROTHER CADFAEL

MEN BEHAVING BADLY: *1. Martin Clunes; 2. True; 3. Kylie Minogue; 4. Barbara Streisand; 5. A security firm; 6. The Crown; 7. B) Plop; 8. Dorothy Bishop; 9. Harry Enfield, Dermot Povey; 10. Kylie.* **OTHER ROLES:** *A) Martin Clunes as Doc Martin, B) Caroline Quentin in Blue Murder; C) Neil Morrissey in Line of Duty; D) Lesley Ash in Merseybeat.*

A Scottish detective fiction programme created by Glenn Chandler. Made by STV Studios for the ITV network. Originally a mini-series, Killer, from 6 -20 September 1983. Full series commissioned and ran from 2 July 1985 until 7 November 2010. 27 Series. 110 Episodes.

1. In which Scottish city was Taggart set?

2. In what fictitious police station did the team operate from?

3. Who played DCI Jim Taggart until his death in 1994 and what was the series named after his death until it finished 16 years later?

4. Blythe Duff and James McPherson played Taggart's two sidekicks. What were their names and ranks?

5. What was Superintendant Jack McVitie's nickname?

6. What was the name of the new bad tempered Detective Chief Inspector who replaced Jardine after his death?

7. The soulful music is *No Mean City,* written by Mike Moran. Who sung the song and also appeared in *Evil Eye* in 1990, playing a fortune teller who was murdered? A) Lulu B) Susan Boyle C) Maggie Bell D) Sheena Easton

8. Where did Glenn Chandler get the names for many of the characters, including Taggart?

9. Which actor was sacked from *Taggart* in a two-minute phone call from someone they'd never met, while taking their children to the supermarket? A) Blythe Duff (Reid), B) Colin McCredie (Fraser), C) Neil Duncan (Livingstone) D) John Michie (Ross)

10. What did Blythe Duff have to pass before she got her *Taggart* contract?

MATCH THESE 8 SCOTTISH CITIES WITH THEIR CORRECT POPULATION

1. DUNDEE	A. 612,040	5. LIVINGSTON	E. 77,220
2. INVERNESS	B. 488,050	6. GLASGOW	F. 57,030
3. EDINBURGH	C. 200,680	7. ABERDEEN	G. 54,080
4. HAMILTON	D. 148,280	8. PAISLEY	H. 47,290

LES MISERABLES: 1. Fred West; 2. For stealing a loaf of bread; 3. Javert; 4. He lifts a carriage wheel off of a trapped man; 5.Two front teeth ; 6. Monsieur Thénardier; 7. Marius; 8. B) ABC group's meeting place; 9. Jumps into the Seine; 10. Cosette.
WHO AM I ?: Sir Derek Jacobi (5pts - Les Miserables; 4pts - Gathering Storm; 3pts - Vicious; 2pts - Last Tango in Halifax; 1pt - Cadfael).

A British sitcom created by Rowan Atkinson and Richard Curtis, produced by Tiger Aspect and starring Atkinson as the title character. The sitcom consisted of 15 episodes that were co-written by Atkinson alongside Curtis and Robin Driscoll. The pilot was co-written by Ben Elton. The series was originally broadcast on ITV, beginning with the pilot on 1 January 1990 and ending with 'The Best Bits of Mr. Bean' on 15 December 1995.

1. The character of Mr. Bean was developed while Rowan Atkinson was studying for his Master's Degree in what at Queen's College, Oxford? History B) Economics
C) Electrical engineering D) Philosophy

2. Mr Bean drove what make of car?

3. Before entering the department store how did Mr Bean get some money to give to the saxophone playing busker?

4. Mr Bean has an ongoing feud with a van. We never see the driver but what type and colour was the van?

5. Mr Bean's girlfriend Irma Gobb expected him to propose on Christmas Day but instead of a ring, what two presents did he actually give her?

6. When visiting the seaside Mr Bean got lumbered with a baby. Which resort was he visiting? A) Brighton B) Margate
C) Weston-super-Mare D) Southsea

7. When Mr Bean went swimming on another beach he surreptitiously changed into his swimming trunks so as not to be noticed by someone nearby. Why did his discretion not matter?

8. Mr Bean celebrated his birthday alone in a restaurant. He orders the least expensive meal on the menu but it turns out to be a raw steak. What meal did he order?

9. What was the name of the drag queen performing at the hotel Mr Bean is staying at? What is Mr Bean's room number?

10. Who was Mr Bean's best friend?

TAGGART: 1. Glasgow; 2. John Street , Maryhill; 3. Mark McManus, it was still titled Taggart; 4. WPC (then DS) Jackie Reid and DS (then DI and DCI) Mike Jardine; 5. The Biscuit; 6. DCI Matt Burke; 7. C) Maggie Bell; 8. A gravestone; 9. B) Colin McCredie (Fraser); 10. Driving Test.
SCOTTISH POPULATIONS: 1D, 2H, 3B, 4G, 5F, 6A 7C, 8E.

The first teenage all-music show on British TV airing in 1958 and 1959. It was produced by Jack Good for ITV. The hosts were Tony Hall and Jimmy Henney. The artists covered a broad spectrum of music including ballads, jazz, skiffle and rock and roll. The show was broadcast live from the Hackney Empire. 40 Episodes, including 2 pilots.

You need to be a certain age to remember this show.
How many of the performers who appeared on the show can you identify?

MR BEAN: 1. C) Electrical engineering; 2. A citron-green 1977 British Leyland Mini 1000 Mark 4 ; 3. He busks to pay the busker by putting down a handkerchief and dancing; 4. A light blue Reliant Regal Supervan (like Del Boy); 5. A picture of an engaged couple and a hook; 6. D) Southsea, Portsmouth; 7. The person was blind; 8. Steak Tartare; 9. Danny La Rue, Room 426; 10. Teddy.

A British fantasy crime drama and police procedural drama television series, serving as the sequel to Life on Mars. The series began airing on BBC One in February 2008. A second series began broadcasting in April 2009. A third and final series was broadcast from 2 April to 21 May 2010 on BBC One and BBC HD. A total of 24 Episodes were made.

1. Who played DCI Gene Hunt?

2. One of Hunt's famous quotes was: "Fire up the ...." Fill in the blank.

3. DI Alex Drake was a policewoman working for the Metropolitan Police who was captured and shot by a madman in 2008. Then something strange happened. She woke up in which year?
A) 1961   B) 1971   C) 1981   D) 1991

4. What was the name of the daughter that Alex left behind in 2008? Anne B) Kathryn C) Helen D) Sarah

5. Throughout each series a mysterious figure haunts Drake at times of life-threatening danger. What sort of figure does she see?

6. Alex passed out and had a dream in which she saw children's TV characters as police officers in Fenchurch East, mocking her daughter Molly. Which two children's characters did she dream about?

7. DI Martin Summers had been, in 1982, a corrupt PC of Fenchurch East police station. In 2008, due to an illness, he fell into a coma and awoke in 1982. Two actors known for playing TV detectives portray the character as younger and older. Who were they?

8. To which seaside town did Hunt say he was going after he was suspended in Series 1?

9. In the first ever episode Alex was called to which London landmark to negotiate with Arthur Layton who had taken a busker hostage?

10. Which future pop star played a Blitz Kid in the coat check at Blitz nightclub in Covent Garden when Danny takes Alex dancing in 1981?

OH BOY!: 1. Alma Cogan; 2. Billy Fury; 3. Lonnie Donegan; 4. The Vernons Girls; 5. Brenda Lee; 6. Dickie Valentine; 7. Marion Ryan; 8. Vince Eager; 9. Cliff Richard; 10. Gerry Dorsey; 11. The Mudlarks; 12. Vince Taylor; 13. Conway Twitty; 14. The Ink Spots; 15. Shirley Bassey; 16. Tommy Steele.

A British sitcom, produced by BBC it ran from 4 April 1975 to 10 June 1978 on BBC 1 and was written by Bob Larbey and John Esmonde. Opening with the midlife crisis of Tom Good, it relates the joys and miseries he and his wife Barbara experience when they attempt to escape modern commercial living by "becoming totally self-sufficient" in their home. 4 Series. 30 Episodes.

1. What age had Tom reached in the first episode of *The Good Life*?

2. What were the surnames of the two families who were neighbours, and in which suburb did they reside?

3. What was the Russian name for their cockerel?

4. Tom and Barbara thought Margot was having an affair but what was she really doing behind the green door?

5. In the *Windbreak-War* Margot employed Mr Bailey to move her windbreak. She stuck a note to the handle of his pickaxe? What colour envelope did she use? A) White   B) Canary Yellow   C) Pale Blue   D) Red

6. Gerry was surprisingly appointed MD at work. Who were the two other candidates? A) Snetterton & Dalby B) Spencer & Marks C) Scully & Mulder

7. Tom and Barbara's latest acquisitions led Margo to call in the Chairman of the Residents' Association, Mr Carter, for help. What did she not want the Goods to have in their garden.

8. Margo asked Barbara to talk on self-sufficiency to the Townswomen's Guild. Which future *To The Manor Born* star appeared as Lady Truscott?

9. In which disastrous musical production did Margot play the lead?

10. Tom discovered that items have been stolen from his front garden, and stays up all night to catch the thief, Harry Bennett, who he then shoots with an air gun. What was stolen?

ANAGRAMS CONNECTED TO THE GOOD LIFE
Can you work them out?

1. MINDFUL SMASH TOLSTOY

2. EMBARGOED TARTLET

3. DELUDING PANTO

4. DAMSONS PROMOTERS

5. REALIGNED

ASHES TO ASHES: 1. Philip Glenister; 2. Quattro; 3. C) 1981; 4. D) Sarah; 5. A Pierrot Clown; 6. Zippy and George; 7. Gwilym Lee (Midsomer Murders) and Adrian Dunbar (Line of Duty); 8. Bognor Regis; 9. The Tate Modern; 10. Boy George.

A British procedural crime drama, produced primarily by Wall to Wall (final year by Headstrong Pictures), and broadcast on BBC One. Began with a pilot episode on 27 March 2003, before a full series was commissioned for 1 April 2004, with it concluding after twelve series on 6 October 2015. 107 Episodes.

1. The series focused on the work of UCOS - a fictional division within London's Metropolitan Police Service. What does UCOS stand for?

2. In the first 8 series the 4 main characters; Sandra Pullman, Jack Holford, Brian Lane and Gary Standing remained unchanged. Which actors played the roles?

3. From series 8 the original cast gradually changed. Characters Steve McAndrew, Dan Griffin, Sasha Miller and Larry Lamb were drafted in. Which 4 actors took these parts?

4. Esther, played by Susan Jameson, is Brian Lane's long-suffering wife: they have been married for nearly thirty years. But who is Susan Jameson married to in real life?

5. Esther and Brian met when he arrested her for trying to steal a copy of which library book? A) Jaws B) Lady Chatterley's Lover C) The Escaped Cock D) Kama Sutra

6. Sandra Pullman believed her dead father, DI Gordon Pullman, suffered a heart attack in 1975. Many years later (in the series) she found out how he had actually died. What did she discover?

7. Where does Jack Holford often speak to his dead wife Mary?

8. What retro car did Gerry Standing drive in the series?

9. Steve McAndrew departed right at the end. What job was he going to do and in which country?

10. Similarly Dan Griffin also decided to change employment in a new country. Again, what job and in which country?

MEET THE BOSS
Deputy Assistant Commissioner Robert Strickland is the team's boss. Who played the role?

*THE GOOD LIFE: 1. 40; 2. Good and Leadbetter, Surbiton; 3. Lenin; 4. Secretly attending a slimming club; 5. C) Pale Blue; 6. A) Snetterton and Dalby ; 7. Two pigs (Pinky & Perky); 8. Angela Thorne; 9. The Sound of Music; 10. Eight leeks. **ANAGRAMS:** 1. Miss Dolly Mountshaft - unseen leading light of the music society; 2. Margot Leadbetter; 3. Paul Eddington; 4. Mrs Dooms-Paterson; 5. Geraldine (goat).*

A British series that aired between 1979 and 1988. Each episode told a story, often with sinister and wryly comedic undertones, with an unexpected twist ending. Every episode of series 1, eight episodes of series 2, and one episode of series 3 were based on short stories by Roald Dahl. 9 Series. 112 Episodes.

1. In *The Landlady* what was the landlady's hobby?
A) Taxidermy B) Basket weaving C) Crocheting D) Stamp collecting

2. In *Parson's Pleasure* what did the antiques dealer believe he had found? A) Harrison watch B) Titanic's telescope C) Chippendale commode D) Goya painting

3. In *The Hitchhiker* what sort of criminal is the hitchhiker?
A) Serial killer B) Bank robber C) Pickpocket D) Rapist

4. In *Lamb to the Slaughter* Mary Marney (Susan George) killed her husband by hitting him A) With what?   B) How did she then dispose of the 'weapon'?

5. In *Edward the Conqueror* Edward's wife believed that the cat was a reincarnation of which composer as whenever she played his music the cat hopped on the piano stool? A) Chopin B) Liszt C) Mozart D) Grieg

6. How do Pamela and Arthur find out that the Beauchamps, their house guests and bridge opponents, are cheating in *My Lady Love, My Dove*?

7. How does crooked antique expert Cyril Boggis dress when he calls upon Suffolk farmsteads offering to take old furniture away for a fee?

8. In *Man from the South* a young American naval cadet boasts about the reliability of his cigarette lighter. Carlos offers to bet his Cadillac against the American's left little finger that the American cannot do what?

9. In *Mrs Bixby and the Colonel's Coat*, Mrs Bixby is having a secret affair with the Colonel and is given a mink coat as a present. Where did she leave the coat to hide it from her husband? A) Church B) Pawnshop C) Railway station D) Library

10. In the *In the Cards* episode what does Madame Myra foretell in a tarot card reading for her client Charlie?

NEW TRICKS: 1. Unsolved Crime and Open Case Squad; 2. Amanda Redman, James Bolam, Alun Armstrong and Dennis Waterman; 3. Denis Lawson, Nicholas Lyndhurst, Tamzin Outhwaite and Larry Lamb; 4. James Bolam who played Jack Holford); 5. B) Lady Chatterley's Lover; 6. Committed suicide when about to be arrested by Jack Holford for shooting a pimp; 7. At her memorial in the garden; 8. A 1977 Triumph Stag roadster (1974 in the pilot!); 9. Private Investigator in Australia; 10. Criminal Analyst for Interpol in Aberdeen, Scotland. MEET THE BOSS: Anthony Calf.

A comedy sketch show originally broadcast by the BBC and the 3rd TV series by Morecambe and Wise. It began airing in 1968 on BBC2, as it was then the only channel broadcasting in colour. This followed the duo's move from ATV, where they had made Two of a Kind since 1961. 9 Series 71 Episodes.

1. In 1968 ITV offered Morecambe and Wise £39,000 for three years. However, the duo turned the offer down and moved to BBC2. What was the principal reason?

2. Just after the final episode of the first BBC series was transmitted the plans for a second series with longer running times had to be shelved. Why?

3. Sid Green and Dick Hills opted to leave Morecambe and Wise and return to ITV after the first series. Which script writer was then recruited by the duo?

4. M&W Christmas shows became legendary. Which BBC newsreader showed her long legs to the world in 1976 in a memorable dancing sketch?

5. The 1977 special included a version of *There Is Nothing Like a Dame* from *South Pacific*. A) Who performed the song and B) Who sung the final long bass note?

6. *Positive Thinking, We Get Along So Easily (Don't You Agree?), Following You Around* and *Just Around The Corner* are all M&W signature songs, but what was their most memorable and popular signature song?

7. Who was the 'lady who comes down at the end', despite having no involvement in the 50 minute show, she strode onto the stage, took a bow and thanked the audience?

8. Frankie Vaughan was butt of a recurring joke and had a lawyer's letter. The premise of the joke was transferred memorably to... Whom?

9. As Cleopatra, which actress delivered the infamous line from an Ernie Wise play: 'All men are fools. And what makes them so is having beauty like what I have got...'?

10. Possibly M&W's finest moment came in the 1971 appearance of which renowned composer, conducting Eric 'playing' Grieg's Piano Concerto?

TALES OF THE UNEXPECTED: 1. A) Taxidermy; 2. C) Chippendale commode; 3. C) Pickpocket; 4. Frozen leg of lamb, she cooks it and feeds it to the investigating detectives; 5. B) Lizst; 6. They hide a microphone in their room; 7. As a Vicar (in Parson's Pleasure); 8. Ignite the lighter ten times consecutively; 9. B) Pawnshop; 10. He will come into a lot of money... but die shortly afterwards.

A British series created and written by British writer and barrister John Mortimer about Horace Rumpole, an elderly London barrister who defended a broad variety of clients, often underdogs. On Thames Television (ITV). There were 7 Series. 44 Episodes.

1. Who brilliantly portrayed Horace Rumpole?

2. How did Rumpole frequently describe his wife Hilda?

3. Which well-known TV actor played the well-connected, if occasionally feckless, Head of Chambers Sir Guthrie Featherstone?

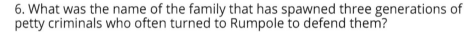

4. Rumpole loved to quote poetry. To which poetry book did he often refer?

5. In which branch of the British Armed Services did Rumpole serve?
A) RAF Ground Staff B) Catering Corps C) Royal Corps of Signals

6. What was the name of the family that has spawned three generations of petty criminals who often turned to Rumpole to defend them?

7. Who was the school-friend of Hilda's that often visited the Rumpoles, much to the displeasure of Horace?

8. Name the wine bar that Horace Rumpole frequently visited for a glass of the house plonk?

9. What was Rumpole's rhyming slang for the feminist barrister Liz Probert?

10. Who played Rumpole's pupil, Phyllida Trant, who was a strong advocate, with definite opinions of her own? Usually, but not always, she sided with Rumpole in Chambers matters. She eventually became a QC, a Recorder, and then a High Court judge.

TRIVIA

Leo McKern played Carl Bugenhagen in which 1976 horror classic?

MORECAMBE AND WISE SHOW: 1. BBC2 could offer colour transmissions; 2. Eric Morecambe had a serious heart attack following a show at the Batley Variety Club; 3. Eddie Braben; 4. Angela Rippon; 5. A) BBC Presenters, B) Peter Woods; 6. Bring Me Sunshine (written by Arthur Kent); 7. Janet Webb; 8. Des O'Connor; 9. Glenda Jackson; 10. André Previn (introduced by Ernie as Andrew Preview).

A second set of trivia about the classic BBC sit-com series Only Fools and Horses. How many can you answer?

1. In *Heroes and Villains* Del and Rodney stopped an attempt to mug Councillor Murray dressed as Batman & Robin and scaring away the thieves. They arrived at the party, unaware the fancy dress is now a wake (a fact that Boycie forgot to mention on the door). They burst into the main room singing the *Batman* theme. Whose wake were the boys attending?

2. In the episode *The Unlucky Winner Is....?* what was the title of Rodney's painting that won the Mega Flakes children's drawing competition?

3. Which darkened, run-down hotel managed by sinister Mrs Cresswell do Del, Rodney and Albert end up staying the night at in *The Jolly Boys Outing*?

4. In *Video Nasty*, Mickey Pearce used Rodney's camera to earn a 'few bob' covering weddings. With girlfriend Amanda he made an adult film. Title?

5. In *May the Force Be With You* what programme was Grandad trying to watch on the microwave oven?

6. In *If They Could See Us Now* Del asks what music Rodney is playing. Trigger says 'It's Mozart's Symphony Number 38 in D Major. It's the .... version.' What word is missing?

7. In *Slow Bus to Chingford*, Sherlock Holmes birthplace in Shoreditch, the summit of Mount Pleasant, the place where Jack the Ripper is buried; were all destinations for Del's latest get rich quick scheme. What was it called?

8. Complete this famous quote from *Time on Our Hands*. 'No Rodney, I'll buy the sandwiches, because ... .'

9. In *Ashes to Ashes* Del and Rodney spent the episode trying to respectfully dispose of the ashes of Trigger's Grandad Arthur. Where did the ashes end up?

10. In *Yesterday Never Comes* Del tried to sell a 'Queen Anne Cabinet' to antique dealer Miranda Davenport. Clearly it was not a historic piece as they found what word stamped on the interior?

RUMPOLE OF THE BAILEY: 1. Leo McKern; 2. 'She who must be obeyed'; 3. Peter Bowles; 4. Oxford Book of English Verse; 5. RAF Ground Staff; 6. Timson; 7. Dodo Mackintosh; 8. Pomeroy's; 9. Miz Liz; 10. Patricia Hodge. TRIVIA: The Omen.

A British sit-com made in the late 1980s and early 1990s satirising the UK's Conservative Party Government of the period. It was written by Laurence Marks and Maurice Gran. The programme was made by the ITV franchise Yorkshire Television between 1987-1992; the BBC made two special episodes in 1988 and 1994. 4 Series. 26 Episodes and 3 Specials.

1. Who played Conservative MP Alan B*Stard?

2. Which constituency did B*Stard represent having gained a majority of 26,738?
A) Haltemprice   B) Gidleigh Park   C) Dibley   D) Crinkley Bottom

3. Both Alan's main opponents in the election from the SDP and Labour parties ended up on life support machines. What happened to them?

4. What was the name of Alan's transsexual accountant and confidante?

5. In the Episode *Live from Westminster*, who hosted the quiz show to which Alan is invited? A) Leslie Crowther B) Jim Bowen C) Bruce Forsyth D) Nicholas Parsons

6. What did B*Stard and his wife Sarah name their daughter?
A) Margaret Hilda   B) Susan Alan   C) Sarah Jane   D) Janet Mary

7. In the Episode *Heil and Farewell in 1992* who played Marlene Dietrich?

8. What character was the elderly, neurotic publican, formerly the Hangman, in Alan's constituency, who infrequently doubled as his assistant?

9. In the Episode *Passport to Freedom* B*Stard sneaked into Thatcher's office and found a copy of which book in her desk drawer?
A) Spycatcher by Peter Wright B) Journey by Tony Blair C) Jaws by Peter Benchley

CONSERVATIVE PRIME MINISTERS
Match the right PM with the date they were first elected as PM

1. ANTHONY EDEN	A. 1957	6. HAROLD McMILLAN	F. 2010
2. THERESA MAY	B. 1990	7. WINSTON CHURCHILL	G. 1970
3. NEVILLE CHAMBERLAIN	C. 1937	8. JOHN MAJOR	H. 1955
4. MARGARET THATCHER	D. 2016	9. DAVID CAMERON	J. 1940
5. ALEC DOUGLAS-HOME	E. 1963	10. EDWARD HEATH	K. 1979

ONLY FOOLS AND HORSES 2: *1. Harry Malcolm; 2. Marble Arch at Dawn; 3. Villa Bella; 4. Night Nurse; 5. The Dukes of Hazzard; 6. Karaoke; 7. Trotter's Ethnic Tours; 8. ... you bought the Rolls; 9. Sucked up by a council cleaning lorry ; 10. Fyffes (as in banana boxes).*

A list of 20 well known catchphrases from the world of television. Can you remember which character uttered the famous sayings, and in what shows?

1. Yeah but no but yeah but...

2. Good moaning

3. Thank you very much Jerry

4. No, no, no, no, yes

5. Oooh Betty

6. Smeghead

7. To me, to you

8. Fan-Dabby-Dozy

9. Ooh I could crush a grape

10. It's good. But it's not right

11. Let's see what you would have won

12. Bernie the bolt

13. They don't like it up 'em

14. (Three words:) Fab-u-LOUS

15. Nice to see you, to see you.....nice

16. Seems like a nice boy

17. Cheap as chips

18. I'm a laydee

19. Ooh suit you sir

20. Smoke me a kipper, I'll be back for breakfast

CATCHPHRASE: *A well-known sentence or phrase, especially one that is associated with a particular famous*

THE NEW STATESMAN: 1. Rick Mayall: 2. A) Haltemprice; 3. B*Stard had the brake lines of their cars cut ; 4. Norman/Norma; 5. D) Nicholas Parsons; 6. A) Margaret Hilda (after Margaret Thatcher); 7. Paul O'Grady (as Paul Svage); 8. Sidney Bliss; 9. A) Spycatcher by Peter Wright; 10. Piers Fletcher-Dervish. CONSERVATIVE PRIME MINISTERS: 1H, 2D, 3C, 4K, 5E, 6A, 7J, 8B, 9F, 10G.

 *A BBC light entertainment series hosted by Noel Edmonds. Set in a large house in the fictional village of Crinkley Bottom, leading to much innuendo. Broadcast live on Saturday evenings in the 1990s on BBC One. The show, once described by a senior corporation executive as "the most important show on the BBC", was cancelled in 1999 due to poor ratings. 8 Series. 169 Episodes and 15 Specials.*

1. Two residents of Crinkley Bottom were known for starring roles as Captain Peacock and Yvette Carte-Blanche. Who are they in real life?

2. What regular feature of the show featured, amongst others, Barbara Windsor, Lionel Blair and Status Quo?

3. What segment featured a celebrity, a perspex box, a fan and lots of banknotes?

4. Who was Barry Killerby?

5. What heralded the arrival of a celebrity?

6. Another popular feature saw a member of the audience with an embarrassing secret, made to wear a lie detector and questioned by Noel. What was it called?

7. Who appeared in a highwayman's outfit—'going cheap at the Maxwell sale'—as Noel's long-lost 'twin', Berasent Edmonds (Bury St Edmunds)?

8. Celebrity appearances included which actor who came in to find the whole audience dressed as his famous accident prone TV character?

9. Which segment from series 6-8 involved small school children being faced with puppets that start talking to them? It featured aliens Phibber the frog and Waffle the Squirrel.

10. In Episode 169, the final episode, Noel made a closing farewell speech. Who playfully attacked him with a fire extinguisher during the speech?

WHO SAID THAT 2: 1. Vicky Pollard in Little Britain; 2. Officer Crabtree in 'Allo 'Allo; 3. Margo Leadbetter in The Good Life; 4. Jim Trott in The Vicar of Dibley; 5. Frank Spencer in Some Mothers Do 'Ave 'Em; 6. Red Dwarf by various characters; 7. The Chuckle Brothers in Chucklevision; 8. Ian & Wee Jimmy Krankie in The Krankies; 9. Stu Francis in Crackerjack; 10. Roy Walker in Catchphrase; 11. Jim Bowen in Bullseye; 12. Bob Monkhouse in The Golden Shot; 13. Lance Corporal Jones in Dad's Army; 14. Craig Revel Horwood in Strictly Come Dancing; 15. Bruce Forsyth in The Generation Game; 16. Larry Grayson in The Generation Game; 17. David Dickinson in Bargain Hunt; 18. Emily Howard in Little Britain; 19. Ken and Kenneth in The Fast Show; 20. Ace Rimmer in Red Dwarf.

A British sitcom written by David Renwick. There were six series and seven Christmas specials over a period of eleven years from early 1990 to late 2000. The first five series were broadcast between January 1990 and January 1995. For the next five years, the show appeared only as Christmas specials, followed by one final series in 2000. A total of 6 series and 42 episodes plus 2 specials.

1. In *The Beast in the Cage* what was the make of Victor's car? (Think about the singing mechanics on the cassette tape in the traffic jam).

2. In the episode *One Foot in the Algarve* the Meldrews and Mrs Warboys embarked on a hellish holiday to Portugal. What follows Victor everywhere?

3. What was Victor's job before he retired, and what replaced him?

4. In *The Return of the Speckled Band* Victor visited a garden centre and unwittingly took something unexpected home in his bag. What was it?

5. In *Who's Listening,* Victor ordered something from a mail order catalogue and, due to an error, 263 of the items turned up. What were they?

6. Which grocer, played by Barbara Windsor, tried to seduce Victor and what did Margaret hit her with?

7. In *Love and Death* what gift did Vince Bluett give to Victor?

8. What did Victor buy that turned out to be radioactive?

9. What unusual prize did Jean Warboys win in a competition and, as she was in hospital, have delivered to the Meldrews house?

10. In the final episode *Things Aren't Simple Any More* Victor attended a disastrous reunion dinner. What happens to him after the 'non-event"?

THEY STARRED IN ONE FOOT IN THE GRAVE

Can you work out the actors' names?

1) ABSENT ERECTION
2) SARDONIC WHIRL
3) DANA YOUNGEST
4) ADKINS JIVE UNIT
5) NAME NEWBORN

NOEL'S HOUSE PARTY: 1. Frank Thornton and Vicki Michelle; 2. Gotcha; 3. Grab a Grand; 4. He was the man inside the Mr Blobby costume; 5. The doorbell would ring; 6. The Big Pork Pie; 7. Ken Dodd; 8. Michael Crawford (Frank Spencer); 9. My Little Friend; 10. Freddie Starr.

A BBC series of annual snooker tournaments held in the UK from 1969-1986. The event carried no ranking points but was vital in popularising the modern game of snooker. Revived in the form of several one-off tournaments throughout the 1990s and up to 2007. Helped transform snooker from a minority sport played by a handful of professionals into one of the most popular sports in the UK.

1. Whose brainchild was *Pot Black*? This renowned natural historian saw snooker as a sport that could exploit the newly available colour television.

2. What was Winifred Atwell's piano theme tune for *Pot Black*?
A)The Entertainer B) Black and White Rag C) Maple Leaf Rag D) Kismet Rag

3. Steve Davis won the first Celebrity Pot Black in 2006. Who was his partner?
A) Vernon Kay B) Bradley Walsh C) Alan Hansen D) Piers Morgan

4. True or False? Commentator Ted Lowe, aware not all had colour TV's, said, 'For those of you watching in black and white, the pink is next to the green'.

SNOOKER STYLE TRIVIA

1 POINT RED QUESTION - What is the pigment 'Dragon's Blood' made from?
A) Pigs blood   B) Tomato puree   C) Tree resin

2 POINTS YELLOW QUESTION - How many colours are there in a rainbow?
A) 5   B) 6   C) 7

3 POINTS GREEN QUESTION - What colour is 'Lapis Lazuli'? A) Blue B) Pink C) Yellow

4 POINTS BROWN QUESTION - What colour is associated with jealousy?
 A) Blue   B) Green   C) Yellow

5 POINTS BLUE QUESTION - Who were Elvis Presley's favourite American football team? A) Buffalo Bills   B) Tennessee Titans   C) Cleveland Browns

6 POINTS PINK QUESTION - The artist Anish Kapoor has acquired exclusive rights to which pigment? A) Whitest white   B) Blackest black   C) Pinkest pink

7 POINTS BLACK QUESTION - Which painter said, 'Yellow is my favourite colour. It stands for the sun'? A) Vincent Van Gogh   B) Jackson Pollock   C) Andy Warhol

8 POINTS WHITE QUESTION - Who is Alecia Beth Moore?
A) Cilla Black   B) Pink   C) Melanie B

ONE FOOT IN THE GRAVE: 1. Honda; 2. Donkeys; 3. Security guard, a box and a recorded message; 4. An Indian python; 5. Garden gnomes; 6. Millicent, a boxing glove; 7. A tombstone; 8. Horse manure; 9. A waxwork model of herself; 10. He got knocked down and killed in a hit and run accident. THEY STARRED IN ONE FOOT IN THE GRAVE: 1) Richard Wilson; 2) Annette Crosbie; 3) Angus Deayton; 4) Janine Duvitski; 5) Owen Brenman.

A 1979 seven-part drama spy mini-series made by BBC TV. John Irvin directed and Jonathan Powell produced this adaptation of John le Carré's novel. The series was shot on location in Glasgow, at Oxford University, at Bredon School in Gloucestershire (where the character Jim Prideaux was a master), and in London, including some of the Intelligence Agency scenes which were shot at the BBC. 7 Episodes.

1. Where did George Smiley live in London?   A) 9 Bywater Street, Chelsea B) 11 Spook Street, Paddington   C) 5 Lock Gardens, Camden Town

2. Where was the headquarters of the British Intelligence Service? A) Whitehall   B) Piccadilly Circus   C) Cambridge Circus

3. Who was George Smiley's aristocratic and faithfully unfaithful wife? A) Lady Charlotte Wooster   B) Lady Ann Sercomb   C) Lady Jane Grey

4. What was the codename used for the mole at the heart of British Intelligence? A) Geoffrey   B) Gordon   C) Gerald

5. In *Tinker Tailor Soldier Spy* where was the safe house in which the Merlin source passed information to British Intelligence? A) 5 Lock Gardens, Camden Town B) 11 Spook Street, Paddington   C) 9 Bywater Street, Chelsea

6. Who was sent to meet a Czech general on a mission that was a trap and he was captured and tortured by the Soviets. A) Oliver Lacon   B) Jim Prideaux   C) Roy Bland

7. Britain's chief spymaster was known simply by what name? A) The Voice   B) Beggarman   C) Control

8. Smiley was recalled to expose the Soviet mole after being forced to retire in the wake of what operation? A) Testify   B) Crossbow   C) Desert Storm

9. Ricki Tarr began to track a Russian agent named Boris in Hong Kong. The result of this surveillance was that: A) Boris' wife fell in love with Ricki   B) Boris turned out to be a CIA agent   C) Boris was shot in the back

10. With the help of his protégé, Smiley gradually uncovered an ingenious plot, as well as ultimate betrayal of country, of the service and of friendship. Who was the protege? A) Peter Guillam   B) Connie Sachs   C) Sam Collins

POT BLACK: 1. David Attenborough (then Controller of BBC2); 2. B) Black and White Rag; 3. A) Vernon Kay;. 4. True. 1 POINT. C) Tree resin; 2 POINTS. C) Seven; 3 POINTS. A) Blue; 4 POINTS. B) Green; 5 POINTS. C) Cleveland Browns; 6 POINTS. A) Whitest White; 7 POINTS. A) Vincent Van Gogh; 8 POINTS. The singer B) Pink.

A British rock/pop music programme broadcast from 9 August 1963 until 23 December 1966. Conceived by Elkan Allan, head of Rediffusion TV. He wanted a light entertainment programme different from the low-brow style of light entertainment transmitted by ATV. The programme was produced without scenery or costumes and with a minimum of choreography and make-up. 179 Episodes were transmitted.

Below are 15 songs featured on RSG and the 15 performers who performed them. Just match up the correct pairings. (There is one very tricky one, just remember the stars didn't just perform their hits on RSG).

SONG	ARTIST
1. APACHE	A. MANFRED MANN
2. BABY'S IN BLACK	B. THE HOLLIES
3. THE PRICE OF LOVE	C. MARIANNE FAITHFULL
4. SAILOR BOY	D. THE EVERLY BROTHERS
5. YES I WILL	E. DUSTY SPRINGFIELD
6. MAKE IT EASY ON YOURSELF	F. THE SUPREMES
7. SHA LA LA	G. THE ROLLING STONES
8. ONE WAY LOVE	H. ADAM FAITH/THE ROULETTES
9. BLOWIN' IN THE WIND	J. THE YARDBIRDS
10. LOSING YOU	K. THE BEATLES
11. LONG LIVE LOVE	L. GOLDIE & THE GINGERBREADS
12. MESSAGE TO MARTHA	M. SANDIE SHAW
13. STOP IN THE NAME OF LOVE	N. CLIFF BENNETT/REBEL ROUSERS
14. I KNOW A PLACE	P. THE WALKER BROTHERS
15. HEART FULL OF SOUL	R. PETULA CLARK

The best known presenters were Keith Fordyce and Cathy McGowan, though early shows were introduced by Dusty Springfield. The show was occasionally presented by David Gell and Michael Aldred.

TINKER, TAILOR, SOLDIER, SPY: 1. A) 9 Bywater Street, Chelsea; 2. C) Cambridge Circus (why the service is often called The Circus); 3. B) Lady Ann Sercomb; 4. C) Gerald; 5. A) 5 Lock Gardens, Camden Town; 6. B) Jim Prideaux; 7. C) Control; 8. A) Testify; 9. A) Boris' wife falls in love with Ricki; 10. A) Peter Guillam.

1. At the end of *Andy Pandy* he climbed into the box with Teddy and sung the final song. What was it called?

2. What year did *Play School* start on BBC?
A) 1954 B) 1964 C) 1974

3. *Dad's Army* stars provided voices for 2 children's shows. Who voiced A) Bod and B) The Mr Men?

4. Fireman Sam was found in the fictional Welsh rural village of …. Where?

5. In *The Magic Roundabout* what part of Zebedee was the source of his power?

6. What was the name of the snake in the *Sooty Show*?

7. What did Windy Miller do in *Camberwick Green*?

8. TISWAS was on TV screens from 1974-1982. A) What do the initials mean and B) What was the character who threw custard pies around the studio?

9. What was the name of Pippa Pig's younger brother?

10. John and Sue were young friends of which character who spent a lot of time in the middle of a field?

11. A) What was the name of the football team in *Murphy's Mob .* B) Which actor from *Auf Wiedersehen Pet* sung the theme song?

PADDINGTON

12. Mr Gruber and Mr Curry were characters in which 1976-1980 animated show about a lovable bear?

13. Who voiced Toad in *Wind in the Willows* 1984/8?

14. Can you name the dinosaur mascot on the desk in *Multi Coloured Swop Shop*?

15. Which Plasticine figure debuted in *Take Hart*?

16. Who insured the thumb and first two fingers on his right hand for £20,000?

17. Who presented Record Breakers from 1972 until his death in 1994?

18. What was the name of the tortoise in *The Flower Pot Men*?

19. What was the name of the green witch, arch-enemy of Rod Hull and Emu?

20. Mr Benn always wore a bowler hat. What hat did the shopkeeper wear?

READY STEADY GO!: 1G (Stones play Shadows over closing titles!); 2K, 3D, 4L, 5B, 6P, 7A, 8N, 9C, 10E, 11M, 12H, 13F, 14R, 15J.

A British police procedural drama series devised by Lynda La Plante. The series follows the female officer's constant battles to prove herself in a male-dominated profession, determined to see her fail. There were 7 Series from 1991-2006. A total of just 15 Episodes.

1. To which fictional Police Station was Tennison assigned in Series 1?

2. Which actor played the murderer George Marlow in the first series?

3. In a meeting with Det Supt Michael Kernan, Who suffered a fatal heart attack?
A) DI Frank Burkin B) DCI John Shefford C) DI Larry Hall

4. Marlow's common-law wife worked as a manicurist. The police realize Marlow's victims were also her clients. What was her name and who played her?

5. In Series 2 the skeletal remains of a teen girl were found in the backyard of a house in a predominantly Afro-Caribbean area. What was the operation called?
A) Operation Maureen B) Operation Whitney C) Operation Nadine

6. In series 3 Tennison accepted a new job as DCI in Metro Vice. Which former nemesis turned into an ally in *Keeper of Souls*?

7. In Series 4 Tennison was promoted to Detective Supt. George Marlow's guilt doubted but Tennison was sure it is a copycat. She was right. What job did the killer have?
A) Prison guard B) Driving Instructor C) Accountant

8. In series 5 Jane was transferred to Manchester to investigate the murder of a drug dealer. The local gang leader (and a folk hero), played by Steven Mackintosh, was a suspect. What was his nickname?
A) The Road B) The Cul-de-sac C) The Street

9. In *The Last Witness* Tennison and her photojournalist friend, Robert West, visited which country to find the truth about the sadist she knows to be responsible for so many deaths? A) Iraq B) Bosnia C) Libya

10. In *The Final Act* Tennison is struggling with alcohol problems and attends an AA meeting. Which old friend is also at the meeting and what happens to him before the end of the episode?

In the 2017 prequel PRIME SUSPECT 1973, who played PC Jane Tennison?

CLASSIC CHILDREN'S TV: 1. Time To Go Home; 2. B) 1964; 3. A) John Le Mesurier, B) Arthur Lowe; 4. Pontypandy; 5. His moustache; 6. Ramsbottom; 7. Cider; 8. A) Today Is Saturday: Watch And Smile, B) The Phantom Flan Flinger; 9. George; 10. Worzel Gummidge; 11. A) Dunmore United , B) Gary Holton (Wayne in AWP); 12. Paddington ; 13. David Jason; 14. Posh Paws; 15. Morph; 16. Harry Corbett (Sooty); 17. Roy Castle; 18. Old Slowcoach; 19. Grotbags; 20. A fez.

A British sitcom. 20 episodes were broadcast by the BBC. 3 series 19641966. In the colour sequel there were 2 Series with 26 episodes . A subsequent 45-minute Christmas special was aired on 24 December 1974.

Whatever Happened to the Likely Lads?

1. In which factory did Bob and Terry both work?
A) Fenner Fashions   B) Ellisons Electrical   C) National Coal Board

2. Bob applied to join the Army and Terry decided to follow suit. But then Bob was refused. Upon what medical grounds did he fail?

3. In 1964 on *Christmas Night With the Stars*, Bob and Terry had an argument over Bob's encyclopedic knowledge of what character's annuals?

4. In *Outward Bound* the boys decided to go camping. In which type of camp did they plan to end up? A) Hippy love-in   B) Butlins   C) Caravan

5. In *Razor's Edge* why was Bob forced into quarantine for 21 days, and when he reappeared why was Terry horrified?

6. In *Anchor's Aweigh* Bob and Terry embarked on a boating holiday in the hopes of meeting some girls. Where did they go for the holiday?

7. Bob married Thelma. What job did she do?

8. Which former Manfred Mann drummer co-wrote the theme to *Whatever happened To The Likely Lads* and also the score for the feature film?
A) Dave Clark   B) Brian Bennett   C) Mike Hugg

9. Which former girlfriend of Bob's with loose morals, was a running gag throughout the series?
A) Deirdre Birchwood   B) Lilo Lil   C) Wendy Thwaites

10. In the 1974 Christmas Special Bob finally passed his driving test. What job did he then take?

What links these two celebrities?

PRIME SUSPECT: 1. Southampton Row; 2. John Bowe; 3. B) DCI John Shefford; 4. Myra Henson, Zoe Wannamaker; 5. C) Operation Nadine; 6. DS Bill Otley (Tom Bell); 7. A) Prison guard; 8. C) The Street; 9. B) Bosnia; 10. Bill Otley, he is shot dead.

The UK channels and independent production companies output a significant amount of TV drama which is shot all over the UK. TV dramas span all genres; they can be a one-off or a series whose air time is usually capped at an hour. Many have been immensely successful in the UK and around the world. Here is a second round of questions on such programmes.

DRAMA *2*

1. *Where The Heart Is* was on from 1997-2006. It centred around two women in Yorkshire, Peggy Snow and Ruth Goddard. What job did they do?

2. Which rural series starred Pauline Quirke as teacher Faith Addis?

3. Which TV copper's wife was murdered by gangster Joe Webster in 1964?

4. How was Nancy Cunard de Longchamps usually known in *Rock Follies*?

5. Which classic vet series was successfully revived with a new cast in 2020?

6. Susannah York played stud owner Rachel Ware in which 1991 series that had Cliff Richard taking the theme song to number 23 in the charts?

7. How did Francis Urquhart kill Mattie Storin at the House of Commons roof garden in *House of Cards*?

8. Father Aidan O'Connell was new priest in which village?

9. In the 1970s who were the *Family at War* on Granada TV?

10. The story of which speed ace was told in the 1988 drama *Across the Lake*?

11. What was Jessie Smeaton's job in *When the Boat Comes In*?

12. Jack Shepherd played a Labour MP in a 1976 series. What was the series?

13. Who did Hudson marry in the final episode of *Upstairs, Downstairs*?

14. Who played Mark, a bank manager out of the rat race in *Telford's Change*?

15. Which 19th century prime minister was played by Sir John Gielgud in *Edward the Seventh* in 1975?

16. Which Australian actress played Faye Boswell, the prison governor in *Within These Walls,* and which actress played her successor Helen Forrester?

17. Who did Michael Caine name as Jack the Ripper in the 1988 mini-series?

18. Which outrageous character did John Hurt play in *The Naked Civil Servant?*

THE LIKELY LADS: *1. B) Ellisons Electrical; 2. Flat feet; 3. Rupert Bear; 4. A) Hippy love-in camp; 5. Bob has chicken pox, he has grown a beard; 6. The Norfolk Broads; 7. She is a librarian; 8.C) Mike Hugg; 9. A) Deirdre Birchwood; 10. A mini-cab driver.* **SPOT THE CONNECTION:** *When Nana (Liz Smith) dies in the Royle family her last words were 'Trevor McDonald'.*

A British quiz show from the BBC, first broadcast in 2003 chaired by Dermot Murnaghan. In 2008 Jeremy Vine became joint chair, then sole chair 2014. A team of 5 quiz & game show champions (Eggheads) is challenged by a team of 5 contestants for prize money. £75,000 is the biggest prize won (2007). 20 Regular Series + 8 Celebrity. 1870 Episodes + 92 Celebrity shows.

TEST YOUR GENERAL KNOWLEDGE WITH SOME EGGHEADS SUBJECTS

1. The expresssion 'The law is an ass' became popular from which Dickens novel: A) Bleak House   B) Nicholas Nickelby   C) Oliver Twist

2. How many times was Leonardo Di Caprio nominated for an Oscar before eventually winning one? A) 6 times   B) 5 times   C) 4 times.

3. In which film does John Cleese play the role of a headmaster obsesses by punctuality? A) Teacher's Pet   B) Time Bandits   C) Clockwise

4. Which of the following cheeses has the lowest moisture content?
 A) Brie   B) Edam   C) Cheddar

5. On which river does Italian city Florence stand? A) Arno   B) Po   C) Tiber

6. Who led the massacre of General Custer and his men at the Little Big Horn in 1876? A) Geronimo   B) Sitting Bull   C) Crazy Horse

7. Who were 'Lost in Music' in 1979?
A) Kool & Gang   B) Sister Sledge C) Rose Royce

8. Who presides over the election of a new Speaker of the House of Commons?   A) Father of the House   B) Existing Speaker   C) Prime Minister

9. Phonetics is study of what? A) Mechanics   B) Texts   C) Speech & Sounds

10. In cricket what colour balls were used by ladies in Edwardian times in case they became excited by red ones? A) Green   B) Blue   C) Yellow

11. In what year did Pablo Picasso die? A) 1953   B) 1963   C) 1973

12. Who won the Brit Award for Best Female Solo artist in 2020?
A) Mabel   B) Billie Elish   C) Freya Ridings

13. French for custard is? A) Crème Brulee   B) Crème Anglais   C) Coutarde

14. Which of these events came first?
A) Burning of Joan of Arc   B) Battle of Trafalgar   C) Great Plague of London

15. Who succeeded Nelson Mandela as President of South Africa?
A) Mangosuthu Buthelezi   B) Desmond Tutu   C) Thabo Abeki

DRAMA 2: 1. District Nurses; 2. Down to Earth; 3. Inspector George Gently; 4. Q; 5. All Creatures Great and Small; 6. Trainer (song was More To Life); 7. He throws her off the roof; 8. Ballykissangel; 9.The Ashtons; 10. Donald Campbell; 11. Schoolteacher; 12. Bill Brand; 13. Mrs Bridges; 14. Peter Barkworth; 15. Benjamin Disraeli; 16. Googie Withers, Katherine Blake; 17. Sir William Withey Gull, one of Queen Victoria's physicians-in-ordinary; 18. Quentin Crisp.

MR SELFRIDGE

A British period drama series about Harry Gordon Selfridge and his department store, Selfridge & Co, in London, set from 1908 to 1928. It was co-produced by ITV Studios and Masterpiece/WGBH[1] for broadcast on ITV. The series began broadcasting on ITV on 6 January 2013. 4 Series 40 Episodes.

1. Who played the title role?

2. Where was a replica of the first Selfridge's store built for external filming?
A) Historic Dockyard Chatham B) Greenwich C) St Katharine Docks, London

3. Who was portrayed by Katherine Kelly?
A) Lady Mae Loxley   B) Irene Ravillious   C) Lois Selfridge

4. Mr Selfridge inadvertently got Agnes Towler fired from Gamage's so he hired her for Selfridge's when he opened. Why had she been sacked?

5. Which famous French aviator appeared in the store with his aircraft?

6. When Harry installed Ellen Love in an apartment what did she do to inspire him to open a cosmetics department in the front of store not hidden away?

7. Selfridge took his wife and daughter to see which famous dancer perform?

8. Which famous writer followed a book signing session by holding a séance?

9. An old family friend and his wife arrive in London to open a 'pile 'em high, sell 'em cheap store in competition with Selfridge's. What was the rival store?

10. Which Royal was invited to after hours shopping, arranged by Lady Mae?

PICTURE QUESTION
For which product was the magician Dynamo seen floating down from the top shelves of a huge warehouse with an item for the supervisor in a 2020 TV advert?

EGGHEADS: 1. C) Oliver Twist; 2. C) 4 times 3. C) Clockwise; 4. C) Cheddar; 5. A) Arno; 6. B) Sitting Bull; 7. B) Sister Sledge; 8. A) Father of the House; 9. C) Speech & Sounds; 10. B) Blue; 11. C) 1973; 12. A) Mabel; 13. B) Crème Anglais; 14. A) Burning of Joan of Arc; 15. C) Thabo Abeki.

A British crime series based on Sir Arthur Conan Doyle's Sherlock Holmes detective stories. Aired from 2010 to 2017 with a special episode aired on 1 January 2016. The series is set in the present day, while the one-off special featured a Victorian period fantasy resembling the original Holmes stories. 4 series. 13 Episodes.

1. What was the minimum rating out of 10 that a case has to be rated by Sherlock for him to leave his flat?

2. What was Lestrade's first name?

3. From which university did John Watson graduate with a Bachelor of Medicine and Surgery degree?
A) Cambridge   B) Oxford   C) King's College, London

4. Why did Mrs Hudson give Sherlock a lower rent?

5. What board game did Watson refuse to play with Holmes?
A) Chess   B) Cluedo   C) Monopoly

6. What name did Moriarty use for his fake actor persona?
A) Richard Brook   B) Martin Freeman
C) John Smith

7. In *The Empty Hearse* Watson discovered Sherlock is alive, when he appeared disguised as a what?
A) Policeman   B) Waiter   C) Busker

8. In *Scandal in Belgravia* we heard Jim Moriarty's ringtone. Was it: A) Bohemian Rhapsody by Queen B) Stayin' Alive by The Bee Gees C) Hello by Lionel Richie

9. What were Sherlock's last words as he leapt from the roof?
 A) Goodbye John   B) Elementary my dear Watson   C) I'm sorry John

10. What item did Sherlock steal from Buckingham Palace?
A) A spoon   B) A mug   C) An ashtray

MR SELFRIDGE: 1. Jeremy Piven; 2. A) Historic Dockyard Chatham, Kent; 3. A) Lady Mae Loxley; 4. She allowed Mr Selfridge behind the counter when he was buying gloves; 5. Louis Blériot; 6. He watches her apply make-up; 7. Anna Pavlova; 8. Sir Arthur Conan Doyle; 9. Woolworth's; 10 King Edward VII. PICTURE ADVERT: Yorkshire Tea.

QUIZ & GAME SHOWs

A game show is a type of genre in which contestants, TV personalities or celebrities, sometimes in a team, play a game which involves answering questions or solving puzzles usually for money and/or prizes. Britain has struck gold when it comes to TV shows of the gaming variety. The options are endless.

1. Who was the first person to win a million pounds on *Who Wants To Be A Millionaire* and go on to appear regularly on *Eggheads*?

2. What are the 4 areas of pachinko-like pegboards called on *Tipping Point?*

3. On which game show would you find Mr Chips?

4. Who was Hughie Green's cockney hostess on *Double Your Money,* who sadly committed suicide in 1994 aged 45?

5. Who made his name presenting *Supermarket Sweep?*

6. Name the three 'Skyrunners' who appeared on *Treasure Hunt?*

7. Who was the original question master on *University Challenge?*

8. Who won the 'Comedian's Special' version of *The Weakest Link* in 2001?

9. Which *Cube* game show host used to sell candy floss on Newquay beach?

10. What were the original four zones on *The Crystal Maze?*

11. Who was the announcer and co-host on *Bullseye* from 1982?

12. Which weapons were used on *The Golden Shot*?

13. Which ex-footballer presented *Friends Like These*?

14. Which host used to call himself 'The Quiz Inquisitor'?

15. Which west born football commentator narrated action on *Robot Wars?*

16. In which comedy panel game did Loyd Grossman and Keith Lemon snoop around celebrities' homes?

17. Which Scots lady co-hosted *The Generation Game* with Larry Grayson?

18. Who presented *Dog Eat Dog*?

19. Which 'Skyrunner' presented *The Interceptor* in 1989/1990?

20. Which newsreader was the first host of *The People Versus* in 2000?

SHERLOCK: 1. 7; 2. Greg; 3. C) King's College, London; 4. Holmes helped her out by ensuring the conviction and execution of her husband in Florida after he murdered two people; 5. B) Cluedo; 6. A) Richard Brook; 7. B) Waiter; 8. B) Stayin' Alive by The Bee Gees; 9. A) Goodbye John; 10. C) An ashtray.

A British sitcom about The Phoenix Club, a working men's club in the northern English town of Bolton, Greater Manchester. The show is a spin-off from the 'In the Club' episode of the spoof documentary series That Peter Kay Thing, and in turn was followed by the spin-off Max and Paddy's Road to Nowhere. It was produced by Goodnight Vienna Productions and Ovation Entertainments, and broadcast on Channel 4. 2 Series. 12 Episodes.

1. Who did Holy Mary impersonate on Stars in Their Eyes' Night?

2. According to the theme song Max and Paddy don't pay what?

3. For which Asda product did Jerry perform singing advertisements?

4. In which town was *Phoenix Nights* set?

5. Which Frenchman delivered faulty, explicit, inappropriate amusements?

6. What was the name of the dwarf that max loved and lost?

7. For which minibus company did Max and Paddy work?

8. How much did Max and Paddy get for killing someone? In the end, they could'nt pluck up the courage to carry out the hit, but kept the money and split it between them.

9. What did staff call Brian Potter behind his back?

10. What was the name of the Phoenix's hated rival club?

11. In the final episode what did Max and Paddy destroy at the start of the episode?

12. In the 5th episode what did Max and Paddy buy from a farm?

13. Who was Brian's arch enemy?

14. Which TV personality opened the Phoenix Club in the very first episode?

15. Julian Sua and Wai Kee Chan were two illegal immigrants from Asia. Whc played the parts?

TV QUIZ & GAME SHOWS: 1. Judith Keppel; 2. Drop Zones; 3. Catchphrase; 4. Monica Rose; 5. Dale Winton; 6. Anneka Rice, Annabel Croft, Suzi Perry; 7. Bamber Gascoigne; 8. Johnny Vegas; 9. Phillip Schofield; 10. Aztec, Futuristic, Industrial and Medieval; 11.Tony Green; 12.Crossbows; 13. Ian Wright; 14. Michael Miles (on Take Your Pick); 15. Jonathan Pearce; 16. Through the Keyhole; 17. Isla St Clair; 18. Ulrika Jonsson; 19. Annabel Croft; 20. Kirsty Young.

A British sports quiz show produced and broadcast by the BBC. It is the 'world's longest running TV sports quiz'. The series has run continuously since 1970 and celebrated its fiftieth anniversary in 2020. Presenter Sue Barker and team captains Matt Dawson & Phil Tufnell, are all due to leave in 2021. 49 series. 1269

1. Stuart Hall presented the pilot show in the north of England, but who presented the first edition of the networked programme in 1970 until 1977?

2. Name the 2 presenters since 1979.

3. There have been 14 regular captains. How many can you name?

4. On the first show in Jan 1970 a guest had won silver in the 400 metres at the 1968 Summer Olympics then two gold medals at the 1969 European Championships. Sadly she died less than a year later. Who was she?

5. The 1,000th Anniversary show in Jan 2010 featured two teams of captains. Apart from Matt and Phil, who else appeared on the milestone show?

6. In 1987 former England and Liverpool football captain Emlyn Hughes mistook whom for jockey John Reid?

7. Another funny moment saw a champion jockey fail to work out an anagram of his own name (below). Who was that?

TAKEN IT FOR RIDE

8. Who won the French Open tennis tournament in 1976, defeating Renáta Tomanová 6–2, 0–6, 6–2?

9. Which World Cup winner scored 834 points during his career with Northampton, London Wasps, England and the British and Irish Lions?

10. Who has a career batting record in Test matches and first class matches combined of 9.13, with a highest score of 67 not out from 408 innings?

PHOENIX NIGHTS: *1. Lulu; 2. Income tax; 3. Black bin liners; 4. Bolton; 5. Dodgy Eric; 6. Tina; 7. Asian Elders; 8. £8,000; 9. Ironside; 10. Banana Grove; 11. A speed camera; 12. A pig; 13. Den Perry; 14. Roy Walker; 15. Ant and Dec.*

A British television serial that began broadcasting on BBC One on 21 February 2016. The Night Manager was nominated for 36 awards and won 11, including two Emmy Awards for director Susanne Bier and music composer Victor Reyes. 1 series. 6 Episodes.

1. Which actor played the part of Jonathan Pine and won a Golden Globe?

2. What other treelike name did Jonathan Pine assume?

3. In which 3 countries was the series filmed?

4. Which actor moved from playing a title role in a long-running American medical series, to an arms dealer. Receiving Golden Globes for both roles?

5. Jonathan agreed to work with an intelligence officer to try and bring down Richard Roper, upon the promise of a new identity for him afterwards. What was the officer's name?

6. What was the name for the operation to place Pine in the Roper organisation and why did Roper sceptically accept Pine as part of his gang?

7. What was the name of Roper's agricultural equipment company which was a front for his arms dealing?

8. Jonathan Pine sent information to Angela Burr using what sharing app?
A) Twitter   B) Instagram   C) ZitterZatter

9. Tom Hollander played Corky. What was his full name?

10. When Pine robbed the Meisters Hotel in Zermatt, Switzerland, how much did he steal?
A) €20,000   B) €30,000   C)€40,000

ODD ONE OUT
6 TV shows and castings, 1 is out of place
2001 - Life and Adventures of Nicholas Nickleby - Lord
2004 - Pride and Prejudice - Mr Collins
2007 - Casualty - Chris Vaughan
2008/10 - Wallander - Magnus Martinsson
2013 - Family Guy - Statue Griffin

A QUESTION OF SPORT: 1. David Vine; 2. David Coleman (1979-1997) and Sue Barker (1997-2020); 3. Cliff Morgan, Henry Cooper, Freddie Trueman, Brendan Foster, Emlyn Hughes, Gareth Edwards, Willie Carson, Bill Beaumont, Ian Botham, John Parrott, Ally McCoist, Frankie Dettori, Matt Dawson, Phil Tufnell; 4. Lillian Board; 5. Willie Carson, John Parrott, Bill Beaumont, Ally McCoist; 6. Anne, Princess Royal; 7. Frankie Dettori; 8. Sue Barker; 9. Matt Dawson; 10. Phil Tufnell.

Since the early days of TV, comedy has been a main segment of the programmes that we have enjoyed on our box. This round comprises questions on all different sorts of shows that have made us laugh. From sitcoms to stand up comedy. How much can you remember from the days of old? Well, here's a second chance to find out.

1. Who famously ate pickled onions in his bath in 1963?

2. In *My Hero* into which Superhero did George Sunday become?

3. Which of Morecambe & Wise's famous guests was always chasing payment?

4. In *Monty Python's FC*, Mr Hilter stood for election in which English seaside town?

5. Paul Shane and Su Pollard appeared in *Hi-De-Hi* but in which sit-com did they play father and daughter?

6. In *The Brittas Empire* which assistant manager, who is also the centre's caretaker, had several skin allergies and a constantly infected hand?

7. In Jack Rosenthal's 1970/71 sitcom who were Geoffrey Scrimshaw and Beryl Battersby?

8. Who wrote *Clarence* under the pseudonym 'Bob Ferris' as an acknowledgement to Dick Clement and Ian La Frenais, the creators of *Porridge*?

9. Who did Frankie Howerd play in Up Pompeii?

10. In *Ripping Yarns*, how did a British expedition cross the Andes?

11. In 1980-82, who played brothers Brian & Steve Webber in *Sink or Swim*?

12. In the 1960s which comedian's opening titles showed him performing an optical trick in a shop window?

13. In the 1990s who were Harry Enfield's two chums?

14. What sit-com ran for 39 episodes and revolved around the romance between a widowed solicitor, Alec Callender) and a much younger woman, Zoë Angell?

15. Which 1970/80s show gave a stage to nightclub and working men's club comedians, including Russ Abbot, Jim Bowen and Bernard Manning?

THE NIGHT MANAGER: 1. Tom Hiddleston; 2. Andrew Birch; 3. Egypt, Spain and Switzerland; 4. Hugh Lawrie (House was the medical series); 5. Angela Burr (Olivia Colman); 6. Limpet , he seemingly saved his son from kidnappers; 7. Tradepass; 8. C) ZitterZatter; 9. Lance Corcoran; 10. C) €40,000. ODD ONE OUT: 2004 - Pride and Prejudice - Mr Collins. The rest were Tom Hiddleston roles, this part was played by Tom Hollander.

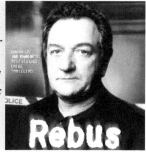

A British detective drama series based on the Inspector Rebus novels by the Scottish author Ian Rankin. The series was produced by STV Studios for the ITV network, and four series were broadcast between 26 April 2000 and 7 December 2007. The first series starred John Hannah as DI John Rebus. After Hannah quit the series, the role of Rebus was re-cast, with Ken Stott appearing as Rebus in three subsequent series, which were produced in-house by STV. Total of 14 Episodes.

1. Gayanne Potter in the first series and Claire Price in series 2-4 played Rebus's sidekick. What was her name?
A) DS Siobhan Clarke B) DS Barbara Havers C) DI Helen Morton

2. In which city was the action played out in *Rebus*?

3. Which football team does John Rebus support?

4. Rebus was on the trail of The Disciple who had the same modus operandi as a prolific serial killer who had killed in the 1980s. What was that killer called?
A) The Archdeacon B) The Preacher C) The Bishop

5. In series 2 Rebus investigated a death of a foreign national who was found dead in a seedy Edinburgh slum with a racist slur left on their head. What nationality was the victim? A) Iraqi B) Libyan C) Kosovan

6. In series 3 Rebus investigated the death of a prostitute who was buried alive beneath which famous Scottish landmark?
A) Edinburgh Castle B) The Five Sisters C) Arthur's Seat

7. In *A Question of Blood* Rebus witnessed a plane crash and was distraught. Why? A) He thought Siobhan was on board B) It crashed on to the pitch of Hibernian FC C) It landed on an Edinburgh tour bus

8. John Rebus was born in Scotland, but his family originated in continental Europe. From which country did his ancestors hail?

9. Which of these was one of John Rebus' favourite drinking establishments?
A) The Bristol Bar B) The London Bar C) The Oxford Bar

10. All good fictional cops have an idiosyncratic car. In the books Rebus drives a Saab, on TV he drove which make? A) Skoda B) Volvo C) Mercedes

Linked anagram: *BEHIND RUG*

BRITISH COMEDY 2: *1. Albert Steptoe; 2. Thermoman; 3. Peter Cushing; 4. Minehead; 5. You Rang M'Lord; 6. Colin Wetherby; 7. The Lovers; 8. Ronnie Barker; 9. Lurcio; 10. By frog; 11. Peter Davison and Robert Glenister; 12. Harry Worth; 13. Kathy Burke and Paul Whitehouse; 14. May to December; 15. The Comedians.*

Chat Show Time

A chat show is a programming genre structured around the act of spontaneous conversation. It is distinguished from other programmes by certain common attributes. In a chat show, a person (or group of guests) discusses various topics put forth by the host. The personality of the host shapes the tone of the show. Chat shows go back to the 1950s.

1. Which diminutive comedian inspired the red chair in *The Graham Norton Show,* allowing members of the public air their most cringe worthy secrets?

2. What was the name of Alan Carr's show that ran from 2009 - 2017?

3. What husband and wife team hosted an evening chat show from 2001-2009 on Channel 4 and included OJ Simpson as a guest on their first show?

4. Who hosted *The Last Resort*?

5. Which Liverpool comedian had a chat show on television channel W from 2016-2018? Guests ranged from Jeremy Corbyn to Professor Green.

6. Which upper-middle class, macho hell-raising actor was extremely drunk when he appeared on the Michael Aspel Show, *Aspel & Company* in 1984?

7. Which famous gardener chaired an afternoon chat show on ITV from 2007-2014?

8. Since 2017, which 'Dublin mother' has opened her house door for a Saturday night show in which she and the family are joined by celebrity guests?

9. On *The Des O'Connor Show* in the mid 80s, a risqué story about a Second World War Polish pilot flying in the RAF got a Liverpool comedian a TV ban. Who was he?

10. Who held *Open House* on Channel 5 from 1998 and 2003?

11. Which mock chat show host's most famous question was probably one she asked Debbie McGee in 1995; 'So what first attracted you to the millionaire Paul Daniels?'

12. Which bird famously wrestled Michael Parkinson to the floor in 1976?

13. Which Aussie journalist presented *Saturday Night Clive* from 1989-91?

14. Which chat show aired 3 nights a week from 1985 - 1991?

15. 'Hello, Possums'. With her wisteria hue hair and face furniture and her favourite flowers, gladdies, which character gave us her Treatment in 2007?

REBUS: 1. A) DS Siobhan Clarke; 2. Edinburgh; 3. Hibernian; 4. B) The Preacher; 5. C) Kosovan; 6. B) The Five Sisters; 7. A) He thought Siobhan was on board; 8. Poland; 9. C) The Oxford Bar; 10. C) Mercedes. LINKED ANAGRAM: Edinburgh.

A British sitcom broadcast by the BBC between 1961 and 1963 and by LWT between 1977 and 1978. The scripts were by Ronald Wolfe and Ronald Chesney, who later wrote Wild, Wild Women, Meet the Wife and On the Buses. Wild, Wild Women was a period variation of The Rag Trade. The action centred on a fictional small clothing workshop (the title is a reference to the textile industry).
There were 5 series. 58 Episodes.

1. What was the name of the clothing company featured in the show?
 A) London Britches   B) Fenner Fashions   C) Freddie's Fabrics

2. Who played the militant shop steward Paddy Fleming, ever ready to strike, with a blast on the whistle and the catchphrase 'Everybody out!'?

3. Which former star of *On the Buses* played pattern cutter Reg Turner?

4. In the first episode in 1961, Fenner was far from happy when factory girl Brenda brought something to work. What was it?

5. Harold Fenner (Peter Jones) installed a vending machine. Lily discovers it accepted buttons. When the girls received their pay packets, what do they find in them?

6. Which actress played the sailor-chasing blonde, and the firm's occasional model, Carole?

7. In series 3, carrying on the role of the 'dumb' blonde came the buxom Judy, whom storylines decreed would act as a love interest for Reg. The actress had also appeared in another role in Series 1. Who played Judy?

8. In series 2 and 3 the character Shirley was played by which actress who, amongst numerous other roles, played Rodney Trotter's mother-in-law?

9. The show ran on BBC from 1961-1963. It was revived on ITV in 1977-1978. Mr Fenner and Paddy returned; but who reprised her Olive role from another sitcom?

10. Which character was courted by a rival firm and sneaked out for an interview under the guise of terrible toothache. She arrives back rather the worse for drink, and having also been seen, whilst out, by Mrs Fenner, she decided to quit?

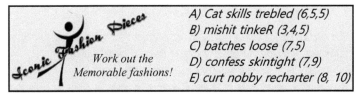

Work out the Memorable fashions!

A) Cat skills trebled (6,5,5)
B) mishit tinkeR (3,4,5)
C) batches loose (7,5)
D) confess skintight (7,9)
E) curt nobby recharter (8, 10)

CHAT SHOW TIME: 1. Ronnie Corbett; 2. Alan Carr: Chatty Man; 3. Richard Madeley & Judy Finnigan; 4. Jonathan Ross; 5. John Bishop; 6. Oliver Reed; 7. Alan Titchmarsh; 8. Agnes Brown, All Around To Mrs Brown's; 9. Stan Boardman (These Fokkers were Messerschmitts!); 10. Gloria Hunniford; 11. Mrs Merton; 12. Emu (with the help of Rod Hull!); 13. Clive James; 14. Wogan; 15. Edna Everage.

Wire in the Blood

A British crime drama series, created and produced by Coastal Productions for Tyne Tees Television. Broadcast on ITV from 14 November 2002 to 31 October 2008. Based on characters created by Val McDermid including University clinical psychologist, Dr Tony Valentine Hill.

1. The series was set in which fictional town, assumed to lie within West Yorkshire? A) Shefton B) Ilkhampton C) Bradfield

2. The show followed the MIT of the Metropolitan Police CID and the assistance provided to detectives by clinical psychologist and serial offender profiler Dr. Tony Hill? What does MIT stand for?

3. The leading role, Dr Tony Hill, was played by a Geordie, who was one half of a chart-topping duo? Can you name him?

4. Tony formed a close bond with Carol Jordan, between them they put many serial killers behind bars.   A) Who played Carol?   B) Tony was later devastated to learn at the end of Series 3 that she had left to go to work in which country?

5. What is Tony often seen carrying around?

6. Carol's successor found that working on murder investigations could cause strain at home, where she was a single mum. What was her name?
A) DI Alex Fielding   DI) Kate Burrows   C) DI Helen Grace

7. In *Unnatural Vices* DC Chris Collins received what shocking token from the killer?   A) Severed finger B) An ear lobe C) A blood stained pendant

8. ITV cancelled the series in 2009, citing high production costs, estimated at how much per episode?   A) £250,000   B) 500,000   C) £750,000

9. Carol Jordan was replaced by DI Alex Fleming for Series 4-6. Who played the role of a detective willing to put in the hours to get the case solved?

10. Of the 24 Episodes, how many were based upon Val McDermid's books?
A) 18   B) 12   C) 4

'The Wire in the Blood'

Where the title came from and what it means...

The phrase 'the wire in the blood' comes from T.S. Eliot's Four Quartets. – 'The trilling wire in the blood/sings below inveterate scars/appeasing long-forgotten wars.'

THE RAG TRADE: 1. B) Fenner Fashions; 2. Miriam Karlin; 3. Reg Varney; 4. A baby; 5. Buttons; 6. Sheila Hancock; 7. Barbara Windsor; 8. Wanda Ventham; 9. Anna Karen (On the Buses); 10. Paddy Fleming. ICONIC FASHION PIECES: A) Little Black Dress; B) The Mini Skirt; C) Chelsea Boots; D) Fishnet Stockings; E) Burberry Trenchcoat.

A British serial made by London Weekend Television for ITV and broadcast from 24 September to 17 December 1978. This period serial starred Francesca Annis in the title role of Lillie Langtry. She had played the same character in the 1975 ATV serial Edward the Seventh. Lillie Langtry, trapped in a loveless marriage, took full advantage of her beauty; attracting many lovers and admirers including the Prince of Wales. 13 episodes.

1. What was Lillie's nickname? A) Silly Lily B) Jersey Lily C) Passion Flower

2. Lillie married a wealthy widower who was a ship owner. What was his name? A) Edward Langtry B) Harry Langtry C) Tom Langtry

3. Where did Lillie live at the start of married life?
A) Portsmouth B) Southampton C) Bristol

4. Whose sketch of Lillie heralded her arrival as a professional beauty in great demand by artists? A) Frank Miles B) John Millais C) James Whistler

5. Which writer, known for his biting wit, flamboyant dress and glittering conversational skill, became a close friend of Lillie?
A) George Bernard Shaw B) Oscar Wilde C) D H Lawrence

6. Which member of the Royal Family did Edward cite in his divorce papers?

7. What was the name of Lillie's daughter of whom she told the world was her niece? A) Victoria Ann B) Sarah Jane C) Jeanne Marie

8. With which wealthy New Yorker did Lillie embark upon a relationship?
A) Peter Stuyvesant B) Freddy Gebhard C) Cornelius Vanderbilt

9. Lillie fell in with a wealthy racehorse owner and amateur jockey. The relationship was abusive and bullying. At the Prince's behest, she did not press charges when one of his beatings nearly killed her. Who was he?
A) George Baird, Squire of Abingdon B) Hugo de Bathe
C) Louis Battenberg

10. Lillie lived at Regal Lodge for 23 years and received many celebrated guests, not least of whom was the Prince of Wales. She sold it in 1919 and moved to a place where she would remain for the rest of her days. Where did she move? A) Jersey B) Guernsey C) Monaco

TRIVIA QUESTION:
Who connects Only Fools and Horses with Lillie?

WIRE IN THE BLOOD: 1. C) Bradfield; 2. Major Incident Team; 3. Robson Green; 4. A) Hermione Norris, B) South Africa; 5. A blue plastic bag; 6. DI Alex Fielding; 7. A) Severed finger; 8. C) £750,000; 9. Simone Lahbib; 10. C) 4 (Only Episodes 1 & 2 of Series 1), The Mermaids Singing and Shadows Rising, 2nd Episode , Series 4, Torment, and 2nd Episode, Series 6, Falls the Shadow.

A British sitcom produced by Yorkshire Television for ITV who originally broadcast the programme from 2 September 1974 until 9 May 1978. It was adapted for television by Eric Chappell from his 1971 stage play The Banana Box (retained as the working title early in the series). Was the highest-ranking ITV sitcom in BBC's 100 Best Sitcoms 2004 poll. 4 Series. 28 Episodes.

1. What was the full name of the miserly, seedy, and ludicrously self-regarding landlord of the run-down Victorian townhouse who rents out his shabby bed-sits to a variety of tenants?

2. In what county was the rundown Victorian townhouse located?

3. What job did the educated, romantic life-long spinster Miss Ruth Jones have?
A) Accountant   B) Teacher   C) College Administrator

4. Who played the likeable, long haired, left-wing medical student Alan Moore?

5. A second generation British African from Croydon was the last of the trio of regular characters. Throughout the series he claimed to be an 'African Prince' and to be the son of an African tribal chief. What was his name?
A) Philip Smith   B) Philip Jones   C) Philip Williams

6. In the first series a professional wrestler known as 'The Animal' is also a lodger. What was the name of the character played by Derek Newark? *(Just his surname!)*

7. Which character, played by Denholm Elliott, preyed on Rigsby's gullibility by conning him out of money, recommending that he bought shares in an oil company which drilled in the Pennines?   A) Daley   B) Seymour   C) Boyce

8. Rigsby thought he had run over his cat Vienna, but it turned out to be;
A) A coat   B) Ruth's fur stole   C) A fox

9. In the Episode *Charisma* Philip told Rigsby of an African love rite whereby the suitor burnt a piece of wood from the 'love tree' outside his sweetheart's hut. Rigsby duly approached Ruth with the wood and she told him to ... What?
A) Extinguish your stick Mr Rigsby   B) Come back later Rupert
C) Come in Rupert

10. Exotic dancer Marilyn moved in with a python she used in her routine. He was harmless but Philip tells Rigsby that he was a Fawcett's python, a deadly snake. Of course he escaped, and the boys scare Rigsby with a stuffed toy python. What was the snake's name?   A) Monty   B) Charlie   C) Farrah

LILLIE: 1. B) Jersey Lily; 2. A) Edward Langtry; 3. B) Southampton; 4. A) Frank Miles; 5. B) Oscar Wilde; 6. Edward, Prince of Wales; 7. C) Jeanne Marie; 8. B) Freddy Gebhard; 9. A) George Baird, Squire of Abingdon; 10. C) Monaco. TRIVIA QUESTION: Dennis Lill played the Prince of Wales in Lillie and Alan Parry in Only Fools and Horses.

A British drama series centred on the work of mobile, uniformed police in Lancashire. Produced by the BBC, it ran from January 1962 until September 1978. The series differed sharply from earlier police procedurals. With a Northern setting, it injected elements of harsh realism into the Police image which some found unwelcome. 12 series. 801 Episodes

1. What was the name of the police station that was the HQ in this series?

2. The title came from the radio call signs allocated by Lancashire Constabulary. What was the non-existent call signs used by the two featured cars?

3. One character appeared throughout the series in 629 episodes. Who rose through the ranks from PC-DC-Sgt-Insp?

4. A very well known star of an eponymous TV detective series which ran from 1987 to 2000 was in 4 episodes of Z Cars as a humble PC. Can you name him?

5. The still instantly recognised theme music was based upon the traditional folk song 'Johnny Todd'. Which football team still plays the tune as their team enters?

6. Terence Edmond was in 78 episodes. His final appearance saw him drown in a heroic but misguided attempt to save a young boy. Which PC did he play?

7. The character of PC Bob Steele, played by Jeremy Kemp, was in the original cast Not a lot of people know that the part was refused, by which actor who became a top film star?
A) Sean Connery   B) Stanley Baker   C) Michael Caine

8. One other actor appeared spasmodically throughout the series. In the very first episode he was Chief Superintendent Robins. Who did he play in the last ever episode *Pressure* in 1978?
A) The Chief Constable   B) A villain   C) A PC

9. PC David Graham was played by a man who went on to become a top screenwriter, winning Best Original Screenplay for Chariots of Fire at the 1982 BAFTA awards. He also won best supporting actor for Kes (1986). Who was he?

10. In episode *Made For Each Other* in 1963, Smith and Weir have just forcefully caught Elena Collins who has been squatting in an unoccupied house. Smith: 'What's you name'? Elena: 'Judy Garland'. Weir: 'Oh aye'. Elena: 'Shall I sing a song, like - prove it?' Who played Elena and went on to become a Dame?

RISING DAMP: 1. Rupert Rigsby; 2. Yorkshire (likely near Leeds); 3 C) College Administrator; 4. Richard Beckinsale; 5. A) Philip Smith; 6. Spooner; 7. B) Seymour; 8. B) Ruth's fur stole; 9. A) Extinguish your stick Mr Rigsby (really a piece of wood from the wardrobe!); 10. C) Charlie.

A British coming-of-age sitcom, which originally aired on E4 from 2008–2010,. Created and written by Damon Beesley and Iain Morris. The misadventures of suburban teenagers involving situations of school life at fictional Rudge Park Comprehensive. 3 Series. 18 Episodes.

1. In the first episode, what pub did the boys visit first?

2. Who was the school bully and juvenile delinquent who often picks on Will in Series 1?

3. Neil was the dim-witted, gentle and gullible nice guy member of the group. What was his surname and which actor plays him?

4. Simon passed a driving test in dubious circumstances. A) What car did his father buy him and B) What colour was the replacement door he bought?

5. Which comedian played Mr Gilbert, the archetypal Head of the 6th Form?

6. Who was Geography teacher at Rudge Park, alleged to be a paedophile?

7. The youngest of the group was obsessed with sex, with almost all of his comments being about the subject. He falsely claimed to be the most sexually experienced of the group. What is his name?

8. What was Charlotte Hinchcliffe's nickname?
A) Big Lips   B) Big Jugs   C) Hot Legs

9. Who moved from an un-named private school to the comprehensive because his mother, Polly, could no longer afford the private school fees?
He is the central character and also the narrator of the show too.

10. Which of the group, who used to stick Lego up his anus when younger, said, 'I stopped believing in God when I realised it was just dog spelt backwards'?

Which of the cast played Private Pike in the remake of Dad's Army and scored the winning penalty for England v the World XI in the 2018 Soccer Aid match for Unicef at Old Trafford in front of 71,965 fans which raised over £6m?

Z CARS: 1. Newtown; 2. Z Victor 1 and Z Victor 2; 3. Bert Lynch; 4. John Thaw; 5. Everton (Watford also used the tune for several years up to 2019); 6. PC Ian Sweet; 7. C) Michael Caine; 8. A) The Chief Constable (he had risen to the very top!); 9. Colin Welland; 10. Judi Dench.

A British drama series produced by Carnival Films and distributed by BBC Worldwide, in which detectives in London's Whitechapel district dealt with murders which replicated historical crimes. The first series was first broadcast in the UK on 2 February 2009 . 4 Series . 18 Episodes.

1. In episode 1, fast-tracker DI Joseph Chandler is posted to Whitechapel by Commander Anderson to lead the investigation into the murder of a woman? Who played the role, and who is his actress wife?

2. The first series revolved around copycat murders that were committed by which unidentified serial killer active in the largely poorer areas in and around Whitechapel in 1888?

3. With time running out fast, Chandler and Miles managed to find and stop the Ripper before he completed his recreation of the murder of Mary Jane Kelly. What then happened to the Ripper?

4. Series two focused on copycat crimes of which infamous twin brothers, main perpetrators of organised crime in the East End in the 1950s /1960s?

5. A man was murdered in an old haunt of the twins. What was the name of the pub in Whitechapel, the scene of a similar murder by Ronnie Kray in 1966?

6. Managing to obtain DNA of Ronnie and Jimmy, Chandler's group managed to confirm what about their 'Kray twins'?

7. In series 3, Chandler and Miles investigated the slaughter of four people at a tailor's fortified workshop? What 1811 crime did they echo?
A) The A6 murders   B) C) Mangle St murders   C) Ratcliff Highway murders

8. In crimes echoing the Thames Torso Murders of the 1880s, what was seen running through the streets with a human arm in its mouth?

9. A 16th century torture, Peine forte et dure, was used on an unfortunate victim in Series 4. It was formerly used in the common law legal system, in which a defendant refused to plead. What did the torture involve?
A)Heavy stones   B) Water   C) Branding

10. When journalist Peter Dunn was visited by the police, he was cooking something that smelt very strange? What did his dinner guests (illegally) enjoy eating?

THE INBETWEENERS: 1. The Black Bull; 2. Mark Donovan; 3. Sutherland, Blake Harrison; 4. A) A yellow Fiat Cinquecento Hawaii, B) Red; 5. Greg Davies; 6. Mr John Kennedy; 7. Jay Cartwright; 8. B) Big Jugs; 9. Will McKenzie; 10. Neil. INBETWEENERS TRIVIA: Blake Harrison (Neil).

A 1967 British sci-fi series about an unnamed British intelligence agent who is abducted and imprisoned in a mysterious coastal village. His captors try to find out why he abruptly resigned from his job. Elements of science fiction, allegory and psychological drama, as well as spy fiction. 1 Series. 17 Episodes.

1. What number was assigned to *The Prisoner*? A) 6   B) 66   C) 666

2. In *Arrival* ice cream was available for the Villagers' enjoyment. What was the flavour of the day? A) Vanilla   B) Chocolate   C) Strawberry

3. In *The Chimes of Big Ben, The Prisoner* told the Colonel the location of the Village. Where did he say it was? A) Morocco, in the desert
B) Lithuania, on the Baltic, 30 miles from the Polish border
C) An uncharted island off France

4. Why did Number 6 complain about his driver, Number 58, in *Free For All*?
A) 'She will not go away, and she doesn't even speak English'
B) 'I need a drink. She drives far too slowly.'   C) 'Just whose side is she on?

5. Seen in the Village. A penny farthing. A moke. A bicycle with awning. A helicopter. Did a car appear in the Village? Yes or No?

6. In *Checkmate,* the Chess Queen asked Number Six whether she may see him again. What did he reply? A) I'll be seeing you   B) Oh, yes, I'm here all the time   C) No, I'll probably be gone by morning

7. In which British seaside town was the cult classic filmed?
A) Barry Island   B) Blackpool   C) Portmeirion

8. Which fearsome method of terror was used to keep people in check?

9. Why was Number 6 in The Village? A) To reveal information
B) Recruited to serve as leader   C) A test subject for aliens

10. The villagers wore colourful apparel. What style is prevalent?
A) Orange hoodies   B) Polka dot waistcoats   C) Striped shirts

CAPTIVE TRIVIA
*On The Prisoner's dwelling there is a sign.
What does it say?
A) 6 PRIVATE B) 6 PENDING C) PRISONER 6*

WHITECHAPEL: *1. Rupert Penry-Jones, Devla Kirwan; 2. Jack the Ripper; 3. He escapes and commits suicide; 4. The Kray twins; 5. The Blind Beggar; 6. They were not related to the original Kray twins; 7. C) Ratcliff Highway murders; 8. A fox; 9. A) Heavy stones (Heavier and heavier stones placed upon chest until a plea was entered, or they died); 10. Rare and endangered animal species.*

A British sitcom shown on BBC1 from 1972 - 1985. Set in London, it follows the misadventures and mishaps of the staff of the retail ladies' and gentlemen's clothing departments in the flagship department store of a fictional chain. 10 Series. 70 Episodes. 1 Special shown on 28 August 2016.

1. Mr Humphries was well known for saying 'I'm free!', but he had another catchphrase when a customer was not sure of a fit. He would say - what?

2. Although we hear a great deal about Mrs Slocombe's pussy, we never actually saw the cat. True or False?

3. Captain Peacock claimed to have fought in which Campaign in WWII?

4. Mike Berry, who had several hit records, joined the cast as Mr Spooner in Series 8. In *The Pop Star* what song did Spooner record for the music company?   A) Tribute to Buddy Holly   B) Don't You Think It's Time C) Chanson D'Amour

5. What part did Mr Lucas play in the *Ballet of the Toys*?
A) Little Boy Blue   B) Humpty Dumpty   C) Little Bo-Peep

6. In *By Appointment*, Miss Brahms spent her holiday having what lessons?

7. What was bumbling floor manager Mr Rumbold's first name?

8. In the episode *A Change is as Good as a Rest*, who was the first (and only) person to resign?   A) Mr Lucas   B) Mr Grainger   C) Mr Humphries

9. In *New Look*, whose voice was used to inform shoppers of special offers?

10. What were Mr Harman's two first names?
A) Warwick Castle   B) Arthur Albert   C) Beverly Harry

2016 REVIVAL CHARACTERS
Can you name the actors?

A) Captain Peacock   B) Mrs Slocombe   C) Miss Brahms   D) Mr Humphries   E) Mr Grainger

THE PRISONER: 1. A) 6; 2. C) Strawberry; 3. B) Lithuania, on the Baltic, 30 miles from the Polish border; 4. A) 'She will not go away, and she doesn't even speak English'; 5. Yes; 6. B) Oh, yes, I'm here all the time ; 7. C) Portmeirion; 8. Giant white balloons; 9. A) To reveal information; 10. C) Striped shirts. CAPTIVE TRIVIA: A) 6 PRIVATE.

A game show with panel of celebrities trying to guess what a person does for a living, or figure out who a mystery guest is. Originally aired on BBC from 16 July 1951 to 13 May 1963. BBC2 from 23 August 1973 to 25 May 1974. ITV from 26 March 1984 to 28 August 1990. 2 regional ITV stations, HTV and Meridian, revived it again from 19 September 1994 to 17 December 1996. Over 500 Episodes. Approximately 23 Series in all.

Celebrities have done some varied jobs in their past.
Can you match each job to a celebrity

CELEBRITY	JOB
1. VICKI McCLURE	A. MODEL
2. HELEN MIRREN	B. SHOWROOM SALES
3. CHERYL	C. REPORTER & FEATURE WRITER
4. KERRY KATONA	D. LUXURY FASHION BUYER
5. KATE MIDDLETON	E. AMUSEMENT PARK PROMOTER
6. MARY BERRY	F. LAP DANCER
7. ANNE HEGERTY	G. RETAIL ASSISTANT IN H SAMUEL
8. ESTHER RANTZEN	H. WAITRESS
9. KATE WINSLET	J. SANDWICH MAKER IN A DELI
10. HOLLY WILLOUGHBY	K. RESEARCHER

CELEBRITY	JOB
1. SEAN CONNERY	A. PROFESSIONAL FIRE EATER
2. MICK JAGGER	B. BUTCHER'S DELIVERY BOY
3. GERARD BUTLER	C. GRAVEDIGGER
4. SIMON COWELL	D. MILKMAN
5. PHILLIP SCHOFIELD	E. PROFESSIONAL FOOTBALLER
6. CHRISTOPHER LEE	F. POST BOY AT EMI
7. PIERCE BROSNAN	G. HOSPITAL PORTER
8. DAVID BOWIE	H. BOOKINGS CLERK
9. ROD STEWART	J. TRAINEE LAWYER
10. MARTIN COMPSTON	K. INTELLIGENCE SERVICE

ARE YOU BEING SERVED?: 1. It will ride up with wear; 2. False (She brought the cat into the and deportment store on one memorable occasion, and we saw her head poking up out of her handbag); 3. North Africa; 4. C) Chanson D'Amour; 5. A) Little Boy Blue; 6. Elocution lessons ; 7. Cuthbert; 8. B) Mr Grainger; 9. Young Mr Grace; 10. C) Beverly Harry. *REVIVAL CAST:* A) John Challis, B) Sherrie Hewson; C) Niky Wardley, D) Jason Watkins, E) Roy Barraclough.

190

A British costume drama series, adapted by the BBC from Flora Thompson's trilogy of semi-autobiographical novels about the English countryside, published between 1939 and 1943. The first episode aired on 13 January 2008 on BBC One and BBC HD. The series is set in the small hamlet of Lark Rise and the wealthier neighbouring market town of Candleford towards the end of the 19th century. The series chronicles the daily lives of farmworkers, craftsmen, and gentry, observing the characters in loving, boisterous, and competing communities of families, rivals, friends, and neighbours. 4 Series. 40 Episodes.

1. In which county was Lark Rise to be found?

2. The main character was Laura. Who were her parents?

3. Interior scenes were shot in a warehouse on Beeches Industrial Estate, which is in: A) Yate, South Gloucestershire B) Pinewood C) Coryton, Cardiff

4. What was Twister's real name? A) Tucker   B) Tom   C) Tim

5. Who played postmistress Dorcas Lane?

6. What was Robert Timmins' job?
A) Gravedigger   B) Train Conductor   C) Stonemason

7. The arrival of a new teacher caused divisions in the two communities. His radical views raised eyebrows in Candleford, but in Lark Rise he endeared himself to the residents. What was his name?
A) Mr Ashlow   B) Mr Delafield   C) Mr Dowland

8. The narrator was an, unseen, adult Laura Timmins. Which actress voiced the introduction to each episode as Laura?   A) Sarah Lancashire
B) Vanessa Redgrave   C) Rebecca Front

9. Laura fell in love with Fisher Bloom, a travelling clockmaker, who was building a clock commissioned by James Dowland. Which *Vera* sidekick played Fisher?

10. The death of Margaret Ellison's father united the communities of Lark Rise and Candleford. Miss Ellison was overwhelmed with grief and oblivious to someone's affection and his desire to marry her. Who ?

ANAGRAM TIME: ADDERS FLORA INTERLOCK

*WHAT'S MY LINE?: WOMEN: 1G, 2E, 3H, 4F, 5D, 6B, 7C, 8K, 9J, 10A.
WOMEN: 1D, 2G, 3J, 4F, 5H, 6K, 7A, 8B, 9C, 10E.*

SECRET ARMY

A drama made by the BBC & BRT (now VRT) created by Gerard Glaister. A fictional Belgian resistance movement in German-occupied Belgium during WW2 dedicated to returning Allied airmen, usually having been shot down by the Luftwaffe, to Great Britain. Made in the UK and Belgium. 3 series were broadcast on BBC1 between 7 September 1977 and 15 December 1979. A total of 43

1. Lisa Colbert ran a Brussels-based resistance organisation that helped Allied aircrew to evade capture and return to Britain via Switzerland or Spain. What was its name?
A) Salvation   B) Sustain   C Lifeline

2. Flight Lieutenant John Curtis a former evader, was sent back by London as a Special Operations Executive liaison officer to coordinate its activity. What was his pseudonym? A) M Maurice   B) M Renée   C) Madame Fanny

3. Which fervent Nazi was assigned to work with Luftwaffe Major Erwin Brandt and close down the evasion line? A) Sturmbannführer Kessler B) Major Franz Ulmann   C) Major Willi Schaeffer

4. Albert Foiret sold Cafe Candide and bought an upper-class black-market restaurant, Restaurant Candide was prominently located in the Grand-Place. Why did London part own and finance the restaurant?

5. Whose character changed from dowdy waitress to sultry chanteuse?
A) Madeleine Duclos   B) Monique Duchamps   C) Mimi Labonq

6. Max Brocard was an expert forger with some obvious communist leanings. What did he do in the evenings in Restaurant Candide?

7. Who was the farmer who acted as the group's wireless operator and passed on messages from London to the Candide? A) Rene Artois   B) Marius Pontmercy   C) Alain Muny

8. Max was shot dead by the Germans and civil police whilst taking part in resistance activities. Their whereabouts had been tipped off by whom?

9. A newly arrived, cynical and world-weary war hero, found himself in constant conflict with Standartenführer Kessler. Who was he?   A) Major Hans Reinhardt   B) Colonel Kurt von Strohm   C) Major Hans Geering

10. Kessler engineered a court-martial of Reinhardt for allowing himself to be captured and for disobeying the orders of a superior officer. Despite there being only flimsy evidence, what is the outcome?

LARK RISE TO CANDLEFORD: 1. Oxfordshire; 2. Robert & Emma Timmins; 3. A) Yate, South Gloucestershire; 4. B) Tom; 5. Julia Sawalha; 6. C) Stonemason; 7. B) Mr Delafield; 8. Sarah Lancashire; 9. Mark McNulty; 10. Pious postman Thomas Brown. *ANAGRAM:* Lark Rise To Candleford.

Every January one programme has the accolade of being named as the most watched programme during the previous year. This round names 20 such programmes, and also the year in which they each came out top. Just match the programme with the correct year that it topped the viewers charts.

PROGRAMME	YEAR
1. BRITAIN'S GOT TALENT - Diversity win (18.29m)	A. 1970
2. ONLY FOOLS & HORSES -French Wine plus Gary! (17.4m)	B. 1973
3. FILM. JAWS - shown on 8 October (23.3m)	C. 1974
4. LIVE AID from Wembley and JFK Stadium (24.5m)	D. 1976
5. APOLLO 13 SPLASHDOWN (28.6m)	E. 1979
6. GAVIN & STACEY - Nessa's proposal to Smithy (17.92m)	F. 1981
7. ROYAL WEDDING - Prince William & Catherine (13.59m)	G. 1984
8. TO THE MANOR BORN - The First Noel (23.95m)	H. 1985
9. CORONATION STREET - Platts and Carmel Finnan (20.73)	J. 1989
10. A MATTER OF LOAF & DEATH - Wallace & Gromit (16.15)	K. 1993
11. ENGLAND V ARGENTINA - World Cup, Beckham off (23.78)	L. 1994
12. NEW YEARS EVE FIREWORKS from London (13.53m)	M. 1995
13. TORVILL & DEAN - Olympics, Bolero!	N. 1998
14. ROYAL VARIETY PERFORMANCE Max & Rowan (20.55m)	P. 2001
15. ROYAL WEDDING - Princess Anne & Mark Phillips (27.60m)	Q. 2002
16. THE SWEENEY - Sweet Smell of Succession (20.68m)	R. 2008
17. ONLY FOOLS AND HORSES - Bankrupt! (21.35m)	S. 2009
18. FILM: CROCODILE DUNDEE - Christmas Day (21.77m)	T. 2011
19. PANORAMA SPECIAL - Princess Diana (22.78m)	U. 2013
20. LOVE THY NEIGHBOUR - Bananas (21.01m)	V. 2019

SECRET ARMY: 1. C) Lifeline; 2. A) Monsieur Maurice; 3. Sturmbannführer Kessler ;
4. To overhear German officers indiscretions and provide better cover for the resistance;
5. B) Monique Duchamps; 6. Accompanies Monique on the piano; 7. C) Alain Muny; 8. Albert;
9. A) Major Hans Reinhardt; 10. Reinhardt is shot by a German firing squad.

A British sitcom about employees in a fictional supermarket, which debuted on Sky One on 4 August 2011 and ended on 23 December 2018. The series was filmed in a purpose-built replica supermarket in the Bottle Yard Studios in Bristol . 7 Series. 71 Episodes. 5 Specials.

1. What was the name of the fictional supermarket in Warrington, Cheshire?

2. Who was the university educated store manager and a long-term employee of the company played by Jason Watkins?

3. Who was appointed manager of a rival discount chain opening a store directly opposite before joining the *Trollied* team as regional manager?

4. Who rose from a lowly role stacking shelves and manning checkouts, through a few traumatic personal problems, to be deputy manager?

5. Brian became the new pharmacist; having previously worked for Boots, but deciding not to reveal why he left. Which actor took the part, a big change from playing DCI Banks?

6. Which senior worker was originally placed on the delicatessen counter before she found a new home with Brian at the store's pharmacy?

7. Which nice guy optimist, who once had everything - the job, the house, the family, had to start again on the shop floor to surprisingly find love?

8. Which gross couple get away with doing as little as possible but show a frankly disgusting level of intimacy with each other?

9. Linda and Sue work together every day. They are as inattentive and unhelpful as is humanly possible. In which section were they employed?

10. Who was the daughter of Brendan O'Connor, the owner of the entire store's empire, who joins the team? *He wanted her to learn the business from the ground up but she is oblivious to concepts like work and not being minted.*

10 Anagrams 1 Link

CAN YOU WORK THEM OUT AND GET THE CONNECTION?

1. ACHIEVE FOOT TORPEDO	6. LAID
2. MINOR ROSS	7. COTES
3. DILL	8. EXCESS PESTER
4. ABYSS RUINS	9. RASP
5. ARISE TWO	10. CRAMPNESS DARKEN

WHAT YEAR WAS IT 2: 1S, 2Q, 3F, 4H, 5A, 6V, 7T, 8E, 9K, 10R, 11N, 12U, 13L, 14G, 15B, 16D, 17P, 18J, 19M, 20C.

A British soap opera created by Granada Television. Shown on ITV since 9 December 1960. The programme typically centres around the residents of a cobbled, terraced street in Weatherfield, a fictional town based on inner-city Salford. Over 10,000 Episodes shown.

1. In December 2012. Which company was named as the new sponsor and, as at November 2020 remains the longest lasting sponsor of Corrie?

2. Hilda Ogden left Coronation Street on Christmas Day. Can you remember which year? A) 1984   B) 1985   C) 1986   D) 1987

3. Two regular characters died in a 2010 tram crash, along with a taxi driver? Can you remember the names of the two regulars who were killed?

4. What was the name of the retirement complex where Ken Barlow and Norris Cole lived, before Ken then decided to go back to Coronation Street?

5. How did Peter and Susan Barlow's mum Valerie (played by Anne Reid) die in 1971?

6. Regarded as one of the best soap villains of all time, Alan Bradley met his end when he was run down b a Blackpool tram in 1989. Can you remember the destination shown on the tram?

A) Fleetwood B) Bispham C) Starr Gate D) Pleasure Beach

7. Ivy Brennan left the show in 1994 after the final collapse of her marriage to Don. Where did she go?

8. In 1997 'Free the Weatherfield One' was the talk of the nation. Who was the 'Weatherfield One' who had the nation supporting her injustice?

9. Butcher Fred Elliott, I say Fred Elliott, lost Weatherfield the prize at the French-English black pudding contest. How?   A) He tried to bribe the French judges B) He switched the entry tags   C) He used Aldi bought products

10. To celebrate Corrie's 50th anniversary in 2010, Corriepedia embarked on a mission to find out who were the fifty all-time favourite Coronation Street characters. Who came number one?
A) Hilda Ogden   B) Vera Duckworth
C) Sophie Webster   D) Blanche Hunt

On Friday, April 8, 2005, seventeen million viewers watched episode 5,998, in which Ken Barlow remarried ex-wife Deirdre Rachid. This was four million more than had watched the real-life Royal Wedding between the Prince of Wales and Camilla Parker-Bowles earlier that day.

TROLLIED: *1. Valco; 2. Gavin Strong; 3. Cheryl Fairweather; 4. Katie McVey; 5. Stephen Tompkinson; 6. Margaret; 7. Neville; 8. Colin & Lisa; 9. Customer Relations desk; 10. Charlotte. 10 anagrams, 1 link: UK Food Supermarkets. 1. The Cooperative Food; 2. Morrisons; 3. Lidl; 4. Sainsburys; 5. Waitrose; 6. Aldi; 7. Tesco; 8. Tesco Express; 9. Spar; 10. Marks and Spencer.*

 A political satire British sitcom written by Antony Jay and Jonathan Lynn. Split over three, seven-episode series, it was first transmitted on BBC2 from 1980 to 1984. A sequel, Yes, Prime Minister, ran for 16 episodes from 1986 to 1988. A mix of questions from both series.

1. When Jim Hacker is chosen for Cabinet, he was Minister of ....?

2. Which multi-award winning Knight of the Realm played Sir Humphrey Appleby, the Permanent Secretary to the Minister?

3. In *Official Secrets* who accidentally told the press that Hacker had tried to suppress the publication of the former Prime Minister's memoirs?

4. In *The Diplomatic Incident* what does the French President propose to hand to the Queen as a present?

5. In *A Patron of the Arts* what does Jim propose to do with the National Theatre?

6. In the *National Education Service* which language does Sir Humphrey speak, that Jim cannot understand? A) French   B) German   C) Latin

7. According to Jim Hacker which newspaper was read by people who think they run the country? A) Daily Mirror   B) Daily Mail   C) The Times

8. What was Sir Humphrey's favourite word to describe decisions with which he disagreed? A) Foolhardy   B) Courageous   C) Unwise

9. Bernard often used to interject into discussions when he observed what linguistic error? A) Mixed metaphor   B) Split infinitive   C) Spoonerism

10. In an episode on media influence, Bernard said, 'Sun readers don't care who runs the country.........'   A) Because they only look at the pictures B) As long as she's got big tits   C) As long as they get their benefits

MAJORITIES AT UK GENERAL ELECTIONS - MATCH THEM UP!

ELECTED PRIME MINISTER	YEAR
1. TONY BLAIR (LABOUR)	A. 1955 - Majority 60
2. MARGARET THATCHER (CON)	B. 1964 - Majority 4
3. HAROLD WILSON (LABOUR)	C. 1983 - Majority 144
4. BORIS JOHNSON (CON)	D. 2005 - Majority 66
5. SIR ANTHONY EDEN (CON)	E. 2019 - Majority 80

CORONATION STREET: 1. Compare The Market; 2. D) Christmas Day 1987; 3. Ashley Peacock and Molly Dobbs; 4. Still Waters; 5. An electric shock when using a faulty electrical outlet in her home; 6. B) Bispham; 7. On a long-term retreat in a convent, where she had a stroke and died. In 1995; 8. Deirdre Barlow; 9. A) tried to bribe the French judges; 10. D) Blanche Hunt.

A Scottish crime drama broadcast from 10 March 2013. Initially based upon the novels of Ann Cleeves. The story takes place largely on the eponymous Scottish archipelago, although much of the series' filming is done on the Scottish mainland, with only some location filming actually taking place in Shetland. Five series have been broadcast as of April 2019. 26

1. Ann Cleeves also wrote another series of novels about a detective that has also been made into a television series. Can you name the other series?

2. Douglas Henshall was the star of the show, what is his character's name?

3. In *Red Bones* elderly Mima Wilson was shot dead outside her croft. What was taking place on her land at the time?

4. Filming locations have included the main port of the Shetland Islands and on the North Link ferry approaching it. What was the name of the port?

5. In *Blue Lightning* a scientist was found dead in what sort of nature centre on Fair Isle?

6. *Series 4. Episode 1* the actors who play Duncan Hunter & Gail Callahan also worked together on Line of Duty in 2012 as DCC Mike Dryden and DS Jayne Akers respectively. Can you name them?

7. In *Dead Water* a journalist died in a suspicious car accident. He was an old friend of Perez's who was chasing a lead about what controversial plan?

8. In *Series 3. Episode 2* the body of a young man, Robbie Morton, was discovered in a shipping container. What identical body modification soon linked the victim to the chief suspect?

9. *Series 5. Episode 1.* Perez realised a modern slave trafficking ring was involved after gruesome remains were washed up on the shore. What was the first body part discovered?

10. From Series 2 Julie Graham appeared as Rhona Kelly. What was her job?

SHETLAND HISTORY
1. What is the Shetland name given to a basket used for carrying fish?
a) A büddhie b) a caisie c) a kishie

2. What was the real name of the Shetland poet we know as 'Vagaland'?
a) Emily Milne b) Thomas Alexander Robertson c) Basil Anderson

3. Who wrote the words to the Up-Helly-Aa song?
a) JJ Haldane Burgess b) Patrick Stewart c) Johnnie Notions

YES MINISTER / YES PRIME MINISTER: 1. Administrative Affairs; 2. Nigel Hawthorne; 3. Bernard Woolley; 4. A puppy; 5. Sell it; 6. C) Latin; 7. A) Daily Mirror; 8. B) Courageous; 9. A) Mixed metaphor; 10. B) As long as she's got big tits. *ELECTION MAJORITIES:* 1D, 2C, 3B, 4E, 5A.

A variety show attended by senior members of the British Royal Family. Held annually in the UK to raise money for the Royal Variety Charity. The evening's performance is presented as a live variety show and consists of family entertainment that includes comedy, music, dance, magic and other speciality acts. 91 Episodes to date.

1. By what name is the show otherwise known?

2. The first ever Royal Variety Performance was held in the presence of King George V and Queen Mary in?
A) 1912   B) 1922   C) 1932

3. Which famous music hall artiste was regarded as too risque to perform in front of Royalty and left out of the line up; so she staged a rival show in a nearby theatre 'by command of the British people'?

4. When The Beatles appeared in 1963 John Lennon said 'Will the people in the cheaper seats clap your hands? And for the rest of you ......?

5. In 1987 the 'Understudy of the evening award' went to which tycoon? He was Eartha Kitt's companion as she sang her distinctive song 'Old Fashioned Girl.'

6. In 1966, which football squad came on to the stage after a major victory?

7. What year did the 'Queen of British Soul' Beverly Knight MBE, perform the national anthem to kick off the show?

8. In 2009 the show was held at the Blackpool Opera House. The cast included Faryl Smith, Michael Buble, Andre Rieu and Lady Gaga. Who was hosting the show on his third Royal Variety appointment?

9. Dennis Waterman and Maureen Lipman as 'A Couple of Swells', brought the house down in front of the Queen and the Duke of Edinburgh in what year?

10. For the Queen's Silver Jubilee in 1977 two American stars were due to co-host the show. Sadly one died just weeks before the show. Bob Hope did appear and paid tribute to whom when he said he was 'A man who meant an awful lot to me and an awful lot to the world. He was the greatest entertainer of them all'?

MOST APPEARANCES ON THE ROYAL VARIETY SHOW
Name the artistes pictured below (number of appearances is shown)

A. 10 *appearances*   **B. 10**   **C. 13**   **D. 10**   **E. 16**

SHETLAND: *1. Vera; 2. DI Jimmy Perez; 3. An archaeological dig; 4. Lerwick; 5. A bird observatory; 6. Mark Bonnar and Allison McKenzie; 7. A new gas pipeline; 8. A tattoo; 9. A severed hand; 10. Procurator Fiscal (prosecutes criminal cases in sheriff courts & investigates sudden, suspicious, & unexplained deaths in Scotland).* SHETLAND HISTORY: *1b, a caisie; 2b, Thomas Alexander Robertson; 3a, JJ Haldane Burgess.*

A British series made by Central Television for ITV between 1995 & 2001. The series features a barrister who is from a working-class upbringing in Bolton, Greater Manchester. It dealt with his battles in the courtroom as well as his domestic dramas, including the death of his devoted and affectionate wife. Later he begins dating a fellow barrister. 6 Series. 27 Episodes.

1. What was the first name of Kavanagh QC?
A) Henry   B) Michael   C) George   D) James

2. What does QC stand for, and what happens to the title if a King is the monarch?

3. At what Chambers was Kavanagh employed as a barrister?
A) River Court Chambers   B) Shoe Lane   C) Equity Court   D) Goldsmith

4. *In God We Trust* Kavanagh, driven by his desire for justice and keenness to help a former colleague Julia Piper, jetted off to assist with the appeal of a convicted murderer. What was his destination? A) Cuba   B) Bosnia   C) Florida   D) Rome

5. Whilst assisting Julia Piper what devastating news did Lizzie Kavanagh receive?

6. *In Mute of Malice* Kavanagh defended an army chaplain, made all the more difficult by the fact that his client was found to be mute of malice and refused to speak. Of what crime was the chaplain accused?

7. *Previous Convictions* - what incident involved a RAF Jet Provost trainer aircraft?

8. In *Innocency of Life* the Bishop of Norfolk asked Kavanagh to defend a young vicar in an ecclesiastical court. Ian Winfarthing had been accused by a pub landlady, Anne Murchison. What was the charge against him?

9. Which football team did Kavanagh support?
A) Manchester United B) Bolton Wanderers C) Leeds United D) Oldham Athletic

10. In *End Game* the practice's faithful clerk, Tom Buckley, set off down the corridor in a war-dance of glee when he heard the news that had also devastated conniving Jeremy Aldermarten QC. What was the news?

JOHN THAW - ONE OF TELEVISION'S GREATS

Here are just a few of the characters he portrayed. Can you name them?

A   B   C   D   E   F

THE ROYAL VARIETY PERFORMANCE: 1. Royal Command Performance; 2. A) 1912; 3. Marie Lloyd; 4. 'If you'll just rattle your jewellery.'; 5. Richard Branson; 6. England Football World Cup winning squad; 7. 2015; 8. Peter Kay; 9. 1985; 10. Bing Crosby. MOST APPEARANCES: A) Arthur Askey; B) Shirley Bassey; C) Max Bygraves; D) Harry Secombe; E) The Tiller Girls.

A musical drama and its sequel. On ITV in 1976/1977. The storyline followed the ups and downs of a fictional female rock band called the Little Ladies as they struggled for recognition and success. Original Series 6 Episodes. The sequel was also 6 Episodes.

1. Who played Nancy 'Q' Cunard de Longchamps, Devonia 'Dee' Rhoades and Anna Wynd; the three members of The Little Ladies?

2. The first soundtrack album reached number one in the charts and the follow up got to number 13. The girls also had a top 10 hit with OK. Which of them notched up a number one single in their own right, and what was the song?

3. All the original songs were written by Andy Mackay. Andy was a founder member of which top 1970s art rock band?

4. One of the trio of stars was quoted as saying how much they were each paid for each episode. How much was it? A) £1,500   B) £800   C) £450   D) £225

5. When the girls met they were struggling actresses auditioning for a West End style play. They got the parts but the show flopped. What was its title?
A) Broadway Annie   B) Funny Boy   C) Hamlet : The Musical   D) Saucy Jack

6. The three singers, with hugely contrasting personalities, unite with their shared catastrophe. The director then says they should form a rock band and have him as manager and songwriter. What was his name?
A) Billy White   B) Derek Huggins   C) Terry Thompson   D) Lou Glade

7. After a failed image change to 1920s style under Stavros, he then decided that another radical change is called for: this time, a pastiche of which American trio who made their name in the 1940s?

8. The girls performed in a new theme club which served food like powdered eggs and bangers and mash, all bought with ration coupons. What was it called?
A) The Shelter   B) The Blitz   C) Rick's Cafe   D) The Canteen

9. In 1977 the girls were into a Pub Tour under a new musical driving force called Harry Moon. Which star of a long-running British hospital drama played the role?
A) Hugh Quarshie   B) Charles Tingwell   C) Derek Thompson   D) David Rintoul

10. Anna left the band. Which Welsh singer replaced her?

KAVANAGH QC: 1. D) James; 2. Queen's Counsel, the title changes to KC; 3. A) River Court Chambers; 4. C) Florida; 5. She has terminal cancer; 6. Killing his brother; 7. It crashes into a crowded moto-cross event killing 22 people; 8. Sexual harassment; 9. B) Bolton Wanderers; 10. Kavanagh was to be the new head of chambers. JOHN THAW : A) DCI Endeavour Morse (Inspector Morse); B) Tom Oakley (Goodnight Mr Tom); C) DI Jack Regan (The Sweeney); D) Henry Willows (Home to Roost); E) Sergeant John Mann (Redcap); F) Stanley Duke (Stanley and the Women).

A British series, based on W. J. Burley's novels about Detective Superintendent Charles Wycliffe. It was produced by HTV and broadcast on the ITV Network, following a pilot episode on 7 August 1993, between 24 July 1994 and 5 July 1998. The series was filmed in Cornwall. 5 Series. 38 Episodes. 2 Specials.

WYCLIFFE

1. Who played the lead role Detective Superintendent Charles Wycliffe?

2. In the pilot programme Carla Mendonca played DI Lane, but throughout the 5 series the role was played by an actress who, before being cast, had just played Princess Diana's sister in *Diana: Her True Story*. Name her.

3. What was the name of the Police force that employs *Wycliffe*?
A) South West Constabulary B) Devon & Cornwall Police C) Cornish Police

4. *Wycliffe* had a musical hobby. What was it?
A) Playing jazz piano B) Singing in a Cornish choir C) Playing guitar

5. There was only one mention of a fictional Cornish town throughout the 5 series. What was the town's name? A) Dreckley B) Eastgate C) Pedrevan

6. In Series 3 when unexplained killings rocked the Bodmin community, locals became convinced that who or what had returned?

7. The detective had to leave silver anniversary celebrations when the corpses of five illegal immigrants were found - where?

8. In *The Last Rites* Rev Jordan arrived at the village church and discovered the partially clothed body of Jessica Dobell spread eagled below the cross. Who was she? A) The curate   B) The churchwarden   C) The church cleaner

9. An attractive local woman in the village of Kergwyns was killed, and the only thing stolen from the scene was her left shoe and stocking. It became apparent that she had left clues about her murder. How?
A) In a diary   B) Held in her hand   C) Embedded in crossword puzzles

10. In *Scope* what decoration was handed to Wycliffe?
A) George Cross B) Queen's Gallantry Medal   C) George Medal

ODD ONE OUT
*Which of the 6 places listed below is **NOT** in Cornwall*

Welcome to
FEOCK PARISH

COCKS
Please drive carefully through the village

A) Greensplat B) Cocks   C) Feock   D) Shaggs   E) Skinner's Bottom   F) Booby's Bay

---

ROCK FOLLIES: 1. Rula Lenska, Julie Covington and Charlotte Cornwall; 2. Julie Covington, Don't Cry For Me Argentina; 3. Roxy Music; 4. D) £225; 5. A) Broadway Annie; 6. B) Derek Huggins; 7. The Andrews Sisters; 8. B) The Blitz; 9. C) Derek Thompson; 10. Rox.

STEPTOE & SON

British sitcom written by Ray Galton and Alan Simpson about a father-and-son rag-and-bone business in London. 4 series were broadcast by the BBC from 1962-965, and from 1970-1974. The show focused on the inter-generational conflict of father and son and Harold's continually thwarted attempts to better himself, and the irresolvable love/hate relationship that exists between the pair. 8 Series. 57 Episodes.

1. Harold was played by Harry H Corbett. What did the H stand for?
A) Henry   B) Henything   C) Horace   D) Hugh

2. Wilfrid Brambell played Albert Steptoe. In which Beatles film was he Paul's grandfather? A) Help   B) Yellow Submarine   C) A Hard Day's Night

3. What was the address of Steptoe & Son's yard and home?
A) 26 Oil Drum Lane, Shepherd's Bush   B) 296 Steel Crescent, Camden Town   C) 32 Windsor Gardens, Hammersmith

4. What was the name of the Steptoe's original horse, and how old was he when he died in Series 5?

5. In *The Economist* Harold bought 4,000 sets of an item, advertised them in The Times and sold none at all. What did he buy?

6. Harold was planning an adventure at the beginning of Series 3, so he put Albert in a home. What adventure was he planning?

7. In *The Desperate Hours* two escaped prisoners from Wormwood Scrubs turned up hoping to find something to steal. The established Irish actor JG Devlin played the older escapee and the younger actor went on to play Rigsby and Reginald Perrin and other great characters. Who was he?

8. In the Episode *Men of Letters* what was Albert's contribution to the church Newsletter that had caused the Vicarage to be raided by the Police, and all copies of the newsletter confiscated?

9. True or False? Albert was fraudulently claiming for £15 per week wages being paid to Muriel his 35 year old daughter, on his tax return?

10. In *The Piano,* when they gave up on the job and leave the piano stuck in a doorway, the man says he will sue them and asked for their names. What comedy duo's names did they give him?

*WYCLIFFE: 1. Jack Shepherd; 2. Helen Masters; 3. A) South West Constabulary; 4. A) Playing jazz piano (Jack Shepherd actually did play the piano scenes); 5. B) Eastgate; 6. The Beast of Bodmin; 7. By Customs in a meat lorry at ferry terminal; 8. C) The church cleaner; 9. C) Embedded in crossword puzzles ; 10. B) Queen's Gallantry Medal. **ODD ONE OUT:** Shaggs, E Lulworth, Dorset.*

A British historical drama series about Queen Victoria's life from her accession to the throne. Created and principally written by Daisy Goodwin, The first series premiered in the United Kingdom on ITV on 28 August 2016 with eight episodes. Two further series, in 2017 and 2019, followed and a Christmas special. 25 Episodes were made in total.

1. In the first episode, *Doll 123,* Victoria told Lord Melbourne she first realised she would be queen when she was....? A) 8   B)10   C)13

2. In *Ladies in Waiting* which member of the Royal Family said that Victoria was insane like her grandfather King George III, in an effort to install a Regent to limit her power? A) Duke of Wellington   B) Duke of Cumberland   C) Lord Melbourne

3. In *Young England* who attempted to shoot Victoria during a carriage ride on 10 June 1840? The first of 8 attempts to assassinate her? A) Edward Oxford B) John Francis C) John Bean

4. Yes or No? In *Clockwork Prince* did Victoria propose marriage to Albert?

5. In *The Engine of Change* what new transportation did Albert want to try, but Victoria did not, as she felt he was trying to upstage her? A) Automobile   B) Railway locomotive   C) Passenger liner ship

6. Who played Queen Victoria? A) Olivia Colman   B) Jenna Coleman   C) Charlotte Coleman

7. At what age did Victoria inherit the throne of the United Kingdom from her paternal uncle King William IV?   A)18   B) 20   C) 21

8. In *The King Over the Water,* following another assassination attempt, Victoria and Albert travelled to the Scottish Highlands to stay with the Duke of Atholl at Blair Castle. During a walk they got lost and were missing overnight. Where had they found refuge? A) A tent   B) An elderly couple's home C) A log cabin

9. In *The White Elephant* , Foreign Secretary Lord Palmerston's public declaration of support for whom, created such bad reaction in Parliament that he was forced to resign?

10. Prince Albert's ambitious big project to celebrate industrial technology proved to be a great success, much to the Royal family's relief? What was it?

STEPTOE & SON: 1. B) Henything! There was already a Harry Corbett in Equity - presenting Sooty - so he needed a different name and just added the H; 2. C) A Hard Days Night; 3. A) 26 Oil Drum Lane, Shepherd's Bush;, 4. Hercules was 39 ; 5. False teeth; 6. Planned to sail around the world in a group of 5 men and 5 women; 7. Leonard Rossiter; 8. A crossword made up entirely of swearwords; 9. True; 10. Jewel and Warriss (Active as a duo from 1934-1966).

LAST TANGO IN HALIFAX

A British comedy-drama series that began broadcasting on BBC One on 20 November 2012. Screenwriter Sally Wainwright loosely adapted the story of her mother's second marriage. The series has been praised for its depiction of the older generation, strong acting, and believable dialogue. It won the British Academy Television Award for Best Drama Series. It has run for 5 Series and 24 Episodes

1. How did Celia and Alan make contact after 60 years and rekindle their former romantic interest?

2. Celia's daughter Caroline was distracted by her own romantic problems involving her adulterous husband and her own relationship with which colleague?

3. Alan and Celia met for the first time in which Yorkshire town?
A) Halifax   B) Skipton   C) Settle   D) Hawes

4. When Celia and Alan got engaged, instead of buying a ring, they celebrated by buying an engagement present to each other. What was it?

5. When the happy couple visited Southowram, a stately home which was a possible wedding venue, what happened to them?

6. Eventually the happy couple had a much simpler wedding. Where was it?

7. Caroline and Kate decided to have a baby. Who did Kate choose as sperm donor? A) John B) Robbie C) Greg D) Paul

8. What terrible secret did a drunken Gillian tell Caroline about her former husband Eddie?

9. Celia was devastated when Alan finally revealed a secret that he had kept from her. She was infuriated by his dishonesty and unsure how to progress. What was the secret?

10. Raff was left speechless when a mural appeared on the wall of the barn at Far Slack Farm. What was the subject of the mural? *(Generous clue here!)*

SONGS AND DANCES
Fill in the blanks to name the missing dances

A. Let's …… Again - Chubby Checker	D. ….. Inferno - Trammps
B. Blame it on the ….. …. - Eydie Gorme	E. …. Talkin' - The Bee Gees
C. Dark …… - Madonna	F. The Last….. - Engelbert Humperdinck

VICTORIA: 1. C) 13; 2. B) The Duke of Cumberland, her paternal uncle; 3. A) Edward Oxford;
4. Yes, she had to as she was the sovereign; 5. B) Railway locomotive; 6. B) Jenna Coleman; 7. A) 18;
8. B) With an elderly couple in their small home; 9. Napoleon III ; 10. The Great Exhibition.

A British sitcom that was broadcast on ITV from 1969 to 1973. It was created by Ronald Chesney and Ronald Wolfe, who wrote most of the episodes. The BBC rejected it, not seeing much comedy potential in a bus depot as a setting. Frank Muir, Head of Entertainment at London Weekend Television, loved the idea and despite a poor critical reception it was a hit with viewers. 7 Series 74 Episodes.

1. What was the title of the series' theme music written by Tony Russell?
A) Happy Larry   B) Happy Barry   C) Happy Harry   D) Happy Days

2. What number bus would you have caught to get to the Cemetery Gates?
A) 11   B) 21   C) 31   D) 41

3. What fictional bus company featured in the series? A) Southdowns
B) Luxton & District Traction Company   C) Butlers   D) Midland Red

4. Stan Butler (Reg Varney) was the lead character but who was his conductor?
A) Joe Brown   B) Joe Harper   C) Jack Harper
D) Jack Brown

5. Cicely Courtneidge played Stan's mother Mrs Mabel Butler in the first series, but who played her throughout the rest of the run?
A) Jean Boht   B) Barbara Lott   C) Doris Hare   D) Pat Heywood

6. How often did the company issue new uniforms?
A) Every year   B) Every 2 years   C) Every 3 years   D) Every 4 years

7. What breed of dog did Arthur and Olive receive from Aunt Maud as a 10th Wedding Anniversary? A) Rottweiler   B) Corgi   C) Poodle   D) Spaniel

8. The Inspector's schemes typically backfired with hilarious consequences, and landed him in trouble with the management or in hospital. What was his name? A) Cyril 'Blakey' Blake   B) Fred 'Jonesy' Jones   C) Joe 'Lewy' Lewis
D) Bert 'Harry' Harris

9. How was Arthur written out of the show?   A) Jailed after a theft
B) Run over by a bus   C) Work on an oil rig   D) Left Olive and divorced

10. Stan left halfway through the last series and went to the Midlands. What work did he have in his new environment? A) Car Salesman   B) Taxi Driver
C) Car Factory   D) Chauffeur

LAST TANGO IN HALIFAX: 1. Facebook; 2. Kate; 3. B) Skipton; 4. A Lexus convertible sports car; 5. They get locked inside overnight ; 6. In the Register Office with 2 passers-by as witnesses; 7. C) Greg ; 8. She had killed him and staged his suicide; 9. He had a secret son Gary; 10. A giraffe. **SONGS & DANCES:** *A) Twist; B) Bossa Nova; C) Ballet; D) Disco; E) Jive; F) Waltz.*

A British biographical documentary, based on the 1952 American show of the same title. Hosted by Eamonn Andrews from 1955-1964, then from 1969 until his death in 1987. Michael Aspel took over until the show ended in 2003. In 2007 Trevor McDonald presented a one-off special. 43 Series. 1130 Episodes.

1. Which famous Spurs and Northern Ireland footballer refused to take part in the programme when confronted by Eamonn Andrews in 1961?

2. Which TV actor was caught out by Andrews, with his red book, at the Prince of Wales Theatre, when he was just 30 years old? Tragically just 16 months later he died of a massive heart attack.

3. Actress Hattie Jacques appeared in 1963. Her husband John Le Mesurier helped to set the surprise up and was featured on the show. Why was it all so clearly rather embarrassing for her?

4. Bob Hope (1970) and Dudley Moore (1987) had unique editions of the show featuring their lives? What was different about the two programmes?

5. In 1962 David Butler, at 17, was the youngest subject on the show. He was surprised in the headmaster's study at his grammar school. Eamonn said 'This is only the first chapter of your life - but what a chapter! Already your complete and absolute triumph over disability is an inspiration to us all.' What had he done to earn this tribute?

6. A TV screenwriter was caught on the cobbles of the Coronation Street set whilst he was celebrating 35 years of the soap on our screens. Who was he?

7. Another Tottenham Hotspur player featured in 1999. He was caught at White Hart Lane and the guests included Gary Lineker and Chas and Dave. This captain, a England international who battled diabetes, had demonstrated with an orange on *Blue Peter* how he injected insulin daily. Who was the football ambassador?

8. In 1972 Eamonn surprised a famous actor, known for playing a bigoted loudmouth, whilst the actor was playing a saxophone at the City Lit Institute in London. Who was the thespian?

9. A Coronation Street actress was fooled by Eamonn at Euston Station when he was dressed as a newspaper vendor. Who was the actress, forever associated in the soap with her 'Hotpot'?

10. In 1991 an English comedian and nightclub owner was caught in his own Embassy Club in Manchester. His act became more controversial as times changed. but he remained a big attraction until his death. Who was he?

ON THE BUSES: 1. C) Happy Harry; 2. A) 11; 3. B) Luxton & District Traction Company; 4. C) Jack Harper; 5. C) Doris Hare; 6. B) Every 2 years; 7. C) Poodle; 8. A) Cyril 'Blakey' Blake; 9. D) Left Oive and they divorced; 10. C) Car factory.

A British crime drama series produced by the BBC, which focuses on a team of forensic pathology experts and their investigations into various crimes. First broadcast in 1996, the series was created by Nigel McCrery, a former murder squad detective. Twenty-three series have been broadcast since 1996. 208 Episodes.

1. What is always quoted as the two main differences between Silent Witness and real life pathologists?

2. Who played the first lead role, Sam Ryan, until she left during the 8th series?

3. The series has been located in London since series 4, but what was the city used as the base for the first 3 series?

4. Emilia Fox joined midway through series 8. She plays a forensic anthropologist. What is her character's name?

5. Leo Dalton, was promoted to professor after Sam Ryan left. His wife and daughter were killed in a car accident. He too died in the finale to series 16, *Greater Love*, when he sacrificed himself saving many others. How?

6. Harry Cunningham (Tom Ward) appeared from series' 6-15. He started as a junior doctor, worked as an apprentice alongside Sam and Leo and left to become a professor. To which major city did he move?

7. What was the name of the character played by Liz Carr from Series 16–23? She was Jack's personal lab assistant, and was disabled by an unspecified condition and used an electric wheelchair.

8. In Series 23, *Deadhead.* A private jet crashed into woodland outside London. Its passengers included Jonathan Kraft, a friend of Nikki's partner Matt. What was Kraft's former high powered position in the UK?

9. In series 20, *Identity.* The team assisted DI Paul Renick, following the assumed suicide of Jamal Al Sham and discovered that he was actually murdered. What dark secret did Al Sham have?

10. Fans somewhat controversially voted series 22 the best ever. In the episode *To Brighton, To Brighton* the Lyell team were summoned to a rubbish dump where body parts had been found. What was a significant aid in identifying the scattered body parts?

THIS IS YOUR LIFE: 1. Danny Blanchflower; 2. Richard Beckinsale; 3. They had split up and she was then living with lorry driver John Schofield; 4. They were broadcast as 2 parts over two weeks; 5. David lost both his legs and a hand when, aged 11. He had found an unexploded bomb on Ivinghoe Beacon; 6. Tony Warren, the creator of Coronation Street ; 7. Gary Mabbutt; 8. Warren Mitchell; 9. Betty Driver; 10. Bernard Manning.

A BBC comedy series in which celebrities are invited to discuss their pet hates and persuade the host to consign those hates to oblivion in Room 101, a location whose name is inspired by the torture room in George Orwell's novel Nineteen Eighty-Four which reputedly contained the worst thing in the world. Orwell himself named it after a meeting room in Broadcasting House where he had sat through tedious meetings. 18 Series 141 Episodes.

1. The show has had three presenters. Can you remember them?

2. The show returned after a five year absence in 2012, with a new host and a new format. How had the show been revamped?

3. Who was the very first guest back in 1994?
A) Bob Monkhouse   B) Ian Hislop   C) Jo Brand   D) Peter Cook

This is a selected list of guests and their choice of banished items. Can you match them up?

GUEST	BANISHED ITEM
1.BOB MONKHOUSE	A. Golf
2. RICHARD WILSON	B. Tie a Yellow Ribbon Round the Old Oak Tree
3. MEERA SYAL	C. Elizabeth Hurley
4. ANNE ROBINSON	D. Cyclists
5. SHEILA HANCOCK	E. Boiled eggs
6. RICHARD E GRANT	F. Marzipan
7. JEREMY CLARKSON	G. Chris Evans
8. LORRAINE KELLY	H. Skin on rice pudding
9. JESSICA STEVENSON	J. Noel and Liam Gallagher
10. TERRY VENABLES	K. Elvis Presley
11. SPIKE MILLIGAN	L. Chiswick Post Office
12. BORIS JOHNSON	M. Songs of Praise
13. PHIL COLLINS	N. Chris De Burgh
14. IAN HISLOP	P. The Welsh
15. BILL BAILEY	R. Paul Merton

SILENT WITNESS: *1. Real life pathologists do not take victims into their own homes and do not interview suspects; 2. Amanda Burton; 3. Cambridge; 4. Nikki Alexander; 5. From a terrorist bomb explosion; 6. New York City; 7. Clarissa Mullery ; 8. The former US ambassador; 9. He was a people smuggler; 10. They are heavily tattooed.*

A British series produced by Parallel Film and Television Productions for the ITV network. The series follows Peter Kingdom, a small-town solicitor whose work revolves around cases brought by the eclectic and eccentric populace of his small town. The series retains a largely episodic format.
3 Series. 18 Episodes.

1. In which fictional Norfolk town was Peter Kingdom based?
A) Studley Constable B) Market Shipborough C) Angelby D) Walton St Giles

2. Peter's half sister Beatrice moved into his spare room after a spell in rehab. Which *Spooks* and *Wire in the Blood* actress played Beatrice?

3. Karl Davies portrayed a trainee solicitor who qualified and accepted a partnership in the practice. He got soaked in almost every episode, from falling in swimming pools to landing in dikes. Name the character.
A) Tate Henderson B) Lyle Anderson C) Robert Sugden

4. Despite being generally stand alone stories, there was a storyline concerning the mysterious disappearance of someone who had allegedly vanished at sea six months earlier. Who was this person, related to Peter?

5. In the last episode of Series 1, Peter learned Lyle intended to take a city job. He handed him a case of a man who has had multiple eviction notices. The man's wartime story so emotionally drained Lyle, he decided to stayat the practice when the eviction order was dropped. Why did the man's story prove so powerful to Lyle?

6. In series 2 the Women's Institute enlists Peter's assistance to save a building which was threatened with demolition. What building was it?
A) Barn B) Church C) Lighthouse

7. The practice was embroiled in a feud between two brothers who battled one another on opposite sides of the same stretch of road. What business did they both operate?

8. Who played the smelly local and a frequent client of Peter who often found ways to sue the local council? Known for *Whose Line Is It Anyway.*

9. What classic 1965 car did Peter Kingdom drive in the series?
A) Alvis B) MG C) Bentley

10. In the second series Peter's half brother was charged with faking his own death when he returned to the town. Where had he been 'in hiding'?
A) Edinburgh B) Lanzarote C) Dublin

ROOM 101: 1. Nick Hancock (1994-99), Paul Merton (1999-2007), Frank Skinner (2012-?); 2. Under Nick and Paul there was just 1 guest, with Frank it increased to 3; 3. A) Bob Monkhouse. BANISHED ITEMS: 1K, 2M, 3H, 4P, 5L, 6B, 7A, 8C, 9F (She is now Jessica Hynes), 10D, 11G, 12E, 13J, 14R, 15N.

A contemporary English music show hosted by Jools Holland. A spin-off of The Late Show, it has run in short series since 1992 and is part of BBC Two's late-night line-up. It features a mixture of both established and new musical artists, from solo performers to bands and larger ensembles. 54 Series. 369 Episodes.

JUST A FEW OF THE ACTS TO BE FEATURED ON THE SHOW IN ITS FIRST 15 YEARS. HERE COME THE GIRLS! CAN YOU NAME THEM?

KINGDOM: 1. B) Market Shipborough; 2. Hermione Norris; 3. B) Lyle Anderson; 4. Simon Kingdom, Peter's half-brother; 5. He was an Auschwitz survivor; 6. C) A lighthouse; 7. They both run Burger vans; 8. Tony Slattery; 9. A) Alvis (TE21 Drophead Coupe); 10. C) Dublin.

A British private detective series. Created by Dennis Spooner and produced by Monty Berman the show was first broadcast in 1969 and 1970. The Series was 26 Episodes. It was remade in 2000, starring Vic Reeves and Bob Mortimer. Two series were commissioned and were broadcast in 2000 and 2001 with the pilot episode airing 18 March 2000. A total of 13 Episodes.

1. What were the first names of the two private detectives?

2. Mike Pratt played Randall and also had a history in the music business, playing in The Cavemen with Tommy Steele and Lionel Bart. He also wrote *A Handful of Songs* and which Spanish flavoured hit for Tommy Steele?

3. In the first Episode *My Late Lamented Friend and Partner*, Hopkirk was killed by the husband of a client. How was he killed?

4. Who was the only person who can usually see or hear Hopkirk, when he returned as a ghost, although characters like mediums can also do so?

5. Randall was depressed after his partner's death, so his wife Jeannie sent him to the Lambert Clinic to see Dr Conrad. The doctor turned out to be a mastermind of many robberies of his wealthy patients. How did he extort information from them?

6. In the episode *That's How Murder Snowballs*, a theatre performer was killed during a performance of a Russian Roulette type trick. The other half of the act, a man called Abel was prime suspect. Which top TV actor played the role? A) David Jason   B) John Thaw   C) Ronnie Barker   D) Roger Moore

7. What sort of car did Randall drive? A) Green Morris Marina   B) White Austin Allegro   C) White Vauxhall Victor   D) Beige Ford Capri

8. In the Episode *But What A Sweet Little Room,* Jeannie was used as a decoy to penetrate a group of middle class men, who it transpired were robbing wealthy widows in the room in the title. What sort of room was it?

9. In *Somebody Just Walked Over My Grave,* which actor, particularly known as a foreign employee at a shambolic Torquay hotel, played an English football commentator?

10. In *The Ghost Talks,* Jeff was in hospital with an arm and a leg in plaster. How did he sustain the injuries?

LATER WITH JOOLS HOLLAND: 1992 - Kirsty MacColl; 1993 - Gloria Estefan; 1994 - Bonnie Raitt; 1995 - Dusty Springfield; 1996 - Eddi Reader; 1997 - Texas; 1998 - Beth Orton; 1999 - Mary J Blige; 2000 - All Saints; 2001 - Anastacia; 2002 - Sugababes; 2003 - Amy Winehouse; 2004 - Macy Gray; 2005 - Sheryl Crow; 2006 - Corrine Bailey Rae.

A British surreal sketch comedy series created by and starring the comedy group Monty Python. The first episode was recorded at the BBC on 7 September and premiered on 5 October 1969 on BBC1. The series stands out for its use of absurd situations, mixed with risqué and innuendo-laden humour, sight gags and observational sketches without punch lines. A total of 4 Series & 45 Episodes were broadcast.

1. What was the title of the theme tune to the show and who composed it?

2. Which Python was responsible for the animations?

3. Why was the Bronzino painting 'Venus, Cupid, Folly and Time' of significance to the show?

4. Why did the customer return to the pet shop with his Norwegian Blue parrot?

5. Complete the lyrics: 'I'm a lumberjack and I'm OK, I sleep all night and I work all day, I cut down trees, I skip and jump, I like to press wild flowers, ... bars'

6. The accountant who wished to be a lion tamer mistook what animal for a lion?

7. In the 'Nudge, nudge' sketch, where did Terry Jones supposedly come from?
A) Harlow   B) Purley   C) Gloucester   D) Scotland

8. Five mentally deficient members of the landed gentry went through a challenging obstacle course, with such events as: walking along a straight line; jumping over a wall of two rows of matchboxes; and slamming a car door loudly. The winner was the first competitor to shoot himself in the head. What award was at stake?

9. Lobster Thermidor aux crevettes with a Mornay sauce, garnished with truffle pâté, brandy and a fried egg on top, and .... What ingredient completed the recipe?

10. A milkman (Michael Palin) got seduced at the door of a house by a lovely woman (Carol Cleveland), and followed her inside, only to get locked in a room. What was in the room?

RANDALL AND HOPKIRK DECEASED: 1. Jeff and Marty; 2. Little White Bull; 3. Killed by a car driven at high speed; 4. Jeff Randall; 5. Hypnotic suggestion; 6. A) David Jason; 7. C) White Vauxhall Victor; 8. A gas chamber; 9. Andrew Sachs; 10. He fell off a balcony trying to apprehend a safe cracker.

A British claymation comedy franchise created by Nick Park of Aardman Animations. The series consists of four short films and one feature-length film, but has spawned numerous spin-offs and TV adaptations. The series centres on Wallace, a good-natured, eccentric, cheese-loving inventor, along with his companion Gromit, a silent yet loyal and intelligent anthropomorphic dog.

1. In which film did Shaun the Sheep make his first appearance?

2. What was Feathers McGraw trying to use the Techno Trousers to steal in the film *The Wrong Trousers*?

3. What was the name of the contraption invented by Wallace to help him sleep?

4. In *A Matter of Loaf & Death* how many bakers were reported missing at the beginning of the film?

5. It is a well known fact that Gromit is a clever, cultured canine. But from where did he graduate?

6. What sort of bird was Feathers McGraw?

7. In *A Grand Day Out*, what colour did Wallace paint the spaceship?

8. What is the name of the Wallace and Gromit's street?

9. Why did Wallace and Gromit go to the moon in *A Grand Day Out*?

10. Wallace's house was overrun by what at the end of *A Close Shave*?

11. What was the name of dog food shown on the box in which Gromit hides during the scene in *The Wrong Trousers*, when he is trying to catch Feathers McGraw out?

12. What was the headline on the newspaper that Gromit reads at the cafe?

13. Who voiced Lady Campanula Tottington?

14. Where did the Police imprison Feathers at the end of *The Wrong Trousers*?

15. What colour tie does Wallace usually wear, and what is his favourite accompaniment to crackers?

MONTY PYTHON'S FLYING CIRCUS: 1. John Philip Sousa (in 1893); 2. Terry Gilliam; 3. It is the source of the squashing foot animation; 4. It is dead; 5. I put on women's clothing and hang around in bars; 6. An anteater; 7. B) Purley; 8. Upper Class Twit of the Year; 9. Spam; 10. Many other milkmen, some of them very old!

A British drama series that debuted on ITV on 29 May 2011 and concluded on 27 April 2016. Scott & Bailey is based on an original idea by Suranne Jones and Sally Lindsay, with Jones commenting that there needed to be more roles for women that weren't 'wife-of, sidekick-to, mother-of, mistress-to, etc'. So, the concept of a programme detailing the lives of two professional women was born. 5 Series. 33 Episodes.

1. What were the first names of Scott and Bailey, who played the two roles?

2. In which part of the UK was the series based?
A) Greater Manchester B) Yorkshire Dales C) Peak District D) Merseyside

3. The former *Coronation Street* actress who played DCI Gill Murray also wrote 3 episodes. What is her name?
A) Sally Lindsay B) Helen Worth C) Amelia Bullimore
D) Sarah Lancashire

4. Which actress was originally intended to play Scott, but withdrew when she became pregnant with twins?

5. In which team did the two detectives work in the fictional Manchester Metropolitan Police Service?

6. The actor who played DS Andy Roper is Scott's lover, he is also her real life husband! Who is he?

7. In *Secret Trust* the body of eight-year-old Dylan Nichols was discovered four days after his initial disappearance. But, as they search for the paedophile killer, they were unaware that the culprit has placed himself at the heart of the child's grieving family. Where was the boy's body found?
A) In a wheelie bin B) On a bonfire C) At a rubbish tip D) In loft of his home

8. In the episode *Cradle* when vulnerable Helen Bartlett (Nicola Walker) approached Janet, she revealed a dark family secret about her long lost brother. What was it?

9. DSI Hodson replaced the retired Gill Murray in series 5. Which *Brittas Empire* actress replaced her?
A) Julia St John B) Harriet Thorpe C) Pippa Haywood
D) Judy Flynn

10. Bailey started out in the series as a DC. What was her rank when the 5th series ended?

INQUIZITION +151 BY THE INQUIZITORS - MIKE, ROB & MO LEWIS IS ALSO AVAILABLE FROM AMAZON FOR JUST £5

WALLACE AND GROMIT: *1. A Close Shave; 2. A diamond; 3. Snoozatron; 4. 12; 5. Dogwarts University; 6. A penguin; 7. Orange; 8. 62 West Wallaby Street; 9. Because it is made of cheese; 10. Sheep; 11. Meatabix; 12. Dog reads newspaper; 13. Helena Bonham Carter; 14. The zoo; 15. Red, Wensleydale cheese.*

A British sitcom created and written by Raymond Allen and starring Michael Crawford and Michele Dotrice. It was first broadcast from 1973 and 1975 and ran for three series, including 2 Christmas specials in 1974 and 1975, after a three year absence it returned for a fourth series in 1978 and returned in 2016 for a one-off special. In all 23 Episodes were made.

1. What was the name of Frank's wife and what was her maiden name?

2. Frank was given the use of a Morris Minor car for his job on a chicken farm and took Betty for a picnic on Dorset's Purbeck coast. Who rescued Frank as he was hanging from the exhaust pipe over a cliff near Swanage?

3. What was the name of the Spencer's cat?
A) Vienna   B) Top Cat   C) Cleopatra   D) Whoopsy

4. In series 3 what type of dancing did Betty and Frank take up?

5. Frank wanted to succeed in his new job as a holiday camp entertainer. His act included very poor ventriloquism, bad jokes about kangaroos, and an interesting rendition of *Early One Morning*. What was the act's climax?

6. In series 2 Frank's impending RAF reunion caused him to relive his brief and disastrous time in training. He managed to make a complete mess of the aptitude tests under the watchful eye of Fowler, who was played by an actor yet to tangle with Fletcher at Slade. Who was he?

7. Frank worked as a motorcycle courier, what was his radio call sign? A) Phantom   B) Demon King   C) Vesuvius   D) Beret Beret

8. In woodwork class what did Frank make for Jessica?
A) A Wendy House   B) A pencil case   C) A wall shelf D) A mobile

9. Later in series 1, Frank was back at the employment exchange, where the new manager Mr Bradshaw insisted that he is employable, and gives him a job himself. Frank managed to wreck the computer link with HQ at which Cheshire town? A) Crewe   B) Chester   C) Northwich   D) Runcorn

10. Frank was looking forward to playing Joseph in the annual Nativity play, but the parish wisely cast another. However Frank got a late call up and with 'help' from Mr Hunter and sandbags, chaos ensued. What role was Frank reluctantly given?

SCOTT AND BAILEY: 1. Janet and Rachel, Lesley Sharp and Suranne Jones; 2. A) Greater Manchester; 3. C) Amelia Bullimore; 4. Sally Lindsay; 5. The Major Incident Team; 6. Nicholas Gleaves; 7. A) In a wheelie bin; 8. He is buried in the cellar of the family home; 9. C) Pippa Haywood; 10. Acting Detective Inspector.

A British drama programme made by London Weekend Television for ITV and shown between 1974 and 1978. The lead character was the well-groomed, genteel governor and episodes revolved around her attempts to liberalise the prison regime while managing her personal life at home. 5 Series. 72 Episodes.

1. The programme portrayed life in a fictional women's prison. What was it called? A) HMP Stone Park B) HMP Slade C) HMP Crown Hill D) HMP Redford

2. Faye Boswell, played by Googie Withers was governor for 3 series. She was replaced by Helen Forrester for Series 4. Who played Helen? A) Amanda Barrie B) Katharine Blake C) Charlotte Rampling D) Diana Dors

3. The final series saw yet another change at the top, as Susan Marshall arrived. Who played Susan? A) Susan Hampshire B) June Ritchie C) Sarah Lawson D) Honor Blackman

4. The creator and writer of the show, David Butler, played the prison chaplain in some episodes. What was the chaplain's name?
A) Henry Prentice B) Ted Crilly C) Neil Boyd D) Mervyn Noote

5. Another familiar TV actress of the time appeared in 55 episodes of the series and also wrote 3 episodes. She played the Chief Officer, Mrs Armitage. Who was she? A) Wanda Ventham B) Mona Bruce C) Dawn Addams D) Sylvia Syms

6. Governor Faye Boswell had been in charge at Stone Park women's prison for one month when a prisoner on remand, Martha Kyle, spread false stories in the newspapers. A political activist, her stories were lies about what?
A) No Sunday Roast each week B) Radio 1 banned C) Mistreatment by prison officers B) Drug taking was rife.

7. Lady Evelyn Smythe arrived on the remand wing. She wrongly thought that because she once met Governor Faye Boswell at an opera, she deserved special treatment. Of what crime had she been convicted? A) Fraud   B) Attempted murder of her husband   C) Shoplifting from Harrods   D) Prostitution

8. Betty and Magda showed up as prisoners in *The Group* episode. The actresses portraying them were Helen Worth and Cheryl Murray, who were to share a flat at number 11 Coronation Street. What were their Corrie characters?

9. True or False? One audience who were unable to watch the series were real-life prison inmates.

10. In *Nemesis* in the final series, Jennifer Rawlings began serving her life sentence for what crime? A) Killing a policewoman B) Killing her son's murderer C) Killing her mother D) Causing a train crash which killed many people

SOME MOTHERS DO 'AVE 'EM: 1. Betty, Fisher; 2. A passing rugby team; 3. C) Cleopatra; 4. Scottish country dancing; 5. He becomes a human volcano with fireworks (which he sets off by accident); 6. Fulton Mackay; 7. B) Demon King; 8. A) A Wendy House; 9. D) Runcorn; 10. The Angel Gabriel.

A panel were shown babies, both beautiful and otherwise, and were invited to guess who the celebrity parent(s) were, and narrow their guesses down with probing questions. Invented by Eamonn Andrews. Produced by Thames for ITV. Hosted by David Nixon (1973), Roy Castle (1977), Leslie Crowther (1982), Bernie Winters (1983-88). 4 Series. 45 Episodes.

Whose Baby?

Here's the twist! 16 celebrities pictured as kids. Who are they?

1. BGT judge
2. Sexy?
3. I think so!
4. Morning person

5. You're fired!
6. BGT again
7. Strictly
8. Fast!

9. 90s Model
10. X Factor!
11. Morning girl
12. Hell's kitchen

13. Hello
14. Legolas
15. Line of Duty
16. Now 80!

WITHIN THESE WALLS: 1. A) HMP Stone Park; 2. B) Katharine Blake; 2. C) Sarah Lawson; 4. A) Rev Henry Prentice; 5. B) Mona Bruce; 6. C) Mistreatment by prison officers; 7. B) Attempted murder of her husband; 8. Gail Potter & Suzie Burchill ; 9. True, lights out in prisons back then was 9pm; 10. B) Killing her son's murderer

217

Since the early days of TV, comedy has been a main segment of the programmes that we have enjoyed on our box. This round comprises questions on all different sorts of shows that have made us laugh. From sitcoms to stand up comedy. How much can you remember from the days of old? Well, here's a third chance to find out.

1. In *Benidorm,* what was the name of the Spanish hotel?

2. In *The Office*, what paper company employed David Brent?

3. What was Blackadder's first name through the series featuring The Middle Ages, The Elizabethan Era, The Regency Period and World War I?

4. Tubbs and Edward ran the local shop in which series?

5. What was the name of Rodney's biological father in *Only Fools and Horses,* as revealed in the last episode?

6. In which fictional town was the Police sit-com *The Thin Blue Line* set? A) Burlingham   B) Harmouth   C) Gasforth

7. Which much loved comedy star died during a live TV show from Her Majesty's Theatre in Westminster, London on 15 April 1984?

8. What was *Dad's Army* originally going to be called?

9. A travelling salesman who sold stationery lived at Birch Avenue, Putney, London with his wife and two teenage children. What was the title of the series?

10. In *The Brittas Empire* where did Carol keep her children during the day?

11. *Roger, Roger* was a lesser know John Sullivan sitcom about a taxi operation. What was the name of the cab company?

12. Bill, Ben and Rhona appeared in which BBC1 sitcom for 9 years?

13. What was the name of Nessa and Smithy's son in *Gavin and Stacey*?

14. In Series 7 of *My Family* Michael succeeded in placing the whole family under Anne Robinson's scrutiny on which TV quiz show?

15. Who played Hyacinth Walton in 2016 *Young Hyacinth,* prequel of *Keeping Up Appearances*? A) Sophia Myles B) Carey Mulligan C) Kerry Howard

WHOSE BABY?: 1. Amanda Holden; 2. Rod Stewart; 3. Penny Lancaster; 4. Phillip Schofield; 5. Baron Alan Sugar; 6. David Walliams; 7. Claudia Winkleman; 8. Lewis Hamilton; 9. Kate Moss; 10. Dermot O'Leary; 11. Holly Willoughby; 12. Gordon Ramsey; 13. Adele; 14. Orlando Bloom; 15. Vicky McClure; 16. Sir Cliff Richard.

HOW MANY ADVERTISING SLOGANS CAN YOU RECALL?

1. Hands that do dishes can be soft as your face.

2. The sweet you can eat between meals.

3. Refreshes the parts other beers cannot reach.

4. If you can't beat 'em, join 'em.

5. Tell them about the honey mummy.

6. For men that don't have to try too hard.

7. Melt in your mouth, not in your hand.

8. Schhh! You know who.

9. Vorsprung durch technik.

10. Your flexible friend.

11. The longest lasting snack.

12. The real thing.

13. The appliance of science.

14. Simply clever.

15. Never knowingly undersold.

16. Have a break.

17. Just do it.

18. The listening bank.

19. Put a tiger in your tank.

20. Splash it all over.

21. Exceedingly good cakes.

22. The mint with the hole.

23. Because you're worth it.

24. It's finger lickin' good.

25. The bank that likes to say yes.

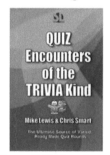

Also available from Amazon

BRITISH COMEDY 3: 1. Solana Resort; 2. Wernham Hogg; 3. Edmund; 4. League of Gentlemen; 5. Frederick Robdal; 6. C) Gasforth; 7.Tommy Cooper; 8.The Fighting tigers; 9. Bless This House; 10. In a cupboard behind the reception desk; 11. Cresta Cabs; 12. 2.4 Children; 13. Neil; 14. The Weakest Link; 15. C) Kerry Howard.

A British sitcom which originally ran on BBC One from 10 November 1994 to 22 January 1998, then from 24 December 1999 to 1 January 2007. It is set in a fictional small Oxfordshire village called Dibley, which is assigned a female vicar following the 1992 changes in the Church of England that permitted the ordination of women. It was placed third in a BBC poll of Britain's best sitcoms. 3 Series. 20 Episodes plus 7 charity shorts.

1. When Reverend Pottle, the vicar of St Barnabas' Dibley, died suddenly, the villagers eagerly await his replacement. How old was Rev Pottle?

2. What was Geraldine's real, unusual first name?
A) Cleopatra   B) Boadicea   C) Bathsheba   D) Drusilla

3. Which villager came out as gay in a radio broadcast, but nobody heard?

4. Dibley's annual Autumn Fayre had raised a measly £270 last year so the vicar was set on getting a celebrity to open the event. After a false Elton John hope, who showed up unexpectedly and did a great job?

5. In the *Christmas Lunch Incident* Geraldine received multi lunch invitations and not wishing to offend anyone attended all of them. How many vegetables did Frank and Jim serve with their lunch?
A) 16   B) 12   C) 8   D) 4

6. A church stained glass window got damaged. Geraldine persuaded Daniel Frobisher to donate the money to replace it. What caused the damage and how much did Daniel eventually donate?

7. Dibley was chosen to host an episode of a weekly religious programme hosted by Pam Rhodes. What was the programme? A) Highway   B) Songs of Praise   C) Stars on Sunday   D) Heaven and Earth Show

8. At the end of every episode Geraldine told Alice a joke that Alice never comprehended. The pattern was broken when Alice married Hugo. Who did Geraldine tell a joke to on this one special occasion?

9. In the Winter Seasonal Special in 1999 how did Alice's portrayal of Mary in the Nativity Play at Owen's farm become very realistic?

10. In *The Vicar in White* Geraldine married Harry and became Mrs ....?
A) Campbell B) Dwight C) Kennedy D) Harris

AS SEEN ON TV 2: 1. Fairy Liquid; 2. Milky Way; 3. Heineken; 4. Tetley Bitter; 5. Sugar Puffs; 6. Denim; 7. Minstrels; 8. Schweppes; 9. Audi; 10. Access; 11. Twix; 12. Coca Cola; 13. Zanussi; 14. Skoda; 15. John Lewis; 16. Kit Kat; 17. Nike; 18. Midland Bank; 19. Esso; 20. Brut; 21. Mr Kipling; 22. Polo; 23. L'Oreal; 24. KFC; 25. TSB.

An English episodic drama programme that ran from 20 February 1988 until 25 August 2002, produced by London Weekend Television for the ITV network. It was based on the 1986 TV Movie of the same name, and focused on the lives of members of the London Fire Brigade. In total there were 14 Series and 172 Episodes.

1. What watch was featured in the show and what is the fictional fire station from which they operated?

2. For the first 10 series the theme music was based upon a children's round of the same name and sung by schoolchildren. Who wrote the new music used for series' 11-13?

3. For the first three series the Assistant Divisional Officer (ADO) was played by James Marcus. Who was the character forced to retire from the service at the end of series 3 after failing a routine medical?
A) Sidney Tate   B) John Coleman   C) John Hallam   D) Doris Webb

4. When Blackwall's first female firefighter arrived to join the watch, most reacted with hostility, ignoring her completely at her first shouts, before she won them over and remained in the show for 3 series. What was her name?
A) Sally 'Gracie' Fields B) Josie Ingham C) Melissa Clark D) Fiona Pearce

5. Roland Cartwright appeared in series 1 and 2. He was portrayed as racist and sexist, but that became less prominent during the series. He drowned when his breathing apparatus malfunctioned underwater, whilst rescuing the occupant of a van which had fallen into a dock. What was his nickname?
A) Charisma   B) Rambo   C) Vaseline   D) Recall

6. The watch played a prank on Colin Parrish, getting him to monitor radioactive particles in the atmosphere. What legislative documents did they persuade him that he needed to sign?

7. Kate Stevens joined the watch as Josie's replacement and she soon fitted in after rescuing a baby from a burning car. Who played the role? A) Kate Beckinsale B) Sara Powell C) Kim Clifford D) Samantha Beckinsale

8. John Hallam was the uptight and hen-pecked husband of Sandra. He tried for promotion several times, but was never successful. How did he get his eyebrows singed at Christmas?

9. Nick Georgiadis, initially a disciplinarian, succeeded Tate as Station Officer in Series 4. What nickname was he given due to his Greek-Cypriot origins?

10. Ronnie 'Hi-Ho' Silver was left devastated in Series 13, when he tried to rescue a girl from a flat fire, but she died from her injuries and he was going to resign. How did Geoff Pearce persuade him to change his mind?

THE VICAR OF DIBLEY: *1.102 years old; 2. B) Boadicea; 3. Frank Pickle; 4. Kylie Minogue;*
5. A) 16; 6.Tree went through it in the Quite Great Storm, £11,000; 7. B) Songs of Praise;
8.David Horton; 9. She gave birth to a baby daughter, later named Geraldine; 10. C) Kennedy.

A British sketch comedy show that was originally broadcast between 1999 and 2003 on Channel 4. In addition to the three principal cast members, the show was written by many writers. Created by Victoria Pile. Caroline Leddy of Channel 4 and Peter Fincham at Talkback believed that audiences would welcome a female orientated sketch show. 3 Series. 23 Episodes + 2 Specials.

1. The theme song *In The Middle of Nowhere* was sung by Jackie Clune. Who took the song to number 8 back in 1965?

2. Who were the three main performers?

3. In the pilot show one of the three spots was filled by an actress and media celebrity who made her TV debut as a 19 year old contestant on *Blind Date* back in 1990. Who is she?

4. The show's title was intended to be a spoof of what?

5. What section of the show concerned different women looking for a partner?

6. Another popular section covers people who pretend to be ill to get free things or special treatment. What was that called?

7. What were *Dangerous Cows* and *Planes Trains and Forks*?

8. The show's main cast play Celtic princesses in a 2004 off-the-wall comedy adventure about three unlikely heroines who set out to save Celtic Britain, by thwarting the Roman invasion. What was it called?

9. Which comedy star and actress went on to an eponymous BBC sit-com series after she appeared in 3 episodes in season 3, which had marked her debut in a comedy series, as well as her debut on TV?

10. Which familiar TV actor appeared regularly on the show and went on to voice Mr Brown in The Adventures of Paddington and appear in shows like *Spy, Luther, Killing Eve* and *The Salisbury Poisonings*?

TRIVIA: Miranda Hart appeared in three episodes of the third season, which marked her debut in a comedy series, as well as her debut on television. Hart later had a lead role in her own sit-com, Miranda (2009), which featured Sally Phillips,

LONDON'S BURNING: 1. Blue watch, Blackwall; 2. Warren Bennett (son of Brian, The Shadows drummer, himself a touring member of the band in later years); 3. A) Sidney Tate; 4. B) Josie Ingham; 5. C) Vaseline; 6. The Official Secrets Act; 7. D) Samantha Beckinsale; 8. His elderly father-in-law poured too much brandy over the Christmas pudding, 9. Zorba; 10. He took him to a cemetery to see a huge plaque, dedicated to London Fire Brigade, listing names of many firefighters who had given their lives and the graves of Joe, Sicknote, and Sub Officer John Hallam. He got the message.

A 1984 British serial about the final days of the British Raj in India during and after World War II, based upon the Raj Quartet novels (1965-1975) by British author Paul Scott. Granada Television produced the series for the ITV network with a star-studded cast. 14 Episodes were broadcast.

1. The serial opened in the midst of which conflict in the fictional Indian city of Mayapore?

2. Hari Kumar was a young Indian man, educated at Chillingborough, a British public school; he identified as English rather than Indian. The bankruptcy of his father, forced him to return to India to live with his aunt. Who played the role?

3. Hari became romantically involved with a young British woman. One night they are attacked by a group of unknown Indian men. Hari is beaten and Daphne is gang raped? Susan Wooldridge played the woman, what was her name?

4. Ronald Merrick was a young lower-middle-class Englishman, was intelligent and hardworking. What was his job?

5. Whilst fighting alongside Merrick, Edward 'Teddie' Bingham (Nicholas Farrell) was killed in an ambush by the Japanese-sponsored Indian National Army (INA). In which country was he killed?

6. After her husband's death and the difficult birth of their son, Susan Layton Bingham suffered a mental breakdown. She later married Merrick, but he is later killed by assassins whilst in a compromising sexual situation. However the official version of his death was that he died in what type of accident?

7. Which future star of *EastEnders* played a Signals Sergeant?
A) Ross Kemp   B) Adam Woodyatt   C) Leslie Grantham   D) Martin Kemp

8. Which prolific TV composer wrote the music for *Jewel in the Crown*?
A) George Fenton   B) Ron Goodwin   C) Ron Grainer   D) Brian Bennett

9. Although Judy Parfitt and Geraldine James played mother and daughter, Mildred and Sarah Layton respectively, there is actually only how many years difference in their ages? A) 5   B) 10   C) 12   D) 15

10. The location filming was done in India, so why did a fire in Granada Studios, Manchester, 5,000 miles away, cause continuity problems?

SMACK THE PONY: 1.Dusty Springfield; 2. Fiona Allen, Doon Mackichan and Sally Phillips; 3. Amanda Holden; 4. Stories that appeared in young girl's annuals; 5. Dating Agency Videos; 6. The Fake Diabetic; 7. Alternative titles for the show that were considered; 8. Gladiatress; 9. Miranda Hart; 10. Darren Boyd.

A British dance contest in which celebrities partner professional dancers to compete in mainly ballroom and Latin dance. Each couple is scored by a panel of judges. Broadcast on BBC One since 15 May 2004, typically on Saturday evenings with a Sunday night results show. The title is a continuation of the long-running series Come Dancing, with allusion to the film Strictly Ballroom. There has been 18 Series. 348 Episodes.

THE FIRST 18 SERIES. LISTED BELOW ARE THE 18 WINNERS AND THE 18 CELEBRITIES ELIMINATED FIRST. EITHER PUT W OR L AGAINST EACH NAME (Winner or Loser)

CELEBRITY	W/L	CELEBRITY	W/L
1. CHIZZY AKUDOLU		18. MARTINA HINGIS	
2. JOHNNY BALL		19. CHRIS HOLLINS	
3. BRIAN CAPRON		20. TONY JACKLIN	
4. TOM CHAMBERS		21. HARRY JUDD	
5. ABBEY CLANCY		22. NATASHA KAPLINSKY	
6. SUSANNAH CONSTANTINE		23. JOE McFADDEN	
7. JAMES CRACKNELL		24. JAY McGUINNESS	
8. EDWINA CURRIE		25. MELVIN ODOOM	
9. PHIL DANIELS		26. ORE ODUBA	
10. ALESHA DIXON		27. NICHOLAS OWEN	
11. STACEY DOOLEY		28. MARK RAMPRAKASH	
12. CAROLINE FLACK		29. LOUIS SMITH	
13. KELVIN FLETCHER		30. IWAN THOMAS	
14. GOLDIE		31. KARA TOINTON	
15. DARREN GOUGH		32. GREGG WALLACE	
16. JILL HALFPENNY		33. QUENTIN WILSON	
17. SIOBHAN HAYES		34. JASON WOOD	

The use of 'Strictly' in the title denotes it's difference from the BBC TV series Come Dancing (1949), which was strictly professional with professional Dance Competition format.

JEWEL IN THE CROWN: 1. World War II; 2. Art Malik; 3. Daphne Manners; 4. Indian Police Superintendent; 5. Burma; 6. Horse riding; 7. C) Leslie Grantham; 8. A) George Fenton; 9. D) 15 years; 10. The interiors were shot in Manchester and the 6 month delay meant some of the cast had put on or lost weight in the meantime.

A British comedy show starring Benny Hill that aired in various forms between 15 January 1955 and 1 May 1989 in over 140 countries. The show consisted mainly of sketches - slapstick, mime, parody, and double entendre. At its peak The Benny Hill Show was among the most-watched programmes in the UK with the audience reaching more than 21 million viewers in 1971. Broadcast 1955-1989. 33 series. 99 Episodes

1. The theme music was played by Boots Randolph. What was its title?
A) Yakety Yak   B) Yakety Sax   C) Chase the Girls   D) Beatnik Fly

2. The show typically closed with a speeded-up chase involving Benny and a crew of scantily clad women (usually with Hill being the one chased). It was a send-up on whose stereotypical chase scenes from silent movies?

3. Another signature of the show was the enthusiastic announcers intro: 'Yes! It's *The Benny Hill Show*!' Often this was done by a regular member of the cast. Which one?

4. The cast also included a straight man who was well-known for presenting *Sale of the Century*. Who was he?

5. How much was it estimated that Benny Hill's shows had earned Thames Television?
A) £25 million   B) £50m   C) £75m   D) £100m

6. In the 1980s, public opinion in Britain was turned against Benny Hill and his show. Two former guest stars successfully lobbied to have the programmes in which they appeared (in 1972 and 1976) pulled from repeat airings in England. Who were they? A) Paula Wilcox & Paul Eddington   B) David Prowse & Rikki Howard   C) Percy Thrower & Anne Shelton   D) Sting & Diana Dors

7. Short, bald Jackie Wright was a frequent supporting player. What physical attack did he often have to suffer from Benny?

8. How were the troupe of attractive young women who appeared regularly collectively known?

9. The Head of Light Entertainment at Thames Television, was cited by the press as the man who sacked Benny Hill. Who was he and in which film had he become famous playing the eponymous lead role in 1948?

10. What spoiled food product killed Ernie (The fastest milkman in the west)?

STRICTLY COME DANCING: 1L; 2L; 3L; 4W; 5W; 6L; 7L; 8L; 9L; 10W; 11W; 12W; 13W; 14L; 15W; 16W; 17L; 18L; 19W; 20L; 21W; 22W; 23W; 24W; 25L; 26W; 27L; 28W; 29W; 30L; 31W; 32L; 33L; 34L.

A British drama series produced by the BBC which was broadcast over three series on BBC One between 22 February 2011 and 31 March 2014. Created by Peter Moffat, the series followed the daily goings on of a criminal law chambers and its members in their personal and professional lives. Silk ended with series 3 because creator Moffat and the lead actress were keen to end at a high point. 3 Series 18 Episodes.

1. The series' main focus was on barrister Martha Costello and her ambition to become Queen's Counsel. Which former *dinnerladies* star played the role?

2. To what does the title of the show refer?

3. What is the name of the criminal law chambers featured in the show? A) River Court   B) Shoe Lane   C) Equity Court

4. In the episode *High and Dry* what does Martha discover about herself during the case about a man accused of raping his ex-girlfriend?

5. In *Touch and Go* how did senior clerk Billy Lamb try to get rid of barrister Clive Reader QC?

6. Clive Reader QC was played by an actor who was in *Spooks* and *Whitechapel*. His real life mother starred in *To The Manor Born*. A) Who is he?   B) Who is she?

7. In Series 2 David Lomas is a pupil who 'endeavoured' to step out of shadowing Martha. Can you identify the actor who played him?

8. What disease was Billy, the ducking and diving senior clerk, secretly battling?

9. In *Wooden Overcoat* Martha defended Michael Ward, a man accused of neglect and manslaughter, of a claustrophobic prisoner in his care. What was his job?

10. The head of chambers was Alan Cowdrey QC. Can you name the actor who played him? *He has had numerous roles including the portrayal of Alan Bennett in The Lady in the Van in 2015.*

WRITER PETER MOFFAT: 'I wanted Silk to be full of politics and intrigue. From my experience at the Bar, I felt life in chambers had all of those components, with big stories and lots of courtroom drama—but I wanted to make it as much about barristers and their life in chambers as about the trials'

THE BENNY HILL SHOW: *1. B) Yakety Sax; 2. Keystone Cops; 3. Henry McGee; 4. Nicholas Parsons; 5. D) £100 million; 6. A) Paula Wilcox and Paul Eddington; 7. Being slapped on the top of his head; 8. Hill's Angels; 9. John Howard Davies, Oliver Twist; 10. A stale pork pie caught him in the eye.*

A series of four BBC One pseudo-historical British sitcoms, plus several one-off instalments, originally aired from 1983-1989. Each series set in a different historical period, with the two protagonists accompanied by different characters, several reappearing in one series or another. Blackadder was voted the second-best British sitcom of all time. 4 Series. 24 Episodes plus 3 Specials.

1. Richard III won the Battle of Bosworth Field only to be mistaken for someone else and murdered, then succeeded by Richard IV. A) Who played Richard III as a ghost who haunted Edmund B) Which former *Z Cars* star played Richard IV?

2. What did Baldrick always have?

3. Nursie always dressed up in the same costume at fancy dress parties. What is the costume? A) A baby B) A nurse C) A cow

4. Mrs Miggins was the name of two characters in the *Blackadder* series. She is a shop owner. Hat type of shop in A) *Blackadder II* and B) *Blackadder III*?

5. What was Edmund's profession in *Blackadder III*?

6. In *Blackadder II* what is Bob's real name? A) Robert B) Kate C) Roberta

7. In *Blackadder Goes Forth* which character played by Hugh Lawrie dressed up as Gorgeous Georgina and performed at music hall?

8. What sort of stick did Blackadder give to Queenie as a present in the *Potato* episode in *Blackadder II*?

9. In the *Corporal Punishment* episode in *Blackadder Goes Forth* Edmund faked bad telephone communications and then shot a carrier pigeon –revealed to be the prized pet of General Melchett. What was the pigeon's name? A) Speckled Jim   B) Nipper   C) Pie

10. 'Well, I'm afraid it'll have to wait. Whatever it was, I'm sure it was better than my plan to get out of this by pretending to be mad. I mean, who would have noticed another madman around here? *(whistles blow along the line, signalling the start of the attack)* ...Good luck, everyone' *(blows whistle).* The final words in *Blackadder Goes Forth*. What was the appropriate title of the very last episode?

SILK: 1. Maxine Peake; 2. Colloquial reference to the gown of someone who has attained QC status; 3. B) Shoe Lane Chambers; 4. That she is pregnant; 5. He asks a senior clerk of another chambers to offer him a job; 6. A) Rupert Penry-Jones B) Angela Thorne; 7. Shaun Evans (star of Endeavour); 8. Prostate cancer; 9. Security van driver; 10. Alex Jennings.

A British crime drama series produced by Granada Television for ITV, created and principally written by Jimmy McGovern. Set in Manchester, it followed a criminal psychologist (or cracker), who worked with the Greater Manchester Police to help them solve crimes. Aired from 1993 to 1995. 3 Series. 25 Episodes plus 2 Specials.

1. What was the name of the criminal psychologist who is the main character?

2. In *The Mad Woman in the Attic* Fitz was called in to help with a woman's murder on a train. What was the surname of the original Police suspect?
A) King   B) Kelly   C) Keane   D) Keith

3. Which top football team's players names were used as character's names throughout the series?

4. In *To Say I Love You*, Bonnie and Clyde clones Sean Kerrigan and Tina O'Brien went on a crime spree and then killed one of the Police detectives. Who was the unfortunate victim? A) DS Hughes   B) DS Neville   C) DS Giggs

5. *One Day A Lemming Will Fly* was the third Cracker episode. A young boy, Timothy Lang, was found hanged in a nearby wood. Who played Timothy's father in this episode that revolved around homophobia?
A) Timothy Spall   B) Jimmy Nail   C) Tim Healy

6. Albie Kinsella survived the Hillsborough disaster but was driven over the edge when his father died and he brutally killed DCI Bilbrough. Who was brought in to find the murderer? A) Ricky Tomlinson   B) Robert Carlyle
C) Christopher Eccleston

7. What did Fitz call DS Jane Penhaligon?
A) Pandemonium   B) Panhandle   C) Pantomime

8. Fitz was married to Judith, who was played by Barbara Flynn. In which sit-com was Barbara Flynn billed as 'the milk woman'?

9. In *Brotherly Love* a dead prostitute was killed and the Police had a suspect in custody. Others were killed whilst the suspect was in custody so it was clear the Police have the wrong man. Who was eventually found guilty of killing the other women? A) Jimmy Beck   B) David Harvey   C) Maggie Harvey

10. The final view of *Cracker* was a 1996 Special, *White Ghost* . Fitz was on a lecture tour of which country? A) Hong Kong   B) Thailand   C) Scotland

---

BLACKADDER: 1. A) Peter Cook, B) Brian Blessed; 2. A cunning plan; 3. C) A cow; 4. A) pie shop, B) Coffee shop; 5. Butler to the Prince Regent; 6. B) Kate; 7. Lieutenant the Hon George Colthurst; 8. A boomerang; 9. A) Speckled Jim; 10. 'Goodbyeee'.

A British crime-action drama series produced by Avengers Mark1 Productions for London Weekend Television (LWT). Aired on the ITV network from 1977-1983. There were 5 Series, a total of 57 episodes filmed between 1977-1981. Created by Brian Clemens, who was a driving force behind The Avengers.

The PROFESSIONALS

1. What were the full names of the two main agents featured ?

2. Major George Cowley was their boss. The actor who played him had moved 'upstairs' from a previous role. Who was he?

3. What colour Ford Capri 3.0S was used by Doyle in Season 1?
A) Blue   B) Beige   C) Red   D) Silver

4. What jobs did the two agents have before joining CI5?

5. By what nickname was Cowley known at A) His old unit; and B) What nickname do his operatives now sometimes call him, though not to his face?

6. In *A Hiding to Nothing* what cover profession did Doyle use?

A) English student   B) Salesman   C) Bus conductor   D) Car mechanic

7. In *Foxhole on the Roof* Bodie and another CI5 agent climbed a factory chimney. The other agent was an ace climber who had scaled the Eiger. What was his name? A) Tensing   B) Murphy   C) Hunt   D) Hillary

8. In *Weekend in the Country* the boys had a break away from the city but are captured by fugitive criminals along with their girlfriends. What was the name of Judy's horse that had to be put down after being struck by a car?
A) Stardust   B) Starlight   C) Starburst   D) Starsign

9. In *The Rack* what graffiti was seen on the wall of the interrogation room?
A) No talking!   B) Vot is your name?   C) They're all murderers   D) Doyle did it

10. What did the C15 team buy for Bodie at the end of *Black Out*? A) A Mickey Mouse watch B) A Dinky model of a Capri C) A beer D) A white stick

TRIVIA TIME
Which character particularly loved Swiss Roll?

CRACKER: 1. Dr. Edward 'Fitz' Fitzgerald; 2. B) Kelly; 3. Manchester United; 4. C) DS Giggs; 5. C) Tim Healy; 6. A) Ricky Tomlinson; 7. B) Panhandle; 8. Open All Hours; 9. C) Maggie Harvey; 10. A) Hong Kong.

A British sitcom, set in Liverpool, North West England, which aired on BBC1 from April 1969 to January 1979, and again in 1996. The show was created by Carla Lane and Myra Taylor. The series charted the ups and downs of two young girls sharing a flat on Liverpool's Huskisson Street. A loose female equivalent of The Likely Lads. There were 10 series and 86 Episodes.

1. Who were the original two characters featured in the first series and who played the parts?

2. There was a change in the second series as Dawn moved out. Who moved in?

3. The final lead change came in series 5 when Beryl left to be replaced by Carol Boswell. Who played that role?
A) Sherrie Hewson B) Harriet Walter C) Elizabeth Estensen D) Liza Goddard

4. Who performed the theme song for the show?

5. The Mother's Day episode opened Beryl singing what number one song associated with another Liverpudlian?

6. In series 3 Beryl and Sandra left the grotty bed-sit to move into where? A) Royal Albert Dock B) Beech View C) Oak Tree Lane D) Scotland Road

7. In *Birds in the Club* Sandra was picked to represent the rugby club in 1972 in what competition?
A) Miss Hot Pants   B) Miss Scrum Down   C) Rear of the Year   D) Miss Earth

8. What football team did Beryl support?
A) Liverpool   B) Everton   C) Tranmere Rovers   D) Southport

9. *Have Hen Will Travel* in the fourth series saw Beryl's persistent oversleeping leading to both girls being sacked. Where were they working?
A) A hotel   B) A chocolate factory
C) A hand cream factory   D) A restaurant

10. In series 5 Carol was left some money by her Uncle Billy and thinks her financial problems are over. How much was she actually left? A) £1,000   B) £500   C) £150   D) £2

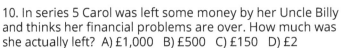

THE PROFESSIONALS: 1. William Andrew Philip Bodie and Raymond Doyle; 2. Gordon Jackson (Hudson in Upstairs, Downstairs); 3. D) Silver; 4. Bodie was a paratrooper and Special Air Service (SAS) soldier, Doyle was a police detective constable; 5. Morris, The Cow; 6. A) English student; 7. B) Murphy; 8. B) Starlight; 9. C) They're all murderers; 10. A) A Mickey Mouse watch.
SWISS ROLL: Bodie.

A British crime drama series about a detective in Amsterdam, based on the novels of Nicolas Freeling. The main character, Simon Piet Van der Valk, was played by Barry Foster from 1972 to 1992, and by Marc Warren in 2020 (more scheduled). All series were produced for the ITV network. 6 Series. 35 Episodes.

1. Which two actors played the title role in the 1972 and 2020 versions of the show?

2. In and around which city did most of the action take place?

3. The theme music for the original series reached No 1 in the UK charts in 1973. What was its title and who performed the hit?

4. In *One Herring's Not Enough* Mr Boersma claimed he had shot his wife and her lover, both with his pistol. When Inspector Johnny Kroon went to investigate, what did he find?

5. When a dead body was found in the canal, Kroon and Van der Valk conclude he must had been gay. It turns out that his mother is an English politician, in Holland for diplomatic talks. What does she do when she sees the dead body?

6. In *A Sudden Silence* in the 4th series, Government minister Van Hoorn had a secret identity and had been accepting bribes. He was killed by someone as he attempted to flee the country. How was he killed?

7. In Season 3, in the *Enemy* episode, Van der Valk ran over a masked woman robber as she was fleeing. Then both Van Der Valk and his wife Arlette face increasing danger as they were stalked and Arlette had a car tyre slashed. What happened to her house plants?

8. *In a Death by the Beach* Van Teesling, a wealthy and influential banker, was found unconscious in his car on the beach. He told police that he and his wife went for a drunken midnight swim, but his wife drowned and he barely escaped with his life. What did Kroon discover that makes Van der Valk suspicious?

9. In *Rich Man, Poor Man* in Season 2 Van der Valk took his wife to a what sort of restaurant for a meal?
A) Indian   B) Chinese   C) Balkan   D) Japanese

10. In the 2020 version where did Van der Valk live?

'I've definitely played my fair share of villains, it's just the face'. MARC WARREN

THE LIVER BIRDS: *1. Dawn and Beryl (Pauline Collins and Polly James); 2. Sandra Hutchinson (played by Nerys Hughes); 3. C) Elizabeth Estensen; 4. The Scaffold; 5. Anyone Who Had A Heart (Cilla Black); 6. B) Beech View; 7. A) Miss Hot Pants; 8. B) Everton; 9. C) A hand cream factory; 10. D) £2.*

A British game show based on a US game show. First shown on ITV 1971 to 1983, hosted by Nicholas Parsons. Special editions aired occasionally, starting on 2 January 1981 with Steve Jones as host. Revived first on Sky from 6 February 1989 to 3 October 1991 hosted by Peter Marshall then on Challenge TV in 1997 hosted by Keith Chegwin.

In this round, you start with £15. Can you get up to £100 or more?

1. For £1. How many people on a UK Jury?

2. For £1. How many are there in a Baker's Dozen?

3. For £1. Who painted the Water Lilies series of paintings?

4. For £1. What nuts are used to make marzipan?

5. For £3. What does www stand for?

6. For £3. In which city would you find the Colosseum?

7. For £3. Who conquered England in 1066?

8. For £3. Babe Ruth is synonymous with which sport?

9. For £4. From which language does the word KETCHUP originate?

10. For £4. What is an endoscope used for?

11. For £4. By what name is Edward Michael Grylls better known?

12. For £4. What colour are the stars on the New Zealand flag?

13. For £5. Gangsta's Paradise was a hit for which US rapper?

14. For £5. The Rijksmuseum is in which European city?

15. For £5. 75% of the world's Vanilla comes from which country?

16. For £5. True or False? Venus is the closest planet to Earth?

17. For £10. How many muscles does a cat have in its ears?

18. For £10. In what year did ITV start broadcasting?

19. For £10. In which city does the Blue Nile meet the White Nile?

20. For £10. Which country hosted the 2005 Elephant Polo World Championship?

'From Norwich – It's The Quiz Of The Week.'

VAN DER VALK: 1. Barry Foster and Marc Warren; 2. Amsterdam; 3. Eye Level, The Simon Park Orchestra; 4. Nothing out of place, certainly not two bodies; 5. Refuses to identify the body as her son; 6. By a machine gun; 7. Sprayed with acid; 8. Van Teesling was a former Olympic swimmer; 9. C) Balkan; 10. On a boat.

A British mystery crime drama series produced by the BBC and written by David Renwick. The title character, worked as a creative consultant to a stage magician while also solving seemingly supernatural mysteries through his talent for logical deduction and his understanding of illusions. The series ran semi-regularly from 1997 to 2004, broadcasting for 5 series. 30 Episodes and two Christmas specials.

1. Who played the title role?

2. What was the title of the first ever episode?
A) Wrestler's Tomb B) The Reconstituted Corpse C) Jack in the Box

3. The windmill used as Jonathan's home is situated in which West Sussex village? A) Pagham B) Shipley C) Earnley

4. What comedian appeared in the 2001 Christmas Special?
A) Sanjeev Bhaskar B) Jack Dee C) Bill Bailey

5. Which significant letter of the alphabet is missing from Jonathan Creek's Typewriter? A) e B) s C) a

6. The theme music, *Danse Macabre*, was an adaptation of a piece of music by which French composer?

7. The name Jonathan Creek was named after?
A) A place in Kentucky B) A brand of whisky C) A highwayman in the 17th century

8. Which real life chat show host did Jonathan subject to a trick involving a peeled banana? A) Graham Norton B) Alan Carr C) Jonathan Ross

9. Which top comedian and TV host appeared in *The Million Joke Man* as a wealthy theatre critic who was a pompous snob with no sense of humour?
A) Jim Bowen B) Bob Monkhouse C) Rik Mayall

10. In *The Curious Tale of Mr Spearfish* Adam Klaus has to deal with a rather awkward court case where a woman claims he asked her to perform unnatural acts with .... what? A) A tennis ball B) A fried egg C) A kipper

There are 12 apples in a barrel.
If you take away 5, how many do you have?

SALE OF THE CENTURY: 1. 12; 2. 13; 3. Claude Monet; 4. Almonds; 5. World Wide Web; 6. Rome; 7. William the Conqueror; 8. Baseball; 9. Chinese; 10. An instrument which can be introduced into the body to give a view of its internal parts; 11. Bear Grylls; 12. Red; 13. Coolio feat LV; 14. Amsterdam; 15. Madagascar; 16. True; 17. 32; 18. 1955; 19. Khartoum, Sudan; 20. Scotland (at Inveraray Castle).

Annual BBC television series which charts the fortunes of British wildlife during the changing of the seasons in the United Kingdom. The programmes are broadcast live from locations around the country in a prime time evening slot on BBC Two. They require a crew of 100 and over 50 cameras, making them the BBC's largest British outside broadcast events. Many of the cameras are hidden and operated remotely to record natural behaviour. Original release 30 May 2005.

1. The original Field Reporter on *Springwatch* and *Autumnwatch* in 2005 left 5 years later. Who was it?   A) Bill Oddie   B) Kate Humble   C) Simon King

2. In which year did current presenter Chris Packham join the shows?
A) 2009 B) 2011 C) 2013

3. In 2011 *Autumnwatch* came from two very different Gloucestershire locations. Can you name them? A) Slimbridge / Westonbirt   B) Aust / Berkeley
C) Forest of Dean / Symonds Yat

4. Which *Rugged Wales* presenter became a regular on the shows in 2019?
A) Iolo Williams   B) Gillian Burke   C) Alex Jones

5. Which of the original presenters was a member of The Goodies?
A) Tom Brooke-Taylor   B) Bill Oddie   C) Graham Garden

6. Who said that 'white, middle-class, old-aged men are an 'endangered species on television after he was axed as a presenter on all 3 programmes?
A) John Craven   B) Johnny Kingdom   C) Martin Hughes-Games

7. What do you call a group of hedgehogs?
A) Prickle B) Array C) Snuffle

8. What percentage of the world's grey seal population is found on the British coastline?
A) 10%   B) 25%   C) 40%

9. Which of the following animals mostly inhabits on the Isle of Mull, Scotland?
A) Turtle Dove   B) Small Blue Butterfly
C) White Tailed Eagle

10. How many earthworms can a badger eat per day?
A) Up to 50   B) Up to 200   C) Up to 500

JONATHAN CREEK: 1. Alan Davies; 2. A) Wrestler's Tomb; 3. B) Shipley; 4. C) Bill Bailey; 5. B) S; 6. Charles-Camille Saint-Saens; 7. A) A place in Kentucky; 8. C) Jonathan Ross; 9. B) Bob Monkhouse; 10. C) A kipper. APPLES: 5.

A British crime drama series based on the Vera Stanhope series of novels written by crime writer Ann Cleeves starring Brenda Blethyn. Only 4 Episodes are based on the books. First broadcast on ITV on 1 May 2011, and to date, ten series have aired, with the latest debuting on 12 January 2020. A total of 40 Episodes

VERA

1. Detective Chief Inspector Vera Stanhope is a nearly retired employee of which fictional Police force?

2. Vera forms a close relationship with her sergeants. The first one, Joe Ashworth, was played by which actor who went on to direct the *Black Ice* episode of Vera. Who was he? A) David Leon B) Jon Morrison C) Kenny Doughty

3. In *Hidden Depths*, the first Vera episode to be broadcast, 15-year-old Luke Armstrong was strangled and placed in a bath. Teacher Lily Marsh was then murdered; throttled and dumped on a beach. What surrounded both bodies? A) Candles B) Flowers C) Apples

4. In *A Certain Samaritan* in Series 2 a shoe found in Newcastle matched another found on a dead body found in a skip in another city. Where? A) Birmingham B) Portsmouth C) Norwich

5. Who is the Detective Sergeant that replaced Joe Ashworth in Series 5? A) Mark Edwards B) Billy Cartwright C) Aiden Healy

6. In *Shadows in the Sky* Owen Thorne plummeted to his death from a multi-storey car park. It transpired that he was pushed by which colleague? A) Mick McKittrick B) Gloria Edwards C) Cameron Thorne

7. In *The Sea Glass* Tom Stonnell, who had been missing for weeks, was dredged up with a load of fish. In the midst of another murder case Aiden had reason to celebrate. Why? A) Birth of a baby B) Promotion C) Passes exams

8. In *Natural Selection* Vera investigated the mysterious death of a wildlife ranger on the shore of a remote island bird sanctuary on which island group?

9. Kingsley Ben-Adir plays Dr Marcus Sumner. What is his profession?

10. What vehicle does Vera drive?

Can you name the four stars of the 1990s comedy series Outside Edge about a local cricket team?

SPRINGWATCH ETC: *1. C) Simon King; 2. 2009 (Winterwatch 2012); 3. A) Slimbridge / Westonbirt; 4. A) Iolo Williams; 5. B) Bill Oddie; 6. Martin Hughes-Games; 7. A) or B) An Array or a Prickle; 8. C) 40%; 9. C) White Tailed Eagle; 10. B) Up to 200.*

A British lifestyle gardening programme that was first broadcast on ITV on 10 June 2011. Series 1 advised viewers how to transform their gardens. Since then the show sees the team visit locations around the UK transforming gardens of people who are described as 'deserving them the most'. 11 Series. 81 Episodes.

1. Alan Titchmarsh presents this long-running, heart-warming show. Can you name his transforming team of three co-presenters?

2. Whilst studying for a Diploma in Horticulture Alan Titchmarsh was employed as a supervisor, and later as a staff trainer, at which major international botanical research and education institution?

3. From 1983-2013 Titchmarsh presented which major flower show on BBC?

4. What was the name of the animated children's television series to get children interested in gardening, on which Alan voiced the main character?

5. From 1997-2005 what was the forerunner to *Love Your Garden* on which Alan, with Charlie Dimmock and Tommy Walsh, performed garden makeovers?

6. Titchmarsh has a wax statue at Madame Tussaud's. What was revealed on TV show *Would I Lie to You?* about cleaning the waxwork, that proved to be true?

7. From 2007-2014 Alan presented *The Alan Titchmarsh Show*. It's discussion of adult themes sparked the 5th largest number of viewer complaints. A regular feature on sex toys proved particularly controversial. Who presented it?

8. On 6 occasions between 1989 and 2020 Alan Titchmarsh presented a BBC religious programme on Sundays. What was its title?

9. In addition to many gardening books Alan has written 14 novels and had them published. What was the title of the first one in 1999?
A) The First Lighthouse Keeper   B) Only Dad   C) Animal Instincts
D) Mr Macgregor

10. Titchmarsh was appointed a Member of the Order of the British Empire (MBE) for services to horticulture and broadcasting. In what year?

GARDENING ANAGRAMS

A. GRADED HENS	E. GEE HOSE RUN
B. ARE FEWER TAUT	F. BRA WHERE OWL
C. ENSURING SHARP	G. WARN ME LOW
D. WANTING CARE	H. BURRO CHEESEBOARD

VERA: *1. Northumberland & City Police: 2. A) David Leon; 3. B) Flowers; 4. B) Portsmouth; 5. C) Aiden Healy; 6. B) Gloria Edwards; 7. A) Birth of a baby; 8. Farne Islands; 9. He is a pathologist; 10. Land Rover Defender.*
OUTSIDE EDGE: (L TO R) : *Timothy Spall, Josie Lawrence, Brenda Blethyn, Robert Daws.*

A detective drama set in modern-day England. The stories revolve around the efforts of Detective Chief Inspector Tom Barnaby, and later his successor, cousin John Barnaby, to solve numerous murders that take place in the picturesque but deadly villages of the fictional county of Midsomer. 21 Series. 126 Episodes.

1. Series 3. Episode 4 – *Judgement Day.* Peter Drinkwater was impaled in the chest with a pitchfork from his farm. Which future film star got the point?

2. Series 19. Episode 1 - *The Village That Rose From the Dead.* Little Auburn, a village that had been abandoned since the second world war, was re-opened to the public for the first time in over seventy years. But on the night of opening, local youngster Finn Thornbury was found dead. What type of vehicle crushed him to death?

3. In the same episode as Q2, Milo Craven played by Hugh Dennis (*Outnumbered*) also met an unpleasant end. What animal ultimately killed him?

4. Series 10. Episode 7 - *They Seek Him Here.* Nick Cheyney, the director of a low-budget film about the French Revolution and the Scarlet Pimpernel, being filmed at Magna Manor, was found dead on the film set. What former method of execution, which ended in 1977, was used to kill both him and Gwen Morrison?

5. Series 11. Episode 1 - *Shot at Dawn.* As Johnny Hammond opened his garage door with a remote and his life was cruelly curtailed. How?

6. Series 6. Episode 4 – *A Tale Of Two Hamlets.* Frank Webster, trying to live a healthy life was killed whilst taking exercise. How?

7. Series 11. Episode 5 - *The Magician's Nephew.* Jean Wildacre, a member of an occult group headed by imperious Ernest Balliol was killed on stage during a magic show? How was she murdered in the middle of a stage act?

8. Series 8. Episode 6 – *Hidden Depths. Otto Benham* was drugged, lured outside and collapsed onto a white target drawn on his lawn, then pinned to the ground by croquet hoops. He was then woken by a bucket of water being thrown over him. How was he killed?

9. Series 15. Episode 6 – *Schooled In Murder.* Debbie Moffett was crushed to death at the factory that produces the world-famous Midsomer Blue. What edible product was used to kill her?

10. Series 13. Episode 2 – *The Sword Of Guillaume.* DCI Tom Barnaby headed off to Brighton on a bus tour arranged by the Mayor of Causton. During the trip the oily property developer Hugh Dalgleish (Tim McInnerny) was decapitated. In which building did his 'unfair' killing take place?

LOVE YOUR GARDEN: 1. David Domoney, Katie Rushworth and Frances Tophill ; 2. Royal Botanic Gardens, Kew; 3. Chelsea Flower Show; 4. Gordon the Garden Gnome; 5. Ground Force; 6 It had to have its face cleaned twice a week to remove all the lipstick smudges on it; 7. Julie Peasgood; 8. Songs of Praise; 9. A) The First Lighthouse Keeper; 10. C) 2000. GARDENING ANAGRAMS: A) Garden shed; B) Water feature; C) Pruning shears; D) Watering can; E) Greenhouse; F) Wheelbarrow; G) Lawnmower; H) Herbaceous border.

Upstairs Downstairs

A British drama series produced by London Weekend Television (LWT) for ITV. It ran for 5 Series, 68 episodes on ITV from 1971-1975. Set in a large townhouse in Belgravia in central London, the series depicted the servants, 'downstairs', and their masters, the family, 'upstairs' from 1903 to 1930, and showed the slow decline of the British aristocracy.

1. The show was created by two actresses, Jean Marsh and Eileen Atkins. What acting roles did they have in the series?

2. At which address did the Bellamy family reside?

3. Mr Hudson's first impression of Sarah Moffat was that she wasn't suited for life below stairs. What did Sarah do to get an initial negative judgement?
A) Caught smoking   B) Came to front door to apply for the job   C) Swore a lot

4. In *Guest of Honour* the Bellamy's esteemed visitor was the king. Which king honoured the family with a visit? A) Edward VII   B) George V   C) Edward VIII

5. Lady Marjorie died in the third series. How did she die?
A) Influenza Pandemic B) She was a passenger on the Titanic C) A Riding accident

6. Where had James Bellamy (Simon Williams) attended school? A) Clifton College   B) Harrow   C) Eton

7. On 15 April 1912 why does Richard hire Hazel Forrest?
A) To type a biography he was writing B) As a Kitchen Maid C) As Parlour Maid

8. Keith Barron joined the series as British sheep farmer living in Australia. He and Rose meet on a tram in April 1914 when he accidentally sat on a plum cake she was carrying. Rose was to marry him but changed her mind. He was later killed by a sniper when he was a sergeant in the ANZACs. What was his name?
A) Thomas Watkins   B) Edward Barnes   C) Gregory Wilmot

9. Eaton Place opened its doors to a group of, initially, troublesome refugees at the start of Series 4. Which country had they come from?
A) Belgium B) France C) Germany

10. During WWI which member of Eaton Place trains as a Voluntary Aid Detachment nurse? A) Georgina Worsley   B) Rose Buck   C) Ruby Finch

Some episodes from the first season are in black and white due to industrial action by the technician's union in a dispute over the introduction of colour TV cameras.

MIDSOMER MURDERS: *1. Orlando Bloom; 2. A military tank; 3. Snake, by constriction, squeezing his body and cutting off his blood flow; 4. The guillotine; 5. was shot by automatic WWI machine gun arranged to start by the same remote; 6. He was electrocuted while riding his exercise bike after it was connected to a main charge; 7. Inside The Cabinet Of Death prop. Knives had been jammed and the blades coated with secretions from the skin of a Poison Dart Frog; 8. By having bottles of wine thrown at him with an antique catapult; 9. A large wheel of cheese; 10. Riding through the House of Horrors fairground ride.*

A British police procedural drama series, first broadcast on 30 August 1980. It ran for 6 series and 88 episodes on BBC1. The theme of the series concerned a female police inspector taking control of a police station in Lancashire. The first series to feature female officers as lead characters.

1. The first female to take charge was Jean Darblay. Which former *Z Cars* and *The Sweeney* actress played the role in the first three series?

2. In series 4 Anna Cartaret took over the lead role. What was her character's name? A) Ellie Miller   B) Kate Longton   C) Maggie Forbes

3. What was the location of the police station?
A) Hartley   B) Angleton   C) Ockleybridge

4. How did the show get its title?

5. What item of police uniform was featured in the opening title graphics?

6. Initially, the long-serving sergeants at the station were sceptical and uneasy about having a female boss. David Ellison and Noel Collins played the roles. What were their characters' names?

7. What car did Jean Darblay drive in the first two series?
A) Yellow Austin Mini Metro   B) Blue Ford Fiesta   C) Orange Austin Mini

8. In *Hostage to Fortune* a ruthless criminal gained access to a bank manager's house by acting as a milk delivery man. Which policeman was held hostage?
A) PC Danny Sparks   B) PC George Dixon   C) PC Tony Stamp

9. In the *Inspection* episode, who was visiting the station?
A) Royalty B) Lord Mayor C) Chief Constable

10. In *Scab* two brothers-in-law are on opposite sides of which national altercation ?

WHAT IS THE LINK BETWEEN

ANNA CARTERET AND HATTIE MORAHAN

UPSTAIRS, DOWNSTAIRS: 1. Jean Marsh was Rose, Eileen Atkins had to withdraw due to theatre commitments and was replaced by Pauline Collins; 2. 165 Eaton Place, Belgravia, London; 3. B) Came to front door to apply for the job instead of the servant's entrance; 4. A) Edward VII; 5. B) She was a passenger on the Titanic; 6. C) Eton; 7. A) To type the biography of his father-in-law, the old Earl of Southwold, which he was writing; 8. C) Gregory Wilmot; 9. A) Belgium; 10. A) Georgina Worsley.

A British quiz programme for competing university teams across the United Kingdom which first aired in 1962 on ITV from 21 September 1962-31 December 1987, quizmaster Bamber Gascoigne. The BBC revived the programme on 21 September 1994, Jeremy Paxman as quizmaster. 48 Series 1,792 Episodes.

STARTER 1. Which planet is principally metal, but shares its name with another metal?

60s
1. What year did William III become king of Great Britain and Ireland?

2. What year was the Open Championship played for the first time at Prestwick?

3. When did Harper Lee publish To Kill a Mockingbird and win the Pulitzer Prize?

STARTER 2. Add together the number of Harry Potter books + Chronicles of Narnia series.

FOOTBALL
1. Which club won the FA Cup 5 times in the trophy's first 7 years, but disbanded a decade later?

2. The first Football League competition took place in 1888/9. Who were winners?

3. Three clubs took part in both the first season of the Football League and the first season of the Premier League 104 years later. Name them.

STARTER 3. In which modern day country is the ancient kingdom of Sheba?

NAME THE TITLES OF AGATHA CHRISTIE BOOKS
1. A typical village murder, or so it seemed, until the last chapter's stunning revelation.

2. The glamorous era of train travel provides Poirot with an international cast of suspects and one of his biggest challenges.

3. Ten people are invited to an island for the weekend. They die one by one!

STARTER 4. What is the chemical element with the symbol Rf and atomic number 104?

UK MOUNTAINS
1. At an altitude of 893 metres, what is the highest point along the Pennine Way?

2. How many Scottish mountains are higher than Mount Snowdon in Wales?

3. What is the highest mountain in Ireland at 1,039 metres high?

JULIET BRAVO: 1. Stephanie Turner; 2. B) Kate Longton; 3. A) Hartley; 4. From the Inspector's call sign J-B; 5. A revolving policewoman's 'bowler' hat; 6. Joe Beck and George Parrish; 7. C) Orange Austin Mini; 8 A) PC Danny Sparks; 9. C) Chief Constable; 10. Miners dispute. LINK: Anna Carteret is Hattie Morahan's mother.

A BBC sitcom, that aired on BBC1 from 1981 to 1982 and from 1985 to 1988. Starring Ronnie Corbett, created and written by Ian Davidson and Peter Vincent for the BBC, both of whom had previously written for The Two Ronnies, of whom Corbett was one half. Sorry! is based around Timothy Lumsden who, 41 years old in the first three series (his age increased to 42 and then 48 in subsequent series. 7 Series. 42 Episodes + 1 short.

1. What was Timothy Lumsden's job?

2. Timothy was dominated by his mother played by Barbara Lott. His father was also henpecked to say the least. What were Timothy's parents names?

3. What was his father's favourite warning to Timothy when he said something that had been misunderstood by him or something he considered offensive?

4. In *For Love or Mummy* Timothy was attracted to Annette, a new member of his amateur dramatic group. Where did he want to take her to a special dance?
A) In the Town Hall   B) On a Riverboat   C) The local Disco

5. In *Buttons* Timothy is cast in the pantomime Cinderella. What part was he given?
A) An Ugly Sister B) Buttons C) The rear end of the horse

6. In *Does Your Mother Know You're Out* Timothy bet a colleague, Victor, that he would take library assistant Caroline to see which film at the cinema?
A) Jaws   B) Gone With the Wind   C) The Godfather

7. In *The Rabbit and the Pussycat* Timothy was involved in a Treasure Hunt, looking for what buried item? A) Treasure chest   B) Money   C) Golden rabbit

8. In *You're Going Nowhere* Timothy's plans to have an exciting Asian break were ruined by mother. Where was Timothy planning to go on holiday?
A) Taj Mahal   B) Gobi Desert   C) Great Wall of China

9. In *The Primal Scene, So To Speak* a local businessman offered Timothy a lot of money and a book contract. Why did he make such a generous offer?

10. In the final episode *Up, Up and Away* Timothy finally escaped and left home to live with his partner. What was her name? A) Pippa B) Dotty C) Muriel

Sorry! Trivia: Ronnie Corbett was almost 52 when this series started, yet he played a 41 year old.

UNIVERSITY CHALLENGE: STARTER 1; Mercury; 1. 1760; 2. 1860; 3. 1960. STARTER 2; 14; 1. The Wanderers; 2. Preston (North End); 3. Aston Villa, Blackburn Rovers, Everton. STARTER 3; Yemen; 1. The Murder of Roger Ackroyd; 2. Murder on the Orient Express; 3. And Then There Were None. STARTER 4; 1. Cross Fell; 2. 18; 3. Carrauntoohil.

An annual marathon event held in London, United Kingdom. Since 29 March 1981, the BBC has broadcast live coverage of the event that was founded by athletes Chris Brasher and John Disley. It is typically held in April. The largely flat course starts in Blackheath and finishes at The Mall. Significant charity running with participants helping to raise over £1 billion since its founding.

1. The 2019 London Marathon raised the highest ever amount for a single-day fund-raising event. How much was raised? A) £42.3m   B) £54.1m   C) £66.4m

2. The London Marathon has seen the marathon world record broken many times. Which British athlete broke the women's world record no less than three times in 2002, 2003 and 2005?

3. There have been 6 major sponsors of The London Marathon. How many can you remember?

4. The theme tune used by the BBC every year is from a film score written by Ron Goodwin, and performed by the Bournemouth Symphony Orchestra. It was originally from the film score of which 1966 film?

5. The first London Marathon was held on 29 March 1981, and more than 20,000 applied to run. 6,747 were accepted. How many runners actually crossed the finish line on Constitution Hill?   A) 6,255   B) 5,985   C) 5,429

6. In 2013 a 30-second silence was held before the start of the marathon to show respect and support to those affected by which tragedy?

7. What are three separate groups of starters?

8. What bridge do runners cross at the half-way point?

9. The race finishes in The Mall, alongside the most senior royal palace in the UK. What is it's name?

10. Firefighter Lloyd Scott wore a 130-pound antique deep-sea diving suit during the 2002 London Marathon. He set a record for the slowest marathon time, a record he then broke at the New York Marathon. What was his London Marathon time? A) 7 days, 2 hours, 12 hours, 3 seconds B) 5 days, 8 hours, 29 minutes, 46 seconds C) 4 days, 18 hours, 12 minutes, 7 seconds.

SORRY! : 1. Librarian; 2. Phyllis and Sidney; 3. Language, Timothy!; 4. B) On a riverboat; 5. Rear end of the horse; 6. B) Gone With the Wind; 7. C) Golden rabbit; 8. B) Gobi Desert; 9. Timothy had accidentally found out that he was having an affair; 10. A) Pippa.

A British drama series of 5 episodes, originally broadcast from 10 October to 7 November 1982 on BBC2. Written by Alan Bleasdale, as a sequel to a television play titled The Black Stuff. The British Film Institute described it as a 'seminal drama series... a warm, humorous but ultimately tragic look at the way economics affect ordinary people'.

1. The main character appeared as a tall man in his mid-thirties who wore predominantly black clothes, and had a distinctive bushy moustache. He always appeared unkempt and unshaven. What was his name?

2. Who played the most prominent female role as Angie Todd, the wife of Chrissie? A) Pauline Collins   B) Janine Duvitski   C) Julie Walters

3. On the way to do casual tarmac laying work on a new housing development the boys met a female student who hitchhiked a lift with them to Leeds. What was the boys' destination? A) Middlesbrough   B) Newcastle   C) Sunderland

4. In *The Muscle Market* Danny Duggan, was a building boss who employed people cheaply by being complicit in social security fraud of his employees and therefore guilty of a crime himself. Which top character actor played the role? A) Pete Postlethwaite   B) Ricky Tomlinson   C) Warren Mitchell

5. In *Jobs For the Boys*, whilst claiming unemployment benefit, they were offered a cash in hand job on a building site for a renovation job. What building does it later transpire that they are working on?

6. Also in *Jobs For the Boys* Snowy Malone, a plasterer, fell to his death trying to flee from whom? A) Police   B) Social security officers   C) Dockers

7. In *Moonlighter* Tom Georgeson appeared as a security guard with the same name as which former legendary England footballer.
A) Roger Hunt   B) Dixie Dean   C) Ian Callaghan

8. In *Shop Thy Neighbour* what pets did Chrissie (Michael Angelis) have to kill to provide food for his family? A) Chickens   B) Geese   C) Pigs

9. In *Yosser's Story* his mental health deteriorated and he went to confession. The conversation went thus, Priest: 'Call me Dan'. Yosser: 'I'm desperate, Dan'. In this episode two Liverpool footballers appeared in cameos. Who were they?
A) Graeme Souness & Sammy Lee   B) Alan Hansen & Ian Rush
C) Phil Neal & Ian Rush

10. In George's Last Ride Chrissie took the dying George in his wheelchair to the place he once worked. Where? A) Coal mine   B) Cotton Mill   C) Docks

THE LONDON MARATHON: *1. C) £66.4m; 2. Paula Radcliffe; 3. Gillette (from 1981 to 1983.), Mars (1984–1988), ADT (1989–1992), NutraSweet (1993–1995), Flora (1996–2009), Virgin Money (since 2010); 4. The Trap; 5. A) 6255; 6. Boston Marathon Tragedy; 7. Elite Women, Wheelchair (Men and Women), and Elite Men followed by Mass Race; 8. Tower Bridge; 9. St James's Palace; 10. B) Five days, eight hours, 29 minutes and 46 seconds.*

DIXON of DOCK GREEN

A BBC series about daily life at a fictional London police station, with the emphasis on petty crime, successfully controlled through common sense and human understanding. In 1955, the BBC was preparing to face competition from the launch of ITN. The BBC resurrected George Dixon for a new series of 'everyday stories of a London policeman'. It ran until 1976. 22 Series 432 Episodes.

1. The character of PC George Dixon was a 'bobby on the beat' from Paddington Police Station in the 1950 film *The Blue Lamp*. What happened to him when he encountered a thug, Tom Riley, played by Dirk Bogarde?

2. *An Ordinary Copper* was the signature tune and it featured Tommy Reilly on harmonica. The Canadian born musician also played the theme for a top radio comedy show of the time. What was the radio show?
A) The Navy Lark   B) Round the Horne   C) Take It From Here

3. In *The Rotten Apple* a young constable, Tom Carr, is enjoying a lifestyle that was more lavish than would be expected on his salary. Gambling debts had got him into a life of crime. Which sit-com star, of more than one hit show, played the young constable?
A) Derek Fowlds   B) Paul Eddington   C) Nigel Hawthorne

4. In *Father-in-Law* Dixon's 23 year old daughter Mary married a policeman. George sung a few songs at the wedding, but who was his new son-in-law?
A) PC Nick Rowan   B) PC 'Laudie' Lauderdale   C) PC Andy Crawford

5. In each episode Dixon broke the fourth wall (spoke to camera). From the 1970s onwards, how did the greeting begin?

6. In *Facing the Music* George Dixon was finally promoted to sergeant. In what number series did he get his stripes? *(Jack Warner was 69!)* A) 4th B) 7th C) 11th

7. In a 1974 episode *Firearms Were Issued*, a notorious gang of bank robbers had performed a raid locally and their whereabouts was known and a raid was authorised. What does Sergeant Dixon issue to the team?
A) Firearms   B) Flak jackets   C) Grenades

8. When Warner was aged 80, George Dixon was shown as retired from the police and was re-employed in a civilian role. What job was he given?
A) Chief constable B) Desk sergeant C) Collator

9. The show was written by a left-winger who became a Baron. Who was he?

10. What service number did George Dixon have on his epaulettes?
A) 49 B) 706 C) 92

BOYS FROM THE BLACKSTUFF: 1. Yosser Hughes; 2. C) Julie Walters; 3. A) Middlesbrough; 4. A) Pete Postlethwaite; 5. C) Department of Employment; 6. Social Security officers working under cover (sniffers); 7. B) Dixie Dean; 8. B) Geese; 9. A) Graeme Souness and Sammy Lee; 10. C) Docks

A cosy British mystery thriller series. The show began on ITV in 2003. The third series ended in August 2007. The theme is murder mysteries in the setting of professional gardening jobs in beautiful English and European gardens. Being gardeners means that they overhear secrets and dig up clues which leads them to handle floral problems, solve crimes and capture criminals. 3 Series. 22 Episodes.

1. What was Rosemary's surname?
1.A) Wrestler B) Fricker C) Boxer D) Smith

2. And which *Good Life* star played Rosemary?
A) Penelope Keith B) Moyra Fraser C) Dolly Mountshaft
D) Felicity Kendall

3. What happened to Laura Thyme's husband Nick, and which actress renowned for playing Ma Larkin in *The Darling Buds of May* played the part?

4. Rosemary said she did not want to buy a new car because the newer models had girly functions, like comfortable seats and power steering. What car did she drive?
A) 1959 Austin Healey   B) 1980 Land Rover Series III   C) 1967 Morris Minor 1000
D) 1975 Triumph Stag

5. True or False? Rosemary's cousin Charles was the murderer in one episode.

6. What was Laura's former profession?

7. From which traditional English ballad lyrics was the title of the show taken?

8. In the episode *In A Monastery Garden* which cathedral was used for the location photography? A) Winchester   B) Chichester   C) Rochester   D) Canterbury

9. True or False? Rosemary had a doctorate in plant pathology and was a University of Malmesbury lecturer in applied horticulture.

10. Rosemary was delighted to be working on the garden of an open-air theatre with Laura when one of the actors is suddenly killed by a prop gun, which police discover had been loaded with live ammo instead of blanks. Where was the real theatre?

A) Minack Theatre   B) Longleat House   C) Woburn Abbey   D) Micklefield Hall

Felicity Kendal was voted Rear of the Year in 1981.

DIXON OF DOCK GREEN: 1. He is shot and later dies in hospital; 2. A) The Navy Lark; 3. B) Paul Eddington; 4. C) PC Andy Crawford; 5. A salute followed by 'Evening all'; 6. C) 11th; 7. A) Firearms; 8. C) Collator; 9. Baron Ted Willis; 10. A) 49.

A UK game show on Channel 4 from 28 December 1982 -18 May 1989, revived on BBC Two 16 December 2002-2 August 2003. Two contestants in the studio used a library of maps & reference materials to solve up to five clues, and communicate instructions via a radio link to a skyrunner who had the use of a helicopter. Presenters: Kenneth Kendall (1982–89),Dermot Murnaghan (2002–03). Skyrunners: Anneka Rice (1982–88), Annabel Croft (1989), Suzi Perry (2002–03).

SOLVE THE 10 CLUES WHICH COVER 10 DIFFERENT UK COUNTIES, THEN USE THE CIRCLED LETTER OF EACH ANSWER TO FIND A MAJOR TOURIST ATTRACTION IN ANOTHER COUNTY OF THE UK.

1. SCOTTISH HIGHLANDS. This was the location of a bloody conflict named after a village 3 miles to the west. - - - - - -(-) - - / - - - -

2. NORTHUMBERLAND. Born in Willington Quay in 1803 this man invented a vehicle to travel very quickly indeed! - - - - -(-)/ - - - - - - - - - -

3. CUMBRIA. This place launched the 7th Invincible in 1977. - - - -(-)- / - - / - - - - - - -

4. NORTH YORKSHIRE . Location at centre of the revival of Alf Wight's memoirs in 2020. - - - - - - - - - -(-)

5. LANCASHIRE. A large underground chamber where coleoptera were seen in the 1960s! - - - / - - -(-)- -

6. POWYS. Under a mile away from this market town at Gigrin Farm in the Brecon Beacons milvus milvus are well fed each day. - (-)- - - - - -

7. WARWICKSHIRE. The myth that this boy picked up a ball at a local school and invented a new sport lives on. - - - - - - - / -(-)- - / - - - - -

8. S GLOUCESTERSHIRE. A local man went to Montserrat and named Needsmust estate after a village near his birthplace (where I live!). - - - - - - -(-)

9. SOMERSET. Since 1970 crowds flock most years to a village where Joseph of Arimathea landed to enjoy this musical event. (-)- - - - - - - - - -/ - - - - - - - -

10. CORNWALL. Oggy, Oggy, Oggy! These baked items have been a favourite since miners had a break in the tin mines. - - - - -(-)-

ROSEMARY AND THYME: 1. C) Boxer; 2. D) Felicity Kendal; 3. He left her for a 23 year old woman, Pam Ferris; 4. B) 1980 Land Rover series III; 5.True (Killed the man who bought out his father's business, causing him to commit suicide); 6. Policewoman; 7. Scarborough Fair; 8. B) Chichester; 9. True; 10. Micklefield Hall, Rickmansworth.

A British series based on the Miss Marple novels by Agatha Christie. It aired from 26 December 1984 to 27 December 1992 on BBC One. All 12 original Miss Marple Christie novels were dramatised. Then, Agatha Christie's Marple was a British ITV programme loosely based on her works. 6 Series. 23 Episodes from 12 December 2004 –29 December 2013. .

1. In the original 1984 series which octogenarian actress played the amateur consulting detective?

2. In which fictional village did Miss Jane Marple live?

3. In the 1961 film *Murder She Said* the actress who played Miss Marple on TV had a minor role. Who played the sleuth in black and white on the big screen?

4. In the first TV story broadcast in 1984 Miss Marple assisted the Bantrys at Gossington Hall when a young girl was found dead in which room of the house?

5. In which story was a handful of grain found in the pocket of a murdered businessman, and Miss Marple sought a murderer who liked nursery rhymes?

6. In which 1987 episode did Miss Marple take a vacation in London and encounter famous adventuress Bess Sedgwick and her daughter Elvira Blake?

7. In the last *Miss Marple* story in 1992, five people were invited to meet a famous film star at a fete in Gossington Hall. Shortly afterwards, one of them is pronounced dead having drunk a poisoned daiquiri. What is the story's title?

8. Geraldine McEwan took over as Miss Marple in 2004. In which story did Mrs Elspeth McGillicuddy travel on a train and see a man strangling a woman?

9. Jacko Argyle died in prison, serving a sentence for killing his adoptive mother. Two years later, Jacko's alibi appeared. The family had to come to terms that Jacko was innocent and that one of them must be the real murderer. What was the story title?

10. Julia McKenzie starred in the very last episode in 2013. Miss Marple wasn't in the original Agatha Christie story when heiress Ellie Thomsen went horse-riding and was found dead the next day with no apparent injuries. Can you remember the title of the episode?

TREASURE HUNT: 1. Drumossie Moor (Battle of Culloden); 2. Robert Stephenson (The Rocket inventor); 3. Barrow in Furness (The Invincible - scrapped in 2005); 4. Grassington (Location for All Creatures Great and Small. Alf Wight was real name of James Herriott; 5.The Cavern (Liverpool, where The Beatles (coleoptera) began; 6. Rhayader. The red kites are fed each day at Gigrin Farm; 7. William Webb Ellis picked up the ball during a game of football at Rugby School; 8. Olveston (James Sturge); 9. Glastonbury Festival; 10. Pasties.
RINGED LETTERS: S-T-O-N-E-H-E-N-G-E.

It is widely argued that the rise of multi-channel television services, together with other 'new media' have led to a decline in family television viewing and the emergence of more individualized media culture within the household. This is a reminder of many, varied perceptions of family television viewing preferences from days gone by.

1. What theme song contained these lyrics? 'We've got some half price cracked ice and miles and miles of carpet tiles, TVs, deep freeze and David Bowie LPs, Ball games, gold chains, what's-names, pictures frames and leather goods, and Trevor Francis track suits from a mush in Shepherds Bush'.

2. In 1999 who were the two original presenters on *Loose Women*?

3. In February 2019, Trevor McDonald presented *The Real Story* about which pair of serial killers?

4. A statue of which famous television comedian was unveiled in his birthplace, Caerphilly, in 2008 by Sir Anthony Hopkins?

5. Fusilier (later briefly Lance Corporal) Dave Tucker and Lance Corporal (later Corporal, and then Sergeant, and then Corporal again) Paddy Garvey were in *Soldier, Soldier*. Off screen they had a number of big hits together. Who were the actors concerned?

6. Which John Sullivan written sit-com ran from 1983-1986 and starred Paul Nicholas and Jan Francis?

7. Which eponymous character, who had been appointed as a High Court judge, actively sought justice in the cases before him, while at the same time trying to rekindle an old romance with his former pupil, Jo Mills QC?

8. Where did Diana Trent, Tom Ballard and Basil Makepeace reside?

9. The Durrell family, Dr Theodore Stephanides and Spiro all appeared together in *My Family and Other Animals*. On which island was the series set in the 1930s?

10. Robert Lindsay played Ben Harper in *My Family from 2000-2011*. What was his profession?

MISS MARPLE: 1. Joan Hickson; 2. St Mary Mead; 3. Margaret Rutherford; 4. The Body in the Library; 5. A Pocketful of Rye; 6. At Bertram's Hotel; 7. The Mirror Crack'd From Side To Side; 8. 4.50 to Paddington; 9. Ordeal by Innocence; 10. Endless Night.

A British sitcom starring Hugh Dennis as a father and Claire Skinner as a mother who were outnumbered by their three children (played by Tyger Drew-Honey, Daniel Roche and Ramona Marquez). The programme received critical acclaim for its semi-improvisational scripting and realistic portrayal of children and family life. There were five series, which aired on BBC One from 2007 to 2014. 35 Episodes + 5 Shorts.

1. What was the family surname? A) Brookman B) Brockworth C) Brockman

2. What was their address? A) 19 Keely Road, Chiswick B) 32 Windsor Gardens, Slough C) 165 Eaton Place, Belgravia

3. What was father Pete's job? A) Geography teacher B) History teacher C) PE teacher

4. Sue was often between jobs as a part-time PA. Who was her hellish boss when she resigned at the end of the first series? A) Tyson B) Veronica C) Andrea

5. In the first episode *The School Run,* what did Karen have that she wanted to keep as pets? A) Mice B) Spiders C) Nits

6. When the family were at the airport in series two, what did Ben consume that made him feel 'Zingy, zangy, zongy' afterwards? A) Four Mars bars B) A double Espresso Coffee with 4 sugars C) Bucket of Popcorn

7. When Jake was bullied when he was 11, what did the bullies steal?
A) His trainers B) His trousers C) His mobile phone

8. In the second series, Frank came to stay with the family whilst recovering from a nasty accident involving a tin of baked beans. What had he inadvertently done? A) Burnt his kitchen down B) Cut his arm C) Dropped the tin on his foot

9. In the *Sport Relief Special* Karen was chosen to be a mascot at Chelsea FC for a televised match, despite being an Arsenal supporter. Which player was she chosen to accompany on to the pitch?
A) John Terry B) Frank Lampard C) Ashley Cole

10. What happened when Pete attempted to become the head of History?
A) He arrives late for the interview B) Fails to give 9 reasons why he should have the job C) He is accused of racism

VARIETY TV: 1. Only Fools and Horses; 2. Kaye Adams and Nadia Sawalha; 3. Fred and Rose West; 4. Tommy Cooper; 5. Robson Green and Jerome Flynn; 6. Just Good Friends; 7. Judge John Deed (played by Martin Shaw); 8. Bayview Retirement Home near Bournemouth (in Waiting For God); 9. Corfu; 10. He was a dentist.

A British spy drama series originally aired on BBC One from 13 May 2002 -23 October 2011. The title is a popular colloquialism for spies. The series follows the work of MI5 officers based at the service's London HQ. It is notable for various stylistic touches, and its use of popular guest actors. 10 Series. 86 Episodes.

1. What was the name of the HQ of MI5 in *Spooks* (and also in reality) since 1995? A) Embankment House   B) Westminster House   C) Thames House

2. What was the name of the operational hub of *Spooks*?
A) The Matrix   B) The Source   C) The Grid

3. Sir Harry Pearce KBE was the only actor to appear in all 10 series of *Spooks*. Which actor played him? A) Peter Firth B) Peter Davison   C) Peter Capaldi

4. Helen Flynn was killed off in series 2. She had her hand, then her head, thrust into a deep fat fryer, before she was shot. Hot fat was not used for the scene which drew many viewer complaints. So what did the film-makers use?
A) Flat Coca Cola   B) Cold tea and food colouring   C) Honey and dry ice

5. Robert Glenister played a senior politician in series 5 to 8. What great office of state did he hold? A) Home Secretary   B) Foreign Secretary   C) Prime Minister

6. In the last episode of series 4. former MI5 officer Angela Wells held everyone hostage, demanding that the service revealed evidence that Harry and MI5 had conspired to kill a senior Royal Family member, or she would detonate a bomb. Who did she think, wrongly, was going to be assassinated?
A) Princess Diana   B) Prince Charles   C) The Queen

7. Tessa Phillips, Senior Case Officer, Section K, defrauded MI5 out of tens of thousands of pounds and was branded a traitor. She fleed the country leaving behind a video for Pearce, in which she gloated about trumping MI5. Who played Phillips? A) Miranda Raison   B) Jenny Agutter   C) Nicola Walker

8. In *New Allegiances* Al-Qaeda positioned a car bomb to explode at a Remembrance Sunday ceremony. Who drove the rigged car to a safe place but killed when it exploded as he was getting out? A) Adam   B) Lucas   C) Malcolm

9. The lamp shades hanging from the ceiling of the operational hub are actually what? A) Ikea bins upside down   B) Christmas decorations   C) Microphones

10. In the last ever episode Sasha blamed Harry for allowing his father to kill his mother and attempted to stab him, who stepped in, took the hit and died?
A) Ruth B) Elena C) Erin

OUTNUMBERED: 1. C) Brockman; 2. A) 19 Keely Road, Chiswick; 3. B) History teacher; 4. B) Veronica; 5. C) Nits; 6. B) Double Espresso Coffee with 4 sugars; 7. C) His mobile phone; 8. A) Burnt his kitchen down after putting a tin of beans in the microwave; 9. B) Frank Lampard; 10. B) Fails to give 9 reasons why he should have the job when the headmaster asks him.

A British sitcom set around a supermarket assistant manager and a promotions rep and their participation in a company car-sharing scheme. The first half of each episode shows John picking up Kayleigh from her house and the pair having conversations about each other's lives as they travel to work. The second half of the episode sees the pair on the car journey home and they discuss what they did at work. 3 Seasons. 12 Episodes (2 Specials).

Peter Kay's
Car Share

1. Who played Peter Kay's co-star Kayleigh?

2. What was the radio station that they listen to on their journeys?

3. What make and model was the car that John drives?

4. What is the nickname of Ray, the supermarket fishmonger, who scrounged a lift with them one day?

5. What fruit fancy dress costume did Kayleigh dress in for National Jam Week?

6. In what store did John meet up with his friend Ian 'Litchy' Litchfield?

7. What song was accidentally played at John's father's funeral? A) Fire by Crazy World of Arthur Brown B) Dizzy by Tommy Roe C) Happy by Pharrell Williams

8. Who did John dress up as for the annual works do?

9. At the end of the first series, Kayleigh, who was moving house and would no longer be car-sharing with John, gave him a CD as a parting gift. Inside was a note dedicating a track to him. A) What was the CD and B) What was the track?

10. In the finale, what did Kayleigh get out of the car to rescue, and what happened to John's car during the resulting stoppage?

The Finale
John and Kayleigh have to travel home on the bus where
they listen to his song and hold hands! Awwwwhhh!

SPOOKS: 1. C) Thames House; 2. C) The Grid; 3. A) Peter Firth; 4. B) Cod tea and food colouring; 5. A) Home Secretary; 6. A) Princess Diana; 7. B) Jenny Agutter; 8. A) Adam; 9. A) Ikea bins upside down; 10. A) Ruth.

A soap opera (or more specifically an operatic drama) is a serial dealing especially with domestic situations and frequently characterized by melodrama, ensemble casts and sentimentality. The term 'soap opera' came from radio dramas originally being sponsored by soap manufacturers.

SOAP WATCH

SOAP CHARACTERS - NAME THE PROGRAMMES IN WHICH THEY APPEARED!

1. LYNN WHITELEY

2. JIMMY STOKES

3. MAUREEN NICHOLLS

4. LUKE MORGAN

5, DANNY BALDWIN

6. SETH ARMSTRONG

7. STELLA RIGBY

8. GLORIA WEAVER

9. DIETER SCHULZ

10 GARRY HOBBS

11. GWEN LOCKHEAD

12. VIV HARKER

13. MRS TARDEBIGGE

14. IDRIS HOPKINS

15. CASSIE CHARLTON

16. JOANNE MINISTER

17. HAYLEY CROPPER

18. DOUGAL LACHLAN

19. SANJAY KAPOOR

20. VINCE PARKER

PETER KAY'S CAR SHARE: 1. Kayleigh; 2. Forever FM; 3. Fiat 500; 4. Stink Ray; 5. Blackcurrant; 6. The Wigan store; 7. B) Dizzy by Tommy Roe; 8. Harry Potter; 9. A) Now 48 double CD B) Hear'say - Pure and Simple; 10. A hedgehog and John's driver's door gets knocked off by a car impatiently overtaking.

An action-comedy series produced by ITC Entertainment, and initially broadcast on ITV and ABC in 1971. The show was called 'the last major entry in the cycle of adventure series that began 11 years earlier with Danger Man', as well as 'the most ambitious and expensive of Sir Lew Grade's international action adventure series'. Filmed in Britain, France, and Italy between May 1970 and June 1971. 1 Series 24 Episodes.

1. Allegedly the two big stars of *The Persuaders* did not really get on off screen. Who were they?

2. What were the names of the two roles the stars played?

3. The American half of the duo was brought up in the slums of which city, before making a success of life and becoming a millionaire in the oil industry?
A) Chicago   B) Washington   C) New York

4. The English half was educated at which private school before going to Oxford University, then becoming a British Army officer and an ex-racing car driver?
A) Harrow   B) Eton   C) Charterhouse

5. A pair of globe-trotting millionaire playboys, where were the two men brought together by retired Judge Fulton (played by Laurence Naismith)?
A) San Francisco   B) Manchester   C) The French Riviera

6. How did the two characters get on when they first met?

7. The two had expensive tastes in cars. What make cars did they drive?
A) Bugatti / Jaguar   B) Ferrari Dino / Aston Martin   C) Bentley / Lamborghini

8. There was only one series of *The Persuaders* due to one of the stars having 'other' commitments. What were those commitments?

9. Which top film music composer of the time wrote the theme music?
A) John Barry   B) John Williams   C) Hans Zimmer

10. An attempt to assassinate Michelle Devigne, an art student, at the Côte d'Azur airport, led Brett and Danny to a syndicate smuggling gold in the form of counterfeit coins, that involved her uncle who was a jeweller. Who played Michelle Devigne? A) Madeline Smith   B) Susan Hampshire   C) Susan George

TRIVIA: The opening titles credit Tony Curtis and Roger Moore by their surnames only.

SOAP CHARACTERS: 1. Emmerdale; 2. United!; 3. Albion Market; 4. Hollyoaks; 5. Coronation Street; 6. Emmerdale; 7. Coronation Street; 8. Emmerdale; 9. Eldorado; 10. EastEnders; 11. Eldorado; 12. Albion Market; 13. Crossroads; 14. Coronation Street, 15. Brookside; 16. Compact; 17. Coronation Street; 18. Take the High Road; 19. EastEnders; 20. Crossroads.

A British sketch comedy series that began as a radio show in 2000 and became a television series between 2003 and 2007. One-off specials were broadcast in 2005, 2007, 2009, 2015, 2016, 2019 and 2020. The programme consisted of a series of sketches involving exaggerated parodies of British people from various walks of life. A guide – aimed at non-British people – to British society. 3 Series. 44 Episodes.

1. Who was the narrator for the show?
A) Tom Baker   B) Colin Baker   C) Richard Baker

2. Ruth Jones was a barmaid in The Scarecrow and Mrs. King pub. Her best friend was 'the only gay in the village' Daffyd Thomas. What was her character's name?

3. Which real life TV personality joined Marjorie Davies at the local Fat fighters Club, only to get spat in her face?
A) Dawn French   B) Lisa Riley   C) Vanessa Feltz

4. What did teenage delinquent Vicky Pollard swop for her baby?

5. At the swimming pool what did 'wheelchair bound' Andy do when his carer Lou's back was turned?

6. What was the name of romance novelist Dame Sally Markham's dedicated secretary? A) Miss Favour   B) Miss Grace   C) Miss Rubens

7. What did the computer always say according to Carol Beer, a bank worker and later a holiday rep and hotel receptionist?

8. Which famous museum did Anne visit?
A) Victoria & Albert   B) The Louvre
C) The Smithsonian

9. Which London born, tough guy actor, was caricatured regularly speaking to his agent and saying things like: 'So they want me to star in it, write the theme tune, sing the theme tune.....?

10. Who has a Thai mail-order bride called Ting Tong?

THE PERSUADERS: 1. Tony Curtis and Roger Moore; 2. Danny Wilde and Lord Brett Rupert George Robert Andrew Sinclair; 3. C) New York City; 4. A) Harrow; 5. C) The French Riviera; 6. They instantly dislike each other and destroy a hotel bar during a fist-fight; 7. B) Ferrari Dino / Aston Martin; 8. Roger Moore accepted the role as James Bond after Sean Connery stepped down 9. A) John Barry; 10. C) Susan George.

A British mystery series, broadcast on ITV between 1994 and 1998, based on The Cadfael Chronicles novels written by Ellis Peters. Produced by ITV Central. The series is set in the 12th century in England, mainly the Benedictine Abbey where Brother Cadfael lives. There are differences between the plots and characters in the novels and on screen in some episodes, as well as the sequence. 4 Series. 13 Episodes.

1. Which knighted star of screen and theatre played the title role?

2. To which order of monks did Brother Cadfael belong?

3. Who were the battling monarchs during the Civil War in which Cadfael was set? A) James VI & George II   B) King Stephen & Empress Maud (Matilda) C) William of Normandy & Empress Maud (Matilda)

4. In *One Corpse Too Many* Cadfael was assigned by the King to dispose of 94 hanged rebels. What did he discover among the corpses?

5. At which Abbey did Cadfael serve? It was destroyed in the 16th century, the nave surviving as a parish church, and today serves as the mother church for the Parish of Holy Cross. A) Shrewsbury   B) Tintern   C) Bath

6. Who was the Abbot of the Abbey throughout most of the series? A) Heribert   B) Oswin   C)Radulphus

7. What was the name of the nobleman who was Cadfael's dear friend who called on him many times to help with the mysteries, and to whom Cadfael was godfather to his son? A) Olivier de Bretagne   B) Hugh Beringar of Maesbury C) Prior Robert

8. What job did Cadfael hold at the Abbey?
A) Detective   B) Hospitaller   C) Herbologist

9. What was the name of the beautiful wealthy widow who disappears in *The Rose Rent* episode?   A) Judith Perle   B) Ariana Dumbledore   C) Lady Ermina

10. In The Sanctuary Sparrow what is the name of the expectant woman who tries to elope with her lover with her father's fortune and his blood on her hands? A) Avice of Thornbury   B) Susanna Aurifaber   C) Eleanor of Maesbury

LITTLE BRITAIN: 1. A) Tom Baker; 2. Myfanwy; 3. C) Vanessa Feltz; 4. A Westlife CD; 5. Jumps off the top diving board; 6. Miss Grace; 7. No!; 8. B) The Louvre; 9. Dennis Waterman; 10. Dudley Punt.

A British game show based on a US show. Aired on ITV from 24 March 1984 to 8 April 1988. Briefly on Sky One for one series as The New Price is Right from 4 September 1989 to 31 August 1990. Returned to ITV in 1995 as Bruce's Price is Right, from 4 September 1995 to 16 December 2001 and again on ITV from 8 May 2006 until 12 January 2007. Two one-off specials aired as part of ITV's Gameshow Marathon in September 2005 and April 2007. 14 Series. Around 691 Episodes.

1. There have been numerous versions of the show in various game-show compilations but only 4 presenters have fronted whole series. Can you name them?

2. Initially there were two pilot programmes made and the winner was selected to front the original UK series of the programme. But, which cockney singer and renowned guitarist, was beaten for the job on that occasion?

3. Three other versions of the show have appeared in more recent times in game-show marathons. Who are the three acts who have presented those versions?

Our version of one of the games featured in the early series. We have picked 10 sundry items available on Amazon as at November 2020. You have up to £50 to spend, no more. How many can you buy without going bust? Answers on next page as usual. GOOD LUCK.

A. KID'S STRETCH BANANA — **B. I'M NOT SLEEPING MUG** — **C. HEINZ BEANS SECRET STASH TIN** — **D. IGLOO HEDGEHOG HOUSE** — **E. ANTI-BULLSHIT MINTS**

F. CLASSIC MOTORBIKE 3D JIGSAW — **G. TELESCOPIC BACK SCRATCHER** — **H. RED HOT CHILLI ADDICT SPICE SET** — **J. MONT BLANC MEISTERSTUCK ROLLER BALL** — **K. I HAVE SEX DAILY BAG**

CADFAEL: 1. Sir Derek Jacobi; 2. Benedictine; 3. B) King Stephen & Empress Maud (Matilda); 4. The body of a murdered man; 5. A) Shrewsbury Abbey; 6. C) Radulphus; 7. B) Hugh Beringar of Meesbury; 8. C) Herbologist; 9. A) Judith Perle; 10. B) Susanna Aurifaber.

A British comedy sketch show created by Bill Cotton for the BBC, it aired on BBC One from April 1971 to December 1987. It featured Ronnie Barker and Ronnie Corbett. The format included sketches, solo sections, serial stories and musical finales based on the Two Ronnies complementary personalities. The two never became an exclusive pairing. 12 Series. 93 Episodes.

1. When the pair met for the first time at the Buckstone Club in The Haymarket in London in 1963 Barker was a rising comedian. What was Corbett doing in the club?

2. One of the scriptwriters was Ronnie Barker himself. What name did he use when he put on his writing hat? A) Gerald Wiley   B) John Hampton   C) Ben Doon

3. The most famous sketch was probably *Four Candles* from 1976. When the shopkeeper took offence over an item on the list, he called his assistant to complete the order. The assistant read the list and opened a drawer marked....what?

4. In the 1980 sketch what subject was chosen by the contestant on Mastermind?

5. The first serial was *Hampton Wick,* a pastiche of costume dramas about a governess called Henrietta Beckett, played by? A) Sue Lloyd   B) Madeline Smith   C) Kate O'Mara

6. *Done To Death* in 1972 featured two fictional private detectives. What were their names?

7. *The Phantom Raspberry Blower of Old London Town* was a Jack the Ripper parody. It was written by Ronnie B and Spike Milligan; but who blew the raspberries? A) Spike Milligan   B) Ronnie Barker   C) David Jason

8. In 1980 Diana Dors guest-starred as Commander of the State Police in a spoof piece of dystopian fiction set in 2012 in which women ruled England. Male and female gender roles were reversed. What was it called?

9. In 1975 the Aldershot Brass Ensemble provided a memorable finale featuring a marching band. What instruments did The Two Ronnies play?

10. Corbett: 'That's all we've got time for, so it's Goodnight from me.' Complete the farewell that concluded every show.

THE PRICE IS RIGHT: *1. Leslie Crowther, Bob Warman, Bruce Forsyth, Joe Pasquale; 2. Joe Brown; 3. Ant & Dec, Vernon Kay, Alan Carr. SUPERMARKET: A) Kid's Stretch Banana £16.81; B) I'm Not Sleeping Mug £8.99; C) Heinz Baked Beans Secret Stash £5.00; D) Igloo Hedgehog House £25.64; E) Anti-Bullshit Mints £6.00; F) Classic Motorbike 3D Jigsaw £20.00; G) Telescopic Back Scratcher £4.95; H) Red Hot Chilli Spice Set £21.99; J) Meisterstuck Roller Ball Pen £276.08 (You're bust if you picked this item!); K) I Have Sex Daily Bag £4.99.*

A British game show produced by Granada Television for broadcast on ITV. It originally ran from 7 September 1977 -20 November 1995, hosted by Gordon Burns. In 1995, the show was heavily revamped, including the introduction of co-host Penny Smith and revived for two series in 2009 and 2010, presented by Ben Shephard. 20 Series. 274 Episodes.

A lot of this show cannot be replicated in a book. However the General Knowledge feature was that for each question answered, the next question contained either the answer to the last question, a word from the last answer, or a word that sounded like it. So here goes......

1. Which superstar singer has had 6 solo number one hits and another one as part of a charity single, they include *Baby Jane* and *Everybody Hurts*. Who is he?

2. What is the name of the parliamentary official who summons the House of Commons to the Queen's speech?

3. What is the name of the body of water and marginal sea of the Atlantic Ocean between Eastern Europe, the Caucasus and Western Asia?

4. Name the Ernest Hemingway novel that won the Pulitzer Prize in 1953 telling the story of a battle between a fisherman and a large marlin?

5. What was the regular description of his father as used by Harold Steptoe in *Steptoe and Son*?

6. What was the 1987 film about a girl on vacation with her family in a Catskill Mountains resort who fell in love with the camp's dancing instructor?

7. What was the title of the TV series that featured celebrities figure skating with a professional partner?

8. What is the phrase that means to do or say something to relieve tension or get conversation going in a strained situation, or when strangers meet?

9. What was the title of the song written by their bass guitarist John Deacon that Queen took to number 3 in 1984?

10. Name the TV sitcom, on our screens from 1984 and 1986, that was about two couples who met while holidaying at a Spanish hotel in Marbella?

THE TWO RONNIES: 1. He was serving the drinks; 2. A) Gerald Wiley; 3. Billhooks; 4. Answer the question before last ; 5. B) Madeline Smith; 6. Piggy Malone (Barker) and Charley Farley (Corbett); 7. C) David Jason; 8.The Worm That Turned; 9. Bass drum (Ronnie B), Cymbals (Ronnie C); 10. Barker: And it's 'Goodnight' from him. Together: Goodnight!

A British sitcom broadcast first on Channel 4 from 2003 until 2015. In 2010. Became the longest-running comedy in Channel 4 history. Never achieved high viewing figures during its original run, but the show received consistent critical acclaim and has since become a cult favourite. There were 9 Series. 54 Episodes.

1. Who played Mark Corrigan, a loan manager at the fictional company, JLB Credit.
A) Robert Webb   B) David Mitchell   C) Matt King

2. Olivia Colman played a co-worker at JLB, who became scruffy and unstable, and served as a love interest for Mark (and occasionally Jeremy) throughout much of the series. What was her character's name?
A) Sophie Winkleman   B) Eliza L Bennett
C) Sophie Chapman

3. Which of these did Jez and Super Hans NOT use to get high at Life08?
A) Snorting spearmint Polo's   B) A can of Coca Cola in one swig   C) Headrush

4. Mark fell for a shy, attractive student in a shoe shop and made an ill-judged visit to his old university where she studied. Where was the university?
A) Camborne   B) Dartmouth   C) Ilminster

5. Sophie left on a business trip, leaving Mark to consider a fling with a woman whom he met at his school reunion. To which German city did Sophie travel?
A) Frankfurt   B) Cologne   C) Dresden

6. What did Mark write on his eyelids during the dinner party?
A) Leave Angus   B) Be mine   C) Love you

7. Which football team did Super Hans support?
A) Spurs   B) Borussia Mönchengladbach   C) Bayern Munich

8. In *Quantocking*, which chocolate bar did Mark ration?
A) Crunchie   B) Dairy Milk   C) Mars

9. What was the name of the block of flats in which Mark and Jez lived?
A) Aphrodite House   B) Apollo House   C) Zeus House

10. What was the name of the dating agency 'for the discerning single professional' that Mark was going to set up with the woman he met on his MBA course?
A) Simpatico   B) First Date   C) DirectDating.com

THE KRYPTON FACTOR: *1. Rod Stewart; 2. Black ROD; 3. BLACK Sea; 4. The Old Man and the SEA; 5. 'You Dirty OLD MAN; 6. DIRTY Dancing; 7. DANCING On Ice; 8. Break the ICE; 9. I Want To BREAK Free; 10. Duty FREE.*

BRIDESHEAD REVISITED

A 1981 British serial produced by Granada Television for broadcast by the ITV network. The serial is an adaptation of the novel Brideshead Revisited (1945) by Evelyn Waugh. It follows, from the 1920s to the early 1940s, the life and romances of the protagonist Charles Ryder—including his friendship with the Flytes, a family of wealthy English Catholics who live in a palatial mansion called Brideshead Castle. 1 Series. 11 Episodes.

1. Who played the leading roles of Charles Ryder and Sebastian Flyte?

2. The stately home of the Flyte family was the real star of this show. Which beautiful real life home was used for the series?
A) Castle Howard   B) Longleat House   C) Chatsworth

3. What was the name of the woman that Lord Brideshead (Bridey played by Simon Jones) married?
A) Lady Celia Mulcaster   B) Mrs Dora Samgrass   C) Mrs Beryl Muspratt

4. In the early days Charles and Sebastian were both at Oxford University. Which of them achieved the better degree?
A) Charles   B) Sebastian   C) Both left without a degree

5. Which Knight of the theatre played Lord Marchmain?
A) John Gielgud   B) Laurence Olivier   C) Anthony Hopkins

6. Sebastian always carried a teddy bear around with him. What was the bear's name? A) Rupert   B) Aloysius   C) Pooh

7. What was the name of Lord Marchmain's mistress with whom he lived in Venice? A) Cara   B) Celia   C) Brenda

8. What is the first thing that Sebastian asked Charles to draw at Brideshead?
A) Himself   B) The fountain   C) Aloysius

9. When Sebastian found drinking was overwhelming him, he moved to Morocco and shared a house with whom? A) Maximilian   B) Marius   C) Kurt

10. Whom did Charles Ryder marry?
A) Lady Celia Mulcaster   B) Lady Cora Crawley   C) Lady Prudence Fairfax

TRIVIA *The ship in the storm scenes was unused footage from The Poseidon Adventure (1972)*

THE PEEP SHOW: *1. B) David Mitchell; 2. C) Sophie Chapman; 3. A) Snorting spearmint Polo's; 4. B) Dartmouth; 5. A) Frankfurt; 6. C) Love you; 7. A) Spurs; 8. B) Dairy Milk; 9. B) Apollo House; 10. A) Simpatico.*

A British police political-thriller series created and written by Jed Mercurio. Produced by World Productions as part of ITV Studios for the BBC. A fictional Police Sergeant is assigned as principal protection officer for an ambitious Home Secretary. The series comments on many issues regarding controversy around government monitoring of private information. 1 Series. 6 Episodes.

1. The plot centred around the fictional character of Police Sergeant David Budd, a British Army war veteran. Who played the role and won the Golden Globe Award for Best Actor in a Television Drama Series?

2. Budd was assigned as the PPO for the Rt Hon Julia Montague MP, the Home Secretary and Conservative Party Member of Parliament for Thames West. Which star of many TV series, including *Line of Duty* and *Ashes to Ashes*, played the part?

3. David Budd was an Afghanistan war veteran. What mental problem does he have as a result of his wartime experiences ?

4. Sergeant David Budd was travelling home to London with his two children when he suddenly discovered what in the train's toilet?

5. Who played bodyguard David Budd's police boss?
A) Pippa Haywood   B) Diana Rigg   C) Haydn Gwynne

6. How did TV political journalists Laura Kuenssberg, Mishal Husain and Martha Kearney turn up in the show?
A) Took part in a heated debate about gun law   B) Contestants on a fictional version of Strictly Come Dancing   C) We heard their voices on news reports

7. Stephen Hunter-Dunn, the Director General of MI5, informed Montague of intelligence suggesting a terrorist plan to attack which target connected to Budd?
A) His car   B) His children's school   C) His wife

8. What happened when Budd cornered the sniper and found him to be Andy Apsted, a friend and former army colleague?

9. What happens whilst Julia is delivering a speech about 'protecting our future' at St Matthew's College?

10. Luke Aikens, a powerful crime lord abducted Budd and fitted him with what deadly contraption?

BRIDESHEAD REVISITED: 1. Jeremy Irons and Anthony Andrews; 2. A) Castle Howard; 3. C) Mrs Beryl Muspratt; 4. C) Both left without a degree; 5. B) Laurence Olivier (Gielgud played Edward Ryder); 6. B) Aloysius; 7. A) Cara; 8. B) The fountain; 9. C) Kurt; 10. A) Lady Celia Mulcaster.

A hapless but caring teacher tried to control his class of unruly kids. The teacher saw much good and potential in his pupils, much to the dismay of his fellow teachers who have long lost hope in the kids. London Weekend Television situation comedy for ITV, created by John Esmonde and Bob Larbey. There were 4 series and 55 episodes between 1968 and 1972

1. When a newly-qualified teacher arrived to start his first job, even he hasn't bargained on what awaited him. What was his name?

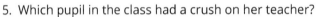

2. Can you remember the name of the school?

3. What class was the 'new boy' given?

4. A member of the art club produced some stunning life studies of one of his unruly class - in the nude. Who was the model? A) Maureen   B) Sharon   C) Daisy

5. Which pupil in the class had a crush on her teacher? A) Maureen   B) Sharon   C) Daisy

6. Who played the cantankerous school caretaker Norman Potter, who claimed to be an ex-Desert Rat and would often complain about class '5C' and their 'dreadful behaviour'? A) Jimmy Edwards   B) Deryck Guyler   C) Windsor Davies

7. Miss Doris Ewell the deputy head was played by an actress who appeared memorably in *Fawlty Towers* as the hard of hearing Mrs Richards. Who was she?

8. Peter Cleall played the wise-cracking Eric Duffy. In real life he became an actor's agent, but how old was he when the filming started in 1968?   A) 20   B) 22   C) 24

9. Trouble ensued when the headmaster, Mr Cromwell (Noel Howlett), decided to implement a new system and do what?   A) Stop competitive sports B) Divide the school into houses   C) Ban smoking behind the bike sheds

10. In the 1971 spin-off film how was a small feud with some stereotypical upper-class children from the posh Boulters School resolved by Sharon?
A) Got them drunk B) She enlisted Hell's Angels friends
C) Made a false rape claim

BODYGUARD: *1. Richard Madden; 2. Keeley Hawes; 3. PTSD (Post Traumatic Stress Disorder); 4. A suicide bomber 5. A) Pippa Haywood; 6. C) We heard their voices on news reports; 7. B) His children's school; 8. Apsted shoots himself; 9. A bomb explodes and kills Montague and others; 10. A suicide vest.*

A British comedy-drama mystery series, based on the picaresque novels about the adventures of the eponymous Lovejoy, by John Grant under the pen name Jonathan Gash. The show ran for 71 episodes over 6 series, was originally broadcast on BBC1 between 10 January 1986-4 December 1994, although there was a five-year gap between the first and second series. Television adaption is by Ian La

1. Who played the eponymous, roguish antiques dealer based in East Anglia?

2. Within the trade, he has a reputation as a 'divvy', a diviner. What does that mean?
A) A bit thick B) Has an eye for exceptional items C) A wide boy

3. Lovejoy would frequently break the fourth wall. What does that mean?
A) Go the extra mile B) Improvised C) Speak directly to the camera

4. The theme tune used in the opening and end credits, as well as the incidental music for each episode, was composed by a man who was also a member of a trio who notched up several chart hits. Who was he?
A) Dec Cluskey B) Michael King C) Denis King

5. In *The Firefly Cage*, the very first episode, Lovejoy acquires a new, enthusiastic, but ever so slightly dim, assistant played by Chris Jury. What was his name?
A) Eric Catchpole B) David Bliss C) Ken Harper

6. In 1977 Ian McShane had a major role in Jesus of Nazareth. Who did he portray?
A) John the Baptist B) Herod Antipas C) Judas Iscariot

7. Lady Jane Felsham, was a nice aristocrat with cash and class to support Lovejoy's operations. Which 'often seen on TV' Scottish actress played the role?
A) Phyllis Logan B) Lindsay Duncan C) Julie Graham

8. In Series 3 Lovejoy borrowed a blue Morris Minor convertible car from Lady Jane, it was a bit rundown, and quite a bit inefficient, but it had history and character. What name had she given the car? A) Mo B) Maurice C) Miriam

9. Caroline Langrishe joined the cast in Series 5 as a replacement for Lady Jane Felsham. An auctioneer, she too was designed as a beauty with a posh accent and susceptibility to roguish charm. What was the character's name?
A) Beth Taylor B) Charlotte Cavendish C) Lavina Pinder

10. In the very last episode Last Tango in Lavenham, Lovejoy proposes marriage to whom when she is considering leaving for New York?
A) Charlotte Cavendish B) Jane Felsham C) Lavina Pinder

PLEASE SIR! *1. Bernard Hedges; 2. Fenn Street Secondary Modern School ; 3. 5C;*
4. B) Sharon; 5. A) Maureen; 6. B) Deryck Guyler; 7. Joan Sanderson; 8. C) 24; 9. B) Divide the
school into houses; 10. C) Made a false rape claim.

A British programme on Channel 4 from 16 January 1994-7 September 2014. Produced by Tim Taylor and presented by actor Tony Robinson. Each episode had a team of specialists carrying out an archaeological dig over three days. Robinson explained the process in lay terms. Also consistently included archaeologists Mick Aston, Carenza Lewis, Francis Pryor and Phil Harding. 20 series. 280 Episodes (including Specials)

TIME TEAM SPECIALS

1. In 2000 A) Which Cornish castle was the team searching for evidence about the myth and mystery of B) Which legendary British leader?

2. In 2001 Tony Robinson and Phil Harding went dinosaur hunting in America, joining a museum dig to excavate the bones of the T-Rex's ancestor. To which part of the US did the boys travel? A) Montana   B) Texas   C) Illinois

3. In 2002 the team went on a dive to recover a wood carved statue from HMS Colossus, one of Nelsons ships at the Battle of the Nile. The ship sank in 1798 near which island? A) Tresco   B) Isle of Wight   C) St Mary's

4. In 2004, to celebrate the 60th anniversary of D-Day the team went to Normandy to retrace movements of the Dorset Regiment on that historic day. On which beach had the regiment landed? A) Omaha   B) Juno   C) Gold

5. In 2005 the *Time Team* went to look at the partial remains of an ancient settlement where spectacular late Bronze Age finds had been discovered. The visit was before new local flood banks were rebuilt. Where was the settlement? A) Bodmin Moor, Cornwall   B) Washingborough, Lincoln   C) Bath, Somerset

6. Also in 2005 the team went to the site of what had been Britain's biggest neolithic henge, which had dwarfed Stonehenge. It's four large concentric circles of postholes would have held extremely large standing timbers. What was the site called? A) Durrington Walls   B) Grimes Graves   C) Avebury

7. In 2006 the team visited the site of Regency era terraced housing that was devastated in the Blitz and later air-raids. It was completely redeveloped in the 1960s/70s. Where was this site that showed housing of the time, and the damage caused by aerial bombing?   A) Shoreditch, London   B) Salford   C) Norwich

8. To celebrate the Queen's 80th birthday which 3 Royal palaces were the team specially authorised to explore in 2008 while the Queen was away?

9. The team excavated a cemetery in a field beside Nelson's first Naval Hospital in 2010. The 1800 bed hospital had cost £100,000 to build in 1753. Where was it?

10. The Time Team cast doubts upon the recognised locations of two famous battles on English soil in 1066 and 1485. Name the two battles.

LOVEJOY: 1. Ian McShane; 2. B) Has an eye for exceptional items (and genuine and forged items); 3. C) Speak directly to the camera; 4. C) Denis King; 5. A) Eric Catchpole; 6. C) Judas Iscariot; 7. A) Phyllis Logan; 8. C) Miriam; 9. B) Charlotte Cavendish; 10. A) Charlotte Cavendish.

A six-episode British drama, adapted by Andrew Davies from Jane Austen's 1813 novel of the same name. BBC1 originally broadcast the 55-minute episodes from 24 September to 29 October 1995. Critically acclaimed and a popular success it was honoured with several awards.

1. Everyone remembers Colin Firth playing Mr Darcy, but who played Elizabeth Bennet? A) Cate Blanchett B) Jennifer Ehle C) Gillian Anderson

2. What was Mr Darcy's first name? A) Fitzwilliam B) Marius C) Jonthan

3. How many daughters did the Bennet's have? A) 3 B) 4 C) 5

4. How did Darcy and his close friend Charles Bingley arrive at Netherfield?
A) Train B) Horseback C) Carriage

5. What was the name of Darcy's huge estate?
A) Cloverfield B) Pemberley C) Manderley

6. Lady Catherine de Bourgh was the aunt of which character?
A) Mr Darcy B) Mr Collis C) Mr Bennet

7. Which scene from the series made Channel 4's Top 100 TV Moments in 1999?
A) The double wedding B) First meeting at the Ball
C) Darcy swims in the lake

8. Two of the actresses were related in real life. Can you name them and also the characters they played?

9. Who was the sycophantic parson who was the distant cousin of Mr Bennet, and holder of a valuable living at the Hunsford parsonage near Rosing's Park, the estate of his patroness Lady Catherine De Bourgh? A) Mr Bamber B) Mr Welby C) Mr Collins

10. When Charles Bingley was persuaded to leave Netherfield, where did he go? A) London B) Italy C) America

What 2001 film is regarded as a modernization of Pride and Prejudice - and even shares a star?

TIME TEAM: 1. A) Tintagel; B) King Arthur; 2. A) Montana; 3. C) St Mary's, Scilly Isles; 4. C) Gold; 5. B) Washingborough, Lincoln; 6. A) Durrington Walls; 7. A) Shoreditch Park; 8. Buckingham Palace, Windsor Castle, Palace of Holyroodhouse; 9. Gosport, Hampshire; 10. Battle of Hastings and Battle of Bosworth (Field).

A British sketch comedy series written by and starring comedy duo Dawn French and Jennifer Saunders. Originally broadcast on BBC Two from 1987 to 1993, and was given one of the highest budgets in BBC history to create detailed spoofs and satires of popular culture, movies, celebrities, and art. 6 Series. 48 Episodes (including 9 Specials).

1. By what name were French and Saunders previously known?
A) Dawn & Jennifer   B) The Menopause Sisters   C) Sharon & Tracey

2. Where did the pair first meet in 1978?
A) Central School of Speech & Drama   B) Guilty Pleasures club   C) Sainsbury's

3. What was the name of the Soho club in which they performed during the 1980s?

4. What was the name of the comedy musical group, consisting of Rowland Rivron and Simon Brint that featured regularly on the show?

5. When did French and Saunders win their BAFTA Fellowship - a lifetime achievement award?
A) 2019   B) 2009   C) 1999

6. Lananeeneenoonoo was a British spoof all-girl group including French & Saunders. A) Who completed the trio? B) With which top girl band did they create a charity single *Help!* which reached number 3 in the UK for Comic Relief in 1989?

7. What cake baking expert was the regular butt of jokes on the show? A) Mary Berry   B) Mrs Brown   C) Jane Asher

8. What material covered the furnishings in the White Room sketches?
A) Newspaper   B) Bubble Wrap   C) Dust Sheets

9. An operatic duo memorably performed a Kylie Minogue hit. What song was it?
A) I Should Be So Lucky   B) Spinning Around   C) Can't Get You Out Of My Head

10. Name the two young women, drama queens obsessed with catalogue shopping, who also put far too much effort into organising a wedding or holiday?

FRENCH AND SAUNDERS DID SOME MEMORABLE SPOOFS OF MAJOR MOVIES · WHICH ONE IS PICTURED LEFT?

PRIDE AND PREJUDICE: *1. B) Jennifer Ehle; 2. A) Fitzwilliam; 3. C) 5; 4. B) Horseback; 5. B) Pemberley; 6. A) Mr Darcy; 7. C) Darcy swims in the lake; 8. Joanna David (Mrs Gardiner) is the mother of Emilia Fox (Georgiana Darcy); 9. C) Mr Collins; 10. A) London.*
MODERN VERSION: *Bridget Jones Diary (Colin Firth).*

A British series set in Whitechapel in the East End of London. Set in April 1889, six months after the last Jack the Ripper killing in Whitechapel. H Division is responsible for policing 1¼ square miles of East London with a population of 67,000 poor and dispossessed. Has the killer returned? 5 Series. 37 Episodes.

1. Which star of the film *Death at a Funeral* played Inspector Edmund Reid, the head of Whitechapel's H Division?

2. Who owned a brothel in Tenter Street for much of the first and second series?
A) Short Sarah   B) Long Susan   C) Lanky Liz

3. Which former US Army surgeon and Pinkerton agent and H Division's forensic expert, was married to a brothel madam?
A) Ronald Capshaw   B) Captain Homer   C) Captain Homer Jackson

4. Deserted by his wife, Emily, Edmund Reid worked most nights in his office at Leman Street. He retired when his daughter is found. What was her name?
A) Mathilda   B) Amelia   C) Jane

5. Reid's daughter had been thought lost during the sinking of which steamer on the Thames in 1888? (Susan Hart then discovered in 1894 that she was being held prisoner by Horace Buckley). A) SS Marchioness   B) SS Ark Royal   C) SS Princess

6. In Series 3 masked hijackers set out to steal a wad of US dollar bearer bonds being transported on the Bishopsgate goods line, but owing to bad luck and misinformation the train crashed and killed how many people?
A) 25   B) 35   C) 55

7. In Series 4 it was 1897 and Queen Victoria's Diamond Jubilee. Reid was retired and living with his daughter in which seaside village in Kent?
A) Hampton on Sea   B) West Bay   C) Whitstable

8. When Reid returned to Whitechapel he was urged by Deborah Goren to investigate the murder of what spiritual figure?   A) A Monk   B) A Rabbi   C) A Priest

9. In *Edmund Reid Did This*, Drake was bitten and mortally wounded. Who killed him?   A) Theodore P Swift   B) Nathaniel Dove   C) Frank Thatcher

10. What is the name of the pub on Leman Street that was close to the location of the train disaster on the bridge?
A) The Brown Bear   B) The White Lion   C) The Red Kite

FRENCH & SAUNDERS: 1. B) The Menopause Sisters; 2. A) Central School of Speech & Drama; 3. The Comedy Store; 4. Raw Sex; 5. B) 2009; 6. A) Kathy Burke, B) Bananarama; 7. C) Jane Asher; 8. B) Bubble Wrap; 9. A) I Should Be So Lucky; 10. Jackie and Leanne.
SPOOF MOVIES: Misery.

A British talent show originally hosted by Hughie Green, with a late-1980s revival hosted by Bob Monkhouse, and later by previous winner Les Dawson. The winning acts were decided by the viewing public. In the ITV version this took the form of a postal vote. The BBC revival was notable for being the first TV show to decide its winner, using the now-standard method of a telephone vote. 22 Series (18 ITV, 4 BBC). 520 Episodes (478 ITV, 48 BBC).

14 OF THE ACTS BELOW APPEARED ON THE SHOW. CAN YOU NAME THEM? ALSO FIND THE ONE ACT THAT WAS REJECTED AFTER AN INITIAL AUDITION!

| 1. 1968 Those Were the Days! | 2. 1974 Just 10 Years Old! | 3. 1971 Mother of Mine! | 4. 1972 Piano Man! | 5. 1972 Welcome Home! |

| 6. 1973 Billy Don't Be A Hero | 7. 1967 A Real Headliner! | 8. 1970 That's Magic! | 9. 1988 Joseph! | 10. 1970 I'll scream & Scream! |

| 11. 1986 Bad Girls | 12. 1986 Large Arena Headliner! | 13. 1971 Steps Back In Amazement! | 14. 1973 Oggy, Oggy, Oggy | 15. 1975 She's A Poet! |

RIPPER STREET: 1. Matthew Macfadyen; 2. B) Long Susan; 3. C) Captain Homer Jackson (really Matthew Judge); 4. A) Mathilda; 5. C) SS Princess; 6. C) 55; 7. A) Hampton on Sea; 8. B) Rabbi; 9. Nathaniel Dove; 10. A) The Brown Bear.

A British period crime drama series created by Steven Knight. Set in Birmingham, the series follows the exploits of a crime family after WWI. The fictional family is loosely based on a real 19th-century urban youth gang of the same name, who were active in the city from the 1890s to the early twentieth century. 5 Series. 30 Episodes.

1. What is the main pub called in the series?
A) Boar's Head   B) The Garrison   C) Blind Beggar

2. What do the Peaky Blinders keep under their hats?

3. What is the name of the Peaky Blinders intro song, and who sings it?

4. What is the official name of the Peaky Blinders family business?
A) Shelby Company Limited   B) The Peak District   C) Wonka Industries

5. Why did Michael kill Father Hughes?
A) Hughes orchestrated his foster mother's death B) To prove his loyalty to Peaky Blinders C) Insinuated Hughes abused him whilst in care

6. Which *Jurassic Park* actor played Inspector Campbell?   A) Jeff Goldblum
B) Sam Neill   C) Richard Attenborough

7. What is the name of Tommy's grey racehorse in series 2? A) Desert Orchid   B) Native Dancer
C) Grace's Secret

8. To which religious movement did Linda Shelby belong? A) Jehovah's Witnesses   B) Scientology
C) Quakers

9. What supposedly cursed gemstone was Grace wearing when she was shot and killed by an assassin?
A) Sapphire   B) Ruby   C) Emerald

10. Inspector Campbell had which animal's head on the top of his walking cane?
A) Cobra   B) Wolf   C) Horse

OPPORTUNITY KNOCKS: *1. Mary Hopkin; 2. Lena Zavaroni; 3. Neil Reid; 4. Bobby Crush; 5. Peters and Lee; 6. Paper Lace; 7. Freddie Starr; 8. Paul Daniels; 9. Darren Day; 10. Bonnie Langford; 11. Debra Stephenson; 12. Lee Evans; 13. Little and Large; 14. Max Boyce; 15. Pam Ayres. **ODD ONE OUT :** 12. Lee Evans was rejected after his audition and did not appear in the TV show.*

Documentary series on Channel 5 following the work of two vets in North Yorkshire. Initially both worked at Skeldale Veterinary Centre in Thirsk. The younger vet moved to another practice following a takeover by Medivat. First episode was shown on 15 September 2015. 11 series with 107 episodes as at August 2020.

1. Name the two Yorkshire veterinary surgeons who have been the stars of the show since 2015.

2. The Thirsk practice was once headed by a vet who became famous as a writer. What was his real name and under what pen name did he gain fame?

3. The series has been narrated by two stars of the original *All Creatures Great and Small* TV series. Who are they?

4. True or False? Julian completed in the 2013 UK Ironman Championship and finished in the top 50.

5. Two of Peter's favourite customers are Mr and Mrs Green. What are their first names?

6. In 2017 a parrot called Dougie was featured. He particularly enjoyed eating what? A) Rice pudding B) Black pudding C) Yorkshire pudding D) Bread Pudding

7. In 2018 Julian was a judge at a … show at Dunsforth. Fill in the blank.

8. Peter obtained his degree in veterinary science from which University in 1981, before rejoining the Thirsk practice in 1982?
A) Bristol   B) Manchester   C) Oxford   D) Liverpool

9. In what other farm based TV programme did Julian appear in 2018-19?
A) Springtime on the Farm B) Countryfile C) Srringwatch D) Our Yorkshire Farm

10. Julian works with which close relative in a vets practice at Boroughbridge?

PEAKY BLINDERS: 1. B) The Garrison; 2) Razors; 3. Red Right Hand by Nick Cave & The Bad Seeds; 4. A) Shelby Company Limited; 5. C) Insinuated Hughes abused him whilst in care; 6. B) Sam Neill; 7. C) Grace's Secret; 8. C) Quaker; 9. A) Sapphire; 10. B) Wolf.

In 1975 the original BBC series adapted novels of Winston Graham. Transmitted between 1975 and 1977. In 2015 the revival follows the titular character on his return to Cornwall after the American War of Independence in 1783. Originally 2 Series and 29 Episodes. The 2015 version was 5 Series 43 Episodes.

1. Who played Ross Poldark in the Series that ran from 1975 and 1977?

2. And who followed suit in the series that started in 2015?

3. Poldark lost his fiancée, Elizabeth, to his cousin Francis. He then married his servant. What was her name?

4. What was the affliction that killed Ross and Demelza's baby Julia?
A) Fetid lung   B) Rancid epiglottis   C) Putrid throat

5. What was the name of the home of the Poldark family?

6. From which battle did Ross return in episode 1 of the 2015 version? A) Battle of Waterloo B) Battle of Virginia   C) Battle of New Orleans

7. What was the name of Demelza's dog?
A)   Garrick   B) Daly   C) Scala

8. Wheal Grace was a mine reopened by Ross Poldark. What metal were they seeking?
A) Copper   B) Tin   C) Gold

9. Charles Poldark had a heart attack during the Christening of his grandson and died. The actor playing Charles also died after completing filming. What was the name of this top TV actor?
A) Ron Moody   B) Warren Clarke   C) Christopher Lee

10. What was the name of Ross Poldark's bitter enemy throughout the series?

THE YORKSHIRE VET: 1. Peter Wright and Julian Norton; 2. Alf Wight, James Herriott; 3. Christopher Timothy and Peter Davison; 4. True; 5. Jean and Steve; 6. C) Yorkshire pudding; 7. Dog; 8. D) Liverpool; 9. A) Springtime on the farm; 10. His wife Anne.

A British general knowledge quiz show broadcast on Channel 4. Originally ran from 11 January 1988 to 19 December 2003 and had a reputation for being one of the toughest quizzes on TV. Presented and produced by William G Stewart. Revived in a 2013 special with Adam Hills and a series in 2014 hosted by Sandi Toksvig. 43 Series. 2635 Episodes.

SOME GENERAL KNOWLEDGE QUESTIONS THAT MIGHT HAVE BEEN ASKED ON THE SHOW

1. What is the capital of Chile?

2. What magazine is the flagship of the Consumers Association?

3. What is the only vowel not used as the initial letter of a US state?

4. Published in 2015, which best-selling novel by Paula Hawkins includes the character Rachel Watson?

5. What is the most famous Mexican beer?

6. What meat is used in Glamorgan sausages?

7. Which football team has won the Champions League (European Cup) most times?

8. Opened in 1801, which waterway links London with the Midlands?

9. Which murder mystery play by Agatha Christie opened in 1952 and celebrated its 25,000th performance in 2012?

10. The saliva of the swiftlet is the main constituent of which Chinese dish?

11. Who was Lord Mayor of London in 1397, 1398, 1406, 1419?

12. What did the Romans call Scotland?

13. The New English Bible was published in which century?

14. In tennis which fruit can be found at the top of the men's Wimbledon trophy?

15. True or False? It is illegal to be drunk in charge of a cow in Scottish law?

POLDARK: 1. Robin Ellis; 2. Aidan Turner; 3. Demelza Carne; 4. C) Putrid throat; 5. Nampara House; 6. B) Battle of Virginia; 7. A) Garrick; 8. A) Copper; 9. B) Warren Clarke; 10. George Warleggan.

A British programme which airs weekly on BBC One and reports on rural, agricultural, and environmental issues in the United Kingdom. Launched as a Sunday morning programme on 24 July 1988 as Country File, it quickly amassed the highest viewers, around 2.5 million, and moved to Sunday evenings in 2009. The show celebrates the beauty and diversity of the British countryside. Now notched up over 1500 Episodes.

1. To whom did John Craven sit with in a meadow, the location of her latest novel, and ask: 'Was there a lot of rumpy-pumpy going on in this field?'

2. True or False? Rock stars Brian May of Queen and Roger Daltry of The Who have both appeared on the programme.

3. How has *Countryfile* raised over £20 million since 1999 for *Children in Need*?

4. Presenter Adam Henson isn't the only presenter with a farming background. Two other regular presenters have farm connections. Can you name them?

5. In March 2013, which Royal Family member was the guest editor for a special edition to mark *Countryfile*'s 25th anniversary?

6. Which country music loving presenter celebrated his Dad's 70th birthday by accompanying him on a pilgrimage to Nashville?

7. For most species of bees, does stinging mean death for the bee?

8. During which epidemic in 2001 was Countryfile broadcast live to bring the nation the very latest on the crisis

9. Whose greatest screen credit was for Mel Gibson's *Braveheart*, supplying two longhorn cattle for filming and then getting a walk-on part towing a cart carrying William Wallace's father's body?

10. In December 2014, which Countryfile presenter took over as President of the Gloucestershire Wildlife Trust from Sir Henry Elwes?

CAN YOU IDENTIFY THESE SPECIES OF BRITISH WILDLIFE?

A   B   C   D

FIFTEEN TO ONE: 1. Santiago; 2. Which magazine; 3. E; 4. Girl on a Train; 5. Corona; 6. None, they are made from cheese; 7. Grand Union Canal; 8. The Mousetrap; 9. Bird's Nest Soup; 10. Dick Whittington; 12. Caledonia; 13. 20th; 14. Pineapple; 15.True (Act of 1872).

All Kinds of Everything

3

A Miscellaneous Round

A round of mixed questions about British TV. This covers categories including Drama, Children's TV, Comedy, Soaps, Cookery programmes, Sci-Fi, News Years, Catchphrases, Crime shows and more! There are 3 sets of these questions throughout the book.

1. Who was the grumpy head of menswear played by Arthur Brough in the sitcom *Are You Being Served*?

2. *Map and Lucia* was a popular 1986 mini-series starring Prunella Scales and Geraldine McEwan. In which fictional town was the series set?

3. In 1960 which female trio would you have likely encountered in The Snug in the Rovers Return Inn?

4. What was the theme song for *The Young Ones*, the 1980s alternative comedy show with Rik Mayall, Adrian Edmondson, Nigel Planer and Christopher Ryan?

5. True or False? *Waterloo Road* was a British drama series about a comprehensive school with the first seven series being filmed in Salford.

6. In 1999-2001, who played Linda La Hughes, an unattractive middle-aged woman who usually wore tight, colourful clothing, in *Gimme, Gimme, Gimme*?

7. Susan Harper was a control freak and very good at getting her way. In which series was she a tour guide who spent a lot of time fretting about her 3 children?

8. Who were the original two presenters on *Loose Women* in 1999?

9. In the seventies Allan Cuthbertson played the straight man to which much loved prop comedian and magician in an ITV series of 9 one hour shows?

10. Which *Doc Martin* actor completely changed character to play Winston Churchill in *Dr Who* in 2010?

11. In the classic 1960 *Missing Page* episode, who borrowed a murder mystery book from the library, *Lady Don't Fall Backwards*, and found that the last page had been torn out?

12. Did summer precede winter in Delia Smith's cookery collections?

13. Which musical quiz show was originally a part of *Wednesday Night Out*?

14. Which 1960's TV personality always ended his show in a white E-type Jaguar?

15. Who was associated with the catchphrase 'Get down Shep'?

COUNTRYFILE: *1. Jilly Cooper; 2. True; 3. With the Countryfile calendar; 4. Matt Baker (brought up on the family farm in Durham) and Helen Skelton (a dairy farmer's daughter); 5. Charles, Prince of Wales; 6. Matt Baker; 7. No; 8. Foot and Mouth Epidemic; 9. Adam Henson; 10. Ellie Harrison.* BRITISH WILDLIFE DRAWINGS: *A) Harvest mouse; B) Peregrine Falcon; C)Puffin; D) Highland cow.*

A British psychological crime drama programme written by Neil Cross. A Detective Chief Inspector (DCI) working for the Serious Crime Unit in series one, and the new Serious and Serial unit from series two. A dedicated police officer, Luther is obsessive, possessed, and sometimes violent. For Luther, the job always comes first. 5 Series. 20 Episodes.

1. Who played John Luther?

2. What job did Luther's wife Zoe have before she was killed at the end of the first series?   A) Librarian   B) Humanitarian lawyer   C) Police detective

3. A colleague tried to frame Luther for the murder of his wife, whereas he was himself the guilty party. Steven Mackintosh played the part. What was his character's name?   A) DCI Ian Reed   B) DCI Martin Schenk   C) DCI Theo Bloom

4. In Series 2 Luther visited the psychiatric hospital where Alice was being kept. After departing the hospital what did Luther put in an apple and throw over the wall for Alice to find?
A) A SIM card   B) a key card   C) a ring

5. What was the first name of Luther's boss DSU Teller who ordered armed Police to shoot Luther, after he had been framed for the murder of his wife?   A) Jenny   B) Zoe   C) Rose

6. In the first series, in what subject did psychopath Alice get a Ph.D when she was just 18?   A) Astrophysics   B) Mathematics   C) Biochemistry

7. DS Ripley was a young policeman who was ambitious and eager. He was eager to be partnered with detective Luther. How long did he have to wait?
A) 3 months   B) 6 months   C) 9 months

8. What game did Luther and Reed play in the psychiatric hospital?   A) Cluedo B) Monopoly   C) Chess

9. What is the theme music to the series? *(Song and performer please)*

10. In 2016 what was the title of the spoof episode for Sports Relief?

ALL KINDS OF EVERYTHING 3: 1. Mr Ernest Grainger; 2. Tilling on Sea; 3. Ena Sharples, Minnie Caldwell and Martha Longhurst; 4. The Young Ones (Cliff Richard's hit performed by the cast); 5. False, it was Rochdale; (then series 8-10 filmed in Greenock); 6. Kathy Burke; 7. My Family (played by Zoë Wanamaker; 8. Kaye Adams and Nadia Sawalha; 9. Tommy Cooper; 10. Ian McNeice (Bert Large); 11. Tony Hancock; 12. Yes it did (1993 and 1995); 13. Name That Tune; 14. Simon Dee; 15. John Noakes (Blue Peter).

A British medical drama series that airs weekly on BBC One. It was created by Tony McHale and Mal Young as a spin-off from the established BBC medical drama Casualty, and premiered on 12 January 1999. It follows the lives of medical and ancillary staff at the fictional Holby City Hospital. 22 Series 1,033 Episodes.

1. Who is the longest serving actor on Holby City?

2. Which surgeon was diagnosed with Parkinson's Disease?
A) Ed Keating   B) Alex Adams   C) Kian Madani

3. Holby City props team regularly produce a mixture of Weetabix, fruit salad, apple juice and soup to create what?

4. To which country did Ric Griffin and Diane Lloyd travel in *Tuesday's Child,* which was broadcast on 5 July 2005?   A) Ghana   B) Tanzania   C) Zambia

5. In 2007 which character had her car stolen, was accused of racism, and then had the hospital board decide that she could not operate without the supervision of a surgeon, Jac Naylor? A) Lola Griffin   B) Cara Martinez C) Diane Lloyd

6. Which character was killed when their car collided with a train on a crossing, which was later ruled as a suicide?
A) Cara Martinez   B) Diane Lloyd   C) Lola Griffin

7. When a patient accused Sacha Levy of sexual harassment, which staff member also commented that he had also been giving her unwelcome hugs?
A) Jac Naylor   B) Chrissie Williams   C) Dominic Copeland

8. A lot of people suffered at the hands of Professor John Gaskell, who was seeking a cure for paralysis. In which hospital had he previously worked?
A) Stockholm   B) Lisbon   C) Madrid

9. How many people died in a shooting spree in the hospital in 2017, carried out by consultant general surgeon Henrik Hanssen's son Fredrik in 2017?
A) 2   B) 4   C) 6

10. Which injury prone former England international footballer played an injury prone footballer in 2011?
A) Darren Anderton   B) Kieron Dyer C) Owen Hargreaves

LUTHER: 1. Idris Elba; 2. B) Humanitarian lawyer; 3. A) DCI Ian Reed; 4. B) A key card; 5. C) Rose; 6. A) Astrophysics; 7. C) 9 months; 8. C) Chess; 9. Paradise Circus by Massive Attack; 10. Meet the Luthers.

A British crime drama series produced by Left Bank Pictures for the ITV network. Broadcast over five series in 2010–2016. Based on Peter Robinson's Inspector Alan Banks novels. Each story over 2 x one hour episodes. Won the drama category at the regional Royal Television Society Yorkshire Programme Awards. 32 Episodes.

1. Who played the eponymous role of DCI Alan Banks?
A) Nathaniel Parker   B) Stephen Tompkinson   C) Damian Lewis

2. Which major character on TV is not featured in the Peter Robinson books?
A) DI Helen Morton   B) DS Ken Blackstone   C) DC Kevin Templeton

3. In *Aftermath* a police officer is killed while responding to a domestic disturbance call. When DCI Alan Banks is called to investigate what is discovered in the cellar?

4. Who calls Alan Banks to his home and asks him to bring home his runaway teenage daughter Emily who has been posing for nude photos on the Internet?
A) DCS Ron McLaughlin   B) DCS Colin Anderson   C) DCS Gerry Rydell

5. In *Strange Affair* which member of Banks' family is found shot dead?

6. Apart from the main character, who is the only actor to appear in every episode, and what role do they play? A) Andrea Lowe   B) Caroline Catz   C) Jack Deam

7. A leading character in all the Peter Robinson books only appeared in the first two series on television before abruptly departing. Which character?
A) DC Taroq Lang   B) DS Winsome Jackman   C) DC Vince Grady

8. Which serial killer in *Aftermath* turns up as the victim in *Friend of the Devil*?
A) Marcus Payne   B) Lucy Payne   C) Maggie Forrest

9. In *Piece Of My Heart,* John Gaunt, a guitarist in an 80s band was killed by a band-mate Martin Hareford, who was imprisoned for manslaughter, serving five years for Gaunt's death. What was the name of the band?
A) The Crystal Kiss   B) Infant Sorrow   C) Mystic Spiral

10. In *A Little Bit of Heart* which senior member of the team placed themselves in danger by going alone to meet a caller and was then violently killed?
A) DS Annie Cabbot   B) DI Helen Morton   C) DS Ken Blackstone

HOLBY CITY: 1. Hugh Quashie (Ric Griffin); 2. B) Alex Adams; 3. Vomit (sorry!); 3. A) Ghana; 4. C) Diane Lloyd; 5. B) Diane Lloyd (as a result of issues in Q5); 7. A) Jac Naylor; 8. B) Lisbon; 9. A) 2 (including the gunman); 10. B) Kieron Dyer.

A British quiz show produced by Banijay for the BBC. In each episode 4 teams of 2 contestants attempt to find correct but obscure answers to 4 rounds of general knowledge. The winning team competes for the show's cash jackpot. A panel of 100 individuals in a pre-conducted public survey are the source of answers. As at December 2019 there have been 24 Regular Series + 13 Celebrity versions. 1193 Episodes + 211 Celebrity.

FOR OUR VERSION WE LIST 5 POSSIBLE ANSWERS TO EACH QUESTION. THEY ARE WORTH 5,4,3,2,1 POINTS. THE MORE OBSCURE THE ANSWER - THE LESS POINTS YOU SCORE. THE IDEA IS TO SCORE THE LOWEST POINTS POSSIBLE.

WHO HAD UK NUMBER ONE HITS WITH ONE WORD TITLES?

A. HELP (1965)
B. VINCENT (2012)
C. MERCY (2008)
D. YOUNG (2012)
E. SHOTGUN (2018)

WHO PLAYED THE ROLE IN EASTENDERS?

A. ALFIE MOON
B. DOT COTTON
C DEN WATTS
D. BIANCA JACKSON
E. KAT SLATER

BRILLIANT BARBARA'S

A. RINGO STARR'S WIFE
B. FUNNY GIRL
C. DAME ROMANCE WRITER
D. CARRY ON TO EASTENDERS
E. WALKIES!

KNIGHTED ACTORS IN FILMS

A. ARTHUR (1981)
B. LIVE AND LET DIE (1973)
C. MURDER ON THE ORIENT EXPRESS (2017)
D. DEATH IN VENICE (1971)
E. BRIDGE ON THE RIVER KWAI (1978)

THE COUNTRY OF WALES

A. CAPITAL CITY
B. PATRON SAINT
C. HIGHEST MOUNTAIN
D. LARGEST NATURAL LAKE
E. SMALLEST NATIONAL PARK

BRITISH BATTLES

A. 1066
B. 1746
C. 1485
D. 1940 (air)
E. 1685

DCI BANKS: 1. B) Stephen Tompkinson; 2. A) DI Helen Morton; 3. Four bodies of girls reported missing; 4. C) DCS Gerry Rydell; 5. His brother Roy; 6. C) Jack Deam who plays DS Ken Blackstone; 7. B) Lucy Payne; 8. B) DS Winsome Jackman; 9. A) The Crystal Kiss ; 10. A) DS Annie Cabbot.

A British current affairs documentary programme aired on BBC. First broadcast in 1953, it is the world's longest-running news television programme. Has been fronted by many well known BBC presenters. It still retains a peak time transmission slot on BBC One. Often controversial and accused of bias.

1. A Daily Mail reporter was the original presenter, but only lasted one episode, after accidentally broadcasting a technical mishap. Who was he?
A) Ian Wooldridge   B) Pat Murphy   C) Daniel Farson

2. After Max Robertson took over for a year the show was then presented by a BBC television legend until his death in 1965. Can you name him?

3. The theme is an adaptation of Francis Lai's *Aujourd'hui C'est Toi*. What is that translated into English? A) Today It's You   B) Bright Outlook   C) Forward

4. Panorama tackles some thorny subjects, however for many people of a certain age, it is best remembered for a 1957 hoax story. What was the subject of the April Fool? A) Swiss Spaghetti harvest B) Instant colour TV   C) UFO lands in London

5. In 2006 Panorama produced *Undercover: Football's Dirty Secrets*. This involved bungs. Which two high profile managers were accused - but never prosecuted of taking bungs?

6. The biggest story was a Martin Bashir interview, conducted in 1995, it is still controversial. Which senior Royal family member, discussed their private life?

7. Sex Crimes and .... Complete the title of the 2006 show that investigated child abuse in the Catholic church. A) The Pope   B) The Cardinal   C) The Vatican

8. Which religion did the show call a cult when it investigated it in 1987?

9. In 1998 Panorama named individuals questioned by police over a bombing. The atrocity, by the Real IRA, claimed 29 lives, in which Irish county town?

10. Who was the leader of the Conservative Party when the programme accused it of militancy? The BBC was forced to pay out huge sums in compensation later.

POINTLESS: **Number Ones:** A. The Beatles (5 points); B. Don McLean (2 points); C. Duffy (4 points); D. Tulisa (1 point); E. George Ezra (3 points).   **EastEnders:** A. Shane Richie (5pt) ; B. June Brown (3 pt); C. Leslie Grantham (4 pt); D. Patsy Palmer (2 pt); E. Jessie Wallace (1 pt). **BARBARAS:** A. Bach (2 pt); B. Streisand (3 pt); C. Cartland (4 pt); D. Windsor (5pt); E. Woodhouse (1 pt). **KNIGHTED ACTORS:** A. John Gielgud (2pt), B. Roger Moore (1 pt); C. Kenneth Branagh (3 pt); D. Dirk Bogarde (5pt), Alec Guinness (4 pt). **WALES:** A. Cardiff (5pt), B. St David (4pt); C. Snowdon (3pt); D. Bala (1pt); E. Pembrokeshire Coast (2pt). **BATTLES:** A. Hastings (5pt); B. Culloden (3pt); C. Bosworth (2pt); D. Britain (4pt); E. Sedgemoor (1pt).

Police and crime dramas have always been very popular in the UK. Throughout this book there are many rounds on individual crime series'. This round is a 'mixed bag'. How well do you know your crime fighters?

1. Which *Birds of a Feather* actress played DI Maisie Raine in 1998/9?

2. *Hazell* was on ITV 1978-1979. James Hazell was a Private Detective played by Nicholas Ball. The series was created by Gordon Williams and which well known former England national football manager?

3. Between 2001 and 2004 Superintendent Susan Blake and Superintendent Jim Oulton led the crime fighting teams in what series set in Liverpool?

4. Which EastEnder starred in the short-lived series McCready and Daughter?

5. Jack Frost's boss was the butt of many of his jokes. Who was he?

6. From 1983 to 1985 which series featured three women who resolved to pull off the same armed robbery that had previously cost their husbands their lives?

7. In what era did DS Cribb of Scotland Yard operate?

8. Mark Williams has played Father Brown on BBC since 2013. Which 50s film star played the role in 13 episodes in 1974?

9. Which Geordie DS had a criminal sidekick named Stick?

10. Sergeant Caleb Cluff was played by Leslie Sands in 1964/5. In which fictional North Yorkshire town was the series set?
A) Darrowby   B) Gunnershaw   C) Aidensfield

11. Liverpool 1 ran for 2 series in 1998/9. Samantha Janus was DC Isobel De Pauli. In what squad did she operate?   A) Vice   B) Specialist   C) Firearms

12. Percy Twentyman was succeeded by Bob Blackett as desk sergeant in which successful 1960s police series?

13. In *The Cops* the Police Station was in the fictional town of Stanton in a road that shared its name with the UK's top selling crime writer. Name that road!

14. What is the name of the police drama series on BBC from 1992/4 and centred upon the eventful life of Detective Superintendant Tony Clark (Neil Pearson)?

15. Name the 1977/78 series set in Southampton that featured the 13th Regional Crime Squad and starred Patrick Mower?

PANORAMA: 1. B) Pat Murphy; 2. Richard Dimbleby; 3. Today It's You; 4. A) Swiss Spaghetti harvest; 5. Sam Allardyce and Harry Redknapp; 6. Diana, Princess of Wales; 7. C) The Vatican; 8. Scientology; 9. Omagh; 10. Margaret Thatcher.

A British series co-produced by the BBC and Universal Studios and screened between 1972 and 1974. The series dealt with Allied prisoners of war imprisoned at escape-proof Colditz Castle during WW II, and their many attempts to escape captivity. Also featured the relationships between prisoners and their captors.

1. In which country is Colditz located?

2. What common bond did the prisoners who were sent to Colditz have?

3. For nearly 100 years, from 1829 to 1924, Colditz was generally reserved for the wealthy and the nobility of Germany for what purposes?

4. What security level did Colditz have and what was its German title as a prisoner-of-war camp ?

5. What type of building was it?

6. An 'appell' was one of the most important things to happen at Colditz. This daily event was better known in the UK as what?

7. Lieutenant Colonel John Preston was the senior British officer. Who played the role?
A) Jack Hawkins   B) Jack Hedley   C) Jack Wild

8. The Kommandant held to the old Army ways of respecting enemy officers and adhered to the Geneva Convention to the best of his ability. Bernard Hepton of Secret Army fame played the role. By what name was he known in the series?
A) Dieter   B)Willi   C) Karl

9. A famous RAF pilot, the subject of the film *Reach For the Sky*, was a prisoner in Colditz and remained there until the liberation. Curiously be was not included in the storyline. Who was he?

10. During 2006 and 2007, the castle underwent a significant amount of refurbishment and restoration which was paid for by the state of Saxony. The castle walls were repainted to recreate the appearance of the castle prior to World War II. For what purposes is the building now used?

WATCHING THE DETECTIVES: 1. Pauline Quirke; 2. Terry Venables; 3. Merseybeat; 4. Patsy Palmer; 5. Superintendent Mullett; 6. Widows; 7. Victorian; 8. Kenneth More; 9. Freddie Spender; 10. B) Gunnershaw; 11. A) Vice Squad; 12. Z Cars; 13. Christie Road (Agatha has sold over 2 billion books); 14. Between the Lines; 15. Target.

A third visit to Mandela House for another set of trivia about the classic BBC sitcom series Only Fools and Horses. By overwhelming numbers this show has produced the most requests from the public to be well represented. I am delighted to comply!

1. During *Strangers on the Shore* Del and Rodney went to France to scatter Albert's ashes, and Del decided to include an illegal booze run as well. Which two Peckham residents did they 'meet' in the hypermarket?

2. 'He made one great film and then you never saw him again'. Trigger's great line in *Time on our Hands*. But to whom was he referring?

3. What was the name of Boycie and Marlene's much-loved Great Dane?

4. What were the names of the two blow up sex dolls Del bought in *Danger UXD*?

5. In *The Second Time Around* Del became re-engaged to an ex fiancee, by now a widow for the second time. What was her name?
A) June Snell   B) Pauline Harris   C) Elsie Partridge

6. Where did the Trotters unsuccessfully clean the crystal chandeliers in *Touch of Glass*? A) Ridgemere Hall Estate
B) Covington House   C) Blandings Castle

7. When Del and Rodney went to Florida in Miami Twice, they met Del's doppelganger, who was a Mafia boss. What was his name?
A) Don Corleone   B) Carlo Civello   C) Don Vincenzo Ochetti

8. When Del got to his feet after falling through the bar what did he say to Trigger? A) Drink up Trig we're leaving   B) Let's try our luck somewhere else Trig C) Come on Trig, we're off to the Nags Head

9. What was Grandad trying to watch on the microwave?

10. What name did the mad axe murderer use to fool the Trotters into letting him into the cottage in *Friday the 14th*?
A) Chief Anderson   B) Chief Sanderson   C) Chief Robinson

What role did this actor play in one memorable OFAH episode?

COLDITZ: *1. Germany (near Leipzig); 2. Officers who were all escape prone; 3. It was a sanatorium; 4. Maximum, Oflag IV-C; 5. A castle; 6. A roll call; 7. B) Jack Hedley; 8. C) Karl; 9. Squadron Leader/Group Captain Douglas Bader; 10. A museum and also guided tours.*

A multi-award winning British reality documentary series set at Battersea Dogs & Cats Home and presented by Paul O'Grady. It has won numerous awards throughout its time on air. Paul meets members of staff to talk about dogs in their care. 8 Series. 79 Episodes.

CAN YOU IDENTIFY THE DOG BREEDS SHOWN BELOW?

1. 2. 3. 4. 5. 6. 7. 8. 9. 10. 11. 12. 13. 14. 15.

ONLY FOOLS AND HORSE 4: *1. Denzil and Trigger; 2. Gandhi; 3. Duke; 4. Lusty Linda and Erotic Estelle; 5. B) Pauline Harris; 6. A) Ridgemere Hall Estate; 7. C) Don Vincenzo Ochetti; 8. A) Drink up Trig we're leaving; 9. The Dukes of Hazzard; 10. C) Chief Robinson.*
ONE EPISODE WONDER: *Phil Pope (Tony Angelino in Stage Fright (the Singing Dustman).*

A music panel show on BBC between 1 June 1959 and 27 December 1967. The series featured celebrity show-business guests on a rotating weekly panel asked to judge the hit potential of recent record releases. By 1962 the programme was attracting 12 million viewers weekly on Saturday nights. Later revived by BBC for one series in 1979 and a further two series in 1989/1990. 12 Series. 463

1. Who were the three presenters of Juke Box Jury throughout its 3 runs?

2. All the records played were declared a 'hit' or a 'miss' – the decision accompanied by what sounds?

3. There were four panellists, if they voted equally, how was the tie-breaker played?

4. 4 July 1964 saw the only occasion that the panel did not consist of four members but five. Why?

5. Which of these celebrities did NOT appear as a panellist on Juke Box Jury?
A) Roy Orbison   B) Alfred Hitchcock   C) Billy Fury   D) Cliff Richard

6. For the first six weeks of the programme, the theme to *Juke Box Jury* was *Juke Box Fury* by Ozzie Warlock and the Wizards. From 1960 to 1967 it was an instrumental called *Hit and Miss* by which band, led by a major film music writer?

7. In 1989/90 the show featured the same theme tune, but it was performed by which British jazz musician?
A) Johnny Dankworth   B) Courtney Pine   C) Ronnie Scott

8. Which Beatle voted all eight records on one programme a 'miss', including Elvis Presley's *(You're the) Devil in Disguise,* which reached number one?

9. True or False? In 1979? Johnny Rotten and Joan Collins appeared together as panellists on the show in 1979?

10. Who, having disrupted rehearsals for the show said, 'Look, we're messing up Mr Jacobs' programme for him. We must behave.'   A) John Lennon   B) Mick Jagger   C) Brian Jones   D) Paul McCartney

PAUL O'GRADY FOR THE LOVE OF DOGS: 1. German Shepherd; 2. English Bulldog; 3. Poodle; 4. Chihuahua; 5. Dachshund; 6. Great Dane; 7. Shih Tzu; 8. Bichon Frise; 9. Basset Hound; 10. Rottweiler; 11. Dalmatian; 12. St Bernard; 13. Greyhound; 14. King Charles Spaniel; 15. Old English Sheepdog.

A British mystery spy thriller series on ITV from 1962-1969. Created by Leslie Charteris in the 1920s. 6 Series. 118 Episodes. Return of the Saint aired for one series in 1978 and 1979 in Britain on ITV.

1. Which future James Bond played Simon Templar, *The Saint,* from 1962-1969?

2. And who succeeded him in the role in *Return of the Saint* in 1978?

3. In the first episode Shirley Eaton was an insurance investigator. In which film was her character painted gold?

4. Which car did *The Saint* drive in A) *The Saint* and   B) *Return of the Saint?*

5. What was the average production budget for an episode of *The Saint* in 1962? A) £10,000   B) £20,000   C) £30,000

6. Which actor and stand-up comedian, best known as Frank Butcher in *EastEnders*, was fired from his role as Roger Moore's underwater stunt double after making fun of the actor's thinning hair?

7. In *Judas Game* Simon Templar rescued Selma Morell (Judy Geeson), a British secret agent who had been captured by which country's secret police? A) Italian   B) Albanian   C) Russian

8. In the *Art Collectors* set in Paris, the Saint met Natasha, who said she wished to sell three priceless paintings by which painter? A) Picasso   B) Da Vinci   C) Van Gogh

9. In *Return of the Saint* episode *Assault Force*, Simon, in error agreed to help a Eurasian woman and her colleague kidnap a politician, who they said was a bad, bad man. In reality the man was actually what?

10. In Duel in Venice an old adversary looking for revenge kidnapped Sally and put a time triggered device on her that will kill her at a specified time. What was the device? A) A necklace B) A bomb C) A gas

TRUE OR FALSE?
Roger Moore wore lifts and a hairpiece to play Simon Templar.

JUKE BOX JURY: 1. David Jacobs, Noel Edmonds, Jools Holland; 2. A bell for a 'hit' or a hooter for a 'miss'; 3. A trio of audience members held up a disc with 'Hit' or 'Miss' displayed; 4. The Rolling Stones were panellists; 5. C) Billy Fury; 6. The John Barry Seven Plus 4 (reached number 10 in the UK charts); 7. B) Courtney Pine; 8. John Lennon; 9. True; 10. C) Brian Jones.

A British sitcom created for the BBC by Roy Clarke, and starring David Jason and James Baxter. It is the sequel to the original sitcom Open All Hours, which both Clarke and Jason worked on throughout its 26-episode run from 1973 to 1985, following a 40th Anniversary Special in December 2013 commemorating the original series. 6 Episodes. 41 Episodes.

Still Open All Hours

1. Granville inherited the shop from his uncle, Albert Arkwright. What relation is Leroy who helps him run the business?

2. Which three main characters from *Open All Hours* have continued their roles in this successful revival?

3. Through which mechanical device does Granville think his late uncle lives on in the shop?

4. After accidentally sending a love note to Delphine Featherstone instead of Mavis, who does Granville encourage to have a relationship with the widow?
A) Wilburn Newbold   B) Gastric   C) Eric Agnew

5. Leroy became committed to winning the affection of a local librarian, despite her values and her lifestyle as a vegan. What is her name?

6. Granville introduced an erotically charged new product called Yaggis. What was it really? A) Spam   B) Salami   C) Chorizo

7. Why did Granville climb a ladder at Mavis's house?

8. Mrs Rossi invited Mr Newbold to Christmas lunch. Which former star of *Only Fools and Horses* joined David Jason in the series to play the exotic Italian lady?

9. The shop that inspired Roy Clarke to write about a little corner shop was based upon a shop that he happened upon one day. Where is the real life shop still operating?
A) Salford, Manchester   B) Thornbury, Gloucestershire   C) Aston, Birmingham

10. When Granville found an old mangle he thought of uses for it, flattening kippers, rolling pizza and then ....?

TRIVIA: The cash till used in this is the same one they used in Open All Hours (1976)

THE SAINT / RETURN OF THE SAINT: 1. Roger Moore; 2. Ian Ogilvy; 3. Goldfinger; 4. A) Volvo P1800 B) Jaguar XJS; 5. C) £30,000; 6. Mike Reid ; 7. B) Albanian; 8. B) Da Vinci; 9. A peace maker; 10. A) A necklace that will garrotte her at a specified time.

A British variety show from the London Palladium. Originally produced by ATV for the ITV network from 1955 -1969, Sunday Night at the London Palladium changed to The London Palladium Show from 1966 to 1969. 3 revivals, 1973 to 1974, 2000, 2014 to 2015 and finally from 2016. 438 Episodes in total.

1. There were 7 regular hosts from 1955 to 1974; then 7 more from 2014 - 2017. How many of the 14 can you name?

2. The show opened with a popular high-kicking dance troupe who had been formed in 1889. Who were they?

3. A game show imported from America was a regular feature for many years. It featured couples having to perform a trick or stunt to win prizes. Name the game.

4. Perhaps the most famous episode took place during a strike by the British acting union Equity in 1961. Exempt from this, Bruce Forsyth and which famous comedian performed the entire show themselves?

5. As the finale to each show, the Tiller Girls, the compère and that night's guests stood and waved and grinned from what mechanism, as the end tune played?

6. In 1967, which famous rock band refused to take part in the finale (see previous question), because it didn't fit their rebellious image?

7. In 1966 the compère once completely forgot a major star's name and introduced her as 'someone who needs no introduction'. Who was the embarrassed host and who was the international singer?

8. Which guest host was knocked unconscious when the heavy clock used to time contestants fell on his head? A) Hughie Green   B) Max Bygraves   C) Max Wall

9. Which acts appearance on the show brought the West End of London to a complete standstill, due to thousands of fans gathering outside the theatre?

10. In 1962 a Liverpool born entertainer, who was still comparatively unknown, took over as host. His catchphrases 'Swinging' and 'Dodgy' were popular. Who was he?

TRIVIA: On one occasion when a power failure blacked out the ITV network, Tommy Trinder ad-libbed for two hours. His first words when the picture was restored were 'Welcome to Monday Morning at the London Palladium'.

STILL OPEN ALL HOURS: *1. His son by a previous girlfriend after a fling in Blackpool; 2. Lynda Baron (Nurse Gladys, Stephanie Cole (Mrs Featherstone) and Maggie Ollernshaw (Mavis); 3. The till; 4. A) Wilburn Newbold; 5. Beth; 6. B) Salami; 7. To deliver a Valentine's card; 8. Sue Holderness (Marlene); 9. B) Thornbury, Gloucestershire (LE Riddiford's - it's still there!; 10. A home trouser pressing service.*

An annual awards ceremony that takes place in December. Devised by Paul Fox in 1954, it originally consisted of just one award. There are currently eight awards presented. The first awards added were the Team of the Year and Overseas Personality awards introduced in 1960. A Lifetime Achievement Award was first given in 1995 and again in 1996, and has been presented annually since 2001. In 1999, three more awards were introduced: the Helen Rollason Award, the Coach Award, and the Newcomer Award, renamed to Young Sports Personality of the Year in 2001.

CAN YOU NAME THESE 15 WINNERS?

| 1. 1959 | 2. 1987 | 3. 2019 | 4. 2009 | 5. 2013/15/16 |
| 6. 1963 | 7. 2018 | 8. 2003 | 9. 2006 | 10. 2003 |

| 11. 1967 | 12. 1971 | 13. 1993 | 14. 1982 | 15. 1975 |

SUNDAY NIGHT AT THE LONDON PALLADIUM: 1. Tommy Trinder , Bruce Forsyth, Don Arrol, Norman Vaughan, Jimmy Tarbuck, Jim Dale, Ted Rogers. Revived series: Bradley Walsh, Stephen Mulhern, Jason Manford, Jack Whitehall, Rob Brydon, Alexander Armstrong, Jimmy Carr ; 2. The Tiller Girls; 3. Beat the clock; 4. Norman Wisdom; 5. A huge revolving stage; 6. The Rolling Stones; 7. Jimmy Tarbuck, Petula Clark; 8. A) Hughie Green; 9. The Beatles (Beatlemania was born!); 10. Norman Vaughan.

A British period drama produced by the BBC between 1976 and 1981. The series starred James Bolam as Jack Ford, a First World War veteran who returned to his poverty-stricken (fictional) town of Gallowshield in the North East of England. The series dramatised the inter-war political struggles of the 1920s and 1930s and explored the impact of national and international politics upon Ford and the people around him. 4 Series. 51 Episodes.

WHEN THE BOAT COMES IN

1. Jack Ford got engaged to whom?
A) Sarah Headley   B) Jessie Seaton   C) Rosie Mason

2. Tom Seaton borrowed money from Jack because he was struggling financially, and his wife Mary was ill. What illness did she have? A) Tuberculosis B) Smallpox C) Scarlet Fever

3. Jack Ford slept with another woman, the widowed sister of a war comrade. Who was she? A) Isobel Murcheson   B) Sarah Headley   C) Dolly Headley

4. When Tom found out about Jack's dalliance he threatened to expose him unless ....what? A) He joined Jack's sheep rustling gang   B) He paid him £5
C) He got him a job

5. Bill Seaton found out that an abandoned coal seam ran under his house. What did he do? A) He dug up his garden   B) He dug up his front room
C) He demolished his garden shed

6. Jessie was impressed by the talent and intelligence of a 14-year-old pupil, Ronnie Fairburn, and tried to dissuade him from working in the mines. But his widowed mother needed the money. What happened on Ronnie's first day down the mine?

7. Whose proposal did Jessie accept?
A) Geordie Watson   B) Stan Liddell   C) Arthur Ashton

8. Why did Jack Ford agree to marry Dolly Headley?
A) He was jealous about Jessie's engagement
B) Dolly was pregnant   C) Dolly was wealthy

9. When widow Downey was evicted Jack broke in to recover her furniture for her. What was the result of his actions? A) He went to prison B) He was assaulted   C) He was fined

10. Later in the story Jack Ford made a fortune from bootlegging, but how did he lose it all? A) Gambling debts   B) Divorce settlement   C) The Wall Street Crash

BBC SPORTS PERSONALITY OF THE YEAR: 1. John Surtees; 2. Fatima Whitbread; 3. Ben Stokes; 4. Ryan Giggs; 5. Andy Murray; 6. Dorothy Hyman; 7. Geraint Thomas; 8. Jonny Wilkinson; 9. Zara Phillips; 10. Michael Owen; 11. Henry Cooper; 12. Princess Anne; 13. Linford Christie; 14. Daley Thompson; 15. David Steele.

Robin Hood was a legendary heroic outlaw. Legend says he was a highly skilled archer and swordsman. Some legends say he was from noble birth. In modern retellings he has sometimes been depicted as having fought in the Crusades and upon returning home, found his land had been taken by the wicked Sheriff. Traditionally dressed in Lincoln green, he was said to rob from the rich and give to the poor.

1. There have been five series about Robin Hood on TV since 1953. Can you name the six actors who have played the legendary, heroic outlaw in those five series'?

2. A noted film director, who won an Oscar for Midnight Cowboy in 1970, played Alan-a-Dale in 2 episodes of *The Adventures of Robin Hood* in 1956 and 1957. Who was he?
A) Alfred Hitchcock   B) John Schlesinger   C) Billy Wilder

3. Robin Hood ran from 2006-2009. The lead actor played the role in 39 episodes and was injured in one staged fight. What bone did be break? A) Clavicle   B) Metatarsal   B) Tibia

4. In one of his earlier roles, a familiar TV actor played Little John 24 times between 1984 and 1986. Who is he?
A) Clive Mantle   B) Matthew Macfadyean   C) Tom Wilkinson

5. Which forest had been occupied by all the merry bands of men?

6. In 1956 two versions of the theme song were hits. Gary Miller reached No 10, and the version used on the show got to No 14. Who was the singer who went on to become a leading music publisher?
A) Caleb Quaye   B) Dick James   C) Michael Holliday

7. 'Guy of Gisborne' married the 'Vicar of Dibley' in 2007, with the 10th Doctor and 2 Daleks in attendance! Which 2 actors were involved?

8. Robin was really a Saxon nobleman, who returned from the Crusades to find a Norman lord living in his ancestral home, Locksley Hall. What was Robin's title?

9. The haunting theme song Robin (The Hooded Man) was part of the soundtrack that won the BAFTA award for Best Original TV Music in 1985. Which band wrote and performed the music?

10. In the final scene of 2009. Robin saw Marian appear and walk to him. Marian said to him 'The greatest adventure is yet to come'. And they embrace. In reality Robin had died. What caused his death?
A) Shot by an arrow   B) Poisoned   C) Fell from a galloping horse

WHEN THE BOAT COMES IN: 1. B) Jessie Seaton; 2. A) Tuberculosis; 3. C) Dolly Headley; 4. A) Join Jack's sheep rustling gang; 5. B) He digs up his front room ; 6. He is killed; 7. C) Arthur Ashton; 8. B) Dolly is pregnant; 9. A) He goes to prison for a month; 10. C) The Wall Street Crash.

And finally! A few more laughs to finish off. If I have missed any TV highlights of your life, let me know. I may be able to produce a second volume at some time. I hope you have enjoyed the book. By the way. Have you noticed that families appearing on TV shows, when asked, never say watching TV is amongst their interests? I don't believe it!!!

Rock on Tommy!

1. As I write this final round, I have just heard that half of a comedy duo who had 9 TV series and 7 specials between 1979-1988 has died. Who was this very funny man?

2. In *The Fall and Rise of Reginald Perrin,* which animal appeared when Reggie thought about his mother-in-law?

3. Who asked, 'What's occurring?' In Gavin & Stacey?

4. What make of car did Basil Fawlty attack with a branch?

5. Who played *Andy Capp* in the 1988 TV series?

6. In the title of the show, what does *QI* stand for?

7. On which floor would you have found 'shirts, socks, ties, hats, underwear and shoes' in Grace Brothers store?   A) 1st   B) 2nd   C) 3rd

8. Father Jack was a drunken old priest in *Father Ted.* What was his surname?

9. At the end of each show Fry and Laurie said 'Soupy twist'. What did it mean?

10. What was John Lacey's profession in *Dear John*?

11. In 1975/6 Reg Varney was a porter in *Down the Gate*. Where did he work?

12. In *The Dustbinmen* Winston Platt played by Graham Haberfield was a die-hard supporter of which football team?
A) Manchester United   B) Manchester City   C) Liverpool

13. What was the name of the girls' landlady in *Girls on Top*?

14. What was Gareth Blackstock's profession?

15. Which Beatle played a lavatory attendant in a sketch in *Not Only...But Also*?
A) Paul McCartney   B) Ringo Starr   C) John Lennon

ROBIN HOOD: 1. Patrick Troughton, Richard Greene, Martin Potter, Michael Praed, Jason Connery, Jonas Armstrong; 2. B) John Schlesinger; 3. B) Metatarsal; (Jonas Armstrong); 4. A) Clive Mantle; 5. Sherwood; 6. B) Dick James; 7. Richard Armitage (Guy of Gisborne in Robin Hood) and Dawn French (Vicar of Dibley); 8. The Earl of Locksley; 9. Clannad; 10. B) Poisoned (Isabella scratches Robin's neck with her dagger which was coated with poison Gisborne had given Isabella to kill herself).

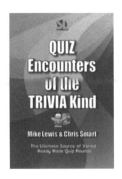

BRITISH COMEDY 4: 1. Bobby Ball (of Cannon and Ball); 2. A hippopotamus; 3. Nessa; 4. Austin 1100; 5. James Bolam; 6. Quite Interesting; 7. A) 1st (menswear) 8. Hackett; 9. Cheers; 10. Schoolteacher; 11. Billingsgate Fish Market; 12. B) Manchester City; 13. Lady Chloe Carlton; 14. He was a chef; 15. C) John Lennon.

Printed in Poland
by Amazon Fulfillment
Poland Sp. z o.o., Wrocław

65376029R10166